CLINICAL STRATEGIES FOR BECOMING A MASTER PSYCHOTHERAPIST

CLINICAL STRATEGIES FOR BECOMING A MASTER PSYCHOTHERAPIST

EDITORS

DR. WILLIAM O'DONOHUE
DR. NICHOLAS A. CUMMINGS
DR. JANET L. CUMMINGS

AMSTERDAM • BOSTON • HEIDELBERG • LONDON
NEW YORK • OXFORD • PARIS • SAN DIEGO
SAN FRANCISCO • SINGAPORE • SYDNEY • TOKYO

Academic Press is an imprint of Elsevier

Academic Press is an imprint of Elsevier
30 Corporate Drive, Suite 400, Burlington, MA 01803, USA
525 B Street, Suite 1900, San Diego, California 92101-4495, USA
84 Theobald's Road, London WCIX 8RR, UK

This book is printed on acid-free paper. ⊚

Library of Congress Cataloging-in-Publication Data
O'Donohue, William T. Clinical strategies for becoming a master psychotherapist / William
O'Donohue, Nicholas Cummings, Janet Cummings.
    p. cm.
  Includes bibliographical references and index.
  ISBN 0-12-088416-X (alk. paper)
 1. Psychotherapy. I. Cummings, Nicholas A. II. Cummings, Janet L. III. Title.
  RC480.O33 2006
  616.89′14–dc22   2005023305

British Library Cataloguing-in-Publication Data
A catalogue record for this book is available from the British Library.

ISBN 13: 978-0-12-088416-2
ISBN 10: 0-12-088416-X

For information on all Academic Press publications
visit our Web site at www.books.elsevier.com

Printed in the United States of America
06 07 08 09 10   9 8 7 6 5 4 3 2 1

Working together to grow
libraries in developing countries

www.elsevier.com | www.bookaid.org | www.sabre.org

ELSEVIER   BOOK AID
              International   Sabre Foundation

CONTENTS

3

THE THERAPEUTIC ALLIANCE: CULTIVATING AND NEGOTIATING THE THERAPEUTIC RELATIONSHIP
JEREMY D. SAFRAN, J. CHRISTOPHER MURAN, MICHAEL ROTHMAN

4

NARRATIVE PSYCHOTHERAPY AS EFFECTIVE STORY-MAKING: AN INTRODUCTION
LOIS PARKER

5

RECOGNIZING AND DEALING WITH CULTURAL INFLUENCES IN PSYCHOTHERAPY
MELANIE P. DUCKWORTH, TONY IEZZI

6

EFFECTIVE UNDERSTANDING AND DEALING WITH MANIPULATION
MICHAEL G. WETTER, JACK WETTER

7

RECOGNIZING AND DEALING WITH TRANSFERENCE
GEORGE STRICKER

8

THE TEMPORAL STRUCTURE OF THERAPY: KEY QUESTIONS OFTEN ASSOCIATED WITH DIFFERENT PHASES OF SESSIONS AND TREATMENTS (PLUS TWENTY-ONE HELPFUL HINTS)
MICHAEL F. HOYT

9

RESISTANCE AS AN ALLY IN PSYCHOTHERAPY
NICHOLAS A. CUMMINGS

10

ENHANCING PSYCHOTHERAPY THROUGH APPROPRIATE ENTRY POINTS

NICHOLAS A. CUMMINGS, JANET L. CUMMINGS

11

DEALING WITH FEELINGS OF DEPRESSION

ALVIN R. MAHRER

12

DESIGNING AND ASSIGNING EFFECTIVE HOMEWORK

RICHARD KAMINS

13

SKILLS TRAINING: HOW THE MASTER CLINICIAN UNDERSTANDS AND TEACHES COMPETENCIES
WILLIAM O'DONOHUE

14

USING TASKS IN ERICKSONIAN PSYCHOTHERAPY
JEFFREY K. ZEIG

15

USING ACCEPTANCE IN INTEGRATIVE BEHAVIORAL COUPLE THERAPY
CHRISTOPHER R. MARTELL, DAVID ATKINS

16

SHORT-TERM DYNAMIC PSYCHOTHERAPY GOES TO HOLLYWOOD: THE TREATMENT OF PERFORMANCE ANXIETY IN CINEMA
LEIGH MCCULLOUGH, KRISTIN A. R. OSBORN

17

THE IMPORTANCE OF NOVELTY IN PSYCHOTHERAPY
BRETT N. STEENBARGER

18

INTERRUPTION REPLACES TERMINATION IN FOCUSED, INTERMITTENT PSYCHOTHERAPY THROUGHOUT THE LIFE CYCLE
NICHOLAS A. CUMMINGS

19

SUICIDAL PATIENTS: THE ULTIMATE
CHALLENGE FOR MASTER PSYCHOTHERAPISTS
JANET L. CUMMINGS

LIST OF CONTRIBUTORS

David Atkins (239), Fuller Graduate School of Psychology, Pasadena, CA 91182

Janet L. Cummings (iii, 1, 145, 309), The Nicholas & Dorothy Cummings Foundation, Scottsdale, AZ 85281

Nicholas A. Cummings (iii, 1, 129, 145, 291), University of Nevada Reno, Reno, NV 89503

Melanie P. Duckworth (71), University of Nevada Reno, Department of Psychology, Reno, NV 89557-0062

Michael Hoyt (113), Kaiser Permanente Medical Center, San Rafael, CA 94903

Tony Iezzi (71), London Health Sciences Centre, London, Ontario, Canada, N6A 4G5

Richard Kamins (189), Magellan Health Services, Public Sector Solutions, Greenwood Village, CO 21046

Eric, R. Levensky (11), University of Nevada, Reno, Department of Psychology, Reno, NV 89557-0062

Alvin R. Mahrer (167), University of Ottawa, Centre for Psychological Services, Ottawa, ON, K1N 6N5

Christopher R. Martell (239), Associates in Behavioral Health and University of Washington, Seattle, Washington 98122

Leigh McCullough (261), Harvard Medical School, Dedham, MA 02026

J. Christopher Muran (37), Beth Israel Medical Center, Albert Einstein College of Medicine, Department of Psychiatry and Behavioral Sciences New York, NY 10003

William T. O'Donohue (iii, 1, 209), University of Nevada Reno, Department of Psychology, Reno, NV 89557-0062

Kristin A. R. Osborn (261), Psychotherapy Research Program, Harvard Medical School Department of Psychiatry, Cambridge, Massachusetts 02139

Lois J. Parker (55), University of Nevada Reno, Counseling and Career Services, Reno, NV 89557

Michael Rothman (37), Beth Israel Medical Center, Albert Einstein College of Medicine, Department of Psychiatry and Behavioral Sciences New York, NY 10003

Jeremy D. Safran (37), New School University, Department of Psychology, New York, NY 10003

Brett N. Steenbarger (277), Clinical Associate Professor of Psychiatry and Behavioral Sciences, SUNY Upstate Medical University, Syracuse, NY 13210

George Stricker (95), American School of Professional Psychology, Argosy University/Washington DC 22209

Jack Wetter (87), Diplomate and Fellow in Clinical Psychology, American Board of Professional Psychology, Los Angeles, California 90024

Michael G. Wetter (87), The Permanente Medical Group, Medical Office Building, Union City, CA 94587

Paula L. Wilbourne (11), Center for Health Care Evaluation, VA Palo Alto Health Care System, Menlo Park, CA 94025

Jeffrey K. Zeig (223), Milton H. Erickson Foundation, Phoenix, AZ 85016

1

THE ART AND SCIENCE
OF PSYCHOTHERAPY

WILLIAM O'DONOHUE

University of Nevada
Reno, Nevada

NICHOLAS CUMMINGS

University of Nevada
Reno, Nevada

JANET CUMMINGS

University of Nevada
Reno, Nevada

Psychotherapy is both an art and a science. Understanding the contribution of both these elements and achieving a proper balance in actual episodes of therapy is essential to optimize therapeutic success. All too often, behavioral health professionals have emphasized one and neglected the other. A major mission of this book is to help redress this imbalance. We have produced other books that have focused on the scientific dimension of the psychotherapeutic enterprise (Cummings & Cummings, 2000; Fisher & O'Donohue, in press; O'Donohue, Fisher & Hayes, 2003). However, this scientific information is incomplete in regard to producing effective psychotherapy. It is incomplete in two important ways. First, it does not cover key problems that if not resolved can impede progress, prematurely end therapy, or result in failure. These problems, if not recognized, confronted, and dealt with well can undermine therapy, even if the therapist is using an empirically supported treatment manual. Moreover, unfortunately, these problems are not rare. Examples of these problems include building a therapeutic relationship, handling resistance, constructing a case formulation, and, on the other end of the therapy time line, terminating appropriately. Second, this

Clinical Strategies for
Becoming a Master Psychotherapist

1

scientific information often does not fully cover the "art" or "craft" of implementing these evidence-based techniques, (i.e., the nuances, the creative maneuvers, the dexterity, the problem-solving strategies when difficulties arise). This book is an attempt to have high-profile, expert "master" therapists discuss the craft of handling these key issues.

Let's examine two examples. The research clearly shows nonspecific factors such as the therapeutic alliance that accounts for a lot of variance in therapy outcome (Thomas, Werner–Wilson & Murphy, 2005). However, this literature is weak in describing the art of establishing and maintaining these nonspecific factors. Thus, a key task in therapy is creating and maintaining an optimal therapeutic relationship. Beginning therapists might mistakenly think that what is involved is simply "being nice." Clearly, this is not it at all. The therapeutic relationship certainly has to involve elements such as empathy, positive regard, and instilling hope — and these can feel somewhat "nice" to the client, but the relationship also must involve persistence in moving the client to explore areas they do not want to; giving honest, useful but perhaps unwanted feedback; drawing clear boundaries (particularly with certain clients such as those with borderline personality disorder); tough love; and so forth Thus, this book contains a chapter by a leading clinical authority, Dr. Jeremy Safran, that describes the art of establishing and maintaining a therapeutic relationship.

Our second example: Although many empirically supported treatment manuals assume clients will always cooperate, do homework, tell us accurate and complete information, clinicians know of the many ways clients demonstrate resistance in psychotherapy. Thus, we have also included a chapter by one of the co-editors, Dr. Nicholas Cummings, on understanding and dealing with resistance.

PSYCHOTHERAPY IS NOT ENTIRELY AN ART

However, another all too common mistake is to view psychotherapy as entirely an art. In this view, each psychotherapist with each client is engaged is some sort of creative enterprise bounded only by the artist's choices among many possible paths in which spontaneous reactions of the artist/psychotherapist are causally related to improvements in the client. In this view, there may be some commonalities (as art can be grouped into schools such as impressionism, Dadaism, cubism, and so on.) so that, although therapeutic styles may be at times grouped into "schools," each artist/psychotherapist is essentially unique. Improvisational jazz is perhaps the best metaphor here. Sometimes, the art argument is based on the uniqueness of each human (applying to both the client and the therapist) and the uniqueness of their problems, thus attempting to justify a radically unique approach to each case. At other times, the argument can be based on the uniqueness of the moment—that each therapist and each client in each moment of psychotherapy is *sui generis* and thus only a corresponding unique response to this can be therapeutic. According to this view, there are few or no general laws then, because this uniqueness defies generalization over common types.

We believe there are three major problems with this view. First, there is the causal problem. In health care we know (painfully so) that not all events lead to the healing effects we want. Not all salves stop poison ivy from itching. Not all treatments stop a cancerous tumor. Not all speech acts stop a suicidal individual. And not all interventions will decrease a patient's belief in a delusion. Some events will have a positive impact on these; many will not. To think that a therapist can simply spontaneously improvise *and* consistently instantiate one of these ameliorative causal factors is either overly optimistic or, when talking about the self, narcissistic in the extreme. A related problem is that even if a particular therapist–artist is wonderful, there is a scalability problem. Is this therapist talented for all patients with all kinds of problems? If this therapist is an excellent artist, it would seem to have very little to do with other therapists and their clients.

The second major problem is that, in most arts, the majority of so called "artists" are not all that good. In fact, most are pretty bad. For every Picasso or Rembrandt or Modigliani, there are thousands of untalented "starving artists" who are reaping the just economic rewards of their talent. Thus, the problem becomes, if psychotherapy is an art, how we can justify the Lake Woebegone claim that "all the artists are above average" and all deserve prizes?

The final problem is that psychotherapy is partly an economic activity (Cummings, in press). We promise our clients that they will efficiently improve and that the therapy we are offering them is the best opportunity—one that has the best value—to resolve their problems. Art is problematic in this regard. Good art typically is very expensive, mediocre art is at least affordable, and bad art is worthless. The same formula might apply to psychotherapy if it were entirely an art. A dysanalogy but an important point is that art rarely harms, but bad therapy can (see Lilienfeld, Wood & Garbe, in press). We would also worry, if psychotherapy is an art, how we can ensure that all these creative spontaneous acts by the therapists would "at least do no harm."

We believe this view misses the point that there are causal relations in therapy that science is best at discovering. Thus, good, effective therapy must rely on known causal relationships. All measurement contains error, and thus knowing the scientific literature about the validity and limitations of the validity of psychological assessments is also essential knowledge in psychotherapy. In addition, only testing can ensure that the intervention is safe. This is important as even a cursory examination of either the history of health interventions or even a reading of a good newspaper will easily show the various iatrogenic and harmful side effects of healthcare interventions. Finally, the advantage of scientific knowledge is that it has a large and known generalizability. We can take information about what constitutes good therapy and teach others to implement this so that many can be helped.

PSYCHOTHERAPY IS NOT ONLY
A SCIENCE

There is something called *scientism*. This construct is used to critique those who have a distorted view of science in that they overestimate it. This view overvalues science and does not see its limitations. Science does not have all the answers. It does not tell you how to love your child. It does not tell you how to be humorous. It does not tell us what is 'the good life'. Carl Hempel (1965), the prominent philosopher of science, has pointed out the irrelevance of science for value and ethical decisions by a thought experiment that evokes LaPlace's demon. The demon is a perfect scientific intelligence that knows all the laws of nature, everything that is going on in the universe at any given moment, and, moreover, can calculate with infinite speed and precision from the state of the universe at any particular moment, its state at any other past or future moment.

Let us assume, then, that, faced with a moral decision, we are able to call upon the Laplacean demon as a consultant. What help might we get from him? Suppose we have to choose one of several alternative courses of action open to us and we want to know which of these we ought to follow. The demon would then be able to tell us, for any contemplated choice, what the consequences would be for the future course of the universe, down to the most minute detail, however remote in space and time. But, having done this for each of the alternative courses of action under consideration, the demon would have completed its task. He would have given us all the information that an ideal science might provide under the circumstances. And yet he would not have resolved our moral problem, for this requires a decision regarding which of the several alternative sets of consequences mapped out by the demon as attainable to us is the best—which of them we ought to bring about. And the burden of the decision world still falls upon our shoulders; it is we who have to commit ourselves to an unconditional (absolute) judgment of the value by singling out one of the sets of conse-quences as superior to the alternatives (Hempel, 1965).

Thus all the value questions that arise in psychotherapy—and there are many—are outside the scope of science.

The other problem with a scientific view of psychotherapy is that it misses that science itself is partly an art and is always evolving. Philosophers of science such as Karl Popper (1972), Paul Feyerabend (1988), and Thomas Kuhn (1962) all agree on this point. Conjectural solutions for problems are scientific for Popper as long as they are falsifiable. However, these conjectures — these guesses — can come from anywhere: from myth, from dreams, from imagination. (See O'Donohue, 1989, for the role of metaphysics in scientific clinical psychology.) The good scientist has good judgment about these matters, but there is no algorithm to spit out the best hypothesis or theory. This is part of the art of science.

In addition, there is an art of experimental design. How does one design a simple, elegant, but persuasive study? Scientists differ on this ability. All these philosophers point out that science also is constantly in evolution or revolution. With the creative acts of paradigm shifting, revolutionary scientists alter science, and these acts render what we thought was the truth into what we now know and believe to be false.

Third, science has revolutions that show that the previously accepted views were wrong. Science does not give us final, objective truth; it is fallible. Thus, science must always be taken with a grain of salt. It may be the best epistemology, but its fallibility should result in a certain humbleness and respect for other points of view. The philosopher of science Paul Feyerabend has pointed out one of the best ways in which the limitations of science has been discovered and rooted out is through extrascientific criticism.

The final problem is that those individuals who see psychotherapy entirely as a science fail to see the entire enterprise of psychotherapy; they narrowly focus on a piece of it. They often focus on important pieces, such as how do we measure this construct with as little error as possible? Or, what causes improvements in this condition? But they miss out on other elements. For example, what should the waiting room look like? How should the patient be greeted and addressed? How should the therapist be dressed? How prompt should the therapist be? What should the therapist's payment policies be? How should the therapist handle the client's no-shows? There is a limit to our scientific knowledge, and therapists still have to practice and thus practice beyond science. They must use their good judgment on these issues. Some of this judgment can come from successes in their personal lives, as general social skills and social intelligence can be keys. However, the point is, the therapist is constantly choosing among alternatives, and science is mute on many of these decisions. The topics that comprise the chapters in this book were selected because we thought that they constitute some of the most important problems that must be addressed in psychotherapy.

O'Donohue (1991) has provided a model for treatment decisions in which all major premises are explicated and form a valid deductive argument. In his model for what treatment methods should be used in this case. His model for deciding what treatment methods should be used is as follows:

1. Treatment goal G entails the realization of states of affairs S1 . . . Sn.
2. F1 . . . Fn are all factors that are known or hypothesized to be causally relevant to S1 . . . Sn.
3. F1 . . . Fn are the most cost-efficient methods and safe methods to obtain S1 . . . Sn.
4. F1 . . . Fn-m are the least restrictive methods to obtain S1 . . . Sn.
5. Client C is fully informed concerning alternative methods, the cost and benefits of these methods, and consents to the use of F1 . . . Fn-m.
6. If 1,2,3,4,5, and if *ceteris paribus* (if all other factors remain constant), then F1-Fn-m are the proper treatment methods to use in this case.
7. *Ceteris paribus*

Therefore, F1-Fnim are the proper treatment methods to use in this case.

PSYCHOTHERAPY IS BOTH AN ART AND A SCIENCE

In O'Donohue's model, treatment decisions can be seen to rely upon several different kinds of information.

- **Empirical information concerning particular facts.** For example, the clinician must assess the goals of a patient. However, there is an art to this (Miller & Rollnick, 2002). Does the client really want the stated goal? Is he after some other goal (see Cummings & Cummings, 2000, for the implicit contract in therapy)?
- **Moral and ethical considerations.** The clinician must decide whether the treatment goal is ethical.
- **Economic information.** Cost and benefits of alternatives must be determined and compared.
- **Causal information.** O'Donohue and Henderson (1999) have claimed that professionals have epistemic duties—requirements to know—and a particular epistemic duty concerns what treatments best produce what outcomes.
- **Pragmatic information.** The therapist must determine what is practically possible. There is an art to this, particularly in overcoming pragmatic obstacles.

The best health practices are a synthesis of science and art. Surgery is a case in point. Although all competent surgeons follow scientific protocols, the best surgeons are masters of the art of surgery and produce better outcomes (e.g., smaller incisions, lower infection and mortality rates). In addition, the best surgeons have a great deal of dexterity because they can handle all the unanticipated problems that arise during the course of surgery. Psychotherapists are in exactly the same position. Psychotherapy is both a science and an art. Sometimes acts of this sort have been called *praxis*—knowledgeable action. This is in contrast to purely theoretical knowledge, which is largely verbal but is not used to interact with the "furniture of the world" to move it around in desired ways. It has also been called *techne*. This implies that there is a distinction between more abstract scientific knowledge and the technical knowledge used to affect the world. All bridges must adhere to certain physical laws of gravity, strain, pressure, and so forth. But, some bridges do this in amazing fashions (the Golden Gate Bridge or the Brooklyn Bridge) whereas others do it in a much more mundane fashion. Sometimes, when some activity is seen as a blending of art and science, it is referred to as a *craft*. We think this is a good word. We know all plumbers must obey the laws of hydraulics; some are better at this craft than others. Unions recognize levels of mastery of a craft—from apprentice to journeyman to master.

AN OUTLINE OF THE PROBLEMS ENCOUNTERED IN THE ART OF PSYCHOTHERAPY

What are the major problems that require a healthful dose of craft that better therapists have? Here is a brief outline.

Clients come to us with various motivations and with various commitments to change. Accurately understanding clients' motivational structure and helping them clarify this and move toward positive, healthy motivations is a key technique in psychotherapy. In Chapter 2 Drs. Wilborune and Levensky deal with the art and science of this issue.

This is no cookbook for establishing a useful working relationship, sometimes called a *therapeutic alliance*. Mistakes can be made in many directions. We can become enmeshed with our clients in counterproductive ways for them and for us. Or we can be too cold and distant, and find that our clients do not return. Some clients are easier to form therapeutic bonds with than others. In Chapter 3, Dr. Jeremy Safran et al. examine the art and science of the therapeutic alliance.

We often seek the client's history—the story of his or her life. Often these stories are fascinating; sometimes they are tragic. It can be useful for the therapist and the client to understand the client's narrative. Seeing recurring themes, seeing tragic flaws, and so forth, can represent insights that both the therapist and the client find useful. In Chapter 4 Dr. Lois Parker describes the art and science of recognizing the patient's narrative.

Culture has become an increasingly important construct in late 20th century and early 21st century psychotherapy. Yet, perhaps because of the infancy of the discipline, it is poorly understood (O'Donohue, 2005). It also might be poorly understood because understanding the client as a person in a cultural context and understanding the particulars of that cultural context is, in part, an art. There are so may factors that can differ: the culture, the degree of assimilation, the degree to which the problem in therapy is a cultural problem (bedwetting would largely not be; responding to discrimination may well be). All render responding to this problem as, at least in part, a craft. Drs. Duckworth and lezzi, Chapter 5, talk about the science and art of dealing with this problem.

Some clients can be quite manipulative. They can want things that we, under normal circumstance, will not provide. I have seen a significant number of sex offenders who tried to fill their court-mandated requirement to be in therapy, manipulatively choose goals such as "help me deal with my stress of the legal system mishandling my case." The legal system wanted to reduce their potential to abuse other children; they wanted to see if they could avoid this issue by focusing on their stress and depression as a consequence of their conviction and incarceration. Individuals with some personality disorders can be particularly manipulative. Therapists have been warned that if they want to avoid malpractice suits, the single most important thing to do is avoid seeing individuals with borderline personality disorder. They can be near geniuses at manipulating therapists into changing their boundaries. In Chapter 6, Drs. Wetter and Wetter talk about the craft of dealing with the manipulative patient.

There is an art of seeing how the client sees us and how we see the client. This "seeing" can involve both the heart and the head. Emotionally we can evoke feelings on the part of the client (rape victims may see us as "males"). To a large extent we cannot avoid our demographics, and sometimes these can play important roles. On the other hand, often we are empathic, caring, and nurturing, and thus can give rise to other images and associated emotions: that of parent, ideal spouse, and so forth. In Chapter 7, Dr. George Stricker examines transference.

There is an art to case formulation and treatment plan development. Case formulation involves putting all the pieces together, arriving at diagnoses (perhaps), and coming up with an acceptable, effective treatment plan. There is no algorithm for this. One cannot just put in some facts and have a case formulation spit out. It takes judgment, and good case formulations take good judgment. If there is a poor case formulation, little success can be expected. In Chapter 8, Dr. Michael Hoyt covers this important skill.

One of the most prevalent and difficult problems is that clients are seldom "putty in our hands." Rather, they are often resistant. They may argue with our suggestions or interpretations. They may do the opposite of what is agreed on during therapy. They may miss sessions, come in late, lie, mislead or do other activities that can make therapy more difficult, or even sabotage it. Accurately seeing and effectively handling client resistance is a key therapy skill and this is covered in Chapter 9 by Dr. Nicholas Cummings.

In Chapter 10, Drs. Janet and Nicholas Cummings describe the craft of recognizing and using therapeutic entry points. Therapy usually can be seen as having some critical moments. The skilled psychotherapist must recognize when it is appropriate to begin to intervene with a particular type of patient and when it is not. Drs. Cummings describe their model of recognizing and utilizing these entry points.

We believe we have given you a flavor of some of the major problems in psychotherapy that this book will address. Others are

- The handling of meaninglessness and despair
- The use of homework
- The use of skills training
- The use of paradox
- The use of acceptance strategies
- The use of insight
- The use of novelty
- The handling of termination/therapy interruption
- The handling of the suicidal patient

We believe that therapists who follow empirically supported treatment manuals and who also have knowledge and skills in these areas will be superior therapists compared to those who follow empirically supported treatment manuals and do not have these skills. Although, at this point, this is an empirical claim waiting experimental testing, it is the hypothesis that is the basis for the editors' undertaking to assemble this book.

We were able to secure an amazing array of masterful psychotherapists. We believe that much of the excellence of the following chapters is a result of the experience and insights of this group. We have asked each chapter author to address the following subtopics:

- Definition of the key construct
- Detection and other assessment issues
- Theory and conceptualization regarding the key construct
- Impact on case formulation
- Clinical strategies
- Key mistakes and miscomprehensions
- Case study
- Summary

In conclusion, we hope that this book will bring insights into the craft of psychotherapy. We believe that the heuristics that are provided in this chapter should be further tested and refined. All psychotherapy should be practiced in the context of quality improvement (Fisher & O'Donohue, in press). Our suggestions, at a minimum, are useful starting points to be further refined in quality improvement processes. However, there may be a limitation to such quality improvement. Some philosophers of science such as Harold Brown (1988) and W. V. O. Quine (1969) state that good scientists simply have better judgment than mediocre or poor scientists. This also may be the case with psychotherapists. Thus, we hope that some of what follows may help refine the judgment of psychotherapists so that, ultimately, clients will experience better therapy.

REFERENCES

Brown, H. I. (1988). Normative epistemology and naturalized epistemology. *Inquiry, 31*, 53–78.

Cummings, N. A. (in press). Psychological treatment and assessment take place in an economic context. In S. O. Lilienfeld & W. T. O'Donohue (Eds.). *Great ideas in clinical psychology.* New York: Bruner-Taylor. (Still in Press)

Cummings, N. A., & Cummings, J. L. (2000). *The essence of psychotherapy: Reinventing the art in the new era of data.* New York: Academic Press.

Feyerabend, P. K. (1988). Knowledge and role of theories. *Philosophy of Social Sciences, 18,* 157–179.

Fisher, J. E., & O'Donohue, W. (Eds.). (in press). *Practitioners guide to evidence-based psychotherapy.* New York: Kluwer Academic/Plenum Publishers.

Hempel, C. G. (1965). Science and human values. In C. G. Hempel (Ed.). *Aspects of scientific explanation.* New York: Free Press.

Kuhn, T. S. (1962). *The structure of scientific revolutions.* Chicago: University of Chicago Press.

Lilienfeld, S. O., Wood, J. M., & Garb, H. M. (2000). The scientific status of projective techniques. *Psychological Science in the Public Interest 1(2)*, 27–66.

Miller, W. R., & Rollnick, S. (2002). *Motivational interviewing: Preparing people for change.* New York: Guilford Press.

O'Donohue, W. T. (1989). The (even) bolder model: The clinical psychologist as metaphysician–scientist–practitioner. *American Psychologist, 44,* 1460–1468.

O'Donohue, W. T. (1991). Normative models of clinical decisions. *The Behavior Therapist,* 14(3), 70–72.

O'Donohue, W., Fisher, J. E., & Hayes, S.C. (Eds.). (2003). *Cognitive behavior therapy: A step-by-step guide for clinicians.* New York: John Wiley.

O'Donohue, W., & Henderson, D. (1999). Epistemic and ethical duties in clinical decision-making. *Behaviour Change, 16,* 10–19.

O'Donohue, W. T. (2005). Cultural sensitivity: A critical examination. In R. G. Wright & N. A. Cummings (Eds.) Destructive Trends in Mental Health: The Well-Intentioned Path to Harm. Pp. 29–44.

Popper, K. R. (1972). *Objective knowledge: An evolutionary approach.* Oxford: Oxford University Press.

Quine, W. V. O. (1969). *Ontological reality and other essays.* New York: Columbia.

Thomas, S. E. G., Werner–Wilson, R. J., & Murphy, M. J. (2005). Influence of therapist and client behaviors on the therapy alliance. *Contemporary Family Therapy: An International Journal, 27,* 19–35.

2

ENHANCING CLIENT
MOTIVATION TO CHANGE

PAULA L. WILBOURNE

Center for Health Care Evaluation
VA Palo Alto Health Care System
Stanford University School of Medicine
Palo Alto, California

ERIC R. LEVENSKY

Center for Alcoholism Substance Abuse and Addiction Albuquergue,
New Mexico

Likewise, there is something special about clients who stick with treatment, take their medications, and complete homework assignments: They are motivated. These clients work hard and they tend to get better (Burns & Spangler, 2000; DiMatteo, Giordani, Lepper, et al., 2002; Finney and Moos, 2003; Kazantzis, Deane, & Ronan, 2000). There is something special about a single session of therapy that performs as well as longer interventions, leads to increased follow-up on treatment referrals, results in increased participation once treatment is started, and produces better outcome one year later (Brown & Miller, 1993; Miller, Benefield, & Tonigan, 1993; Project MATCH Research Group, 1997). There is also something special about therapists with certain characteristics that inspire more consistent improvement in the clients they treat (Fiorentine & Hillhouse, 1999; Valle, 1981). What do these all have in common? These clients, treatments, and therapists capitalize on the client's intrinsic strengths. This approach to therapy is founded in an empathic, collaborative relationship to build motivation and instigate change (Valle, 1981). This chapter provides a definition of motivation, a description of how people change, and an outline of an intervention that has been empirically supported for helping people get motivated and make changes.

DEFINITION

Motivation is the probability that individuals will enter into, continue, and adhere to a specific change strategy or to specific behaviors that direct them toward a goal (Miller & Rollnick, 1991). It can involve making a decision to make a change, as well as behavioral strategies or actions that can facilitate such a change. Motivation is a dynamic state that can be influenced by internal and external factors. It is highly sensitive to a person's environment and to the influence of a therapist. Additionally, therapists can be most effective when motivation is evoked from the client rather than imposed from the outside.

Consistent with this framework for understanding motivation, Prochaska and DiClemente (1982) outlined the transtheoretical model, which defines stages of change through which individuals pass as they make changes. These stages include precontemplation, contemplation, determination, action, maintenance, and relapse. As individuals progress through these stages, they experience fluctuations in problem recognition, in ambivalence about making changes, and in their willingness to take action (Fig. 2.1).

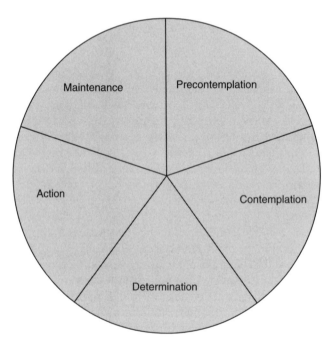

FIGURE 2.1   Stages of change. The use of a wheel to illustrate the stages of change reflects the fact that most individuals will go through these stages, or around the wheel, several times during the process of making lasting change.

A client in the precontemplation stage is not considering making changes. Although this individual may experience distress or problems related to an issue of clinical concern, she or he has not yet identified the issue as a problem that requires consideration. For example, a person may experience a number of problems related to alcohol consumption, such as hangovers, marital conflict, or difficulties at work, without identifying drinking as a problem that merits reflection or action.

As this individual's awareness of the problem increases, he enters contemplation, a stage that is characterized by ambivalence. Ambivalence reflects the experience of a client who simultaneously wants to change and wants to stay the same. Contemplating clients may alternate between outlining the reasons that they should change and outlining the reasons to keep things they way they are. When this balance tips in favor of making a change, the client moves into the determination stage. A client in the determination stage is aware that something has to change, and makes future plans to change. Individuals in determination may plan to make a change even though they may not identify their problems in the same ways as their provider (e.g., embrace the label of alcoholic, describe themselves as mentally ill). When individuals begin taking steps to instigate change, they have moved into the action stage. When small actions by the client come together to change that individual's life, this person can be thought to have entered the maintenance stage. Maintenance can vary in its stability and may include "slips" to previous behaviors.

ENHANCING MOTIVATION
FOR CHANGE

Motivational interviewing (MI) is a directive, client-centered approach for enhancing motivation to change by exploring and resolving ambivalence (Miller & Rollnick, 2002). In the 25 years since its inception, it has earned strong empirical support (Burke, Arkowitz, & Dunn, 2002; Burke, Arkowitz, & Menchola, 2003). Typically, MI is used as a brief intervention of one to four sessions. However, adaptations of MI have ranged from interventions as brief as 5 to 15 minutes in medical settings (e.g., Rollnick, Heather, & Bell, 1992) to a manualized four-session therapy (e.g., Project MATCH Research Group, 1997). The MI approach has been used to help engage clients in treatment, to help individuals instigate change in the context of ongoing treatment, and as an effective stand-alone intervention. In recent years, MI has become a widely used treatment for problem drinking, and has also been adapted to promote health behavior change in a number of other areas, including drug abuse, smoking, HIV risk, exercise, diet, sexual offending, diabetes, and chronic pain (see Dunn, Deroo, & Rivera, 2001; and Miller, 1996 for reviews of this literature). MI has empirical support in many of these applications, including the treatment of the behavioral targets of alcohol problems, drug problems, diabetes adherence, hypertension adherence, dual diagnosis, bulimia, dietary changes, treatment attendance, and increasing physical activity (Burke et al., 2002, 2003). Mixed support has been demonstrated for MI in the treatment of cigarette smoking and enhancing dietary adherence in clients with hyperlipidemia (Burke et al., 2002)

MI emphasizes the autonomy of the client and the client's ultimate responsibility for deciding, committing, and following through with changes. Therapists facilitate this process through the use of empathic listening and acceptance in combination with more directive, structured techniques. Clients and providers work in collaboration. Therapists avoid the use of authority, education, confrontation, or argumentation to persuade or convince clients to change. In this vein, practitioners strive to avoid taking responsibility for one side of the client's ambivalence, based on the assumption that advocacy for change by the therapist will result in client's advocating to stay the same. Instead, clients are encouraged to experience explicitly and take responsibility for the discomfort that results from simultaneously considering both sides of their own ambivalence. Therapists strive to convey acceptance of the client's perspective while assisting the client in shifting this perspective.

Consistent with the brief intervention model, the client is seen as the primary agent responsible for framing the clinical issues and generating the strategies for change. A key assumption in MI is that clients have many capabilities, skills, and resources that can be utilized to effect change with minimal education or skills training involved in this therapy. Therapists use affirmation to support clients' awareness of their own strengths and resources for change. Miller and Rollnick (2002) have described five principles that are core to MI: expressing empathy, developing discrepancies, avoiding argumentation, rolling with resistance, and supporting self-efficacy.

EXPRESSED EMPATHY

In this framework, expressed empathy includes communication of acceptance of the client's perspective and the use of reflective listening. Empathy may also involve normalizing the client's ambivalence about making changes. Moyers, Martin, and Manuel (2005) describe this as the "therapist's interest in making sure they have understood what the client is saying" and "all efforts that the therapist makes to [en]sure that they are truly understanding the clients perspective or a complex story." Empathy includes the therapist's efforts to deepen the shared appreciation of the client's experience through the use of metaphor or by reflecting the emotions that may not be explicitly described by the client.

DEVELOPING DISCREPANCIES

The second principle refers to the MI practitioner's efforts to increase the client's awareness of discrepancies between the client's current behavior and his or her values, goals, or more modest hopes for the near future. Clients' awareness of the discrepancy between their current situation or current trajectory and the desired situation often prompts them to outline the reasons they need to change, make plans to start changing, and make lasting commitments to maintaining these changes. Open-ended questions, affirmations, and formal assessments are tools that therapists may use to assist clients in becoming aware of their hopes and values.

AVOIDING ARGUMENTATION

The third defining principle in MI highlights the importance of avoiding argumentation. When considering clients' ambivalence, it is important that the client experience responsibility for both sides of the argument regarding change (i.e., the good things about the status quo and their reasons for making a change away from the status quo). When practitioners advocate or push for change, clients may experience a reduction in personal responsibility for that side of the ambivalence. This approach often leaves clients feeling defensive and puts them in the position to argue against making a change. In MI, resistance and argumentation are interpreted as clear signs to shift therapeutic strategies.

ROLLING WITH RESISTANCE

The fourth defining principle, rolling with resistance, highlights the strategies that are used when clients voice resistance to change or the therapeutic process. Resistance is generally seen as a signal to the therapist to try something different. Using an MI framework, therapists never directly oppose resistance. Instead, they may empathize with the client, attempt subtly to redirect the client's momentum, or simply change the clinical focus away from the area of resistance. Therapists may use tools such as reflections, reframing, or agreement with a twist when clients outline reasons not to change or when they show resistance in a clinical setting. These techniques are outlined in Table 2.1.

SUPPORTING SELF-EFFICACY

The final defining principle of MI underscores the importance of clients' belief in their ability to carry through with change successfully. To foster this sense of belief and confidence, therapists may inquire about times when this problem was better (e.g., "What was your life like when you were getting

TABLE 2.1   Examples of the Therapist "Rolling with Resistance" Client Statement: "I could never quit drinking. All my friends and coworkers drink. I could never stand to refuse them."

Therapist Response	Clinical Technique
"You may be right about that. You may decide that it is not worth it to stop drinking. Ultimately, you will have to decide."	Affirmation, emphasizing choice, assigning responsibility for the decision to change
"It might be intolerable."	Simple reflection
"You may lose all your important relationships if you choose to stop drinking."	Amplified reflection
"These relationships are important to you. You would have to evaluate your relationships to these people if you were going to make some changes in your drinking."	Reframe
"Tell me some of the things you like about your drinking."	Shifting focus, open question

more exercise?"), inquire about difficult changes the client has made in other domains (e.g., "You mentioned that you quit smoking several years ago. How did you make that change?"), inquire about areas of strength for a particular client (e.g. "You mentioned a certainty that you could quit anytime you would like. Hypothetically speaking, tell me a little about the steps you would take if you decided to make that change."), and affirm strengths that are evident in the client ("You are a graceful person. I am sure you would find a way to turn down dessert/a drink/etc. without hurting anyone's feelings."). Therapists may also share strategies or information about how other clients have made similar changes to increase self-efficacy.

Rollnick and Miller (1995) argue that it is essential for the therapists delivering MI to understand fully, and act in accordance with the "spirit" of the approach, rather than merely following the strategies and techniques that make up the treatment. A useful way to convey the "spirit" of MI is to contrast it with other common approaches to behavior change. Miller and Rollnick (2002) provide three tables contrasting the important elements (e.g., principles, strategies, and techniques) of MI with the elements of *confrontation of denial, skills training*, and *nondirective* approaches to behavior change. These contrasting elements are presented in Table 2.2. Some important points about the nature of MI illustrated in these tables are that MI is an inherently nonconfrontational, yet quite directive, approach that attempts to produce change through creating and mobilizing a client's intrinsic motivation rather than producing change through external forces or skills training.

TABLE 2.2   Contrasts among Motivational Interviewing and Other Common Methods of Producing Behavior Change

Confrontation-of-Denial Approach	Motivational Interviewing Approach
Heavy emphasis on acceptance of self as having a problem; acceptance of diagnosis seen as essential for change	Deemphasis on labels; acceptance of "alcoholism" or other labels seen as unnecessary for change to occur
Emphasis on personality pathology, which reduces personal choice, judgment, and control	Emphasis on personal choice and responsibility for deciding future behavior
Therapist presents perceived evidence of problems in an attempt to convince the client to accept the diagnosis	Therapist conducts objective evaluation, but focuses on eliciting the client's own concerns
Resistance is seen as "denial," a trait characteristic requiring confrontation	Resistance is seen as an interpersonal behavior pattern influenced by the therapist's behavior
Resistance is met with argumentation and correction	Resistance is met with reflection
Goals of treatment and strategies for change are prescribed for the client by the therapist; client is seen as "in denial" and incapable of making sound decisions	Treatment goals and change strategies are negotiated between client and therapist, based on data and acceptability; client's involvement in and acceptance of goals are seen as vital

Skills Training Approach	Motivational Interviewing Approach
Assumes that the client is motivated; no direct strategies are use for building motivation	Employs specific principles and strategies for building client motivation for change
Seeks to identify and modify maladaptive cognitions	Explores and reflects client perceptions without labeling or "correcting" them
Prescribes specific coping strategies	Elicits possible change strategies from the client and significant others
Teaches coping behaviors through instruction, modeling, directed practice, and feedback	Responsibility for change methods is left with the client; no training, modeling, or practice
Specific problem-solving strategies are taught	Natural problem-solving processes are elicited from the client and significant others

Nondirective Approach	Motivational Interviewing Approach
Allows the client to determine the content and direction of counseling	Systematically directs the client toward motivation for change
Avoids injecting the therapist's own advice and feedback	Offers the therapist's own advice and feedback when appropriate
Empathetic reflection is used noncontingently	Empathetic reflection is used selectively to reinforce certain processes
Explores the client's conflicts and emotions as they exist currently	Seeks to create and amplify the client's discrepancy to enhance motivation for change

Reprinted with permission from Miller, W. R., & Rollnick, S. (1991). *Motivational interviewing: Preparing people for change.* New York: Guilford Press.

ASSESSMENT

A number of assessment tools are available for measuring client motivation. Other assessment tools produce information that is useful in getting clients motivated. Tools aimed at measuring motivation directly include the University of Rhode Island Change Assessment Scale (URICA), the Stages of Change Readiness and Treatment Eagerness Scale (SOCRATES), and the Readiness Ruler (Bernstein, Bernstein, & Levenson, 1997; DiClemente, Carbonari, Montgomery, & Hughes, 1994; McConnaughy, Prochaska, & Velicer, 1983; Miller & Tonigan, 1996). Some tools focus on placing the client into a particular stage of change, whereas others measure dimensions thought to be related to the stage of change and motivation. These dimensions include the client's degree of ambivalence, the degree to which a client identifies his or her behavior as a problem, and the degree to which the client is already taking steps to change his behavior. It is recommended that practitioners interested in formal assessments consult the readings at the end of this section for more detailed information on the utility of these measures.

Other information gained through assessment can be used as part of clinical interventions that help increase motivation. Readiness Rulers can be used to assess the client's readiness to make change, the importance the client places on making change, and the client's confidence that he can make changes. Typically, the clinician might ask, "On a scale of one to ten, one being not at all important and ten being the most important, how important is it for you to make changes in your diet?" When the client gives a number associated with the importance of change, the clinician can then use this anchor point to explore further the importance the client places on change and as a tool to prompt the client to outline his reasons for change. If the client were to choose the number five, the clinician could respond by stating, "A five. What makes that number a five instead of a one?" Asking this type of "backward" question, generally prompts clients to explain their desire for change, their reasons for change, and their need for change. In contrast, a "forward" question such as, "What would it take to increase that number up to a six or a seven?" can help the client begin to articulate and imagine what it would take to get even more serious about making a change. When using the ruler to assess confidence, readiness, and importance, it is important to avoid asking clients why they did not choose a higher number, because this tends to elicit resistance.

The Personal Values Card Sort assists in clarifying clients' fundamental values (Miller, C'de Baca, Matthews, & Wilbourne, 2003a). In a typical administration, clients are asked to sort 83 value cards into three groups: very important, important, and not important. Clients can then be asked to look through the values located in the very important group to identify and then rank order the five to ten values that are the most important to them.

Although identifying a client's values is useful in itself, it can be particularly helpful in developing discrepancies between the client's current behavior and her most important values and goals. Open-ended questions asking clients how the behavior of interest fits in with their most important values can provide a new perspective on an entrenched problem behavior.

When possible, assessments are designed to generate normative feedback. This is feedback that compares the client's responses with that of the general population or with that of a relevant, clinical population. The focus of these assessments can vary based on the issue of clinical concern. Behaviors such as drinks consumed, calories consumed, or cigarettes smoked are relatively easy to assess for target behaviors of problem drinking, obesity, or smoking cessation. Lab results with clear upper limits and a demonstrable relationship to the client's behavior are also good targets for assessment feedback. Useful objective assessments that include blood pressure, body weight, lipid levels, and blood glucose can be used when clients are struggling with hypertension, hyperlipidemia, or diabetes. Assessment feedback can also focus on healthy limits, such as normal blood pressure, safe blood sugar, or upper limits of safe or typical behavior. The results of these assessments are given back to the client in a nonjudgmental, nonconfrontational manner that is described in greater detail next.

THEORETICAL UNDERPINNINGS OF MOTIVATIONAL INTERVIEWING

Surprisingly, MI did not grow out of a theory about how to motivate people. It grew out of a set of intuitive principles that were specified before the treatment began to gain its current empirical support. Its creators, Miller and Rollnick (1991, 2002), suggest that MI produces behavioral change by creating an uncomfortable discrepancy between the life a client would like to lead (i.e., their values and goals) and how the client is currently living (e.g., consequences of the behavioral problem). They argue that clients are motivated to reduce this uncomfortable discrepancy and, in the context of a directive, reflective, supportive, and nonconfrontational therapeutic interaction, will do so by making behavioral changes that are consistent with their life goals and values. This perspective assumes (1) that client motivation must come from within the client (as opposed to external forces) and that (2) the therapist has an important role in eliciting and in enhancing this motivation.

MI assumes that (1) clients are ambivalent about changing their behavior, (2) it is this ambivalence that keeps clients immobilized, and (3) the primary task of the therapist is to help clients understand and resolve this ambivalence in a manner that produces behavioral change. Ambivalence is thought of as a state in which clients have compelling reasons for both changing their behavior and not changing it. An example of such ambivalence would be an individual wanting to stop smoking to increase the quality of his health and spousal relationship, and not wanting to stop because in doing so he would lose the stress reduction and weight control benefits he attributes to his cigarette use.

Research supports the existence of four underlying mechanisms in MI (Miller et al., 1993; Miller, Yahne, & Tonigan, 2003b; Amrhein, Miller, & Yahnes, 2003). First, MI has been shown to reduce client resistance (e.g., arguing, interrupting, defending reasons not to change) in session. Second, client resistance has a strong relationship with a lack of change. Third, MI has been shown to increase "change talk" in session. Change talk is defined as statements made by the client that outline clients' own desire to change, their ability to change, the reasons to change, and the need to do something different. Research suggests that this kind of change talk predicts commitments to change, which is in turn linked to observable changes. Finally, an intriguing relationship between change talk and change has been observed. The simple amount of change talk does not predict change. However, change talk that increases throughout the session and leads to a verbal commitment to change leads to observable behavior change.

THE PRACTICE OF MOTIVATIONAL INTERVIEWING

GETTING STARTED IN MOTIVATIONAL INTERVIEWING

As stated earlier, MI is as much a stylistic approach to interacting with clients to produce behavior change as a specific set of techniques. Therefore, what is most important in conducting MI is that the therapist adheres to the "spirit" of MI by adhering to its core therapeutic principles. This section describes MI so that therapists can come to understand the fundamental principles and techniques of this approach. MI can be a rather technically complex intervention, and a comprehensive description of its techniques is beyond the scope of this chapter. However, it is hoped that the information included here will provide the basis for faithful implementation of the basic approach. Readers are encouraged to refer to the more comprehensive descriptions of MI techniques listed in the recommended readings section at the conclusion of this chapter.

PHASE I: SPECIFIC STRATEGIES FOR ENHANCING MOTIVATION FOR CHANGE

The essential task of the therapist in MI is to engage in very specific sets of behaviors that will enhance clients' *intrinsic* motivation to make behavioral changes and facilitate clients' translation of that motivation into change-related behaviors. It can be useful to think of two phases of MI. The first phase is best thought of as focused on building motivation to change; with the second phase, as focused on strengthening commitment to change and making a plan for change. Phase one can also involve providing clients with personalized, normative feedback on their behavior and it's consequences. During both phases of MI, the therapist engages in specific behaviors to help the client to identify and resolve his or her ambivalence about change. These behaviors typically include eliciting and reinforcing self-motivating statements through asking open-ended questions, listening reflectively, summarizing, and affirming the client (Miller & Rollnick, 2002, Rollnick & Miller, 1995).

Asking Open-Ended Questions

In MI, the therapist works to help the client identify his or her reasons for and against making a change. If the target behavior is causing significant distress in the client's life, the reasons for changing will likely become more compelling to the client than the reasons against change. The *therapist* does not attempt to resolve ambivalence by presenting arguments to the client for the existence of a problem or for the need for change; rather, the therapist assists the client in articulating and generating these arguments. Specifically, the therapist attempts to elicit self-motivational statements, or change talk, from the client by encouraging him or her to discuss the behavior and its consequences in the context of the client's values and goals. The therapist elicits these statements by asking open-ended questions (i.e., cannot be answered with yes or no) regarding the problem behavior and its consequences. It is often useful to begin with disarming questions that focus on the reasons for keeping things the way they are (e.g., What do you like about smoking/drinking/isolating?). Open-ended questions include

- What do you like about using cocaine?
- What are the not-so-good things about using cocaine?
- What concerns you about your diet?
- What have been some of the problems you experienced as a result of smoking?
- You mentioned that your wife is worried about your avoidance behaviors, but what are some of your concerns about them?
- Why do you think you need to make a change in your amount of exercise?
- Why does making a change in your gambling feel important to you?

It can be useful to follow open-ended questions with reflections and additional follow-up open questions. Doing so helps to ensure that the therapist understands the client's perspective, and it also tends to elicit more change talk. Examples of such questions include, "How else has your drinking impacted your relationships?" and "What else do you enjoy about smoking?" Additionally, open-ended questions about the client's goals for the future, and the impact of the problem behavior on the client's ability to reach these goals, can be useful in developing discrepancies between client's hopes and the targeted behavior.

PERSONALIZED FEEDBACK OF ASSESSMENT RESULTS

Another method for eliciting self-motivational statements is to provide the client with individualized assessment feedback regarding the behavior of interest and its consequences. This type of feedback is very different from educational information about the effects of the problem behavior or feedback about the interpersonal consequences of the client's behavior. MI-consistent feedback does not include interpretations or the therapist's opinions. Rather, MI-consistent feedback includes assessment results with normative comparisons with other people. For example, a 45-year- old male client who indicates that he is currently drinking 20 drinks per week could be told that compared with other American men his age, he is drinking more than 90% of them. This approach to feedback can be used with lab results as well. Normative feedback can be provided on any assessment dimension for which information on the occurrence of the condition in the general population or a clinical population is available, including body weight, blood sugar, infection rate, and so forth. Assistance with normative data on substance use can be obtained from the online Web sites listed in the recommended readings section at the end of this chapter. When assessment feedback is given, the clinician uses reflective listening, affirmation and open-quesions to explore the client's reactions to the feedback. For example, "Does that sound about right to you?" or "How do you make sense of this information?".

Listening Reflectively

Reflective listening serves as the primary mode of interacting with the client throughout the entire MI process. As the client responds to the open-ended questions and feedback, the therapist uses several reflective listening techniques to facilitate the exploration and resolution of the client's ambivalence. These techniques include (1) listening carefully to the content and meaning of what the client is saying; (2) repeating back the content, meaning, and affect of what the client has said, or rephrasing, paraphrasing, or summarizing it; (3) "mind reading," or reflecting back what the client may be feeling or thinking but has not said directly; and (4) validating or affirming the client, or communicating to the client that his or her thoughts and feelings (including ambivalence) are understandable. The primary functions of reflective listening are to highlight and reinforce the client's self-motivational statements and to reduce his or her resistance to change. However, skillful reflective listening likely serves other important functions, including (1) making the client feel respected, listened to, and understood; (2) ensuring that the therapist understands what the client is saying; (3) encouraging the client to discuss issues around his or her ambivalence; and (4) helping the therapist understand the nature of the client's ambivalence (Miller, Zweben, DiClemente, & Rychtarik, 1992).

Several approaches help to ensure that reflective listening techniques achieve their intended functions (Miller & Rollnick, 1991). First, reflections that highlight self-motivational statements, as opposed to other content, are most likely to guide the client's awareness toward change and will likely result in further elaboration and more "change talk." Second, the reflections must not be biased. That is, if the client states both the reasons for changing and for not changing, both sides of this ambivalence should be reflected by the therapist. Related to this, the therapist should not appear to be confrontational, have an agenda of change, or be judgmental about the behavior. Any of these would likely result in resistance, which would derail the change process. Third, although the therapist is not confrontational about change, the therapist is quite directive in that he or she systematically uses open-ended questions and empathic listening skills to highlight the costs of inaction and the benefits of change, and encourages clients to weigh the pros and cons of changing the behavior. An overarching goal is to help clients perceive the discrepancy between problematic behaviors and important life goals and core values by reflecting the client's own statements. Fourth, the accuracy of reflections are important. Reflections that miss the mark will likely lead the client to feel misunderstood, and may lead to resistance. Fortunately, clients usually give nearly instantaneous feedback regarding the accuracy of a reflection. Having emphasized the importance of accurate reflection, it is valuable to note that skilled listeners can use reflective listening in a strategic manner. Reflections that amplify resistance often lead to a reduction in resistance. Reflections that understate a client's concerns generally lead to further elaboration. The following is a brief example of the use of reflective listening in conjunction with eliciting self-motivational statements:

Client: "I have tried cutting back and I have tried quitting. I have taken pills and used the patch. You name it, I have tried it. "

Reflection with understatement: "You have a bit of experience with trying to quit."

Reflection with amplification: "You have tried it all. Nothing is ever going to work for you."

Summarizing

It can be useful to summarize periodically what the client has said during the session. Summarizing ensures that the therapist understands the client's perspective and highlights all the "change talk" articulated by the client. It also demonstrates to the client that the therapist has been listening. It is crucial that the therapist include a summary of the client's self-motivational statements. However, the summary should also include other important elements of the client's ambivalence. Summary statements should not include the therapist's interpretations.

Affirming the Client

Affirmations are statements that communicate acceptance, respect, appreciation, encouragement, and faith in the client's abilities to make changes. Clients with long histories of mental illness or substance use may have little experience with being affirmed. When sincere, the process of affirmation can bolster clients' faith in themselves, validate clients for their efforts, reinforce engagement in the therapeutic process, enhance the therapeutic relationship, and support self-efficacy. Affirming statements can be made throughout the therapeutic process, but they should only be offered when the therapist believes them. Table 2.3 provides examples of affirmations of support and appreciation as well as of a client's strengths and character.

STRATEGIES FOR RESPONDING TO RESISTANCE

Resistance is thought of as behaviors that interfere with behavior change or the therapeutic process. These can include arguing, not following through with therapy homework, denying that behavior change is needed, lying, not listening, and interrupting (Miller & Rollnick, 2002). In MI, resistance is not considered to be a pathological characteristic of the client, but rather is thought of as the result of the therapist misjudging the client's readiness to change and proceeding toward change faster than the client is ready to do so, or the result of the client feeling invalidated or misunderstood. MI assumes that a client's readiness to change will fluctuate throughout the change process. Therefore, it is up to the therapist to monitor continually the client's

TABLE 2.3   Examples of Affirmations

Affirmations of Support and Appreciation	Affirmations of the Client's Strengths or Character
"You're coming up with great ideas."	"You really care about your family and want to make sure you are there for them."
"I think you are on to something important." "That sounds like a very workable plan."	"You are a very good problem solver. You have a wonderful ability to find creative solutions to overcome challenges."
"I know that talking about these things is difficult, and I appreciate your willingness to do it."	"You have central personal values, and it's important to you that you live up to them."
"I think most people in your situation would feel stressed."	"It's very important to you to treat people with respect and kindness."
"It makes sense to me that you would be concerned about that."	"You have overcome a lot in your life and you have the ability to make difficult changes in your life."
	"You have a lot of inner strength that helps you overcome difficult times."

readiness to change and act accordingly (see a later section, "Assessing Readiness to Change").

Although it can be tempting, the therapist never responds to client resistance in a confrontational or change-focused manner (arguing, confrontation, persuading, coercing, pathologizing, threatening, and so on). Such behaviors only strengthen client resistance. Rather, the therapist responds to resistance with a number of alternate responses consistent with the spirit of MI (Miller & Rollnick, 1991). See Table 2.4 for descriptions of these types of alternate responses, as well as examples of each.

PHASE II: STRENGTHENING COMMITMENT AND MAKING A PLAN FOR CHANGE

Once a client appears motivated to make behavioral changes, the focus of treatment in MI typically transitions from phase I (building motivation) to

TABLE 2.4   Strategies for Handling Client Resistance

Simple reflection: Reflecting the resistant statement
Client: "My diet is pretty much fine the way it is."
Therapist: "You're fairly content with your diet as it is."

Reflection with amplification: Amplifying the resistant statement
Client: "I don't think my smoking is a problem."
Therapist: "Your smoking hasn't caused you any problems at all."

Double-sided reflection: Highlighting both sides of the ambivalence in response to a resistant statement
Client: "If I stop smoking, I'm sure I will gain a ton of weight."
Therapist: "On one hand, you're worried that quitting will cause you to gain weight, and on the other, you are worried that continuing to smoke may harm your relationship."

Shifting the focus: Shifting the topic away from the object of the resistant statement
Client: "My life is way too chaotic right now to make a change in my diet."
Therapist: "Let's not jump into the kinds of changes a person might make. You mentioned earlier that you had some concerns about your health. Would you mind telling me a little more about those?"

Paradox: Going along with the resistance to promote a shift to a direction of change
Client: "I've been drinking for 20 years. I can't even imagine my life without it."
Therapist: "You have been drinking for a long time. It may be too hard to quit now."

Reframing: Recasting resistant statements in a manner that favors change without challenging the content of the statement
Client: "I can handle my cocaine much better these days. I rarely get too high anymore."
Therapist: "When people have used a lot of cocaine they will often build up a tolerance to it."

Emphasizing personal control: Communicating that it is up to the client to decide whether he or she will change and what he or she will do to make the change
Client: "I really don't think I need to stop smoking"
Therapist: "This is entirely your decision. You get to decide whether you will stop smoking."

Adapted from from Miller and Rollnick, 1991.

phase II, which involves strengthening the client's commitment to change and the development of a specific plan for change. Many of the same basic skills used in phase I (i.e. open questions, affirmation, reflective listening, evoking information from the client) will be important when the focus shift towards change planning in phase II. Miller and Rollnick (2002) and Miller et al. (1992) discuss several guidelines for making this transition.

Assessing Readiness to Change

Before moving into the behavior change planning phase, the therapist must determine whether the client is sufficiently motivated to make such a change. Underestimating a client's ambivalence (or overestimating their motivation/ commitment) about change can often lead to resistance or failure to follow through with a change plan. Miller and Rollnick (1991) suggest several factors the therapist can look for as signs that the client is motivated for change:

- The client is less resistant (e.g., stops arguing, denying the problem, and raising objections).
- The client asks fewer questions about the problem.
- The client appears more resolved (e.g., peaceful and settled).
- The client asks questions or makes statements indicating that he or she is oriented or open to change (e.g., recognizing the need to change, asking about how to change, imagining life with behavior change).
- The client makes attempts at behavior change or takes steps to prepare for change (e.g., smokes fewer cigarettes, looks into a membership at a gym). (p. 115)

Although these behaviors can indicate a client's readiness to move on to the change planning phase, it is important to note that readiness to change is not a fixed client trait; rather, it is an ever-fluctuating state. Therefore, it is typically necessary for the therapist to be on the lookout for resistance or ambivalence, and use the techniques mentioned during phase I.

Discussing a Change Plan

Once the therapist has determined that the client is sufficiently motivated to change, the therapist begins to facilitate the client's movement toward and commitment to a course of action. Consistent with the spirit of MI, it is useful to start out by asking the client to suggest the course of action. The therapist can facilitate the beginning of this process by asking the client several key questions and responding with reflection and affirmation:

- What would you like to do about this?
- Where do you see yourself going from here?
- If you were to make a change, were would you start?

MI fundamentally assumes that clients have many capabilities, skills, and resources that can be utilized to effect change. Therefore, the therapist should always look for opportunities to identify, elicit, highlight, and affirm the client's change-related strengths so that these can be used in the change plan.

If the client does not generate, on his or her own, ideas for change, the therapist can ask the client open-ended questions about how he or she would like to go about making them. Examples of such questions include

- What do you think the change plan should include?
- What are some important things for us to think about when planning this kind of change?
- How have you made changes in the past?
- What has helped you in the past to make difficult changes?
- Now that you have some ideas about how to proceed, what might get in the way? What has gotten in the way in past change attempts? How did you manage these things?
- What do you think we might be missing in this plan?

The therapist responds with reflection, emphasizes the client's free choice, and does not tell the client what changes to make or how to make them.

Providing Information and Advice

MI therapists use care when providing information or advice. There are several strategies that are key to doing these things in an MI consistent manner. First, therapists should elicit information about the issue from the client. This starts with open-ended questions and continues with reflective listening, affirmation and more open questions. For example, an MI consistent approach might include asking the client what they already know about controlling their blood sugar. The therapist would then affirm elements that they want to reinforce and attempt to reframe areas where the clients information on the topic is insufficient. Exploring the client's existing knowledge is not done in a perfunctory manner, but with sincere effort to elicit the client's expertise. After the clinician has thoroughly explored the clients existing knowledge, the clinician has several options for adding offering information. Educational information can be framed as information for the client's consideration rather than information that is handed down from an authoritarian therapist. Clinicians can also ask the client's permission to share information in order to make the process of educating the client more collaborative and MI-consistent.

The process of offering advice can unfold in a similar manner. There may be instances when the therapist feels ethically compelled to give advice or when the client requests advice. In these instances, it is important for the therapist to ask the client's permission and to provide clear and accurate information. It can also be useful to frame suggestions or recommendations as issues for the client's consideration, rather than prescriptions for what he or she should do. Additionally, when possible, the client should be presented with several options or a menu of change options from which to choose.

Nature of the Change Plan

A common hazard in the development of change plans is insufficient direction and specificity. Therefore, it is important that the therapist facilitate the client's specification of (1) the change the client wants to make, (2) why the client wants to make that change, (3) the specific steps the client will take to make the change, (4) the barriers that may hinder change or result from change, (5) the things that would help the client to carry out the change plan, and (6) how the client will know that the plan is working (Miller et al., 1992). Also important to this process is setting achievable goals, and identifying and evaluating alternative change options. A particularly useful strategy for assessing clients' confidence that a change plan will work is to have them rate their confidence in making the change on a scale of one to ten, where one is not at all confident and ten is very confident. Therapists can the use "forward" questions to assess what might be useful for increasing confidence. Affirmations that express the therapist's faith in the client's ability to follow through may also increase the client's self-efficacy for change.

COMMON THERAPIST TRAPS

Therapists often get stuck in particular interactional patterns when doing MI. These patterns, or traps, are worth mentioning, because even the most skilled and well-intentioned therapists can fall into them, and doing so significantly undermines the effective delivery of MI. Moreover, if the therapist falls into these traps early in the session, it may set the stage for problematic interactions throughout the remainder of the session.

The Question–Answer Trap

In MI, a therapist can easily fall into a pattern of asking several questions in a row to which clients respond to with short answers. This pattern can emerge when the therapist needs to obtain a lot of initial background information, when the therapist is feeling the need to control the session, or when the client is uncomfortable with discussing specific issues. This trap is particularly problematic because it establishes the client in a passive role in therapy. Solutions to avoiding this trap include having clients complete questionnaires on which they can provide initial intake information (as opposed to the therapist asking these questions in session), asking open-ended questions, and responding to the clients responses with reflective listening rather than additional questions. Alternatively, MI therapists can develop skill in listening for specific information (age, marital status, problem identification, and so on) in the client's narrative responses to open-ended questions.

The Taking Sides Trap

For good reasons, therapists are typically in favor of clients engaging in certain behaviors as opposed to others (e.g., attending therapy and completing treatment recommendations as opposed to not doing so), and making specific behavioral changes (e.g., reducing substance use and increasing self-care). This bias is typically well-intentioned. However, clients are often ambivalent about making changes, and when therapists argue for change, clients will often respond by arguing for the opposite (no change) and can tend to convince themselves not to change. As is the case with the question–answer trap, the solution to this trap is to ask specific, open-ended questions followed by selective reflective listening to help the clients resolve their own ambivalence in favor of change.

The Expert Trap

Therapists know a lot about behavioral problems and strategies for making behavioral changes. Understandably, therapists may believe that the way best to help clients is to offer their opinions about behaviors that are problematic and suggestions about how to make changes. However, this therapist behavior is inconsistent with MI in that it prevents clients from actively identifying their own behavioral problems, deciding to make specific changes, and developing and carrying out change plans—all of which are believed to be important to the process of making lasting changes. In MI, the role of therapist is to guide, rather than direct, the client in the change process through using the strategies described earlier, and to capitalize on clients' own strengths and abilities, which are often significant if explored. In this way the therapist shifts his expertise from active advice giver to active change facilitator.

The Labeling Trap

Therapists often use labels when referring to clients and client behavioral problems (e.g., addict, noncompliant, mentally ill, obese). Some theoretical orientations emphasize clients' acceptance of these labels as an important indication of motivation to change. However, clients often have a history of being labeled, feeling judged and stigmatized by these labels, or otherwise are not ready or willing to be labeled. Therefore, clients may have a negative reaction to being labeled, and the ensuing debate about labels can steer clients away from their personal reasons for change. Additionally, many clients who are not ready to identify a problem, or to be labeled as having one, may be nonetheless willing to start making changes. Therefore, motivational approaches deemphasize labels and help clients to focus on specific behaviors they wish to change.

The Premature Focus Trap

This refers to the tendency of therapist to "jump on" a specific problem too quickly, and potentially divert attention from the client's most pressing concerns. The result of this premature focus can be client resistance or working on less clinically relevant issues that were initially "spotted" by the therapist. Asking sufficient open-ended questions to assess the client's behavior problems and the skillful use of reflective listing to understand the importance of these problems can assist therapists in avoiding this trap.

The Blaming Trap

Clients sometimes feel unfairly blamed for their behavioral problems, or feel that others are at fault for these problems. Therapists sometimes believe that clients must take responsibility for their problems and can feel compelled to have client see their role in them. As a result, clients can feel blamed by the therapist and respond with resistance. In MI, the "fault" for the client's problems is not relevant. Rather, what is of concern is what behaviors the client sees as a problem and what the client is willing to do to make changes. Miller and Rollnick (2002) suggest establishing a "no-fault" policy with the client at the onset of therapy.

SPECIAL POPULATIONS

MI has demonstrated efficacy in assisting individuals to change conditions that involve specifiable behavioral targets. It has earned empirical support for the treatment of these conditions in a range of clinical populations, including individuals with relatively isolated behavioral concerns (treatment compliance), as well as those who are dually diagnosed with conditions such as affective disorders, psychotic disorders, and personality disorders (Graeber, Moyers, Griffith, Guarjardo, & Tonigan, 2003; Martino, Carroll, Kostas, Perkins, & Rousanville, 2002; Swanson, Pantalon, & Cohen, 1999). It has gained empirical support assisting individuals across the life span, including adults and adolescents (Aubrey–Lawendowski, 1998; Berg–Smith, Stevens, Brown, et al., 1996). At this point, it has not been well tested in children. It is not clear that children experience ambivalence in the same way as adults. Furthermore, children may not always have the cognitive and emotional capacity to weigh the pros and cons of their behavior and to choose more value-consistent options. Although it may be the case that this intervention and these processes do have useful parallels in children, this has not been demonstrated at this point. For now, MI may be most useful to children through the ways that it assists their parents to provide effective care to them.

CASE EXAMPLE

Many of the therapeutic techniques of MI have been outlined throughout this chapter. The therapist–client dialog presented in Table 2.5 is a brief example of how these techniques and principles might come together in a single case example. The client in this case is Mr. X, a 54-year-old married man who has been court referred to treatment after receiving his second DUI. He states that he typically drinks about 20 drinks per week, with a

TABLE 2.5   Sample Case Dialog

Client and Therapist Content	Clinical Strategies Used
T: Tell me some about what brings you to treatment?	The therapist begins with opening questions that invite the client to tell his story.
C: The courts sent me here.	The client's response is guarded.
T: You didn't really choose to come here and you are feeling a little angry about having to be here.	The therapist uses a reflection to take a guess about how the client might be feeling about coming to therapy.
C: I don't understand why everyone is making such a big deal of this. I can hold my liquor. A couple of drinks doesn't really change the way I drive.	
T: You don't see this as a big problem. You feel like everyone is blowing this out of proportion. C: It isn't just the police. It's my wife, too. She is riding me all the time now.	The therapist communicates that he hears what the client is saying, without agreeing with the client's formulation.
T: She is really concerned about what is going on with you.	The therapist reframes the situation with his wife to suggest a more positive way of thinking about it.
C: Yeah, I guess so.	
T: Tell me some of the things you enjoy about your drinking.	Therapist begins with a disarming request that focuses on the good things about the target behavior.
C: I drink to relax and to have a good time with my friends.	
T: It helps you wind down and have a good time. What else?	The therapist reflects the "good" things the client likes about drinking. The therapist probes for any additional information.
C: It is just something I do and I have always done. You know, a part of my day-to-day life.	
T: It has always been with you.	
T: What about the other side? What are the not-so-good things about your drinking?	The therapist explores the other side of the ambivalence.
C: Well there is all this trouble with the law. You wouldn't believe all the hoops they have me jumping through. And my family. Between my wife and the kids, you would think I was the town drunk.	
T: Everyone else has the problem with your drinking. You don't see any problem at all.	The therapist uses amplified reflection in the hope of getting the client to back off his resistant stance related to the consequences of his drinking.

(Continues)

TABLE 2.5   *(Continued)*

C: I am not saying that there are no problems. I mean, I can tie one on every now and then. I used to get into some serious brawls in my day. Sometimes, I can feel pretty lousy in the morning.

T: You have gotten into fights when drinking and you don't like the hangovers in the morning. What other problems have you noticed?	The therapist uses reflections and open-ended questions to probe the other side of the ambivalence.

C: Well, every now and then my boss gets on my case about it. It's the craziest thing. I know he drinks his share. He can get pretty mad when I don't make it in on the weekends.

T: Sometimes it can cause a little tension at work.	A minimizing reflection is used here in the hope of getting the client to talk more about it.

C: I'd say it is more than a little tense. Last Christmas he threatened to lay me off if I missed another Saturday.

T: Let me see if I have got this straight. You drink to have a good time with your friends and relax a bit. You stated earlier that you are drinking less than you used to. You aren't quite sure why everyone is making such a fuss. On the other hand, your drinking has gotten you into some hot water with your family and caused some trouble at work. Besides that you don't really enjoy the hangovers that can come along with it.	The therapist summarizes what the client has said, including both sides of the client's ambivalence. This communicates that the therapist is listening and ensures that the therapist understands the client's ambivalence.

C: That's about it.

T: Supposing things stay just the way they are with your drinking. Where do you think you are headed in the next couple of years?	The therapist asks a "looking forward" question to start building a discrepancy between the client's drinking and what he hopes to be doing in the future.

C: Well, I don't know about that. I can't afford to get another DUI. I think they might take my license and never give it back. Besides all that, my wife won't let me take the kids anywhere on the weekend. That is really burning me up. It isn't like I have ever had an accident or anything.

T: You don't like where this is headed. You cannot afford another DUI.	The therapist reflects the client's expression of worries about the negative consequences of continued drinking.

(Continues)

TABLE 2.5   *(Continued)*

C: Oh no. I cannot. I hate these DUI classes they have got me going to. I am a good husband and a hard worker. I don't like being treated like a criminal.	
T: It is important to you to be reliable and trustworthy.	The therapist uses affirmation to highlight the client's important values and to continue to build the discrepancy.
C: It is. I have better ways I want to be spending my time. My time and my money. I want to retire. Spend some money traveling. My oldest son is headed to college. I hate for him to see all this. I don't need to be messing around with all this.	
T: There are more important things you would like to be doing—enjoying your retirement, setting a good example for your son, traveling. Tell me this, where do you see yourself headed from here?	The therapist reflects the client's hopes for the future and uses a key question to transition from phase I to phase II.
C: Well, I have got to get a handle on my drinking. I can't afford to get into this trouble again.	
T: You said that you have cut back on your drinking in the past. How did you do that?	The therapist starts moving the focus toward change. He initially focuses on what has worked before. As the session goes on, he will work with the client to make sure the plan for change is likely to work.

maximum of six drinks per day. On measures of motivation he scores low in ambivalence, low in problem recognition, and moderately higher in taking steps. These scores are likely accounted for by his belief that he does not have a drinking problem (low problem recognition, low ambivalence) and his emphasis on how much less he drinks now than in the past. Because of the space constraints of this chapter, these techniques are somewhat abbreviated.

SUMMARY

MI is a client-centered, directive method for resolving ambivalence and strengthening a client's commitment to change. It has earned empirical support as an effective treatment across a number of behavioral domains. It has demonstrated effectiveness in adolescents and in clients who are dually diagnosed. MI relies on the skillful use of open questions, reflective listening, and affirmation to resolve ambivalence and instigate change. This chapter serves as an introduction to the practice, the philosophy, and the techniques of MI. Many of the skills used in MI are likely to be familiar to the experienced therapist. Those who are interested in learning more about MI are encouraged to build on this introduction by accessing the recommended Web sites and reading the materials listed in the following section.

RECOMMENDED READING AND ONLINE RESOURCES

RECOMMENDED READING

Miller, W. R., & Rollnick, S. (1991). *Motivational interviewing: Preparing people to change addictive behavior.* New York: Guilford Press.

Miller, W. R., & Rollnick, S. (2002). *Motivational interviewing: Preparing people for change (2nd ed.).* New York: Guilford Press.

Treatment Improvement Protocol (TIP) Series 35: Enhancing Motivation for Change in Substance Abuse Treatment. Substance Abuse and Mental Health Services Administration Center for Substance Abuse Treatment. DHHS publication no. (SMA) 99-3354. Available at www.ncbi.nlm.nih.gov/books/ bv.fcgi?rid=hstat5.chapter.61302.

ONLINE RESOURCES

General information on motivational interviewing: The motivational interviewing homepage contains a great deal of useful information on the theory, the practice and the empirical support for MI.

http://www.motivationalinterview.org

Treatment manual: This is a link to a free manual on motivational interviewing that is available through the SAMHSA/CSAT website.

http://www.ncbi.nlm.njh.gov/books/bv.fcgi?rid=hstat5.chapter.61302

Assessment and Assessment Feedback Tools: The following links will connect you to assessment and feedback tools that can be useful for practitioners who are interested in printable materials.

www.ncbi.nlm.nih.gov/books/ bv.fcgi?rid=hstat5.chapter.61302

ASSESSMENT AND ASSESSMENT FEEDBACK TOOLS

http://casaa.unm.edu/inst.html

http://casaa.unm.edu/inst/ Personal%20Feedback%20Report.pdf

www.drinkerscheckup.com/

www.sf.med.va.gov/CHCE/default.asp

REFFERENCES

Amrhein, P. C., Miller, W. R., & Yahne, C. E. (2003). Client commitment language during motivational interviewing predicts drug use outcomes. *Journal of Consulting & Clinical Psychology, 71*, 862–878.

Aubrey–Lawendowski, L. (1998). Motivational interviewing with adolescents presenting for outpatient substance abuse treatment. *Dissertation Abstracts International, 59-03B*, 1357.

Berg–Smith, S. M., Stevens, V. J., Brown[1], K. M., Van Horn[2], L., Gernhofer[2], N., Peters[2], E., Greenberg[3], R., Snetselaar[4], L., Ahrens[4], L., and Smith, K. (1999). A brief motivational intervention to improve dietary adherence in adolescents. *Health Education Research* 14(3), 399–410.

Bernstein, E., Bernstein, J., & Levenson, S. (1997). Project ASSERT: An ED-based intervention to increase access to primary care, preventive services, and the substance abuse treatment system. *Annals of Emergency Medicine, 30*, 181–197.

Brown, J. M., & Miller, W. R. (1993). Impact of motivational interviewing on participation and outcome in residential alcoholism treatment. *Psychology of Addictive Behaviors, 7*, 211–218.

Burke, B. L., Arkowitz, H., & Dunn, C. (2002). The efficacy of motivational interviewing and its applications: What we know so far. In W. M. Miller & S. Rollnick (Eds.). *Motivational interviewing: Preparing people for change* (2nd ed., pp. 217–250). New York: Guilford Press.

Burke, B. L., Arkowitz, H., Menchola, M. (2003). The efficacy of motivational interviewing: A meta-analysis of controlled clinical trials. *Journal of Consulting & Clinical Psychology, 71*, 843–861.

Burns D. D., & Spangler D. L. (2000) Does psychotherapy homework lead to improvements in depression in cognitive–behavioral therapy or does improvement lead to increased home-work compliance? *Journal of Consulting and Clinical Psychology, 68*, 46–56.

DiClemente, C. C., Carbonari, J. P., Montgomery, R. P. G., & Hughes, S. O. (1994). The alcohol abstinence self-efficacy scale. *Journal of Studies on Alcohol, 55*, 141–148.

DiMatteo, M. R., Giordani, P. J., Lepper, H. S., et al. (2002). Patient adherence and medical treatment outcomes: A meta-analysis. *Medical Care, 40*: 794–811.

Dunn, C., Deroo, L., & Rivara, F. (2001). The use of brief interventions adapted from motivational interviewing across behavior domains: A systematic review. *Addiction, 96*, 1725–1742.

Finney, J. W., & Moos, R. H. (2003). Effects of setting, duration and amount of treatment outcomes. In A. W. Graham, R. K. Schultz, M. G. Mayo–Smith, R. K. Ries, & B. B. Wilford (Eds.). *ASAM principles of addiction medicine* (3rd ed., pp. 443–451). Chevy Chase, MD: American Society of Addiction Medicine.

Fiorentine, R., & Hillhouse, M. P. (1999). Drug treatment effectiveness and client therapist em-pathy: Exploring the effects of gender and ethnic congruency. *Journal of Drug Issues, 29*, 59–74.

Graeber, D. A., Moyers, T., Griffith, G., Guarjardo, G., & Tonigan, J. S. (2003). A pilot study comparing motivational interviewing and educational intervention in patients with schizo-phrenia and alcohol use disorders. *Community Mental Health Journal, 39*, 189–201.

Kazantzis, N., Deane, F. P., & Ronan, K. R. (2000). Homework assignments in cognitive and behavioral therapy: A meta-analysis. *Clinical Psychology: Science and Practice, 7*, 189–202

Martino, S., Carroll, K., Kostas, D., Perkins, J., & Rousanville, B. (2002). Dual diagnosis motivational interviewing: A modification of motivational interviewing for substance-abusing patients with psychotic disorders. *Journal of Substance Abuse Treatment, 23*, 297–308.

McConnaughy, E. A., Prochaska, J. O., & Velicer, W. F. (1983). Stages of change in psycho-therapy: Measurement and sample profiles. *Psychotherapy: Theory, Research and Practice, 20*, 368–375

Miller, W. R. (1996). Motivational interviewing: Research, practice, and puzzles. *Addictive Behaviors, 21*, 835–842.

Miller, W. R., Benefield, R. G., & Tonigan, J. S. (1993). Enhancing motivation for change in problem drinking: A controlled comparison of two therapist styles. *Journal of Consulting & Clinical Psychology, 61*, 455–461.

Miller, W. R., C'de Baca, J., Matthews, D., & Wilbourne, P. L. (2003a). *Personal Values Card Sort.* University of New Mexico, Albuguerque. Center of Alcohol Abuse, Alcoholism and Addic-tion. Also available at http://casaa.unm.edu/inst/Personal% 20Values%20Card%20Sort.pdf.

Miller, W. R., & Rollnick, S. (1991). *Motivational interviewing: Preparing people to change addictive behavior.* New York: Guilford Press.

Miller, W. R., & Rollnick, S. (2002). *Motivational interviewing: Preparing people to change addictive behavior* (2nd ed.). New York: Guilford Press.

Miller, W. R., & Tonigan, J. S. (1996). Assessing drinkers' motivation for change: The Stages of Change Readiness and Treatment Eagerness Scale (SOCRATES). *Psychology of Addictive Behaviors, 10*, 81–89.

Miller, W. R., Yahne, C. E., & Tonigan, J. S. (2003b). Motivational interviewing in drug abuse services: A randomized trial. *Journal of Consulting & Clinical Psychology, 71*, 754–763.

Miller, W. R., Zweben, A., DiClemente, C. C., & Rychtarik, R. G. (1992). *Motivational enhancement therapy manual: A clinical research guide for therapists treating individuals with alcohol abuse and dependence* (Project MATCH monograph series, vol. 2). Rockville, MD: National Institute on Alcohol Abuse and Alcoholism.

Moyers, T. B., Martin, T., & Manuel, J. K. (2005). Assessing competence in the use of motivational interviewing. *Journal of Substance Abuse Treatment, 28*, 19–26.

Prochaska, J., & DiClemente, C. (1982). Transtheoretical therapy: Towards a more integrative model of change. *Psychotherapy: Theory Research and Practice, 19*, 279–288.

Project MATCH Research Group. (1997). Matching alcohol treatment to client heterogeneity: Project MATCH post-treatment drinking outcomes. *Journal of Studies on Alcohol, 58*, 7–29.

Rollnick, S., Heather, N., & Bell, A. (1992). Negotiating behaviour change in medical settings: The development of brief motivational interviewing. *Journal of Mental Health, 1*, 25–37.

Rollnick, S., & Miller, B. (1995). What is motivational interviewing? *Behavioural & Cognitive Psychotherapy, 23*, 325–334.

Swanson, A.J., Pantalon, M.V., Cohen, K.R. (1999). Motivational Interviewing and Treatment Adherence Among Psychiatric and Dually Diagnosed patients. *Journal of Nervous and Mental Disease* 187(10): 630–635

Valle, S. K. (1981). Interpersonal functioning of alcoholism counselors and treatment outcome. *Journal of Studies of Alcohol, 42*, 783–790.

3

THE THERAPEUTIC ALLIANCE: CULTIVATING AND NEGOTIATING THE THERAPEUTIC RELATIONSHIP

JEREMY D. SAFRAN

New School for Social Research
Department of Psychology New York, New York

J. CHRISTOPHER MURAN

Beth Israel Medical Center
Albert Einstein College of Medicine
Department of Psychiatry & Behavioral Sciences New York, New York

MICHAEL ROTHMAN

Beth Israel Medical Center
Albert Einstein College of Medicine
Department of Psychiatry & Behavioral Sciences New York, New York

Decades of empirical research have consistently shown that the therapeutic alliance is the most important component of change within psychotherapy (Horvath & Symonds, 1991; Martin, Garske, & Davis, 2000). Since the late 1980s we have been researching the therapeutic relationship, in particular focusing on the ongoing negotiations between the therapist and patient as they do the work of psychotherapy. We have identified and classified types of therapeutic ruptures that we believe are germane to dyadic

Portions of Chapter 3 are adapted from Safran, J. D. & Muran, J.C. (2000). Stage-Process Models of Alliance Rupture Resolution. In Negotiating the Therapeutic Alliance: A Relational Treatment Guide (pp. 140–174). Guilford Press: New York. Copyright 2000 by The Guilford Press.

relating, and we have devised a process of rupture resolution and incorporated it into the framework of a relational treatment that has evolved into a model of psychotherapy. In this chapter we outline our understanding of the therapeutic alliance, our theoretical perspective, and offer our conceptualizations and strategies for cultivating and negotiating a healthy and strong relationship with patients.

DEFINITION

In our understanding of the therapeutic alliance, we have been heavily influenced by Edward Bordin (1979), who suggested that a good alliance is a prerequisite for change in all forms of psychotherapy. He conceptualized the alliance as consisting of three interdependent components: *tasks*, the specific covert and overt activities in which the patient must engage to benefit from the treatment; *goals*, the general objectives toward which the treatment is directed; and the *bond*, the affective quality of the relationship between patient and therapist. The bond, task, and goal dimensions of the alliance influence one another in an ongoing fashion. The quality of the bond affects the extent to which the patient and therapist are able to negotiate an agreement about the tasks and goals of therapy, and the ability to negotiate an agreement about the tasks and goals of therapy in turn mediates the quality of the bond.

In our conceptualization of the alliance we highlight the importance of this process of negotiation between patient and therapist around the tasks and goals of therapy. We assume that there will be an ongoing negotiation between therapist and patient at both conscious and unconscious levels about the tasks and goals of therapy. As Stephen Mitchell (1993) emphasizes, it is the negotiation between the patient's desires and those of the therapist that is a critical therapeutic mechanism. Stuart Pizer (1992) has argued that the ongoing process of negotiation between therapist and patient is the essence of therapeutic action. He suggests that therapists in their interventions and patients in their responses are recurrently saying to each other, "No, you can't make this of me. But you can make that of me" (p. 218). Pizer (1992) includes in this process all aspects of therapy, including frame issues such as the agreement on fees and scheduling. He summarizes that "the very substances and nature of truth and reality . . . are being negotiated toward consensus" in the therapeutic relationship (p. 218). It is negotiation that both establishes the necessary conditions for change to take place and functions as an intrinsic part of the change process.

Inherent in our view of the alliance as a relational push-and-pull is an understanding that therapeutic alliance ruptures are inevitable. Any intervention may have a positive or negative impact on the quality of the bond between the patient and therapist, depending on its idiosyncratic meaning to the patient; and, conversely, any intervention may be experienced as more or less facilitative depending on the preexisting bond. For example, one patient may find the task of exploring an emotional experience especially difficult. Another may experience structured cognitive–behavioral exercises as reassuring and containing, whereas a different patient may experience a therapist's suggestion to do homework between sessions as challenging and domineering. Elsewhere we have defined therapeutic ruptures as a "negative shift in the quality of the existing alliance or as difficulty establishing one" (Samstag, Muran, & Safran, 2004, p. 188). Alliance ruptures are mutually influenced as the patient and therapist "bring to the table" their own relational styles that have been shaped and formed by their own prior relational experiences. Our research findings have reinforced our belief that the identification and processing of these ruptures with the patient plays a critical role in the exploration of and ultimately restructuring of patients' maladaptive relational schemas (Muran, 2002; Muran & Safran, 2002; Muran, Safran, Samstag, & Winston, in press; Rothman, Muran, & Safran, 2004; Safran, 1993a,b; Safran & Muran, 1996, 2000; Safran, Muran, Samstag, & Stevens, 2002; Safran, Muran, Samstag, & Winston, in press; Samstag et al., 2004).

IDENTIFICATION

Given our vital belief in the role of resolving impasses in the therapeutic relationship, we would like to provide an overview of the ways in which we define and detect therapeutic ruptures. It should be noted that ruptures might occur at any time, be a single event or part of a larger process, be related to disagreements about the alliance, be related to the emotional connection (or lack thereof) between the patient and therapist, or can involve an interaction of technique and relationship factors.

Following Heather Harper (1989a,b), we have found it useful to organize ruptures into two subtypes: *withdrawal* and *confrontation*. In withdrawal ruptures, the patient withdraws or partially disengages from the therapist, his or her own emotions, or some aspect of the therapeutic process. Withdrawal ruptures can manifest in many different forms. In some cases, it is fairly obvious that the patient is having difficulty expressing his or her concerns or needs in the relationship. For example, a patient may express concerns in an indirect or qualified way, or in other cases may subtly comply with the perceived desires of the therapist. Thus it is not uncommon for therapists and patients to form a type of pseudoalliance. In such cases, therapeutic progress may take place at one level, but the treatment relationship will nevertheless perpetuate a self-defeating aspect of the patient's style.

Confrontation ruptures are often less subtle, because the patient directly expresses anger, resentment, or dissatisfaction with the therapist or some aspect of the therapy.

Each rupture begins with a specific *marker*, a patient statement or action that signals the beginning of the rupture event. Examples of some markers for withdrawal ruptures include moments when the patient is engaging in denial, storytelling, talking about other people and events, shifting the topic, or engaging in storytelling. Markers for confrontation ruptures might include multiple complaints directed toward the therapist: challenges of the therapist's competence, complaints about the parameters of the sessions (such as time, duration, and frequency), complaints about a lack of progress, or complaints about the therapist's personal style. As we elaborate further, you will see that the detection of these markers is a critical first step in the rupture resolution process.

Depending on different characteristic styles of coping or adaptation, different patients are likely to present a predominance of one type of rupture over another. During the course of treatment, however, both types of ruptures may emerge with a specific patient, or a specific impasse may involve both withdrawal and confrontation features. Thus, it is critical for therapists to be sensitive to the specific qualities of the rupture that are emerging in the moment, rather than becoming locked into viewing patients as exclusively confrontation or withdrawal types.

THEORY AND
CONCEPTUALIZATION

Our conceptualization of the therapeutic process has been greatly influenced by contemporary relational thinking. A more thorough review of our theoretical stance can be found elsewhere (Safran & Muran, 2000), but for purposes of this chapter we will highlight some of the more salient positions. These positions shape how we view the clinical process and, in particular, therapeutic impasses.

One assumption we hold is that agency and relatedness are fundamental human needs. By agency we refer to one's need to exercise self-efficacy or independence, whereas relatedness has more to do with the satisfaction of security operations and affiliative needs. These needs are dialectically opposed to each other, and individuals fluidly shift back and forth in their efforts to meet them both. Aron (1996) argues that these two elemental and conflicting human needs must be incorporated into an understanding of therapeutic interactions. This dialectic tension lies at the core of interpersonal ruptures. In withdrawal ruptures, by engaging in compliant behaviors or by avoiding difficult interactions, patients strive for relatedness by sacrificing their need for agency or self-definition. In confrontation ruptures, patients negotiate this conflict by favoring the need for agency or self-definition by explicitly asserting their needs in a way that tries to foreclose the need for relatedness. Relationships are therefore comprised of two individuals negotiating their own agency and relatedness struggles while simultaneously relating to each other. Learning how to negotiate this interpersonal situation constructively provides an important framework for therapeutic change.

Jessica Benjamin (1990) was one of the first to suggest that the process of negotiation between two different subjectivities is at the heart of the change process. Accordingly we view the therapeutic relationship as an ongoing interplay of separate subjectivities. The relatively recent proliferation of writings in the area of intersubjectivity has been influential in our conceptualization of the alliance as an intersubjective construct. According to this theory, developmentally, as our object relating matures, we begin to understand others as subjects—that is we begin to experience them as independant centers of subjectivity, rather than exclusively as objects of our own needs and desires (Safran, 1993). As Benjamin (1990) indicates, the appreciation of the subjectivity of the other is not developed and cultivated in a static way, but actually shifts discontinuously between subjectivity and objectivity. The therapeutic dyad can therefore be described as a mutual process of recognizing the respective subjectivities of the participants, and negotiating the ongoing shifts between subjectivity and objectivity, as well as the desires and needs of both the patient and the therapist.

Given that much of interpersonal relating involves a process of negotiation, it is useful to include in this discussion our understanding of what it is that each participant brings to the negotiation. We view the person as a relational phenomenon (Muran, 2001; Safran, 1998; Safran & Muran, 2000; Safran & Segal, 1990). On the basis of one's interactions with others, such as attachment figures who contribute to the development of one's first relational blueprint, one develops a relational schema. These schemas provide the cognitive and affective expectancies, procedures, and strategies for negotiating relationships. Thus, relational schemas shape one's perceptions of the environment, which leads to thoughts and behaviors that influence the environment in a manner that confirms the schema. For example, if a woman fears that others will find her undesirable and therefore engages with others in a guarded and self-deprecating way, it is more likely that others will keep their distance from her. This erroneously reinforces the idea, and her schema, that she is undesirable, rather than the possibility that it is the preemptive, and perhaps anxiety-derived distancing behaviors that others find undesirable. These schemas lead to entrenched and redundant patterns of interactions that limit the possibilities of new interpersonal experiences. We refer to the individual's self-perpetuating cycle of interpersonal representations as a *relational matrix*, and we use the term *relational config-uration* to characterize the interaction between the respective relational matrices of patient and therapist at a given time.

We believe that the therapeutic alliance is crucial for facilitating change in relational schemas. As we outline in more detail in the following sections, the therapeutic relationship can be used to introduce a different kind of relation-ship—one that disconfirms previously held beliefs. To achieve this it is first important to be able to cultivate an awareness of one's adaptive and mal-adaptive relational schemas. So entrenched are these schemas that they operate reflexively and typically outside our own awareness. We have found the Eastern notion of mindfulness to be key in helping one "disembed" from the intricacies of one's relational matrix. "Mindfulness involves directing one's attention in order to become aware of one's thoughts, feelings, fantasies or actions as they take place in the present moment" (Safran & Muran, 2000, p. 57). The work of the therapy can focus on directing the patient's attention to different states of awareness ("What are you aware of as you say this?" or "What are you experiencing right now?") at different moments of relational enactments. We also value the therapist's disclosure of his or her own experi-ence in the moment, such as, "It feels as though you are pulling away from me right now, and I'm not sure how I can be helpful." These kinds of disclosures model mindfulness for the patient and focus attention on the relational patterns between the therapist and the patient. They shift the awareness of these patterns from an implicit realm to an explicit realm and cultivate deeper exploration. Deeper exploration and a sense of collaboration during mo-ments of rupture or impasse can serve to deepen the connection between the therapist and the patient, and ultimately disconfirm the relational schema. It is this process of mutually derived disconfirmation that challenges old sche-mas and promotes the development of newer and healthier ones.

CASE FORMULATION

We do not endorse a traditional case formulation model. Case formula-tion is typically driven by theory and is used to shape the intervention strategies of the treatment. For example, a psychodynamically oriented therapist might formulate a patient's depression as rooted in unresolved, intrapsychic anger toward one's mother. In contrast, a more cognitive–behavioral therapist might understand the depressive symptoms as resulting from maladaptive self-recriminatory beliefs. These therapists will approach the treatment of the depression differently and use different clinical strat-egies. Given our emphasis on the in vivo processing of relational material as central to therapeutic growth, our intervention strategies are independent of case formulation. We believe that irrespective of the formulation that is developed regarding the understanding of the patient's problem, maintaining a commitment to resolving alliance ruptures is a key part of the therapeutic process.

Because case formulations serve as organizing principles for clinicians, we would like to offer a few of our own organizing principles for clinicians that reflect our sense of case formulation as a fluid and ever-changing relational process. The position we assume within our treatment is that a focus on the therapist–patient relationship yields important information regarding the patient's own relational schema. As we discussed earlier, the exploration and cultivation of awareness of these schemas contribute significantly to change. Although we certainly do not dismiss the patient's presenting issues and the clinical material about extratherapeutic relationships, it is not the lens with which we choose actively to attend.

We believe that a relational treatment should begin with a collaborative discussion about the tasks and goals of the treatment. Consistent with what Bordin (1979) recommends, the explicit establishment of the rationale for the treatment plays a critical role in the formation of the alliance. Patients are informed about our philosophy of therapy, which sets the stage for our focus on the therapeutic relationship and our explicit goal of cultivating an improved awareness of one's emotions, beliefs, fantasies, and relational self. The clinician needs to bear in mind that regardless of how explicit or how much time is devoted to clarifying and explicating treatment tasks and goals, it is inevitable that there will be shifts and that this will be negotiated and renegotiated on an ongoing basis.

The negotiation process is constantly changing and evolving with the therapeutic relationship. So it is important that even formulations regarding relational patterns be viewed with great flexibility, because they will shift with a wide range of subtlety over the course of a treatment. Staying in the here-and-now should obviate the pitfall of becoming too wedded to particular formulations. We detail the specific strategies we use during the negotiation process in the following section.

CLINICAL STRATEGIES

The process of negotiation involves many tasks for the therapist, and we consider these tasks and this process to be the organizing principle from which our strategic interventions are derived. Therapists must be able to shift their attention between the process and the content of the session—not just *what* is being said, but *how* it is said. Awareness of the process keys the therapist into the interpersonal communication the patient is making about the relationship with the therapist. The interpersonal field should be monitored for levels of relatedness, connection, or disconnection at any given moment. Shifts in affective engagement are important clues to the patient's experience of the therapeutic material as well as the therapeutic relationship.

These shifts should be explored in an effort to help the patient not only become aware of tendencies to avoid or defend against certain experiences, but also to understand the reasons for and ways of doing it. In addition to tracking the patient's experience, it is very important for the therapist to track his or her own internal experience, because this can serve as an emotional compass for gauging emotional closeness and distance with one's patients. As the therapist shifts back and forth between his or her self and other experiences it is critical to maintain a mindfulness that he or she will become embedded in a maladaptive relational matrix with his or her patient.

This is an inevitable part of treatment and a critical part of helping the patient become aware of his or her maladaptive relational schemas and how they operate. Often therapists will feel stuck as they repeatedly find themselves embedded in these relational dynamics. It is essential that therapists help cultivate an awareness of this processs for the patient and acknowledge their own experience as a part of this matrix. It is important that the therapist has faith in and trusts the process, particularly the notion that being stuck is part of the process, and conveys this faith to the patient.

Turning now to the actual strategy and specific technique of communicating these complex relational dynamics to patients, we borrow the term *metacommunication* (Kiesler, 1996) to characterize our intervention. "Metacommunication consists of an attempt to step outside of the relational cycle that is currently being enacted by treating it is as the focus of collaborative exploration: that is, communicating *about* the transaction of implicit communication that is taking place" (Safran & Muran, 2000, p. 108). It is a communication effort designed to introduce a dialogue about a mutual relational process and, as such, should be introduced in the spirit of collaborative inquiry. Metacommunication can be considered to be "mindfulness in action", because it is a deliberate effort to focus awareness on the process of what is being communicated.

We have elsewhere outlined both general and specific principles of metacommunication (Safran & Muran, 2000), but in the interest of space we delineate a select few here. Metacommunication should be based upon feelings and intuitions that are emerging for the therapist in that moment. We encourage clinicians to *recognize that the situation is constantly in flux*, because what was true during one session may not be true during the next, and what was true at the beginning of a session may not be true later in that same session. Therapists must begin by accepting and working through their own feelings in the immediacy of the moment, rather than trying to be somewhere they are not. The focus, therefore, should be on the *here-and-now* of the therapeutic relationship and on the current moment, rather than on events that have taken place in the past (i.e., either in previous sessions or at different points in the same session). The point here is not to make interpretive leaps about other relationships, but to stay focused on the only relationship present—the therapeutic one. The intervention should also *focus on the concrete and specific*, rather than on general ideas. This promotes experiential awareness, rather than abstract, intellectualized speculation. This type of concreteness and specificity helps patients to become observers of their own behavior, thus promoting the type of mindfulness that fosters change.

When metacommunicating, it is important that the therapist *explore with skillful tentativeness* while *establishing a sense of collaboration and we-ness*. The exploration of one's relational dynamics can be a difficult process, and inviting the patient to join in a gentle and tentative discussion can help mediate the loneliness and demoralization so commonly felt by patients during therapeutic impasses. By framing the impasse as a shared experience, the therapist begins the process of transforming the struggle by acknowledging that the therapist and patient are stuck together.

Along these lines, therapists should always *accept responsibility* for their contributions to the interaction, which may ultimately lead to a *judicious disclosure and exploration of one's own experience*. It is critical to bear in mind that, as therapists, we are always unwittingly contributing to the interaction with the patient. When therapists accept responsibility for their contribution to an impasse, patients can become aware of feelings they were having a hard time articulating, receive validation of their own perception of what is happening, and have their own self-doubts reduced, which ultimately decreases defensiveness. Therapists can begin the process of working through an impasse by sharing their own experience with their patients. The process of articulating one's feelings to patients can begin to free the therapist to intervene more effectively. Furthermore, the process of acknowledging one's contributions to the patient can play a critical role in beginning to clarify the nature of the vicious cycle.

Throughout the process of metacommunication, it is essential that the therapist *gauge the patient's relatedness*. Therapists should monitor their intuitive sense of emotional closeness with or distance from patients on an ongoing basis. This continuous assessment provides information about the quality of relatedness with patients in a given moment, and reflects an ongoing interplay between interpersonal and intrapsychic dimensions. To the extent that patients are feeling safe, accepted, and validated by the therapist, they will find it easier to access their inner experience in a genuine fashion. And the extent that therapists are in contact with their inner experience, they will experience a greater sense of relatedness to the patient. A sudden shift in the direction of decreased relatedness may signal that the therapist's intervention has been hindering, rather than facilitative, and may indicate the need to explore the way in which the patient has construed or experienced the intervention. Conversely, a sudden shift in the direction of increased relatedness may signal that the therapist has developed a more attuned understanding of the patient's internal experience.

We advocate the use of metacommunication at various stages of treatment, but particularly when one is engaging in rupture resolution. Our research program has led to the development of two models of rupture resolution that capture the process of negotiation for both withdrawal and confrontation ruptures (Safran & Muran, 2000).

In the first stage of the stage–process model for negotiating withdrawal ruptures, the patient exhibits a *withdrawal marker*, such as being overly deferential to the therapist or being passively nonresponsive. In the second stage the therapist actively engages in a process of *disembedding and attending to the rupture marker*. During this stage the therapist metacommunicate to the patient in an effort to disengage from the enactment by bringing attention to the rupture. A therapist might for example say, "I'm aware of my attention wandering. I'm not sure what's going on, but I think it may have something to do with a kind of distant sound in your voice. Any sense of what's going on for you right now?" This curious and empathic focus on the here-and-now dyadic process can result in one of two parallel pathways — an *experiencing pathway* or an *avoidance pathway*.

Following the experiencing pathway implies a deepening is taking place, and in this next stage the patient begins to express thoughts and feelings about the rupture. We call this stage *qualified assertion*, as the patient begins tentatively to assert his or her underlying wishes. It is often helpful for the therapist to facilitate the patient's assertion by aiding in the differentiation and exploration of various self-states, providing the patient with feedback about the way he or she qualifies statements, or encouraging greater emotional awareness. Working carefully with a patient during the *qualified assertion* stage should ultimately lead to *self-assertion*, the final stage of the model. During this stage the patient accesses and expresses underlying needs in a manner that entails an acceptance of responsibility and implies a certain degree of individuation from the therapist. Thus the trajectory of resolving withdrawal ruptures involves identifying the patient's actual withdrawal behaviors and then exploring the patient's underlying, unacknowledged motivation to withdraw, so that the patient can begin to assert his or her own needs and move from a withdrawn stance toward one of richer engagement.

We anticipate that the negotiation process is often not a linear one, hence the *avoidance pathway* is a common route during attempts at rupture resolution. As its name suggests, when efforts at resolution lead toward avoidance, the patient is typically inhibiting deeper exploration of the identified withdrawal marker. In some instances this may be the result of the patient's expectation of how the therapist will respond, and it is helpful for the clinician to explore the avoidance from an empathic stance (e.g., "I'm aware that you're shifting the topic. Do you have any sense of what makes it so difficult to talk about what I've mentioned?"). In other instances the avoidance can be attributed to the patient's self-doubts or self-criticism, and here it is useful for the therapist to draw the patient's attention to the way in which he or she shifts into a state of self-criticism when beginning to contact self-assertive feelings. Then the clinician can help the patient frame the experience as a conflict between two different parts of the self. Typically, a resolution process involves an ongoing alternation between *experiencing* and *avoidance pathways*, with the exploration of each pathway functioning to facilitate a deepening of the exploration of the other.

Dealing with confrontation ruptures is often a big challenge for therapists because it can arouse a plethora of negative affect and can be difficult both to deal with and believe one can survive. Akin to the withdrawal model, the first stage is indicated by the existence of a marker, in this case a *confrontation marker*. In working toward resolution, the process of *disembedding* is a critical stage and involves extricating oneself from the vicious cycle of hostility and counterhostility that is being enacted. Metacommunicating with the patient about the current struggle is a key tactic for disembedding, because it is often very important for the therapist to acknowledge his or her own contribution to the interaction while commenting on the experience as being a mutual struggle. For example a therapist might say, "It feels like you and I are in a power struggle right now, with me trying to hold you responsible for your frustrations with therapy, and you trying to pin the blame on me." The explicit articulation of the struggle by the therapist serves a number of important goals. It reestablishes the therapist's own internal space because it disembeds him or her from the relational reenactment while providing distance from the emotional experience of the initial attack, it provides the patient with feedback, and it ultimately helps the patient stand behind his or her actions as implicit demands are made more explicit. By metacommunicating about the interaction rather than simply retaliating or withdrawing, therapists can ideally begin the discussion of what is actually going on in the interaction and the *exploration of the patient's construal* of it.

During this exploration, the therapist's task is to elucidate the nuances of the patient's perceptions. The exploration here should focus on those experiences that are on the edge of awareness, but not yet fully explicit. It is critical for patients to come to experience any feelings of anger, hurt, or disappointment that exist as valid, acceptable, and tolerable before they can begin to explore primary yearnings that are more vulnerable in nature. It is often helpful for therapists to acknowledge their own contributions to the relational matrix. So as patients articulate the nuances of their perceptions, therapists begin to understand them from an internal point of reference. When this happens, they are less likely to take things personally and less likely to respond defensively. At the same time, patients begin to feel understood and validated, and some of their pent-up fury and rage start to dissipate. During the process of disembedding and exploring their construal, patients may experience guilt or anxiety about their explicit articulation of their anger and hostility. This results in a subtle dance in which they express aggression and then attempt to undue the harm they feel they have inflicted.

Further complicating things is that patients may then be further angered by feeling guilty about their expression of hostility. It is very useful for therapists to track the cycles of this *avoidance of aggression*, and help patients become aware of the internal processes that lead to these shifts. In some cases the unpacking of the construal constitutes the resolution process, and in other cases things move to a deeper level of exploration of underlying wishes that are more vulnerable in nature.

In some cases a patient will engage in an *avoidance of vulnerability* that will entail a withdrawal from vulnerable feelings into a more familiar and secure state of aggression. Again, here it is important to draw the patient's attention to the shifts. For example, the therapist might note, "My sense is that you began to contact some sadness there and then suddenly shifted into a harder or more aggressive stance. Did you have any awareness of this?" If the patient is able to become aware of the shift, the therapist can then explore his or her internal processes by asking, "Any sense of what went on inside just before the shift took place?" This type of inquiry helps the patient cultivate an awareness of his or her own triggers for shifts in his or her self-states. Processing *vulnerability* is often the final stage of resolving confrontation ruptures. As shifts in the patients' relationship to their vulnerability, and the experience of being vulnerable with their therapist, take place, the need to defend against it is lessened. Ultimately, and ideally, the defensive use of aggression as a way to manage intolerable vulnerable feelings will dissipate, and with it the frequency and intensity of confrontation as well.

Although we have highlighted a strategic intervention tool and guidelines for negotiating impasses, it is worth iterating that metacommunication is an ongoing process rather than one discrete intervention, and the process of rupture resolution can take place over a number of sessions. As we address in the next section, treating these processes as discrete, linear events can lead to greater failure in negotiation, which is more of an ongoing, ever-changing process.

KEY MISTAKES

Throughout the years we have noticed certain common mistakes that therapists make when attempting to implement our model. Often therapists will discontinue the resolution process if their initial metacommunication is not well received. There is often a notable reluctance to pursue rupture resolution explicitly because of a fear that this will jeopardize the alliance. It is critical that therapists expect resolution attempts to lead to more ruptures and expect to revisit ruptures repeatedly. No matter how hard clinicians attempt to follow the principles of metacommunication, there is always a risk that it will further aggravate the alliance rupture and perpetuate a vicious cycle. Moreover, even in a situation when the therapist's communication is not defensively motivated, there is always a risk that it will place a greater strain on the alliance by implicitly suggesting that patients should be saying or doing something other than what they are currently doing. In this regard, it is important for therapists to overcome reluctance to metacomunicate and to recognize that it is but one step in the process of resolution, rather than an ultimate intervention. Furthermore, as we have previously stated, it is quite common for therapists to find that the same impasse is being revisited again and again. When therapists relate to an impasse as simply a recurrence of a previous impasse, it becomes impossible to relate to it in its own terms and appreciate the unique configuration of the moment, and the likelihood of cultivating a new and different relational experience is greatly diminished.

Along these lines, it is important for the clinician to attend to patients' responsiveness to all interventions. Therapists should monitor the quality of patients' responsiveness to interventions on an ongoing basis. It is important here for the therapist to attend to subtle intuitions about the quality of patients' responsiveness. If an intervention fails to deepen exploration or further inhibits it, or if the therapist senses something peculiar in the patient's response to it, it is critical to explore the way in which the patient experienced it. Over time, this type of exploration can help to articulate patients' characteristic way of construing interpersonal relationships and can gradually lead to a fleshing out of their relational schemas. It can also lead to a progressive refinement in therapists' understanding of their own contribution to the interaction.

In general, we view all clinical mistakes as opportunities for furthering the understanding of how they arose, the patient's and therapist's contribution to the mistake, and the patient's and therapist's experience of the mistake. A failure to follow up on metacommunication indicates that the therapist is somehow stuck, either further entrenched in a reenactment and/or genuinely removed from the relationship. Often therapists new to this model who have difficulty facing ruptures directly have more difficulty believing that "sticking it out" will deepen the connection to the patient rather than intensify it. As we have discussed elsewhere (Safran & Muran, 2000), much of the work we do as supervisors is to help therapists negotiate their own internal struggles with being in this relationship with their patients.

CASE STUDY

Much of our work is about the moment-to-moment interactions between a therapist and a patient, and we are less heavily influenced by broader case conceptualizations. Rather than provide an in-depth case study, we believe it will be most illustrative for us to provide case material that demonstrates metacommunication and the rupture resolution process at work. The following is an annotated transcript of a segment of a session that began with a withdrawal rupture.

Lisa is a 32-year-old woman who sought treatment because of a general lack of direction in her life and a difficulty maintaining a long-term relationship. At the start of the fifth session she announces that her work schedule is in flux and it will be difficult for her to schedule regular appointments. In the *withdrawal marker* stage Lisa is somewhat equivocal about her intentions regarding whether she can or will stay in treatment, and she seeks guidance from the therapist in a needy and demanding fashion. The therapist responds to her vacillating in a flippant and mildly irritated manner. When Lisa asks him if he could suggest any names of therapists who might be able to accommodate her schedule better he responds, "I can probably come up with one or two." In the following segment the therapist *disembeds and attends to the rupture*:

T: I guess I'm a little curious and kind of taken by surprise. Because when we started you were aware that you were going to be starting a new job.
L: Yeah, but I didn't know exactly what my schedule would be.
T: Anything else going on for you?
L: No, that's about it. What would you do if you were in my situation?
T: I'm not sure, to be frank.
L: Well, I'm only doing what's right... right for me, anyway.
T: I'm wondering what's going on for you inside.
L: I'm wondering what you're thinking.
T: I guess, I'm aware of feeling like I'm being kind of withholding with you. Does that fit with your experience at all?
L: Yeah, I guess, a little.
T: Can you say anymore?
L: Well, I'm not sure if you're really giving me what I need. Maybe that was true last session as well.

Although the therapist was initially involved in an enactment with Lisa in which her requests were met with irritability, he is eventually able to metacommunicate about a feeling he has that he is being withholding. This facilitates a deepening and Lisa appears assured enough to supply new information about feeling dissatisfied by her experiences in the prior session. As they tentatively pursue a further understanding of the situation, Lisa acknowledges that she is feeling frustrated in the therapy, which leads to her questioning herself, and then wondering if she is "really giving things a chance." As they dig deeper into the here-and-now experience, Lisa states that in the moment she is feeling "a little frustrated... but maybe I'm being demanding." This statement is an example of *qualified assertion* as Lisa begins to articulate her own self-awareness. However, when asked to explore her frustration a little further, Lisa retreats into *avoidance*:

T: Are you open to exploring your frustration a little more?

L: I don't know.

T: Any sense of what your reservations are?

L: Well, I wouldn't want to say something that you took the wrong way.

T: What might happen if I took it the wrong way?

L: I don't know...you might take it personally.

T: And what if I took it personally?

L: I might hurt your feelings (long pause and the patient looks pensive).

T: Any sense of what you're experiencing right now?

As is somewhat typical of withdrawal ruptures, at this moment Lisa is sacrificing her own self-expression for fear that she might be hurtful, which might ultimately harm her connection to her therapist. Put in other words, she is engaging in the dialectic struggle between agency and relatedness. Now, in touch with this fear, Lisa and her therapist move into the stage of *self-assertion*.

L: ...maybe a little angry.

T: Uh-huh, can you put some of your feelings into words?

L: Why should I have to worry about your feelings? I don't see any progress. I guess I want to know what's going to make me function better. Like I want you to tell me what it is about me that stops me from being a functioning person. Why is it that I'm always getting into these predicaments? I guess I want you to tell me what to do.

T: Okay. So I'm going to see if I'm understanding what you're saying.

L: Okay.

T: You can tell me whether or not I've got it. You're saying, "I want to know what's going on...what's blocking me from doing what I want to do, or from being more happy and contented."

L: Yeah.

T: And sort of, "I want you to tell me or show me in a way"...something like that. Can you say a little more?

L: Basically, I want to hear what you have to say. I mean I've given you the facts, and I guess you know what my insights are. I guess I want you to wrap it and tell me what you think. (At this point, Lisa makes an emphatic gesture with her hand.)

T: (The therapist mirrors the gesture.) When you make that gesture, what kind of feeling goes with it?

L: I don't know. It's like...it's your show or something.

T: It's your show?

L: Yeah...you know...the ball's in your court.

T: Okay..."the ball's in your court." It sounds like it feels like I keep putting the ball back in your court rather than really taking responsibility for helping you.

L: Yeah...I guess that's it.

During the course of this exploration Lisa has gotten closer and closer to her anger and frustration with her therapist. Her implicit communication eventually becomes explicit, "Help me" and "Tell me what to do." Lisa is looking for concrete guidance, and the therapist is able to articulate his role in the continuing frustration as he keeps returning the responsibility to her ("I keep putting the ball back in your court"). Moments later Lisa compares this dilemma with one a child faces when seeking help from someone. "You're a little hesitant, a little shy maybe, you know, insecure about it. Why should they help you?" What begins to emerge from this interaction is Lisa's underlying need for nurturance. As the treatment continued it became clearer that this wish has been disavowed by Lisa because of a strong fear of abandonment, an expectation that if she expressed her wish for nurturance she would be disappointed. This translated itself into a perpetual vacillation between resentful compliance and indirect demands for nurturance.

This case highlights a number of different aspects of our work. The reflective pursuit of the here-and-now process in the face of a surface-level resistance to commit to a treatment schedule facilitated a much richer awareness of the relational matrix contributing to the impasse. Repeated metacommunication efforts were essential in facilitating the resolution of this withdrawal rupture, which ended with the patient more genuinely present and beginning to develop an awareness of the different cognitive and affective components that influence her relational behavior.

SUMMARY

The therapeutic alliance is a key ingredient of therapeutic change and growth. Like all relationships, the therapeutic relationship takes work and is complicated. It is an ongoing push and pull of each person's own needs and wishes. Both therapist and patient embark on the treatment with their own cognitive and affective beliefs and expectations about others. These schemas interact as each member of the therapeutic dyad contributes their own relational self to the alliance. What results is an intersubjective process of negotiation.

We believe that this ongoing negotiation process lies at the core of therapeutic change. When a therapist is committed to cultivating a patient's awareness of how his or her internal relational world influences his or her external relational world, not merely through interpretation but through sharing the actual experience of the patient in the room, a new experience is created for the patient. Through repeated experiences like this, patients become aware of when, in what ways, and perhaps why they withdraw or confront others. They learn to negotiate agency versus relatedness needs with an active awareness, ideally without the defensive posturing that arises from having disavowed needs. By using metacommunication the therapist demonstrates and encourages mindfulness, in this case an openness to being in the present while in the presence of another. This focus on the here-and-now process provides the patient with feedback about the relationship in the room, the only relationship in an individual treatment for which actual interpersonal data exist. By attending to relational drifts, picking up on rupture markers, and engaging in a dialogue with patients about the inter-personal field, we hope to stimulate a process of self-discovery and self-awareness that leads to a shift in the relationship to the therapist, which can ultimately lead to shifts in self-definition.

REFERENCES

Aron, L. (1996). *A meeting of minds: Mutuality in psychoanalysis*. Hillsdale, NJ: Analytic Press.

Benjamin, J. (1990). An outline of intersubjectivity: The development of recognition. *Psychoanalytic Psychology, 7,* 33–46.

Bordin, E. (1979). The generalizability of the psychoanalytic concept of the working alliance. *Psychotherapy: Theory, Research, and Practice, 16,* 252–260.

Harper, H. (1989a). *Coding guide I: Identification of confrontation challenges in exploratory therapy*. Sheffield, England: University of Sheffield.

Harper, H. (1989b). *Coding guide II: Identification of withdrawal challenges in exploratory therapy*. Sheffield, England: University of Sheffield.

Horvath, A. O., & Symonds, B. D. (1991). Relation between working alliance and outcome in psychotherapy: A meta-analysis. *Journal of Counseling Psychology, 38,* 139–149.

Kiesler, D. J. (1996). *Contemporary interpersonal theory and research: Personality, psychopathology, and psychotherapy*. New York: John Wiley.

Martin, D. J., Garske, J. P., & Davis, M. K. (2000). Relation of the therapeutic alliance with outcome and other variables: A meta-analytic review. *Journal of Consulting and Clinical Psychology, 68,* 438–450.

Mitchell, S. A. (1993). *Hope and dread in psychoanalysis*. New York: Basic Books.

Muran, J. C. (2001). Meditations on "both/and." In J. C. Muran (Ed.). *Self-relations in the psychotherapy process*. Washington, DC: APA Books, 347–372.

Muran, J. C. (2002). A relational approach to understanding change: Plurality and contextualism in a psychotherapy research program. *Psychotherapy Research, 12,* 113–138.

Muran, J. C., & Safran, J. D. (2002). A relational approach to psychotherapy: Resolving ruptures in the therapeutic alliance. In F. W. Kaslow (Ed.). *Comprehensive handbook of psychotherapy*. New York: Wiley, 253–282.

Muran, J. C., Safran, J. D., Samstag, L. W., & Winston, A. (in press). Evaluating an alliance-focused treatment for personality disorders. *Psychotherapy*.

Pizer, S. A. (1992). The negotiation of paradox in the analytic process. *Psychoanalytic Dialogues, 2,* 215–240.

Rothman, M., Muran, J. C., Safran, J. D. (2004). *From the earth to the moon: An intensive case study of rupture resolution*. Paper presented at the annual international meeting of the Society for Psychotherapy Research, Rome, Italy.

Safran, J. D. (1993a). Breaches in the therapeutic alliance: An arena for negotiating authentic relatedness. *Psychotherapy: Theory, Research, & Practice, 30,* 11–24.

Safran, J. D. (1993b). The therapeutic alliance as a transtheoretical phenomenon: Definitional and conceptual issues. *Journal of Psychotherapy Integration, 3,* 33–49.

Safran, J. D. (1998). *Widening the scope of cognitive therapy*. Northvale, NJ: Jason Aronson.

Safran, J. D., & Muran, J. C. (1996). The resolution of ruptures in the therapeutic alliance. *Journal of Consulting & Clinical Psychology, 64,* 447–458.

Safran, J. D., & Muran, J. C. (2000). *Negotiating the therapeutic alliance: A relational treatment guide.* New York: Guilford.

Safran, J. D., Muran, J. C., Samstag, L. W., & Stevens, C. (2002). Repairing alliance ruptures. In J. C. Norcross (Ed.). *Psychotherapy relationships that work* (pp. 235–254). New York: Oxford University Press.

Safran, J. D., Muran, J. C., Samstag, L. W., & Winston, A. (in press). Evaluating an alliance-focused intervention for potential treatment failures. *Psychotherapy.*

Safran, J. D., & Segal, V. Z. (1990). *Interpersonal process in cognitive therapy.* New York: Basic Books.

Samstag, L. W., Muran, J. C., & Safran, J. D. (2004). Defining and identifying alliance ruptures. In D. Charma (Ed.). *Core concepts in brief dynamic psychotherapy* (pp. 187–214). Mahwah, NJ: Lawrence Erlbaum Associates.

4

NARRATIVE PSYCHOTHERAPY AS EFFECTIVE STORY-MAKING: AN INTRODUCTION

LOIS PARKER

University of Nevada
Reno, Nevada

"The kind of story you want to tell yourself about yourself has a lot to do with the kind of person you are, and can become."

—Frank McConnell (1979, p. 3)

The most distinctive feature of the process we call *psychotherapy* is its quality of narration, especially its quality of *oral–aural narration*. Yet this feature has been largely neglected in much of the literature. Given that, I invite you to explore in this chapter psychotherapy's narrative quality, as well as its neglect, but explore it in the spirit of what David Rubin (1995) calls "a phenomenon in search of a theory, not a theory in search of support" (p. x).

WHY A NARRATIVE APPROACH TO PSYCHOTHERAPY?

The simplest answer to this question is that clients come into psychotherapy bearing *their stories*. However disjointed these *stories* may be, however drenched with emotions, or however poorly they may be worded, they are nonetheless the *stuff* of which psychotherapy is made. Another answer is that the stories of myth and literature, as humanity's early efforts to explain our universe and how we function within that universe, preceded by far the

My deep appreciation is expressed to Drs. Stephen Bertman, Classicist, and Shernaaz Webster, Psychologist, for their generous expertise in editing this paper, without which it would lack much clarity. My appreciation likewise goes to Kirsten Lowry and Aki Masuda for their technological help.

profession of psychology and our modern efforts to do the same. Moreover, psychotherapy itself, very early on, drew upon these same literary arts for many of its major concepts: Freud, Jung, Laing, and May, to mention a few, all had thorough backgrounds in the humanities, from which they developed their theories as well as their practices. Still another answer to the question of why a narrative approach to psychotherapy is that the principles of narration, especially those of *oral–aural narration*—the oldest of the literary arts—are clearly applicable to the practice of therapy, which itself is largely a process of *oral–aural narration*. It is *oral* because the process depends on a *spoken* exchange; and it is *aural* because what is spoken remains inert unless it is *heard*. Still, this body of knowledge is essentially untapped in today's mainline psychology. What might we learn if we tapped into this knowledge? How might it apply, both conceptually and practically, to the process of psychotherapy?

CONCEPTUALIZING PSYCHOTHERAPY AS ACTIVE STORY-MAKING

Narrative notions of psychotherapy are, of course, far from new. In modern-day psychology, they began with Freud (1917/1963, p. 330), who cited the steady progression within Sophocles' drama, *Oedipus Rex*, as analogous to what takes place in psychoanalysis. Following Freud, Roy Schafer (1980) discussed narration as part of the psychoanalytic dialogue, whereas Donald Spence (1982) proposed that psychoanalysis itself constitutes a search for narrative, as opposed to historical, truth. Conversely, from a Jungian or analytical perspective, James Hillman (1975) discussed case studies as a kind of story-making activity. Later, Theodore Sarbin (1986) and Karl Scheibe (1993) presented differing contextual–cognitive–behavioral notions of narrative psychotherapy—Sarbin from the perspective of human conduct and Scheibe from that of drama. In fact, two emphases are found in the annals of psychology and literature: one that emphasizes life itself as a story-making process (and thus, the story-making notion of psychotherapy), and another that emphasizes the influence of stories on our individual lives (see Parker, 1985). These emphases are by no means mutually exclusive, but they nevertheless pertain.

The approach presented here incorporates aspects from all these authors, while also integrating both emphases in the literary equation: psychotherapy as a story-making process *and* the influence that some stories have not only on that process, but on life itself. Beyond this, I freely draw from literature, myth, folk and fairy tales, as well as from the language of literary criticism and oral narration for conceptual and descriptive applications to this process of story-making. My preference for the term *story-making,* as opposed to *narrative,* is based on the simple fact that it more accurately describes the actual *activity* we call *psychotherapy.* It is not to imply that we are engaged in creating fiction. Quite the contrary! Indeed, we are engaged in the most meaningful professional activity possible: that of seeking to find the *time-honored truth* (one of the original meanings of the term *myth*) that rightly belongs to a given life. That it is *time honored* and implies *truth*—in the most basic sense of that word—enriches the psychotherapeutic, story-making task, while also moving our clients' lives forward.

In what follows, I shall first propose a conceptual framework for this notion, then describe various clinical practices that, although not exhaustive, apply within that proposed framework. Finally, I locate this notion within the context of neglect, which is to say, within the context of our modern world, where an atmosphere of fragmentation and disrespect for history, even story itself, seems now to prevail. My emphasis throughout will be on story-making as an *active, experiential, phenomenological process* and will be limited to individual, one-on-one psychotherapy, inasmuch as both couples and group psychotherapy present a series of dynamics that go beyond the scope of this chapter (even though they, too, can be discussed as effective story-making). The process is *active* in that it requires participation by both clients and therapists. It is *experiential* because full participation requires seeking from within, as well as from without, again for both clients and therapists. And it is *phenomenological* in that this seeking aims for us to *see* our worlds differently. Moreover, my emphasis will be on the story itself, as opposed to any given theory, because I maintain that the story and the creative process that fashions it, although certainly subject to discussion and explanation, have been distorted far too often in support of some given theory.

A SUGGESTED CONCEPTUAL FRAMEWORK

In the spring of 1953, M. H. Abrams (1958, p. 6) outlined the elements of literary criticism, showing that the *work* itself is the central focus, the artist or *narrator* is a second element, and the *audience* a third. But he then explained that there was still a fourth element—namely, that of the *universe* in which the work, the narrator, and the audience exist. Much later, Parker (1998, p. 184) drew the coordinates of the oral storytelling performance in an attempt to show the dynamics of interactions between and among the story, the teller, the audience, and the world in which the performance takes place. More recently, Stephen Bertman (personal communication, September 2004) diagramed for me his notion of the creative process as seen through the various relationships between a core myth, the story derived from that myth, the perception of an artist retelling the story of that myth, the varied perceptions of members of an audience witnessing that story, and how all these perceptions (those of both artist and audience) are filtered through not only each participant's "sensibilities and experience," but how they are likewise filtered through "the social issues and events of the day." Thus, for Bertman, any given story derived from a core myth probably yields many interpretations.

Drawing upon these various schemes for a conception of psychotherapy as story-making, we have first, the *story* (or potential *text*) as told or retold by the client; next, the *client* (or primary *author*) telling or retelling her story; then, the *therapist* (initially, the *audience*) listening to the story and observing how it is told; and, finally, the *universe* in which all this takes place, which includes not only the therapeutic setting, but as Bertman would have it, all the "sensibilities and experiences" of both the client and the therapist, as well as all "the social issues and events of the day." And I would add that the *interactions between and among* these varied parts contribute also to how any story is eventually refashioned.

The complexity of this situation is not to be underestimated, especially because therapy is most often sought when individuals perceive their life stories as somehow having gone awry, which is not to say that the life stories of therapists are always on firm ground either. Having now recognized this complexity, how can we effectively go about the task of psychotherapy? How, that is, can we enter into the therapeutic, story-making process with any degree of confidence? Let us begin with the story.

THE PSYCHOTHERAPEUTIC STORY

In the traditional sense, a story has a beginning, middle, and an end, which is to say it has *continuity;* and that continuity usually revolves around the steps taken, however awkward they may be, to resolve some conflict in which the hero or heroine currently finds him- or herself. Within that continuity also may be certain patterns of behavior exemplified by the characters in the story, the discovery of which usually contributes to the enjoyment of any story's given audience. The variations on this basic theme are endless, as every psychotherapist who has practiced more than a few years must know. What we often do not know, however, are the other characters contributing to our clients' presentations. We only hear *about* them from our clients and thus have secondary views of these other characters and of how they impinge upon the stories heard during therapy. Although recognizing this and recognizing that the story being heard may have other versions-in-the-making, we must nevertheless focus on the one at hand and bring elements of our own story to bear upon it. Even though our client's story is our primary focus and is presumably the one that we are asked to help *re*make, we unavoidably become a part of that story, as any client effectively becomes a part of ours. For it is from that relationship between two people and between their two evolving stories that another, more satisfying one hopefully emerges—one that is primarily for the client, but in an odd sense is also for the therapist.

Many approaches to psychotherapy emphasize this relationship between clients and their therapists, none of which we deny. But, here, that relationship additionally implies a bonding that is focused on a joint endeavor of story-making, an endeavor that is not unlike that created between a storyteller and his audience, if the story is to be a dramatic success.

But, you say, how can we ever know the *whole* story of our client? In actuality, we cannot. The *whole* story is never known to us, not just because we have only one version of it as now being told to us, but because most psychotherapy in today's world, where limited sessions are regulated by insurance companies, focuses essentially on episodes from a larger context. But that is not the point. The precise point is that the principles of narration, especially those of *oral–aural narration* have more to offer to this process than we have yet acknowledged.

CLIENTS AS PRIMARY NARRATORS—*OUTSIDE THE CITY GATES*

In this process, our clients are the primary narrators. As such, they reveal to us those aspects of their lives that they perceive as conflicting, what is hurting or confusing them, what is important to them, and, hopefully, what they would like to change. Or, from this perspective, they reveal what it is they would like to *tell* in another way. They also reveal their perceptions of others who are helpful or impeding their efforts to make their story a satisfying one. And in so doing, they present to the therapist the greatest *gift* any one person can give to another—namely, a gift of oneself, a revealing of one's soul. Clients nevertheless often register surprise when, at the end of a session, I say, "Thank you for coming," or "Thank you for sharing with me!" But that is the way it is, for in my heart-of-hearts, I too know something of the difficulty of sharing one's private thoughts, of being vulnerable, of revealing one's soul. As therapists, it is important for us to recognize that our clients are here through courage or desperation to trust us with a gift that somehow describes their own private story, now in turmoil.

But allow me to say it another way. In the stories of Greek mythology, a character that was *outside the city gates* was one who, for some reason, was not acceptable to be within the city—that is, he or she was an outcast. Such was the story of *Oedipus at Colonus;* such was also the story of Procrustes. But, whereas Oedipus, by the retelling of his story by Sophocles, is known to us as having eventually grown in great wisdom, Procrustes forever remains an outlaw. How important is it, then, to have one's story told or retold? Or, more important, how many of our clients in today's world are *outside the city gates?*

He had the most engaging smile I thought I had ever seen, so I was curious to learn why he had come into therapy. He responded by saying that he "did not feel that [he] belonged anywhere." I asked him when he had last felt that he belonged. He said it was when he "had been a member of a gang." My heart skipped a beat, for I knew something about what happens to young men when they try to leave a gang. But he was rushing on, saying that he knew where he would be had he not left the gang, that he "would now be in prison with [his] friends." He added that he wanted his life to mean something more, that he aspired to go to medical school.

He only came in a few times, but something must have happened during that first session, although exactly what was never clear to me. What was clear was that emblazoned in my mind was the sad fact that such an engaging young man could feel that there was no place for him to "belong" in our society today.

Three years later, I was attending an award ceremony where some of our students were being recognized. Standing there before the beginning of the ceremony, I realized that someone had approached me from behind, someone who, with hands now on my shoulders, was turning me around. Once again, I found myself face to face with that engaging young man. I asked him how he had been. He explained that he had been studying abroad. I asked him about medical school. He said he was still working on it.

Although I never saw him again, I still feel his pain, his feeling of not belonging anywhere. I can only hope that our brief encounter, or some other, helped him find his way back *inside the city gates.*

THE THERAPIST AS AUDIENCE, INITIALLY

In response to clients, in response to those who feel they are *outside the city gates,* and in response to the conflicted stories they present, an attentive therapist *initially* functions as a good audience: one who is fully *engaged,* actively *listening, observing,* and poised for *dialogue;* one who is respectful, not at all passive; and one who can recognize patterns.

The Quality of Engagement

Simply put, to be *engaged* means to be involved and ready to respond, ready to participate, readily committed. It is the same kind of engagement that we use when we attend a movie and allow ourselves to be swept along with the progression of events on the screen, except that—and this is a key—we must be immediately present to the whole scene that encompasses our client, present in a way that no movie could ever command. To be present in this manner is to bring not just our attention to the situation at hand, but to bring a lifetime of experience and learning that we are ready to commit to this new experience of story-making. Or, to put it another way, to be *engaged* and *present* means to *listen* with our hearts as well as our heads.

Actively Listening

So listening, a therapist must bring into play all the elements of Carl Rogers' (1961) client-centered therapy: empathy, unconditional positive regard, and acceptance, both for clients and for oneself. But therapists attuned to the *oral–aural narrative* process bring into play something beyond this—namely, the ability to listen with still another ear: one that not only registers the content being reported and the emotions that accompany that content (both of these, to be sure), but one that registers also a literary assessment, however crude it may be, of the story being told. What this means is that therapists from this persuasion pay attention to the *language* used by clients, including metaphors, images, and word patterns embedded in that language, and attention also to the *voice* used by clients to narrate the events being described. *Voice*, as used here, means both the *style* of narrating and the *tone* used for narrating. To be sure, the ability to listen in this manner takes some practice, but it also has its rewards. These rewards are the same as those reaped by ancient storytellers in oral cultures—namely, an enhanced memory and an ability to transmit what is valuable from what is heard (see Gentili, 1985/1988, p. 21).

Clinical and Interview Observations

Observations begin with the initial handshake in the waiting room. The client's damp palm may reveal something about his or her level of anxiety; or, a grasp that is firm or weak may say something about the client's sense of vulnerability, a vulnerability that rightly accompanies any trip to therapy. Then, there is the walk down the hall and the way in which the therapist's room is entered; these tell the practiced eye something, however tentative that may be.

Once the therapist has welcomed a client, he must then pay close attention to the client's opening statement. This is critical. For, despite earlier observations, this is the true beginning of the story-making process. Compare it, if you will, with the opening line of any fairy tale, wherein "Once upon a time" or "In those days" is designed to immediately capture the attention of any audience. In just such a manner, the opening statement of a client should capture the therapist's attention, inasmuch as that initial statement is the client's open *invitation,* however hesitantly expressed, to *hear* me and *hear* my story.

> He had been referred to me by our judicial affairs office, because he had frightened one of our young instructors with a gesture that she had interpreted as sexually threatening. He greeted me in the outer office with a military salute and a click of his heels. But once in my office with the door closed, he slumped into a chair, his long frame awkwardly fitting, and began to sob openly. I waited, reassuring him as gently as I knew how that it was okay to cry. But, finally, he blurted out, "I know I'm a man, but I don't want to be a man, as I feel like a woman inside."

How could any therapist not realize the turbulence of his emotions? How could any therapist not recognize his macho façade (a pattern) as an intentional gloss for an anguish that positioned him squarely *outside the city gates?* How could any therapist not hear his plea to have his story heard?

And hear it we will, if we are observing with our full attention the inflections of voice, the emotions that coincide with those inflections, and the nuances accompanying the way in which the story is told.

Poised for Psychotherapeutic Dialogue

Dialogue as a story-making genre dates from Plato and the *Book of Job.* As such, it has a long history of being an effective way for dealing with life's most critical problems. But what does *dialogue* mean in the psychotherapeutic sense?

The term itself has two parts: the first of these (*dia-*), as clarified by Dr. Stephen Bertman, a classicist (private e-mail, October 28, 2004) comes not "from the Greek number two, but from the Greek preposition that means 'through' or 'across'," whereas the second part (*-logue*) means *conversation* or *discourse.* Thus, as Bertman explains, *dialogue* "would literally be 'a talking across'." And in psychotherapy, this "talking across" is of a particular kind, in that it describes *a life-defining process of story-making.* For my own purposes, I like to think of this dialogue in terms of what Martin Buber (1958) called the *I–Thou relationship,* wherein both honor and compassion flow between two people who recognize each other as a *Thou,* not as an *It.* Initially, clients are seldom able to engage the therapist in this manner, but with the therapist modeling such a dialogue, they, too, eventually enter it with both compassion and honor. Indeed, when this happens, it is a clear sign that therapy is moving toward effectiveness.

But we have said that the therapist must be *poised* for dialogue. This means that, although initially the therapist functions as an audience, just as the client functions initially as the primary narrator, a moment comes when a true exchange begins. In that moment, a shift takes place: That shift joins therapist and client together as partners, now locked into a task of *re*making a story. Although the roles of *narrator* and *audience* still apply, a mutual dependence now exists, just as it exists between an author and a reader, or between a performer on stage and an observing audience. To have either without the other surely creates an impossible void.

SUGGESTED CLINICAL PRACTICES FOR NARRATIVE PSYCHOTHERAPY

What, then, are some elements of that dialogue that might effectively move the process forward? Or, what clinical practices might a therapist use for it is nothing less than *work* to assist clients to find more satisfying stories? Let us now proceed with a discussion, however partial, of some basic terms: the *problem that is presented,* the client's *history*, and *other elements of story-making.*

To *re*make a story, or to *tell* it in another way, both client and therapist must first develop some awareness of what the story is. They must acquire an understanding of what *continuity,* if any, applies, both currently and historically. Each of these follows a distinct course of action, because the current issue, as well as the developmental history of the client, although invariably related, has its own set of dynamics.

THE CURRENT ISSUE AS PRESENTED

What needs to be known about the current issue is: How is it perceived? When did it arise? In what way is it interfering with current functioning? And, what was happening in the client's life at the time of onset—not necessarily the precise time, but the time frame that comprises a six-month period prior to the beginning of the emotional discomfort? The first three of these (how, when, and what way) are usually clarified quickly. But teasing out what happened in the client's life at the time of onset, or what happened in a period of time just prior to that onset, may take more time. The reason for this six-month time frame is that emotions do not always surface at the time of the triggering event—a good point to remember in assembling the various parts of a story.

There are many strategies for working with these scenarios. Here are a few. Ask clients to project their experience of the troubling events onto an imaginary canvas, as though painting it. Ask what colors they are using, what shapes are taking form, which side of the canvas seems open to change, and what their reactions are to what they are creating. Then ask them to move their vision along the periphery of their imaginary canvas and talk about what they see there—that is, talk about what lies beyond the picture they have created. The purpose of this image-exercise is twofold: It allows clients to project their troubling situation outwardly, where they hopefully can gain some sense of control, and it also allows them to move cognitively into their imaginations.

Or again, for those clients who seem overly resistant, those who seem to see only the shadows of life, ask where they are standing in relationship to the sun, if the shadows always fall in front of them. The answer is simply that they are facing away from the sun. Then ask what they need to do to see the sun. Again, the answer is simply that they need only to turn around. This may seem too simplistic, so it is always needful for the therapist to explain that the act of turning around does not in any sense make the shadows disappear, because they are still there. Rather, what it effectively does is refocus a client's attention so that something other than the shadows can now be seen.

Such exercises are endless, limited only by the disinclination of either therapists or clients. It is, in fact, a sad commentary on our current society that our imaginative capacities are all too often bereft, leaving some clients *and* some therapists in a never-never land, unable to venture into this richest of all cognitive areas.

THE CLIENT'S HISTORY—DEVELOPMENTAL
AND BEYOND

Clients' histories, both developmentally and beyond, are necessarily integral to the story-making process. From such historical information we often find roots for any patterns now being enacted. What needs to be known developmentally involves the client's family history: What supportive relationships, if any, did he or she experience while growing up? What traumatic events occurred, and at what age? What messages were received from family members with respect to him- or herself? What kind of imaginative activities did the client engage in as a child? Which were his or her favorite childhood stories? And what family ties are currently being maintained? Although each story is different, the richness of this material is inexhaustible. This family history tells us a great deal about the story currently in the making, as well as any connections between that story and its historical antecedents.

What needs to be known beyond the developmental history involves what has happened since the client left home: What relationships, if any, has he or she pursued? What was the style of pursuit and was it successful? Who is currently significant in his or her life? What work or other activities have been of interest? What dreams have been abandoned or pursued? What values are currently held?

Most of this information can be gained simply by asking the right questions, as would happen in any good dialogue. In fact, such questions usually accompany any other strategies that might be used.

What is emphasized here, however, are the *messages* that clients receive during their developmental years, especially those that have been internalized, those that dictate behaviors that readily evolve into patterns. In this regard, R. D. Laing's (1972) notion of *mapping* is helpful. By *mapping*, Laing meant those messages that children receive that tell them who they are and what is expected of them—messages such as: "You are just like your uncle Sid," or "You are the smart one," or "You'll never amount to anything." Such messages, if believed, can evolve into patterns of behavior that were never intended.

To get at these messages and thus learn some of the themes and motifs that characterize a given life, an image exercise introduced by Akhter Ahsen (1972), but used here somewhat differently, is sometimes helpful: Ask the client to see both parents in front of him or her, then ask the client to bring either parent's face into close proximity to his or her own (like holding up a mirror). Then ask him or her to look into that parent's eyes to see what messages were received from those eyes. Once that image has been explored, ask the client to replace it with the other parent's face, and repeat the same questions. This exercise often evokes a great deal of emotion, not just because such messages may still be painful, but because all too often the act of acknowledging them is likewise painful.

Once messages have been identified, we then must explore just how they have influenced our clients' lives. If they are messages of self-loathing, for example, it is absolutely imperative that we eventually supplant them with other, more fruitful messages, those that can break dysfunctional patterns of behavior and set our clients on more productive paths of story-making. Depending on how ingrained such messages have become, the duration of this task may seem endless.

Amazingly, children often find other sources of meaning! One of these may be the stories they read. Such stories can serve as a kind of projective test to reveal which imaginary characters they identified with as children, what fantasies they built about life, and what ways they found to enrich their lives, despite other, more negative experiences. It was, in fact, Marie Louise Von Franz (1972) who maintained that, in order for psychotherapy to be truly effective, this information is always needed. For our purposes, it reinforces the other side of the equation, wherein literature influences us in more ways than we might imagine.

> She said the children at school had singled her out as the one to be picked on. Thus, not being accepted by the group, she had come to feel that she must be different. The teachers, she said, never saw what was happening, because these kids were clever enough not to get caught. She described how one of the girls had once pulled her hair from the right side, while another pulled it from the left, thus making it difficult for her to defend herself. She said that she still felt angry about that incident and sometimes found herself taking that anger out on her friends.
>
> Because she had told this part of her story in a dispassionate voice, I asked her what she would like to do, now that she was an adult, for that little 11-year-old girl, the one who was being picked on. She began to cry. Still sobbing, she said that she wanted to give that little girl all the love and protection that she deserved.

SELECTED ELEMENTS OF PSYCHOTHERAPEUTIC STORY-MAKING

The history of the client is essential to the story-making process, for, without it, we have no foundation on which to build. Not only does it connect the past with the present, but it provides the continuity needed to recognize the themes, motifs, and patterns within the story. Unfortunately, we cannot change history. At best, we may assist clients to perceive their histories differently. To do this, we must have some points of reference that easily apply within an *oral–aural* framework of narration. The following selected elements, although not exhaustive, may be helpful: *indiscriminate characters, intergenerational features, looking at the flip side, critical moments,* and *continuity.*

Indiscriminate Characters

In the story of *Rumpelstilskin*, and again in the story of *Psyche and Eros,* the father of the young maiden whose story is being told disappears from the story in the first few paragraphs. We simply never hear of him again. Yet the father in both these stories was fully instrumental in the events that followed. He set the action in motion.

In psychotherapy, we often have similar situations wherein clients tend to focus on one particular character, ignoring the roles played by others. It is the responsibility of the therapist to make sure that these *indiscriminate characters,* as I have elsewhere termed them (see Parker, 1998, p. 136), are identified, and that their roles are integrated into the story-making process. To do this, one need only acknowledge that any presentation will have its own biases, and that our memories, however keen they may be, are always, to some extent, flawed, even selective.

Intergenerational Features

By the expression *intergenerational features,* I refer to the histories of those others within the client's immediate family who have impinged upon the client's own. As is generally known, parents often come off poorly in psychotherapy. But to get the story right, a new perspective is needed. Mothers and fathers also have their stories, and many of them were really doing the very best they could, given their own human limitations. This is not to excuse abuse; rather, it is to say that sometimes it is helpful for our clients to look through the lens of their parents' own eyes, and in so doing to learn of *intergenerational features* that might somehow explain what happened ever so long ago.

Looking at the Flip Side

A story is found in William George Jordan's (n.d., pp. 34–35) *The Majesty of Calmness* that I sometimes paraphrase for those clients who are much concerned with their "failures." That paraphrase goes something like this: Early in the 20th century, logs were shipped by chaining them together on a raft for floating them to their destination. One such shipment was being floated down the eastern seaboard when a storm came up, ripped the chains apart, and scattered the logs far and yonder, leaving them to float out to sea. Thus, they never reached their intended destination, so we might call that *failure.* (At this point, clients usually express agreement.) However, so the story goes, these logs were spotted all over the ocean by astute sea captains, the result of which was the charting of the currents for the first time ever. So, I ask, was this failure or success?

The point is: We simply cannot know sometimes. Given that, it is often wise to look at the other side of the story, what I call *the flip side,* where failure and success, for example, are simply seen as two sides of the same coin.

Critical Moments

Sometimes in life, even sometimes in psychotherapy, we experience sudden insights that, seemingly coming from nowhere, give us glimpses into our lives that heretofore were unavailable to us. Such glimpses often tell us not just about the past, but tell us something about the future as well. Where might these come from? And how might they be accessed more readily for psychotherapy?

Poets, of course, have always known about this deep reservoir within. T. S. Eliot (1987, p. 146) referred to it as a "sense" involving a "perception, not only of the pastness of the past, but of its present." Stephen Bertman (2003, p. 67) described it as that pose that the Greek sculpture Myron chose for his statue *The Discus Thrower*. That pose, so Bertman explains, embodies "the moment between the wind-up and the release, the moment that sums up what has gone before and points to what is yet to come." And, Shelly (cited in Abrams, 1958, p. 131) described such moments as "interlunations" — the moon which disappears sometimes, but is nevertheless there, or the moon within.

According to these authors, such glimpses into our lives encompass all that has gone before and something of what may yet follow. Such glimpses, then, are essential to this life-defining process. But how, in such a busy world, can we ever be open to them?

The trick, I suggest, is to listen to our own deep thoughts, those thoughts buried within the recesses of mind, heart, and soul, that tell us what is truly important to us. It may be helpful just to slow down and listen, but, in my experience, such glimpses come at such odd, unexpected moments that I suggest we must practice not pushing them aside, but practice, instead, listening to our own deeper selves as we move through the fray of our lives. Of course, this is not easy in a world where multiple demands and distractions tend to focus our attention elsewhere. Yet, we must attempt to raise the awareness of our clients to these inner resources, to the *interlunations* that await them, to those insights that are all too ready to inform their better selves, as well as the world beyond.

Continuity

Such critical moments can become touchstones for the *continuity* that is sorely needed for effective story-making. They can sometimes let us see our parents for whom they really were, or open our eyes to the energy that lies available beyond what seemingly makes us a failure, or give us the hope that is needed to finish something that was begun long ago, or point us in a direction to other more fruitful patterns of life. Indeed, when our inner ear becomes attuned to the *interlunations of life,* we'll be able to tell our stories in more satisfying ways and, in turn, assist our clients to do the same.

A STORY UNFINISHED

She was an attractive woman in her mid 30s, who had returned to school after her divorce and, in fact, was doing quite well with her studies. But she had what seemed to be a "thought disorder," a delusional system working within her mind, one that told her that all the members of a worldwide religion, a church to which she no longer belonged, were now out to harm her. They entered her apartment when she was not there; they followed her and tried to harm her in various ways. Week after week, she came faithfully, reciting a litany of these strange experiences in a voice that echoed that of a small child. Listening carefully, I tried to discover what truth, if any, might be in her report. I never told her that I did not believe her, as many other therapists had, until one day she asked. Choosing my words carefully, as I had no desire to offend her, I explained that it was difficult for me to comprehend how millions of strangers would all be focused on hurting her, but that I was absolutely certain that this was how she was experiencing her world.

She continued through the end of the semester, but failed to come in at the beginning of the next one. I wondered what had happened, but had no reliable contact information. About midway through the semester, she came into the office and asked to see me. Having an open hour, I saw her immediately. Once she was seated in my office, she lowered her face into her hands and cried uncontrollably. I waited, but eventually asked why she had dropped out of therapy. Had I offended her in some way? She explained that she had been unable to pay a fee from the previous semester and, thus, had not been allowed to re-enroll in school. So, being keenly aware that she could seek services in our office only as a student, she had dropped out. Then I asked her why all the tears when she had first come in that day. She said that my office was the only place in the whole world where she felt truly safe.

That was ever so many years ago. Still, I think of her, think of her story that forever remains, for me, unfinished.

STORY-MAKING'S UNIVERSE, OR NARRATION'S NEGLECT IN PSYCHOTHERAPY

In fact, most therapeutic stories remain unfinished for therapists. But that does not mean that psychotherapy does not have a great deal in common with other story-making endeavors. Indeed, it does! That the story being retold at a time of some individual's crisis requires both a teller and an audience, and that this teller and audience must together engage in a life-defining endeavor seem obvious. What do not seem obvious are the effects that the *universe* in which all this takes place might have on this process. Those effects, I suggest, are closely related to the *neglect* of the narrative tradition in psychotherapy itself.

Because that narrative tradition is, by definition, traditional, and because tradition is largely devalued in today's world—a notion that, having been documented by Stephen Bertman (1998, 2000) and others, needs no further elaboration here—story-making as a possible reference point for psychotherapy is simply unfashionable. This is particularly true for mainline psychology, in which research and its tendency to fragment *lived experience* have long prevailed. Such a tendency simply does not lend itself to approaches for which a longer view of life is required. And this is not to demean psychological research per se, because its wealth of information relative to human behavior continues to enrich all that we do. But it is to demean the fragmentation of life. For, unless we come to recognize those *interlunations* that link past with present, unless we find ways to identify the *continuity* that defines our lives, and unless we learn to assist our clients to do the same, then we are surely destined to live out unfinished stories *outside the city gates*.

A STORY RETOLD

For a number of weeks, I had heard about a young woman who was causing problems in our residence hall at the university. The resident directors had lost patience, as had several of our younger therapists who had tried in vain to keep the young student in therapy. So I told our receptionist that this student would have to see me, should she need to be referred to our office again. And referred she was. She arrived in a state of high agitation, delivering her opening statement about how unfair everyone was in a voice that was so unsure of itself that I had trouble distinguishing her words. But I had decided to hear her story, for I surmised that if I listened I would probably learn more than was evident from all the reports. What I learned was that she was desperately homesick for her mother, that she came from a divided household where she sometimes still had problems, that she had experimented with drugs and sex during high school, but that she now wanted to live differently and to do well in school, because she had come to realize the folly of her high school days. The problem, as she saw it, was that the party atmosphere in the residence halls was interfering with this. I learned also that she idealized her grandmother—a point that, in view of my age, could explain why she continued in therapy with me.

Within weeks, having found herself a job and an apartment, she moved from the residence halls, continued with school, and subsequently finished the semester with good grades. Although she went home for the summer, she returned to therapy in the fall, still essentially self-supporting herself. In short, she became a very responsible young woman. Then one day she told me she did not think she needed to come in anymore. I agreed.

Three years later, seeing her name on my schedule, I wondered what had happened. When she came in, she seemed her usual self. After bringing me up to date on what had been happening in her life, she said that she had recently talked with her grandmother, and that her grandmother had suggested that she come in to tell me what a difference therapy had made in her life.

Such return visits after termination are really quite rare. But if I never have another, this one is quite sufficient to assure me that the story-making process in psychotherapy can have far-reaching results, results that somehow evolve from a meaningful dialogue between two people working together in an uncertain universe to discover a more satisfying story.

REFERENCES

Abrams, M. H. (1958). *The mirror and the lamp: Romantic theory and the critical tradition.* New York: WW Norton & Company. [Original work published 1953.]

Ahsen, A. (1972). *The eidetic parents test and analysis.* New York: Brandon House.

Bertman, S. (1998). *Hyperculture: The human cost of speed.* Westport, CT: Praeger.

Bertman, S. (2000). *Cultural amnesia: America's future and the crisis of memory.* Westport, CT: Praeger.

Bertman, S. (2003). *Climbing Olympus: What you can learn from Greek myth and wisdom.* Naperville, IL: Sourcebooks.

Buber, M. (1958). *I and Thou* (2nd ed.). (R. G. Smith, Trans.). New York: Charles Scribner's Sons.

Eliot, T. S. (1987). Tradition and the individual talent. In V. Lambropoulos & D. N. Miller (Eds.). *Twentieth-century literary theory: An introductory anthology* (pp. 145–151). New York: State University Press.

Freud, S. (1963). General theory of neurosis. In J. Strachey (Ed., Trans.). *The standard edition of the complete psychological works of Sigmund Freud.* London: Hogarth. [Original work published 1917.], 243–495.

Gentili, B. (1988). *Poetry and its public in ancient Greece: From Homer to the fifth century.* (A. T. Cole, Trans.). Baltimore: John Hopkins. [Original work published 1985.]

Hillman, J. (1975). The fiction of case history: A round. In J. B. Wiggins (Ed.). *Religion as story* (pp. 123–173). New York: Harper & Row.

Jordan, W. G. (n.d.). *The majesty of calmness.* Westwood, NJ: Fleming H. Revell. [Dust jacket indicates essays written 1900.]

Laing, R. D. (1972). *The politics of family and other essays.* New York: Vintage Books.

McConnell, F. (1979). *Storytelling and mythmaking.* New York: Oxford University.

Parker, L. (1985). Between storytelling and storyliving. *The National Storytelling Journal, Winter,* 14–17.

Parker, L. (1998). *Mythopoesis and the crisis of postmodernism: Toward integrating image and story.* New York: Brandon House.

Rogers, C. (1961). *On becoming a person.* Boston: Houghton Mifflin.

Rubin, D. C. (1995). *Memory in oral traditions: The cognitive psychology of epic, ballads, and counting-out rhythms.* New York: Oxford University.

Sarbin, T. R. (Ed.). (1986). *Narrative psychology: The storied nature of human conduct.* Westport, CT: Praeger.

Schafer, R. (1980). Narration in the psychoanalytic dialogue. *Critical Inquiry, 7,* 29–53.

Scheibe, K. E. (1993). Dramapsyche: Getting serious about context. In S. C. Hayes, L. J. Hayes, H. W. Reese, & T. R. Sarbin (Eds.). *Varieties of scientific contextualism.* Reno, NV: Context Press, 191–205.

Spence, D. P. (1982). *Narrative truth and historical truth: Meaning and interpretation in psychoanalysis.* New York: WW Norton.

Von Franz, M. L. (1972). *The feminine in fairytales.* New York: Spring Publications.

5

RECOGNIZING AND DEALING WITH CULTURAL INFLUENCES IN PSYCHOTHERAPY

MELANIE P. DUCKWORTH

Department of Psychology
University of Nevada Reno, Nevada

TONY IEZZI

Behavioral Medicine Service
London Health Sciences Center
London, Ontario, Canada

Although therapists commonly recognize and deal with clients of different cultures, they often neglect to focus on the effects of cultural influences on psychotherapy. In fact, out of an idealistic belief that "we are all the same," some therapists purposely ignore cultural influences on psychotherapy. However, this perspective would be inconsistent with the reality of everyday life that clients of diverse cultures experience.

Consider the following features of two case presentations:

A 54-year-old married Lebanese woman with three children works as a cashier at a small department store. She has been residing in a small northern US city for the last five years since leaving her country because of political pressure. She recently developed chronic low back pain as a result of a motor vehicle collision, and she is a devout Muslim.

A 28-year-old single Vietnamese woman just started working as an accountant in a prominent firm. After immigrating from Vietnam approximately 10 years ago, she has been living in a large city on the western coast of Canada. She does not suffer from any particular ailments. Her religious and philosophical orientation is

Clinical Strategies for
Becoming a Master Psychotherapist

71

consistent with Buddhism. Although she has acknowledged being in a relationship for the past four years, she considers herself-bisexual.

Consider the following features of two therapists:

A 40-year-old single African-American woman was born and raised in New Orleans, Louisiana. She has a devout Catholic upbringing and works as a university professor in a relatively small city in the western United States. She has recently developed insulin-resistant syndrome.

A 45-year-old married Italian-Canadian with three children was born and raised in Montreal. He is a nonpracticing Catholic and works as a staff psychologist in a general medical hospital in a city in Ontario, Canada. He has a 27-year history of chronic knee pain that significantly affects his quality of life and during the last few years he has had to undergo cataract and retinal detachment surgeries unexpectedly.

Although the clinical cases are fictitious, they do represent a compilation of features previously seen in a number of clients. These two fictitious cases would not be all that unusual to full-time practicing therapists. The two therapists represent the first and second authors of this chapter. Regardless of clinical presentation, therapeutic relationship between the client and therapist does not occur in a vacuum. Even without other important historical information (e.g., developmental, social, interpersonal, vocational, and psychiatric.), readily available information can be used heuristically to start the hypothesis testing process about a client's clinical presentation. In addition, the hypothesis testing process is influenced by cultural characteristics present in the therapist. The client and therapist interact on a background of historical, sociopolitical, and cultural influences.

Although historical and sociopolitical influences on therapy have been recognized, cultural influences have received greater clinical and research attention during the last 20 years. The primary aim of this chapter is to review different terms used to describe and define cultural influences in the psychotherapy context. The secondary aim of this chapter is to review a select literature of client cultural influences and therapist cultural influences that impact the psychotherapeutic relationship. The overall aim of this chapter is to increase cultural competence in therapists. Increased cultural competence will result in increased mastery of clinical skills and more effective management of culturally diverse clients.

DEFINITION OF CULTURE
AND OTHER TERMS

Before discussing cultural influences on psychotherapy, a presentation of definitions of culture and related terms is indicated. Draguns (1997) defines culture as "the shared social experiences of a group defined on the basis of its origin and/or morphological or 'racial' characteristics" (p. 214). Examples of this type of cultural grouping include African-Americans, Italian-Australians, and Finnish-Canadians. A more explicit definition provided by Hays (1996) states that culture refers to "all the learned behaviors, beliefs, norms, and values that are held by a group of people passed on from older members to newer members, at least, in part to preserve the group" (p. 333). Interpersonal and social aspects of culture are emphasized rather than physical similarities. Ethic identity refers to the historical and cultural patterns and collective identities shared by groups of people from a specific geographical region of the world (Betancourt & Lopez, 1993). In a face valid fashion, ethnicity provides more insight into a client's heritage and value system than race (Atkinson, Morten, & Sue, 1993). Human diversity refers to group-specific factors salient for the client (Roysircar, 2004). These include gender, socioeconomic status, age, religion, race, ethnicity, regional/national origin, sexual orientation, and ability status. All these factors shape a client's and a therapist's identity, worldview, attitudes, values, and beliefs. It should be understood that clinicians and researchers use *culture, race, ethnicity*, and *diversity* somewhat interchangeably. This sometimes makes it difficult to establish common reference points when using these terms. In addition, these constructs are also emotionally laden terms and they can create awkwardness or discomfort in the therapist, client, and researcher. Overall, when compared with race and ethnicity, and other similar terms (e.g., *minority group*), *culture* is viewed and conceptualized as more comprehensive in its influences on the human condition.

The increasing recognition of cultural influences in the psychotherapeutic context is a reflection of increased cultural diversity in society. According to the US Census Bureau (2001), Caucasians (81%) make up most of the current US population, followed by African-Americans (12.7%) and Hispanic-Americans (12.6%). Although "white" is used in the U.S. Census Bureau Document, Caucasian will be used throughout the current chapter except when referencing the work of the other authors. By the year 2050, the US Census Bureau (2001) projects that the Caucasian population will decrease by approximately 10% and that Hispanic-American and Asian-American populations will at least double in size. A slight increase of several percentage points for the African-American population is expected. It is anticipated that one quarter of the US population will consist of Hispanic-Americans by the year 2050. At this time, only 6% of psychologists are of African-American, Hispanic-American, Asian-American, and Native American descent (American Psychological Association, 1997). Thus, a significant number of culturally diverse clients seeking mental health assistance will be assessed and treated by a Caucasian therapist. Given that clients generally prefer a therapist of similar background (Sue, 1998), most therapeutic interventions involving culturally diverse clients begin with a client–therapist cultural mismatch. Obviously, clients of diverse cultural backgrounds will need more therapists with a diverse cultural background. However, Caucasion therapists can still assist the needs of culturally diverse clients by increasing their cultural competence.

RECOGNIZING AND DEALING
WITH CULTURAL INFLUENCES
IN THE CLIENT

Studies examining the influence of culture on psychopathology have been shaped by two distinct conceptualizations (Draguns, 1997). One conceptual model views culture as permeating all aspects of psychological distress. Culture and psychopathology are intertwined and are part of a holistic experience. Based on this model, there would be no advantage to comparing psychological distress across cultures because of the uniqueness of each culture. Alternatively, the second model discourages the role of culture in defining psychological experiences. In this model, the focus is on examining common psychological experiences that go across different cultures.

These two conceptual models have led to the use of two distinct approaches in conducting cross-cultural research: the emic approach and the etic approach. The emic research model favors qualitative and descriptive research that tends to demonstrate the uniqueness of a culture and discourages Western conceptualizations of psychological distress. For example, this type of model would value the role of familism (*familismo*; La Roche, 2002) in the etiology of psychological distress experienced by Hispanic-Americans. Although there may be a similar construct, for example, in an Asian culture, the interest would be in how the perception of familism from a Hispanic-American perspective might lead to unique psychological experiences and repercussions. Other culture-specific experiences can be reviewed in the following articles: For African-American experiences, see Fuertes, Mueller, Chauhan, Walker, & Ladany, 2002; for Asian-American experiences, see Kim, Yang, Atkinson, Wolfe, & Hong, 2001; and for Arab-American experiences, see Erickson & Al-Timimi, 2001.

Another example of the emic research approach is the classic research conducted by Kleinman (1984a, b), which examines culture, affect, and somatization in Asian samples. His research identified differences between Eastern and Western populations in the use of somatic symptoms as an expression of psychological distress. Interestingly, this initial research may have led to the perception or stereotype that persons of Eastern culture and other foreign cultures tend to focus on somatic symptoms as a means of expressing psychic distress. More recent research suggests that Westerners are increasing their rates of somatization in spite of, or maybe because of, recent advancements in medical assessment and treatment (Gureje, Simon, Ustun, & Goldberg, 1997; Kirmayer & Young, 1998).

An etic research model is based on concepts, methods, and measures that apply to all cultures. This model would essentially capture a construct of interest and attempt to measure it in a standardized manner (e.g., paper–pencil measure and/or diagnostic interviewing) across different cultures. For example, familism would be conceptualized as those common family-related etiological factors that could be assessed across Hispanic-Americans, African-Americans, Asian-Americans, European-Americans, and other cultural groups.

The etic approach is well demonstrated by a study evaluating attachment in African-American, Asian-American, Hispanic-American, and Caucasian students (Wei, Russell, Mallinckrodt, & Zakalik, 2004). Specifically, the authors examined attachment anxiety, which taps into the need for approval from others and sensitivity to interpersonal rejection by others; and attachment avoidance, which attempts to assess an excessive need for self-reliance and discomfort with interpersonal closeness. The four cultural groups were compared using the Experiences in Close Relationship Scale (Brennan, Clark, & Shaver, 1998). The results indicated that Hispanic-Americans displayed greater attachment anxiety, whereas, African-Americans and Asian-Americans displayed greater attachment avoidance than their Caucasian peers. The investigators also found that attachment anxiety was associated with negative mood for all groups but the relationship was stronger for Asian-Americans than African-American and Caucasian peers.

Other studies have looked at differences in psychopathology across certain cultures. Major depression appears to occur at a greater frequency for Western and Latin-American countries and at a lesser frequency for Asian countries (Kawakami, Shimuzu, Haratani, Iwata, & Kitamura, 2004). One of the most extensive epidemiological studies of African-Americans, Hispanic-Americans, and Caucasians used the Diagnostic Interview Schedule to examine anxiety disorders (Robins & Regier, 1991). Findings indicated that generalized anxiety disorder was greater for African-Americans than Caucasians when panic and depression were excluded. Hispanic-Americans had the lowest rates of generalized anxiety disorder. No consistent differences were found for panic disorder. The rates for phobias were greater for African-Americans than for Caucasians and Hispanic-Americans. There is also extensive literature examining cultural differences in other clinical presentations (e.g., schizophrenia, alcohol abuse, eating disorders).

A review of studies examining all the possible permutations of cultures and psychological conditions is beyond the scope of this chapter. The select emic and etic research studies described here were presented to familiarize the reader with these two distinct conceptualizations of the role of culture in human experiences and the influence of these conceptual models on the conduct of culture-related research. As important as the contribution of these two conceptual models to the conduct of culture-related research is the potential contribution of these models to the competent conduct of clinical assessment and psychotherapy. Although emic and etic approaches are on opposite ends of the continuum, they can be seen as complementing each other (Draguns, 1997). The emic approach provides information about abnormal behavior and experiences that is unique in terms of the historical and sociocultural background of the individual, whereas the etic approach leads to generalizations about psychological experience that allows for an appreciation of the shared aspects of psychological experiences. An understanding of these two perspectives helps the therapist to assess and manage psychological distress more effectively in culturally diverse clients. It is interesting to note that regardless of perspective, psychological distress and its manifestations remain essentially the same across the world (Draguns, 1997). However, when working with diverse cultural clients, an emic approach to cultural influences seems to be the most relevant to establishing workable and working therapeutic relationships with clients, and maximizes the therapist's effectiveness as an agent of change in the therapeutic process. The emic model also lends itself well to the single-case research design, an analysis strategy necessary to the process of evaluating the effectiveness of a given therapeutic intervention used with a given client.

DEALING AND RECOGNIZING CULTURAL INFLUENCES IN THE THERAPIST

Everything being equal, obtaining a successful therapeutic outcome with culturally diverse clients is likely to be more of a challenge than when working with clients of a similar cultural background. It should be understood that therapists working with clients of a diverse background need to accept the burden of adjusting to new circumstances. Therapists should not be quick to blame either the client or the culture if psychotherapy does not result in the desired outcome. Instead, modifying the therapeutic approach and adapting it to the specific needs of clients will result in a more positive therapeutic outcome and in an overall positive experience throughout the therapeutic process.

It should be understood that no therapist, no matter how skilled, knows everything that there is to know about every culture. However, there are a number of strategies on which a skilled clinician can rely to improve cultural competence and therapeutic outcome with clients of different cultures and backgrounds. The focus in the following sections is on increasing knowledge and awareness of attitudes, biases, and assumptions related to culturally diverse clients.

A good starting point in increasing knowledge in working with culturally diverse clients is becoming familiar with available ethical guidelines. The American Psychological Association has sponsored a number of reports on culture, ethnicity, age, gender, and sexual orientation: *Guidelines for Multicultural Training, Research, Practice, and Organizational Change for Psychologists* (American Psychological Association, 2003a); *Guidelines for Providers of Psychological Services to Ethnic, Linguistic, and Culturally Diverse Populations* (American Psychological Association, 1993); *Guidelines for Psychological Practice with Older Adults* (American Psychological Association, 2003b); and *Guidelines for Psychotherapy with Lesbian, Gay, and Bisexual Clients* (American Psychological Association, 2000). The Council of National Psychological Association for the Advancement of Ethnic Minority Issues has published relevant documents related to ethnic minorities: *Guidelines for Research in Ethnic Minority Communities* (Council of National Psychological Associations for the Advancement of Ethnic Minority Issues, 2000) and *Psychological Treatment of Ethnic Minority Populations* (Council of National Psychological Associations for the Advancement of Ethnic Minority Issues, 2003). Being familiar with these guidelines will not only assist with recognizing biases and assumptions therapists might have about culturally diverse clients, but will also result in clinical practice that is in keeping with the American Psychological Association and other regulatory bodies.

Even when familiar with the available guidelines, the therapist needs to recognize that ethical guidelines generated for one cultural context may need to be modified for use in another cultural context (Pedersen, 1995). Pedersen (1995) makes the point that therapists need to be aware that they have to differentiate "fundamental" ethical principles (e.g., no physical abuse of a child), which cannot be negotiated, from more "discretionary" ethical principles (e.g., a parent has to discipline a child and that discipline can sometimes include corporal punishment).

Borrowing from Berry and colleagues (1992), Pedersen (1995) describes cultural ethics as guided by one of three perspectives: relativism ("to each his/her own"), absolutism ("mine is best"), or universalism ("we are both the same and different") (Berry, Poortinga, Segall, & Dasen, 1992). The relativist perspective attempts not to make value judgments and emphasizes the importance of understanding each cultural context on its own terms. The assessment of something as right or wrong is determined entirely by the culture of the client, and judgments made by therapists outside the culture are discouraged. Thus, the therapist is removed as a moral agent from the discussion with the client.

The absolutist perspective applies the same evaluative criteria across cultures in a fixed and standardized manner. In other words, the cultural context is actually considered irrelevant to the discussion between therapist and client. The emphasis is on cultural similarity with the dominant group.

The universalist perspective assumes that psychological processes (e.g., pain and pleasure) are universal across all cultures, but the way these are manifested or expressed may be specific to each culture. Therapists will find that ethical decisions based on relativist (the culture of origin is right) and absolutist perspectives (the dominant culture is right) easiest to follow. However, Pedersen (1995) believes that, in more difficult and challenging clinical circumstances, the universalist position, which recognizes cultural differences but also tries to find commonalities with the dominant culture, is most effective. Although he is supportive of the American Psychological Association guidelines, Pedersen (1995) noted some weaknesses in the guidelines: the lack of an explicit philosophical principle, the maintenance of dominant culture, and a minimization of culture in ethical decision making.

Much of the credit for recognizing and valuing cultural competence in psychotherapy goes to Stanley Sue. In a seminal position paper, Sue (1998) indicated that the ingredients for culturally competent therapists include being scientifically minded, having skills in "dynamic sizing," and acquiring knowledge about a cultural group. Scientifically minded therapists are individuals who apply the scientific method to the therapeutic process. Instead of making premature conclusions based on biases or assumptions about cultural factors, these therapists form hypotheses, develop ways to test the hypotheses, and try to provide services consistent with the obtained data. Of course, most therapists are versed in the scientific method, but they sometimes forget to apply this in the clinical context, especially in a context when they may know relatively little about a cultural group.

Sue (1998) defines dynamic sizing as the ability to know when to generalize and be inclusive and when to individualize and be exclusive. This construct is similar to Pedersen's (1995) universalist perspective on guiding ethical choices when working with clients of diverse backgrounds. Sue (1998) recognizes that therapists' perceptions of clients are influenced by stereotypes, and these stereotypes can take away from specific characteristics in culturally different clients. In other words, dynamic sizing helps the therapist to avoid applying stereotypes to members of a particular cultural group while appreciating the importance of the cultural group.

Finally, Sue (1998) emphasizes the need for therapists to acquire knowledge that is relevant to the cultural group of interest. This includes seeking information from the literature, colleagues, community representatives (e.g., translators), or previous clients.

Daniel, Roysircar, Abeles, and Boyd (2004) discuss the importance of self-awareness in the therapist. The authors focus primarily on racism, heterosexism, and ageism, but their suggestions for increasing the therapist's skill level also apply to other important cultural markers, such as disability, religion, social status, and gender. Daniel et al. (2004) note that therapists residing in the United States are likely to be exposed to different stereotypes that could lead to biases and unwarranted assumptions about culturally diverse clients. They astutely point out that therapists are likely to subscribe to them, consciously or unconsciously. It is particularly at the unconscious level that therapists are most vulnerable to their biases and assumptions of clients culturally different from them. The authors encourage self-awareness of attitudes, biases, and assumptions. The therapist's persona and self-awareness is viewed as essential in establishing a therapeutic alliance with the client. Therapists can rely on self-report measures, journaling, and review of clinical notes and critical incidents to begin the process of increasing self-awareness. Daniel et al. (2004) also recommended seeking feedback from clients, peers, supervisees, and relevant others as a means of increasing self-awareness.

Among a number of conclusions made in relation to knowledge about working with culturally diverse clients, Daniel et al. (2004) conclude that therapists should recognize that there is a growing body of literature on the topic of cultural competence. They note that there is more than one way to conceptualize and provide services to culturally diverse clients. Providing culturally relevant services should not override the theoretical model being used to guide assessment and psychotherapy. Daniel et al. (2004) also conclude that cultural markers (e.g., race, ethnicity, age, (sexual orientation) are dynamic and influence other issues that come up in psychotherapy.

Roysircar (2004) expands on suggestions for increasing cultural self-awareness. She encourages the therapist to become aware of his/her respective cultural influences, explore his/her own cultural heritage, and appreciate this in relation to understanding the cultural influences that are relevant to clients. Roysircar (2004) borrows from Sue, Arredondo, and McDavis (1992) and quotes, "A culturally skilled therapist is one who is actively engaged in the process of becoming aware of his or her own assumptions about human behavior, values, biases, preconceived notions, and personal limitations" (p. 481). Culturally sensitive therapists demonstrate their skills when they can discuss diverse cultural factors openly. Therapists need to know when to and when not to refer to salient cultural factors in the client. Therapists' awareness of culture is a precursor for effective, culturally relevant psychotherapy. Therapists have to be aware of negative views of clients. Self-awareness allows for an exploration of barriers to effective psychotherapy, including defensiveness, projections, anxieties, fears, and guilt in managing clients of different cultures.

Cardemil and Battle (2003) note that that there are no clear rules for how and when to address certain potentially sensitive issues with culturally diverse clients during the psychotherapeutic process. The authors provide a number of recommendations to assist therapists in integrating multicultural issues in psychotherapy. Although they focus primarily on race and ethnicity, their recommendations also apply to other cultural indicators. With regard to race and ethnicity, Cardemil and Battle (2003) encourage therapists to suspend conclusions about race and ethnicity of clients and that of family members until confirmed by clients. Making assumptions about race and ethnicity without verification could lead to potential pitfalls in psychotherapy. For example, a client may prefer to be described as an African-American person rather than a black person. When in doubt about the importance of race and ethnicity in treatment, Cardemil and Battle (2003) encourage directly asking the client: "How would you describe your racial background?" They encourage therapists to recognize that clients may be quite different from other members of their race and ethnic group. As noted by others (Roysircar, 2004; Sue, 1998), this reduces the likelihood of stereotyping clients. Therapists also need to consider how differences in race and ethnicity between therapist and client might affect psychotherapy. For example, cultural differences between a therapist and client could lead to differences in perception of physical space (e.g., distance between therapist and client) and verbal (e.g., directive vs. nondirective statements) and nonverbal (e.g., smiling, hand shaking, or eye contact) behaviors. Mismatches in perceptions can lead to awkwardness in the psychotherapeutic relationship. Finally, Cardemil and Battle (2003) recommend that Caucasion therapists acknowledge that power, privilege, and racism might affect the therapeutic relationship. Therapists have to recognize that being part of a majority culture has provided them greater power and privilege. This magnifies the power differential already inherent in the therapeutic relationship (i.e., client seeking help from therapist). Again, therapists are encouraged to discuss these issues openly and nondefensively as they come up in therapy, or at least to look for opportunities to manage potential barriers to effective therapy.

Hays (2001) also makes a strong argument for recognizing and understanding the influence of bias and power in therapy. She defines bias as a tendency to think, act, and feel in a particular way. In some individuals these biases may lead to some correct hypotheses and quicker understanding of someone, but in other situations these biases can lead to embarrassingly wrong conclusions. Biases often emerge in combination with two other cognitive processes: categorization and generalization. These cognitive processes often help to facilitate learning and social interactions. However, according to Hays (2001), when these assumptions become fairly set, the result is stereotyping. She notes that power is closely tied to social bias. Similar to Cardemil and Battle (2003), Hays (2001) suggests that, because members of a high-status group hold more power, they can exert more control over their own situations and the situations of members of lower status groups. In *Addressing Cultural Competencies in Practice: A Framework for Clinicians and Counselors*, Hays (2001) summarizes earlier work on the topic of social bias and power (Hays, 1996), concluding that "stereotypes and bias, when combined with power, form systems of privilege known as 'isms' (e.g., racism, sexism, classism, heterosexism, ageism, ableism, and colonialism)" (p. 24). She indicates that underprivileged groups are socialized into seeing differences between those who have and those who have not. In contrast, privileged groups are not socialized to see these differences, largely because they do need to.

According to Hays (2001), the most important quality or characteristic in doing cross-cultural work is the therapist's ability to be humble and yet think critically. To think humbly and critically and to prevent premature conclusions, Hays (2001) recommends examining the functional value of assumptions, asking how the therapist has come to a given understanding about the client, asking whether other alternative explanations are possible for the client's experience, and trying to generate a more positive interpretation of culturally influenced behaviors, beliefs, or feelings.

Hays (1996) developed a very helpful approach to becoming more aware of cultural influences on therapy and to identifying potential sources of bias. Her model is called *ADRESSING* and is designed to organize and recognize systematically complex cultural influences on the therapeutic relationship. The acronym stands for age, disability, religion, ethnicity, social status, sexual orientation, indigenous heritage, national origin, and gender. The two fictitious cases as well as two descriptions of therapists presented at the beginning of this chapter essentially follow the ADRESSING model. The ADRESSING model does not cover all possible cultural influences, but it does focus on variables that have been recognized as important by the American Psychological Association and other organizations (Hays, 1996). The model can be used not only to examine a therapist's bias, but also to examine the client's self-assessment of cultural identity. The model recognizes that no therapist can possibly have an insider's view on all cultural influences. Hays suggests that beginning with these basic indicators can help to make a therapist more aware of cultural influences on the psychotherapeutic relationship.

CASE ILLUSTRATION

The following is a case illustration designed to highlight cultural influences in the client and the therapist. It also provides an example of adjustments that a therapist needs to make to meet best the needs of the culturally diverse client. The client was seen within the context of the second author's clinical activities. A number of changes were made to the case presentation to maintain the privacy of the client.

The client is a 47-year-old married Lebanese woman with two daughters and three sons. She has been residing in a large metropolitan city in Ontario since 1995. Before coming to Canada, she completed a university degree in child care in France. She obtained a position as a child care worker within four years of immigrating to Canada. She incurred a slip-and-fall injury while working at a child care center in 2001. As a result of her work-related injury, she developed chronic neck and head pain, and associated sequelae (e.g., reduced quality of life and emotional distress). She was initially referred to a pain psychologist at another medical center who suggested that she consider a mindfulness-based treatment approach to her chronic pain and depression. Although fluent in both Lebanese and French, she was reticent about pursuing this treatment approach because of her relatively limited mastery of the English language. Although her command of the English language was serviceable in everyday interactions, she did not feel competent in being able to understand and express more subtle aspects of her thoughts and feelings.

She was then referred to the second author because of his ability to speak and write in French. A standard assessment was conducted and treatment options were presented to her. It was agreed that her mastery of the English language was not sufficient to conduct an intervention in English. The option of a referral to a female therapist who could speak in French was considered, but the therapist was not skilled in psychological pain management. Because chronic pain was so prominent in affecting the client's life, she chose to pursue treatment with a male therapist. The client and I agreed to conduct psychological management in French, recognizing that I sometimes might not be able to use the right word in French and might even make grammatical speaking errors. We both agreed to ask questions when not certain about language use and expression.

Although the standard treatment protocol for a chronic pain patient consists of 12 biweekly sessions and is based on an empirically validated cognitive–behavioral management, this approach had to be quickly abandoned. It became clear that a therapeutic alliance had to be established first, and that this would require more time than typical. When working with culturally diverse clients, therapists sometimes think that therapy is failing when a positive outcome is not readily noticeable. Because cultural differences (e.g., ethnicity, race, education, language, age, gender, and religion) between the client and therapist need to be worked through, the normal assessment and treatment timetables need to be amended and expanded.

It was readily apparent at the beginning of therapy that direct questions about thoughts and feelings were ineffective. These questions met with silence or long quite pauses. When asked why this was the case, the client expressed feeling threatened by such a direct approach. She expressed that such direct questioning was considered inappropriate in her culture. Although I was well versed in cognitive behavioral techniques, I had to use other less familiar therapeutic approaches. It was agreed that the client would keep a dream journal and that we would use dream interpretation as a means of slowly exploring psychological processes. Within a year of therapy, the client began to return to a favorite past time of painting. She then began to bring her artwork to therapy and we used her artwork to explore psychological processes further. Throughout her therapy, we were able also to address pain issues and other threatening material (e.g., discussions about family and marriage) as they came up. Therapy is still ongoing and the client has much improved. Currently, therapy largely focuses on existential issues (e.g., "meaning of life"). A year ago, the client stated that my initial willingness to do therapy in French was very beneficial. Even though French was not my first language, doing therapy in French provided her with a forum to pursue discussions about her thoughts and feelings. Without this, she expressed that she would likely have not continued in therapy. She also stated that my willingness to be vulnerable by expressing myself in French helped her to be more comfortable in becoming more open with her thoughts and feelings.

SUMMARY

It is almost impossible to be involved in psychotherapy and not have some prominent cultural influence affecting the psychotherapeutic relationship. Even when the cultural background between clients and therapists is similar, there is still a need to recognize and deal with cultural influences. Becoming a skilled therapist requires an appreciation for the influence of cultural factors on both the client and the therapist, with this active appreciation of cultural influences ultimately resulting in culturally competent psychotherapy. Increasing knowledge about cultural influences; increasing self-awareness about cultural biases, assumptions, and beliefs; and open communication about sensitive issues related to culture result in a more positive psychotherapy experience. In addition, this approach to psychotherapy results in perspectives that enhance and transform emotional and social relations in the world experience.

REFERENCES

American Psychological Association. (1993). Guidelines for providers of psychological services to ethnic, linguistic, and culturally diverse populations. *American Psychologist, 48,* 45–48.

American Psychological Association. (1997). *Commission on ethnic minority recruitment, retention and training in psychology (CEMRATT).* Washington, DC: Author.

American Psychological Association. (2000). Guidelines for psychotherapy with lesbian, gay, and bisexual clients. *American Psychologist, 55,* 1440–1451.

American Psychological Association. (2003a). Guidelines for multicultural education, training, research, practice, and organizational change for psychologists. *American Psychologist, 58,* 377–402.

American Psychological Association. (2003b). *Guidelines for psychological practice with older adults.* Washington, DC: Author.

Atkinson, D. R., Morten, G., & Sue, D. W. (1993). *Counseling American minorities: A cross-cultural perspective.* Dubuque, IA: William C. Brown.

Berry, J. W., Poortinga, Y. H. Y., Segall, M. H., & Dasen, P. J. (1992). *Cross-cultural psychology: Research and applications.* Cambridge, UK: Cambridge University Press.

Betancourt, H., & Lopez, S. R. (1993). The study of culture, ethnicity, and race in American psychology. *American Psychologist, 48,* 629–637.

Brennan, K. A., Clark, C. L., & Shaver, P. R. (1998). Self-report measurement of adult attachment: An integrative overview. In J. A. Simpson & W. S. Rholes (Eds.). *Attachment theory and close relationships* (pp. 46–76). New York: Guilford Press.

Cardemil, E. D., & Battle, C. L. (2003). Guess who is coming to therapy? Getting comfortable with conversations about race and ethnicity in psychotherapy. *Professional Psychology: Research and Practice, 34,* 278–286.

Council of National Psychological Associations for the Advancement of Ethnic Minority Issues. (2000). *Guidelines for research in ethnic minority communities.* Washington, DC: American Psychological Association.

Council of National Psychological Associations for the Advancement of Ethnic Minority Issues. (2003). *Psychological treatment of ethnic minority populations.* Washington, DC: Association of Black Psychologists.

Daniel, J. H., Roysircar, G., Abeles, N., & Boyd, C. (2004). Individual and cultural diversity competency: Focus on the therapist. *Journal of Clinical Psychology, 60,* 755–770.

Draguns, G. (1997). Abnormal behavior patterns across cultures: Implications for counseling and psychotherapy. *International Journal of Intercultural Relations, 21,* 213–248.

Erickson, C. D., & Al-Timimi, N. R. (2001). Providing mental health services to Arab-Americans: Recommendations and considerations. *Cultural Diversity in Ethnic Minority Psychology, 7,* 308–327.

Fuertes, J. N., Mueller, L. N., Chauhan, R. V., Walker, J. A., & Ladany, N. (2002). An investigation of European American therapists' approach to counseling African-American clients. *The Counseling Psychologist, 30,* 763–788.

Gureje, O., Simon, G. E., Ustun, T. B., & Goldberg, D. B. (1997). Somatization in a cross-cultural perspective: A World Health Organization study in primary care. *American Journal of Psychiatry, 154,* 989–995.

Hays, P. A. (1996). Addressing the complexities of culture and gender in counseling. *General Counseling and Development, 74,* 332–338.

Hays, P. A. (2001). *Addressing cultural complexities in practice: A framework for clinicians and counselors.* Washington, DC: American Psychological Association.

Kawakami, N., Shimuzu, H., Haratani, T., Iwata, N., & Kitamura, T. (2004). Lifetime and six-month prevalence of DSM-III-R psychiatric disorders in an urban community in Japan. *Psychiatry Research, 121,* 293–301.

Kim, B. S. K., Yang, P. H., Atkinson, D. R., Wolfe, M., & Hong, S. (2001). Cultural value similarities and differences among Asian-American ethnic groups. *Cultural Diversity in Ethnic Minority Psychology, 7,* 343–361.

Kirmayer, L. J., & Young, A. (1998). Culture and somatization: Clinical, epidemiological, and ethnographic perspectives. *Psychosomatic Medicine, 60,* 420–430.

Kleinman, A. (1984a). Culture, affect, and somatization. Part I. *Transcultural Psychiatric Research Review, 21,* 159–188.

Kleinman, A. (1984b). Culture, affect, and somatization. Part II. *Transcultural Psychiatric Research Review, 21,* 237–262.

La Roche, M. J. (2002). Psychotherapeutic considerations in treating Latinos. *Harvard Review in Psychiatry, 10,* 115–122.

Pedersen, P. B. (1995). Culture-centered ethical guidelines for counselors. In J. G. Ponterotto & J. M. Casas (Eds.). *Handbook of multicultural counseling* (pp. 34–49). Thousand Oaks, CA: Sage Publications.

Robins, L. N., & Regier, D. A. (1991). *Psychiatric disorders in America. The epidemiologic catchment area study.* New York: Free Press.

Roysircar, G. (2004). Cultural self-awareness assessment: Practice examples from psychology training. *Professional Psychology: Research and Practice, 35,* 658–666.

Sue, S. (1998). In search of cultural competence in psychotherapy and counseling. *American Psychologist, 53,* 440–448.

Sue, D. W., Arredondo, P., & McDavis, R. J. (1992). Multicultural counseling competencies and standards: A call to the profession. *Journal of Multicultural Counseling & Development, 20,* 64–88.

Tsai, J. L., Yeng, Y., & Lee, P. A. (2000). The meaning of "being Chinese" and "being American": Variation among Chinese American young adults. *Journal of Cross Cultural Psychology, 31,* 302–322.

United States Census Bureau. (2001). *Profiles of general demographic characteristics 2000: 2000 census of population and housing: United States.* Washington, DC: Author. Retrieved from www.census.gov/ipc/www/ usinterimproj/>.

Wei, N., Russell, D. W., Mallinckrodt, B., & Zakalik, R. A. (2004). Cultural equivalence of adult attachment across four ethnic groups: Factor structure, structured means, and associations with negative mood. *Journal of Counseling Psychology, 51,* 408–417.

6

EFFECTIVE UNDERSTANDING AND DEALING WITH MANIPULATION

MICHAEL G. WETTER

Kaiser Permanente Medical Center

JACK WETTER

Diplomate and Fellow in Clinical Psychology
American Board of Professional Psychology

The term *manipulation* often carries with it a stigma of malice or deceit, most specifically when associated with the actions of the borderline patient. All clients, however, are capable of exhibiting manipulative behaviors, regardless of pathology. It is interesting to note that when the therapist offers a suggestion, interpretation, or "behavioral intervention," it is conceptualized far differently from a "manipulative" act. Yet, manipulation of behavior and cognitions are, to a very strong extent, exactly what we are hoping to achieve. Manipulation, as defined by The American Heritage Dictionary of the English Language (2000), Fourth Edition by Houghton Mifflin Company (p.540), is "to handle and move in an examination or for therapeutic purposes." Yet, it is also defined as "to influence or manage shrewdly or deviously."

When a patient engages in readily recognizable manipulative behavior repeatedly, it is not surprising to discover that therapists later dismiss threats made by the client simply because they believe them to be a manipulative technique. Common examples include

- Threats of suicide, if not given medication or prescribed inappropriate medication
- Threats of violence, including veiled threats such as "I don't think I can control myself much longer" (a common one from people awaiting trial for violent assault because they think a diagnosis of anger problems will mean a reduced sentence)
- Emotional blackmail, such as the suggestion that the professional is making things worse by not letting them have their own way and thus is a "bad" practitioner
- Showing up late to sessions or withholding payment for services because they are disappointed with their "progress"
- Waiting until the session is over before disclosing critical information (e.g., death of a loved one, former childhood abuse)

Some individuals achieve their objectives by instilling guilt or fear in people. Others manipulate in more aggressive ways, such as through intimidation or threats. Still others may use more passive forms of manipulation to get their needs met, such as through conning others, seeking pity, requesting rescue, or using flattery. Consider the following types of manipulative styles:

- **Overreacting:** These individuals respond to requests with plaintive protests such as, "There is *No way* I can do that!" When the requester persists, they are met with a display of ill temper. Often, these individuals are perceived by others as those who rant, rave, or threaten.
- **Self-declared victim:** These people get their objectives met by whining, crying, engaging in the "silent treatment," or pouting for hours. Somatic complaints are also a very common tactic of this type.
- **Hypersensitive:** When approached with a particular request or denied a particular request, these individuals take extreme offense to serve their agenda. Common reactions include tearfulness, immediate fleeing from a situation, or claiming sudden physical illness.
- **Passive aggressive:** These people are most likely to conceal antagonistic behavior. They will often appear helpless while infuriating others. Often, they lack the confidence to challenge others directly, and, instead, express anger indirectly. They are prone to show late for appointments, fail to pay bills, and so forth. They are likely to offer an apology, but typically it is superficial in nature.
- **The sycophant:** These individuals are likely to lavish praise and kudos to seek ulterior motives: undeserved praise is a form of manipulation.

When faced with manipulation, it is not uncommon to "disattend". Quite simply, this refers to ignoring the threat effectively and demonstrating the pointlessness of manipulation. Often clients learn this lesson very quickly, and then real work can begin on the actual problems. This does not mean that the manipulation is not a symptom of the disorder; often it is, but focusing too much upon threats of self-injury or whatever just clouds the issue.

Of course any one of these threats could also be a statement of fact from a genuinely distressed client. Often, mental health professionals are so used to manipulation that they can quickly tell the difference. For example the intoxicated young man who ends a relationship with his girlfriend, takes an overdose of aspirin, and then calls her to get the ambulance is more likely to want her to feel guilty than to end his life. Many therapists resent getting out of bed at three in the morning to interview such cases, and the resentment grows as the frequency of such acts increase.

To deal effectively with manipulative behavior, it is essential for us to understand better its purpose. Behavior does not occur in a random or unorganized fashion. People behave purposefully, and their behavior attains meaning as a function of the context—situation or circumstances—that exists in a particular environment (Maag, 1992). The meaning a behavior has for an individual is a function of the context in which that behavior is displayed: Lifeguards have more meaning by the side of a pool than on a ski slope; singing out loud has more meaning at a rock concert than it does in a library (Howell, Fox, & Morehead, 1993). In addition, very few behaviors could be universally considered inappropriate or appropriate apart from the context in which they occur. Running and yelling provide obvious examples. Within the context of a math lesson, these behaviors would be considered inappropriate, whereas they would be acceptable, or possibly valued, in the context of playing basketball. Perhaps a more striking, yet less apparent, example that nevertheless makes the same point involves cutting someone's throat with a knife—clearly a behavior most people would consider aberrant, especially within the context of attacking someone. However, it would be quite appropriate if someone was performing an emergency tracheotomy on a choking person. In essence, almost all behaviors are appropriate given some context or frame of reference.

The word *manipulation* often has a negative connotation. However, manipulation may not be as negative as it often appears. The very process of teaching is manipulative: Teachers manipulate materials, curricula, and instructional techniques. In fact, every interaction with others can be considered a manipulation because the goal is usually to elicit a response (Watzlawick, 1978). Can't we consider this true in psychotherapy as well? Manipulating context can have a profound impact upon reducing resistance (Maag, 1991). This assertion is based on the previous discussions of (1) how behaviors derive meaning from context and (2) how context serves as a cue that elicits certain behaviors. Therefore, it is axiomatic that when the context surrounding a behavior changes, the meaning, purpose, and desire to engage in the behavior also change.

Let us consider this perspective further. Manipulative behavior is a skill. Like any skill, it can be used effectively or it can be used detrimentally. When we examine manipulation as a skill while recognizing the importance of the context of such behavior, it then becomes less likely to view manipulation as "pathological." Take, for example, an adolescent male who grows up in an urban neighborhood plagued with gang warfare, chronic violence, and pervasive drug use. In his efforts to remain safe and out of harms way, one might describe his behavior as hypervigilant and possibly distrusting of strangers. Would we consider this behavior pathological, given this context? Unlikely. Now, place the same individual in a college environment or a small suburban community. With this change in context, the behavior is now likely seen as paranoid, distant, and isolative. What was once a survival skill is now viewed as a symptom of pathology. The same perspective can be applied to manipulative behavior. At some point in the patient's lifetime, perhaps the only way to get critical emotional or developmental needs met was through effective acts of manipulation. When considering such behavior as a survival skill, it becomes apparent how intricately woven and critical manipulative behavior is to the patient's emotional survival and existence. Therefore, an expectation of immediately "calling out" manipulative behavior and expecting to extinguish such behavior is likely to be unrealistic—even detrimental. Yet, how does one work with the patient in decreasing the likelihood of continued manipulative behavior?

Manipulation is achieved when one uses his or her power over a weaker party to influence behavior or ideation. In therapy, there should be no one of power over the other, yet we both attempt to manipulate the other. In fact, efforts to manipulate the patient into changing behavior are quite ineffective. Rather, the patient will resist the manipulation, just as we, the therapist, resist their manipulative behavior. A more effective strategy in motivating the patient for behavior change is to reframe their behavior as a skill. Acknowledging how such behavior has been instrumental to the patient's emotional and physical survival during times of distress validates the patient's efforts of living and surviving the best they can.

One of the most persuasive and effective manipulative behaviors are acts of self-harm or threats of self-harm. Suicidal ideation and behaviors can be explored and addressed within the context of this cooperative doctor–patient relationship, with the ultimate goal of reducing suicide risk. At the same time, the therapist should recognize that an individual who is determined to die may not be motivated to develop a cooperative doctor–patient relationship and indeed may view the therapist as an adversary. Appreciating the patient's relationship to and with significant others can help inform the clinician about the patient's potential to form a strong therapeutic relationship.

In caring for potentially suicidal patients, the therapist needs to manage effectively the often conflicting goals of encouraging the patient's independence yet simultaneously addressing safety. In addition, the therapist should be aware of his or her own countertransference to the suicidal patient that may influence the patient's care. Therapists should acknowledge the unique role that they may serve in a patient's life, very often representing the only relationship of stability or consistency. Behavior often referred to as *manipulative* (e.g., trying to extend length of sessions, frequent phone calls) could therefore be interpreted as attempts of seeking ongoing support and stable reassurance. At the same time, the clinician must be cautious of falling into the role of "knight in shining armor." Suicidal patients may wish to be taken care of unconditionally or, alternatively, to assign others the responsibility for keeping them alive. Therapists who find themselves in the role of savior with suicidal patients often act on the assumption (be it conscious or unconscious) that they can provide the love and concern that others have not and, therefore, can effectively change the patient's wish to die into a desire to live. In producing false or unrealistic hopes, however, or setting the pretense for a relationship that can never match idealistic expectations, the therapist may ultimately disappoint the patient by not fulfilling those expectations. Thus, it becomes imperative that we realize, when taking responsibility for a patient's care, it is not the same as taking responsibility for the patient's life. Making this distinction can help to minimize the feeling of being manipulated by the patient.

Whether conscious or unconscious, however, manipulative behavior is designed for the clear purpose of getting one's objective met, deceitfully or otherwise. Yet, if the patient is being encouraged to "give up" the only skill they consider to be effective in getting his or her needs met, the therapist must be prepared to offer another set of skills in exchange. There is also the challenge of convincing the patient that manipulative behavior is not as effective as he or she believes it to be. This is a delicate process, because most people consider that as long as they get their primary objective met, manipulative behavior or otherwise is effective.

Often, when patients exhibit manipulative behavior, they are in pursuit of a focused, tangible goal: a primary goal. The primary goal is perhaps best defined as the single objective most critical to the individual; all other factors or consequences associated with that interaction are ignored. In essence, the individual resembles the horse with blinders on: Their only focus is on the attainment of that one need or objective.

Consider, for example, the patient who frequently argues with her spouse. Although her spouse has made repeated attempts to visit his family living in another state, each time he brings up the subject, the patient notes how she does not want to go, and if he leaves her alone, she will likely do something to hurt herself. On face value, the patient believes she is successful in her goal of avoiding her in-laws, and is also successful in not being left alone for any given time. It becomes imperative, however, to highlight for the patient that although she appears victorious, her success is, in fact, a pyrrhic victory. One would need to question if maintaining a healthy, amicable, and loving relationship with her husband is also a goal of the patient. If so, how is denying him the chance to be with family going to effect that goal? How does she believe her husband feels or thinks about her as a result of her threats? Furthermore, how does her behavior make her feel? Does it bring up feelings of guilt? Does it bring about feelings of anxiety? Is not another goal of the patient's to maintain or improve self-respect? Acknowledging these other meta-goals is a pathway to a more skillful manner of interpersonal interaction.

Marsha Linehan's (1993) model of dialectical behavior therapy (DBT) offers a wonderful structure for more effective skills in communicating needs and getting objectives met in such a way as not to sacrifice healthy relationships or self-respect—both often casualties of manipulative behavior. Interpersonal response patterns taught in DBT skills training are very similar to those taught in many assertiveness and interpersonal problem-solving classes. They include effective strategies for asking for what one needs, saying no, and coping with interpersonal conflict.

Linehan (1993) refers to skills of "interpersonal effectiveness" such as focusing on situations where the objective is to change something (e.g., requesting someone to do something) or to resist changes someone else is trying to make (e.g., saying no). The skills taught are intended to maximize the chances that a person's goals in a specific situation will be met, while at the same time not damaging either the relationship or the person's self-respect. This is accomplished by helping the person understand that in each interpersonal interaction, there are, in actuality, three goals to keep in mind, not just one primary goal. They are as follows:

1. Getting primary objectives met in a situation
2. Getting or maintaining a healthy relationship
3. Maintaining or improving self-respect

Again, many patients who tend to exhibit manipulative behaviors are often successful in obtaining their primary objective. The primary objective, however, is moreover obtained at the sacrifice of the latter two goals. Individuals are often blind to this effect, and therefore are unlikely to attribute the loss of relationships or poor self-respect to manipulative behavior. It is more likely, in fact, that these losses will invariably lead to a cyclical increase in manipulative behavior. It therefore becomes critical to highlight how being more skillful in interpersonal situations can actually result in better outcomes to getting what people really want: their primary goal met, as well as the maintenance of healthy relationships and continued self-respect.

When all is said and done, the key to responding effectively to manipulative behavior in therapy is to understand effectively the function it serves. If the therapist subscribes to the belief that the patient is merely trying to "take advantage of a situation" or exploit a given circumstance, it is unlikely that an interpretation of the manipulative behavior will result in an effective outcome. Rather, it is more likely that the therapist's comments or reactions will lead to an increase in the patient's defensiveness. Manipulative behavior should be viewed primarily as skill that, although effective in obtaining some primary goals, is ineffective in sustaining others. The skilled therapist, therefore, should work with the patient in determining whether the benefits of such behavior are truly in the best interest of the patient for the long term; in other words, helping patients learn to see the forest through the trees.

REFERENCES

Howell, K. W., Fox, S. L., & Morehead, M. K. (1993). *Curriculum-based evaluation: Teaching and decision making* (2nd ed.). Pacific Grove, CA: Brooks/Cole.
Linehan, M. (1993). *Cognitive behavioral treatment of borderline personality disorder*. New York: Guilford Press.
Maag, J. W. (1991). Oppositional students or oppositional teachers? *Beyond Behavior, 2,* 7–11.
Maag, J. W. (1992). Integrating consultation into social skills training: Implications for practice. *Journal of Educational and Psychological Consultation, 3,* 233–258.

7

RECOGNIZING AND DEALING WITH TRANSFERENCE

GEORGE STRICKER

Argosy University
Washington, DC

Transference as a theoretical concept is inextricably linked to psychoanalytical theory. The theory takes myriad forms and the definition of transference differs, sometimes in significant ways, within the various versions of the theory. Regardless, transference is one of the twin pillars of the technical approach to psychoanalysis, along with resistance. Transference as a process is present, in greater or lesser intensity, in all approaches to psychotherapy, regardless of whether the approach has a theoretical concept that recognizes the existence of the process. In fact, although transference technically refers to a relationship between a patient and a therapist, something akin to transference occurs in many human relationships outside the therapeutic setting. Finally, transference, in this omnipresent sense, is the basis of a good deal of human dysfunction, and the ability to deal with it effectively underlies much that is reparative in psychotherapy. There are a great many ideas in this paragraph, and I will now unpack them for greater clarity.

DEFINITION

The notion of transference, of course, can be traced to the writings of Sigmund Freud, and it was first mentioned as early as 1895 (Breuer & Freud, 1895/1961), although it later was elaborated in more detail (e.g., Freud, 1912/1961). Among the many definitions that have been given, Greenson's (1967) is representative of the more classical view of transference:

Transference is *the experiencing of feeling, drives, attitudes, fantasies, and defenses*
toward a person in the present which do not befit that person but are a repetition of
reactions originating in regard to significant persons of early childhood, unconsciously
displaced onto figures in the present. (p. 171, italics in original)

The critical features of this definition are the view of transference as
repetitive, based on past experiences, and unsuitable to the current object
of the feelings. Thus, it is a displacement to the therapist of feelings that
originated with previous significant figures in the patient's life, most usually
parents.

The relationship between the patient and the therapist often is seen
as having three components: the transference, the real relationship, and
the working alliance (Weiner, 1998). The distinction among these components is important and is illustrative of the change that has occurred in the
concept of transference. Although Freud initially distinguished among
the positive, negative, and unobjectionable components of transference,
what he termed *unobjectionable* later was elaborated and became the core
of the working alliance (Greenson, 1967). The working alliance, which is
covered in greater detail elsewhere in this book, refers to the agreement
between the therapist and the patient to work in a particular fashion in
the service of the goals established for the treatment, and the patient's ability
to perform according to that contract. The agreement may be to report
everything that comes to mind, as in free association in psychoanalysis, or
the agreement that the patient will perform certain assignments, such as
may occur in cognitive–behavioral therapy. A perfect relationship would
consist only of this rational and goal-directed component, but such is never
the case.

The working alliance always is colored by the real relationship between
the doctor and the patient and the transference that the patient feels toward
the therapist (the issue of countertransference is a major topic that must be
considered elsewhere). The notion embraced by the classical theorists, as
exemplified by Greenson, is that transference originates in the patient,
provides clues to the patient's manner of construing the world, and can be
clouded by the imposition of the real relationship, which constitutes countertransference and is to be avoided. However, more recent relational theorists
view the real relationship as an inevitable portion of the therapeutic situation
and the transference as coconstructed by the patient and therapist in response to the cues provided by the therapist as well as the needs occasioned
by earlier experience. Thus, in contrast to Greenson's (1967) definition, there
is the relational model that states:

> The patient's experiences, associations, and memories can be integrated or organized
> in innumerable ways. The organizational scheme arrived at is a dual creation, shaped
> partly by the patient's material but also inevitably shaped by the analyst's patterns of
> thought, or theory. The "meaning" of clinical material does not exist until it is
> named — it is not uncovered but created. (Mitchell, 1993, p. 58)

In this view, transference is not a displacement onto the therapist, but a creation, with the therapist, of a manner of relating that also typifies other relationships that the patient has and has had. The transference can be better thought of as an enactment, a repetition with the therapist of a pattern of behavior.

The contrast that has been noted can be seen as two diametrically different views of psychotherapy. In one view, transference is an irrational displacement and in the other it is a constructed enactment. However, it may also be valuable to look at these as existing on a continuum, for even so classical an author as Greenson (1967) acknowledges:

> In adults, all relationships to people consist of a varying mixture of transference and reality. There is no transference reaction, no matter how fantastic, without a germ of truth, and there is no realistic relationship without some trace of a transference fantasy. All patients in psychoanalytic treatment have realistic and objective perceptions and reactions to their analyst alongside of their transference reactions and their working alliance. (p. 219).

Thus, in considering transference, I will not take a position on the psychoanalytical controversy (indeed, many therapists are not practicing any variant of psychodynamic treatment, but these concerns still exist), but instead will keep in mind that any response of the patient to the therapist is a combination, in varying proportions, of internally generated and externally stimulated responses.

The concept of transference is closely related to the concept of parataxic distortion first mentioned by Sullivan (1953), a forerunner of the current relational theorists. For Sullivan, a parataxic distortion is one way a person has of dealing with anxiety. It generalizes early means of dealing with and avoiding anxiety to current relationships where it may not be appropriate (hence, distortion). One such current relationship is the therapeutic relationship, where the presence of a parataxic distortion provides a clue to the patient's means of coping with anxiety. However, these distortions occur in all relationships and are not restricted to the therapeutic. Freud also acknowledged the presence of transferencelike phenomena outside of therapy, but preferred to reserve the term for the patient–therapist relationship.

Several other definitions are in order, because they refer to terms frequently used in relationship to transference. The distinction between positive and negative transference initially referred to attitudes in the transference, so that positive transference referred to good feelings toward the therapist and negative transference to bad feelings. However, it is now more typical to view positive and negative transference as indistinguishable (Menninger & Holzman, 1973). In fact, it has been asserted that all transference is negative in that it represents an unrealistic view of the therapist and disregards his person in favor of a view rooted in earlier experience (Singer, 1970). The concept of a transference neurosis (or transference psychosis) represent extremes in intensity of involvement of the patient with the therapist, and are unlikely to occur outside the psychoanalytic situation and so are less relevant to this presentation. Finally, transference cure refers to changes in the patient that are made to please the therapist. Initially, these were disparaged as superficial and transient, but more recent evidence suggests that they may be more stable and should not be as easily ignored (Gabbard, 2000).

DETECTION AND OTHER
ASSESSMENT ISSUES

The detection and assessment of transference is not easy, because it can never be observed directly, but rather is always a matter of inference from a derivative. Nonetheless, there are some clear indicators of the presence of transference, and it is important to attend to these. The key in recognizing transference is to understand that transference always is inappropriate. Even when transference is considered mutually constructed, the contribution of the patient will seem disproportionate in the case of a transferential response.

Greenson (1967) highlights several characteristics of transference that can be used for its detection. In every case, the inappropriateness of the response, along many dimensions, is the critical factor. One such dimension is intensity. An exaggerated response, or the absence of a response, can be considered as an indicator of transference. Transference responses often are ambivalent and can be changeable rapidly. They also may be split, so that one response is expressed to the therapist and the opposite to another person outside the treatment. Thus, a patient may be expressing very positive feelings toward the therapist while suddenly becoming angry at a significant other. Transference responses also can be either capricious or tenacious, both of which are exaggerated and inappropriate responses. This often will vary with diagnosis, so that patients with more hysterical defenses will develop rapid but superficial responses to the therapist, whereas more obsessional patients will develop responses more slowly but quite tenaciously. This leads to a time dimension in that more capricious responses develop early and more tenacious ones develop later in treatment.

Weiner (1998) also provides helpful indices of transference, listing his from the most indirect to the most direct expressions. Beginning with the indirect, there may be changes in the appearance or behavior of the patient. These vary as to whether the transference is marked by positive or negative feelings. With more positive transference, for example, the patient may arrive early for appointments, whereas negative transference may be accompanied by late arrival. The patient may make remarks about the therapist's office or profession, an indirect way of making comments about the therapist, and the nature of these remarks will be an indicator of the characteristic of the transference. As transference responses become more direct, the comments may be more clearly about the therapist, with the most direct expressions being of feelings toward the therapist. It is important to remember that these must be inappropriate to be considered transference. A patient who criticizes a therapist for coming late is not expressing transference if the therapist indeed was late, although an exaggerated set of comments may indicate a mixture of transference with the realistic response.

A dream, always helpful in expressive therapy, is a rich source of information about the transference. The therapist may appear in the dream, and the first time this happens often is considered a particularly informative capsule of the nature of the feelings about the therapist. Therapist surrogates, such as confidantes, may also appear in dreams and be thinly disguised representatives of the therapist and the nature of the transference.

The therapist should be alert to the possibility of an acting out of the transference. This occurs when attitudes toward the therapist are displaced onto figures in the life of the patient. For example, the development of an affair, or a love relationship, with a person who is a stand-in for the therapist may indicate an unexpressed aspect of the transference and should be explored with the patient.

Finally, it is important during the course of diagnosing the presence of transference for the therapist to engage in careful self-monitoring. For more traditional therapists, there still may be a contribution that they are making to the response they are drawing, and transference can only be present when it is developed by the patient inappropriately, rather than in a reasonable way to the cues being given by the therapist. For more relational therapists, the contribution of the therapist is critical and must be understood to understand the nature of the contribution by the patient. Failure to self-monitor can result in participation in an enactment, a destructive course of conduct that will perpetuate, rather than resolve, dysfunctional behavior.

THEORY AND CONCEPTUALIZATION

Much of the theory underlying the concept of transference has been reviewed when we considered the definitions that have been proffered. The contrast between the extremes of a continuum of definitions is also the contrast between a one- and a two-person psychology. The earlier, more classic definitions are based on a one-person conception that views transference as a distortion of reality originating in the patient and generalized to the therapist. The more contemporary two-person conception views transference as coconstructed between the patient and the therapist, and expressed in enactments that are not distortions of reality but reflections of current interactions.

The two approaches, different as they may be, do share some common ground. In both, the transference is a repetition of past experiences and relationships, whether that repetition is displaced or enacted in the current relationship. In both, this process is unconscious, so that the making of the unconscious conscious is an important part of the treatment. In both, the same process occurs outside as well as inside the treatment room (the concept of parataxic distortion is particularly valuable in this regard), so that the identification of the pattern allows the patient to generalize the learning to external settings and modify behavior that has proved dysfunctional.

To the extent that the transference is successfully interpreted, that patient should move toward therapeutic success. The success of the interpretation rests, in one view, on the capturing of past experiences, and on interpretation of the current relationship in the other. For both, the ability to interpet the transference successfully rests on a firm foundation of positive transference. However, to the extent that the positive transference alone impels the patient to recover, a transference cure is made likely, an outcome seen both traditionally and more currently as a danger, but one that may not be a source of difficulty after all (Gabbard, 2000).

This contrast of the two approaches again makes it appear as though they are opposed views of transference rather than views that exist on a continuum. This is wisely contradicted by Wolitzky (2003), who notes that the therapeutic relationship

> ... is simultaneously a new experience as well as a reenactment of earlier experiences. The "modernist" view of transference (Cooper, 1987) stresses the aspect of new experience; the "historical" view emphasizes the aspect of reliving the past. In the historical view, the experiencing of the "here-and-now" transference is important not only in its own right but as a path toward the revival and recovery of childhood memories and the interpretive reconstruction of the past. In the modernist view, successfully analyzing the "here-and-now" transference is sufficient. Keep in mind that these are matters of emphasis, not either–or distinctions. (p. 40)

In both approaches, the patient is seen as enacting his style of functioning, either as an expression of his character viewed objectively by a distant therapist or in combination with the therapist engaging in a mutually constructed enactment. In either case, if the patient is allowed to continue to enact previous ways of being in an unconscious and almost reflexive fashion, there is no opportunity for insight, self-awareness, or change. Interestingly, for traditional therapists, these needs of the patient must be understood and renounced, but some contemporary theorists, such as Kohut, suggest that the needs must be met in order for the patient to be able to move on in development (Gabbard, 2000). Finally, it should be noted that the unaddressed presence of transference can serve as a resistance and interfere with the patient's ability to adhere to the therapeutic contract and to make changes.

IMPACT ON CASE FORMULATION

The initial and significant issue in case formulation is the recognition that transference may well develop before the first appointment. There is a marked difference between a patient who was referred to you with a glowing recommendation from a trusted, perhaps transferential, person and one who got your name from the Yellow Pages. Patients also bring transference predispositions, probably best thought of as parataxic distortions, to the first session. The nature of this initial transference may affect the extent to which the patient is open and cooperative, and should be addressed directly at an early time if it is not to serve as a resistance (Gabbard, 2000).

The manner in which the therapy is conducted will affect the development of the transference. Other things being equal, the more frequent the sessions, the more intense the transference. The more anonymous the therapist, the more intense the transference. In planning the treatment, if transference is to be a central part of the efforts, multiple sessions per week should be considered, and the therapist should plan on being less active. For this reason, some therapies do not place transference as a central concern because it does not occur in a dramatic fashion. These include such approaches as cognitive–behavioral therapy, in which sessions typically are weekly and the therapist plays a directive role, factors that would reduce the likelihood of the intense development of transference.

Diagnostic concerns also affect the nature and quality of the transference. As has been noted, patients with more hysterical defenses are likely to develop rapid and superficial transference whereas those with more obsessive defenses will develop slower and more rigid transference reactions. In planning treatment with these patients, it would be necessary to accentuate the conditions that encourage transference with more obsessive patients, whereas more hysterical patients can be seen less frequently without hampering the development of the transference. It also is possible that a diagnostic error may be made and the treatment plan will have to be changed as the more correct diagnosis becomes apparent. This is most likely seen with a borderline patient who may present in a more intact manner, and as the borderline dynamics become clear, it will be necessary to reduce the frequency and perhaps become more supportive in the treatment situation (Weiner, 1998).

Another diagnostic dimension that affects transference, although one not within the standard nomenclature, is that between the introjective and anaclitic patient (Blatt, 1992). Introjective patients are most concerned with their self-concept and are good candidates for insight-oriented approaches. Anaclitic patients are more concerned with relatedness and are more likely to benefit from supportive approaches that place less stress on the transference (Gabbard, 2000). A variation on this is that patients whose difficulty is more primitive are more helped by relationship factors, and those who are more concerned with Oedipal issues are more able to deal with insight and transference considerations (Wolitzky, 2003).

There also are cultural considerations that must be taken into account. There are some patients whose backgrounds are more responsive to direction and authority, and are not likely to thrive in an environment with a silent and anonymous therapist. They require more activity, and therefore we can expect less intense transference to develop. In taking culture into consideration, we also should be careful not to stereotype the patient and direct interventions toward them based on cultural preconceptions. Rather, culture should be evaluated and considered appropriately in treatment planning.

The critical distinction that has been raised is whether the treatment should be based on insight, which would argue for a less active therapist and a more intense transference, or on the relationship, which would lead to more supportive interventions and less of a focus on transference. It should be noted that more relational approaches would question this dichotomy and approach the treatment with more activity, but not with less of a focus on transference. However, even more traditional therapists also question the stark contrast that has been presented. Wolitzky (2003) describes this well when he states:

> Broadly speaking, the curative factors created by the foregoing conditions have been divided into two main categories — insight and the relationship. This is a potentially misleading distinction because insight based on interpretation can only take place in the context of a relationship. Thus, an interpretation leading to an emotionally meaningful insight can be, and often is, simultaneously experienced as a profound feeling of being understood (perhaps the strongest expression of a solid holding environment). Nonetheless, the distinction between insight and relationship factors is retained in order to assign relative influence to the element of enhanced self-understanding versus the therapeutic benefits of the relationship per se. Among the benefits of the latter one can include the support inherent in the therapeutic relationship, the experience of a new, benign object relationship with a significant person (i.e., one who does not recreate the traumatic experiences that the patient suffered in relation to the parents), and identification with the analyst and the analytic attitude, including a softening of superego self-punitiveness and feeling understood and supported, even by interpretations that arouse some degree of anxiety. (p. 51)
> The distinction between relationship and insight is important to maintain as long as one also considers that these are matters of relative weight rather than mutually exclusive approaches.

Finally, there is the need to consider termination. Again, we have contrasts between the two primary approaches to theory. "From the intersubjective perspective, both patient and therapist experience termination as a suspension of face-to-face meeting. It is acknowledged that the relationship continues even though regular meetings do not. The model is one of separation, not death" (Buirski & Haglund, 2001, p. 98). In both these models, transference is prominent, but in one, the transference must be resolved before successful termination can occur, whereas in the other, it is assumed that the co-constructed transference will continue with no harm to the patient. In both, however, it is likely that transference will diminish in intensity as the end of treatment draws near.

Gabbard (2000) mentions two other mechanisms related to a transference cure that relate to termination and the nature of change. The first, transfer of the transference, occurs where the supportive elements of the relationship are transferred to another significant person in the patient's life, often a spouse, allowing the gains to be maintained even in the absence of insight. The other, the antitransference cure, is one achieved through defiance of the therapist. This resembles a less manipulative use of paradox, which characterizes strategic family therapy (Haley, 1973), and a less consciously devised response to a reactant patient (Beutler & Harwood, 2000).

CLINICAL STRATEGIES

Many of the strategies for dealing with transference have been prefigured in the discussion of the various meanings given to the concept. First, however, must be the recognition that transference is ubiquitous in all human relationships, perhaps more widely conceived as parataxic distortion, and it is ignored at the peril of the therapist (and, unfortunately, of the patient). The failure to recognize how relationships are replicated in the consulting room opens the door to the continuation of dysfunctional habits and behaviors, regardless of whether the concept is recognized by the theory of the practitioner. One of the saddest cases that I know was a case of sexual misconduct in which the practitioner, a cognitive–behavioral therapist, was charged with mishandling the transference. This is a common legal strategy to make the case coverable by insurance. The practitioner denied that it was possible because cognitive–behavioral therapy does not include the concept of transference. Perhaps if he had been more attuned to transference, the misconduct could have been avoided. In any case, the first strategy, then, is to understand that transference occurs and to be prepared to deal with it, either directly or by finessing it while remaining cognizant of its impact. In any case, as long as the transference remains ego syntonic for the patient, there will be little motivation to deal with it, and so the first task might be to help the patient to recognize the impact of the transference on the treatment, and to be motivated to deal with it.

Not only does transference exist, but it begins before the treatment does, and the wise practitioner will be alert to the attitudes that the patient brings into the treatment, for these may lead to cooperation, submission, or defiance, depending on the patient's previous experience with authority figures. When the attitude facilitates the treatment, it is possible to postpone attending to it, or even neglect dealing with it directly, but when it acts as an impediment to treatment, it should be discussed immediately. In treatments that do not focus on transference, this same principle should be followed, with transference ignored until it begins to interfere with the treatment.

Transference has a different role depending on whether the treatment is primarily expressive or supportive. If it is an expressive treatment, transference will be interpreted and used as a vehicle for behavior change. If the treatment is primarily supportive, transference will be allowed to remain unexplored unless it is negative and an impediment, and may provide the basis for a transference cure.

The strategy for choosing to consider and interpret transference is described well in the following statement:

> The actual extent to which transference interventions are used during any session or phase of treatment is determined by three factors; (1) the therapists identification of material that can be understood as plausibly related to transference issues (Hoffman, 1983); (2) the patients current receptiveness to examining his or her experiences in the patient–therapist relationship; and (3) the therapists attentiveness to overt or disguised patient references to their relationship, as well as his or her attentiveness to countertransference reactions. (Binder, Strupp, & Henry, 1995, p. 59)

The three factors identified — the internal state of the therapist, that of the patient, and the content of the session — are all crucial to any clinical strategy.

The foundation of any treatment is a good working relationship between the patient and the therapist. This is separate from the transference, and may be considered the unobjectionable part of the relationship. Beginning with this, if the therapist chooses to foster transference, this can be done by increasing the frequency of meeting and reducing the directiveness of the interventions. In addition, it also is helpful for the therapist to act in a way that fosters the union with the patient. This can be done by using the patient's words, reflecting the patient's posture, and including the patient in communications by phrases such as "As we know..." or "As you and I have seen...". This is not intended as an artificial mocking of the patient's style, which it can be seen as if the therapist does not do it artfully, but rather as a means of communicating empathy and a sense of being in it together. Kohut (1977), for one, believes that this communication of empathy is the prime mutative factor in treatment, independent of any insight that may occur.

It also should be noted that the strategy for dealing with transference is directly related to the goals of treatment. If the treatment is intended to reduce the intensity of a particular symptom, it is unlikely that transference will play a large role in the treatment unless it begins to interfere with the progress toward that goal. When the goal is self-understanding or the modification of characterological patterns, transference is more likely to be important. However, even in these cases, the only point to interpreting transference is to further these goals, and not simply because transference is there and can be identified.

The stance of the therapist should be one of neutrality, but it is important to realize that neutrality does not mean aloofness. Rather, the therapist must be nonjudgmental, nonintrusive, but at the same time humane in his relationship with the patient. This requires a delicate balancing of empathy and therapeutic distance. Although the therapist is exhorted to be nonjudgmental, it is inevitable that judgments will occur, because they determine what is chosen for response and what is ignored. Similarly, it is inevitable that influence will occur, and it is the hope for salutary influence that brings the patient to psychotherapy. A more classical approach to treatment will argue for not gratifying the patient through the transference. However, more contemporary approaches see that the patient is seeking gratification as a necessary step in growth, and will not be as forbidding of such a stance, as long as it is directed to therapeutic goals. However, there is danger to providing gratification, such as in erotic transferences, and these must be monitored carefully. Perhaps the best advice that can be given to the therapist is to behave in a natural and genuine way rather than in an artificial, stilted, and pseudoprofessional manner.

The issue of therapeutic action requires a word about self-disclosure. The issue is not whether to disclose, because disclosure occurs inevitably simply by such matters as the dress and speech mannerisms of the therapist and the decor of the office. Rather, it is what to disclose, when to disclose it, and toward what purpose. The best rule of thumb for self-disclosure is that it should always be in the service of a therapeutic goal and never simply for the gratification of the therapist. Disclosure about events in the session are much more desirable than disclosure of life events, although the latter may be useful only if they can be instructive to the patient and are consistent with the general stance of the therapist. The patient may ask questions of the therapist, and these should be examined for the possible meaning that they have. However, there are some questions that the patient has a right to ask, particularly early in the treatment, and these should be answered in a matter-of-fact way, along with the possibility of an inquiry as to why they are being asked. If the therapist should make an error, such as coming late to a session, it is wise to acknowledge having done so, but not to spend much time discussing the countertransferential motivation for having made the error.

It is typical to ask the patient to reflect on his feelings, particularly toward the therapist, when such is part of the ongoing fabric of the treatment. The more affect that is being expressed, the more necessary such inquiry is. Sometimes if the therapist names the patient's affect, this is helpful in focusing on the issues, conveys an empathic connection, and helps the patient to deal with difficult matters. Keep in mind that there are times that extreme expressions of affect toward others are really disguised ways of speaking about the therapist, and this is ripe for transferential inquiry. There also is a need to remember that asking for elaborations of positive affect has the possibility of being a seductive and self-serving exercise, and should be limited to times when it is necessary to do so to pursue the goals of the treatment. The pursuit of negative affect almost always is indicated, because negative transference can be an impediment to treatment, but this may be modulated in the case of seriously disturbed patients.

It is critical that the therapist, while asking the patient to engage in self-reflection, should be doing the same thing himself. This is the only protection against being caught up in destructive enactments. The patient will bring his natural way of acting into the treatment room, and this includes treating the therapist as he treats others, providing important clues to the patient's functioning. The difference in psychotherapy is that the therapist will not react in the same way as everyone else (unless a destructive enactment is taking place), but instead will provide a corrective emotional experience (Alexander & French, 1946) that may be central to the mutative process of psychotherapy. Viewing the alliance as central, which it is in any psychodynamic approach, whether as a foundation for insight, the basis of transference, or the vehicle for change, makes it necessary to detect and heal any ruptures in the alliance. This is best done by attending to negative transference, a frequent source of ruptures. However, it also should be remembered that such ruptures are inevitable, and that, when handled properly, often are necessary for growth, because the patient must learn to tolerate disappointments and failures of gratification.

It is usually useful to attend to the interpretive triangle, because patterns that occur in the transference also occur in contemporary and past experience. To the extent that the therapist can link transference observations and interpretations to these other events, they become more meaningful and are likely to be more powerful. As the transference comes closer to consciousness, interpretations regarding the transference are more "experience near" and are likely to be more meaningful and more linked to change. This is particularly so if they are connected to events outside the consulting room. This leads to the question of timing of interpretations. It usually is the case that interpretations delivered too early are likely to be seen as meaningless or to be absorbed in an intellectual fashion, whereas interpretations that are too late may be overwhelming because the affect has built to an unmanageable proportion. Knowing when it is the right time is a matter of clinical skill, but it often is linked to how experience near the recognition is for the patient.

Perhaps the most important recognition is that the dysfunctional behaviors, patterns, and affect that the patient brings to treatment really do serve a purpose. When the patient was treated badly, he developed a self-protective means of dealing with this danger. Although the defense may have become dysfunctional in a larger sense, it still is useful, and it will not be discarded until the patient is able to deal with the danger in a more adaptive manner. It is here that the corrective emotional experience may provide a platform for attempting new patterns that can be more functional, and it is in the empathy that produces the recognition of the patient's need for the pattern that treatment can occur.

Finally, there are special considerations as termination approaches. It is at this point that negative transference often can emerge, or will be accentuated, because the patient may either feel more free or, more likely, will be resentful of the loss of a valuable relationship. If the treatment was expressive, it is important to explore this negative transference with the recognition that its continued expression will undermine some of the gains of the treatment. If the treatment was supportive (or not psychodynamic), the therapist might emphasize the gains that have been made, so that the patient can leave with a better sense of accomplishment and a willingness to return to treatment should it become necessary. Of course, these suggestions must be tempered by the theoretical considerations already mentioned, for more relational approaches do not see the resolution of transference as integral to the termination of treatment.

Weiner (1998) offers an excellent summary of the overall strategy suggested in this section:

> [I]ndirect expressions of mild positive transference attitudes should receive the least interpretive attention and direct expressions of intense negative transference the most. The appropriateness and potential utility of interpreting transference increases as positive transference elements shade into negative ones, as mild transference reactions become moderately intense, and as indirect expressions of transference grow increasingly direct. (p. 226)

KEY MISTAKES AND MISCOMPREHENSIONS

In many ways, the key mistakes that can be made are the inverse of the strategies that have been suggested. For example, either ignoring the transference or using it for the therapist's gratification is a critical mistake. Rather than simply repeat the previous suggestions in a negative form, I will try to identify some other areas where mistakes can occur.

For Greenson (1967), "the most frequent cause of a patient's prematurely breaking off his psychoanalytic therapy is the improper handling of the transference situation" (pp. 270–271). At a later point he suggests, and Wolitzky (2003) agrees, that the major problem usually can be traced to countertransference. One way this can have a pronounced effect is in the failure to recognize an enactment, so that the therapist will be drawn into the dysfunctional patterns of the patient and be unable to extricate himself or to offer the patient an alternative view of the possibilities inherent in the situation.

There are also several technical errors that can be made in any therapy, but that are exacerbated by their implications for transference. These often have their roots in countertransferential issues that the therapist has not dealt with adequately. For example, excess gratification of dependency will slow the process of therapy and may lead to an interminable treatment situation, largely because of the transferential nature of the relationship. Lack of attention to boundaries, such as with time or fees, carries with it the promise of a special relationship that grows from the transference and can be very destructive. Needless to add, extratherapeutic contact has this same problem, and is even more likely to lead to difficulties. These errors fall in the general class of seductive therapist behavior, and this is most harmful when it encourages an erotic transference.

The lack of skillfulness of the therapist also is a source of difficulty. This includes problems in the timing and frequency of interventions. The use of jargon and intellectualization as a means of delivering interpretations also is a potential source of trouble. There also is the temptation to impose values and worldviews on the patient, something easier to do when there is a transferential connection that can be exploited. This does not allow the patient to develop, and threatens an increase in dependency. Finally, unfamiliarity with the cultural background of the patient can lead to many therapeutic gaffes and a decided failure in an empathic connection.

Weiner (1998) cites several research studies that are relevant to the issue of mistakes. He states that the most common reason for a patient to drop out of therapy is a therapist who is perceived as "distant and uninvolved" (p. 212). He also notes that early dropouts felt less well liked and respected by their therapists. Both these findings underline the importance of establishing a respectful and mutual working alliance as a foundation for treatment, and anything that diminishes such a relationship is likely to interfere with the course of the treatment.

CASE STUDY[1]

Saul is a 50-year-old man who was married for 20 years to his wife Sharon. They have two sons, age 16 and 11. He is a practicing attorney who worked in a family firm operated by his father Eli along with his older sister. The year prior to treatment his father retired, the firm closed, and Saul felt that he had been given fewer and less desirable clients. He and Eli (as he refers to his father) were battling over payments due to his father, which Saul did not want to provide because of the unfair division of accounts. Saul was depressed, short-tempered, and unmotivated, with some teariness, trouble sleeping, and weight gain. He did not want to consider medication. He described himself as an honest, straightforward man with little pretense, soft and easily taken advantage of, and now being taken advantage of by his father and sister. Initially he spoke about how much confidence he had, but this appeared to be bravado as he had trouble speaking concretely about the situation and clearly felt he never had been appreciated, was mistreated and exploited in business by Eli from the beginning, and never was able to act independently. He now wanted to establish himself but didn't have the energy to do it effectively. He came to treatment at the urging of Sharon. I saw him once weekly for a year in assimilative integrative psychodynamic psychotherapy (Gold & Stricker, 2001; Stricker & Gold, 2002).

The tone for the treatment was set at the first session. Saul did not come of his own volition and, because of his conflicted relationship with his father, was distrustful and wary. Thus, we began with a clear instance of mild negative transference. I responded by listening carefully, speaking gently, only asking

---

[1] This case was presented previously (Stricker, in press-a) in a similar form, but with more detail and less commentary about the impact of transference on the therapeutic process.

necessary questions, and never making any judgments about what he was telling me. I did not address the transference directly, but noted it and responded in a way to minimize it. Had this not been successful, I would have discussed it with him. Gradually, Saul seemed to relax slightly, agreed to treatment with the goal of helping him with his depression, and made clear that he did not want to talk about the past. He had bad feelings about the past because he had been in treatment as an adolescent when his parents thought that there was something wrong with him, and now Sharon recreated the situation by sending him to treatment. I explained the structure of treatment to him, including his responsibility for a $15 copay according to the terms of his insurance contract. He agreed and left two bills on my desk. He never has handed me money directly, but always leaves it for me so as not to contaminate our relationship by needing to pay for it. As he was leaving, I looked at the money and called after him. He asked what I wanted, I told him that one of the bills was not a ten, he angrily wondered what it was, and I told him it was a hundred dollar bill. He sheepishly exchanged it, but his contentious attitude was dropped and he was very cooperative and involved in treatment after that. I did not inquire about the motivation behind the overpayment, as there was not a need to challenge him or to invite defensiveness, and at that time he had not yet developed curiosity about his actions. However, it was interesting that he acted in a way that asked to be taken advantage of, and by not doing so, I took on a unique role in his life.

In the next session, Saul responded to my inquiry by saying that he felt very upset and angry after the first session, then felt a fog rolling over him, was too depressed to work the next day, but the fog then lifted and he felt better until it was time for another session, when he felt the fog returning. I suggested that the problem might not be depression as much as it was his difficulty with anger, his defense being the fog, and the depression being subsequent to it. This made sense to him, and we spoke about various ways he has of dealing with anger. Foremost among these are walks and solitude, and he had not been doing that. Saul seemed much lighter, left feeling somewhat better, and vowed to do more to take control of his life.

Almost immediately, Saul spontaneously began to talk about some of his early experiences, despite his initial expression of a wish not to do so. This seemed responsive to the positive transference that was established by my early interpretation of his depression. The most interesting experience he related was a symbolic incident in which he left home as a teenager, functioned well in California, but then returned home to go to college at Eli's request. I asked whether there were any colleges in California, and he recognized how he had abandoned his independence to return to the safety and security of his father's shelter. This incident captured the conflict between his wish for independence and apparent ability to function well on his own, and his insecurity about that ability and reliance on his father for assurance about his competence. Unfortunately, his father has not provided that reassurance, always having favored his sister and expressed his disappointment with Saul. Saul internalized this view of himself and it is behind the anger he feels over the unfair division of the firm, accompanied by his inability to deal comfortably with the prospect of being on his own.

During the early portion of treatment Saul talked about many of his early experiences, usually with his father, and his subsequent sense of inadequacy and disrespect. These were related to his current experiences, with his father, with others in his life, and with me. The key to the therapy was his experiencing of these past events and current connections in the context of his relationship with me, thus making the interpretive triangle meaningful to him. In me, he found an older man whom he experienced as understanding, accepting, and prizing of him. This allowed him the freedom to explore his feelings and to experiment with new behaviors. It represents a good illustration of the corrective emotional experience, resting on a firm positive transference, and Saul enjoyed and profited from it.

When Saul achieved some clarity about dynamic issues, I began to introduce some behavioral interventions designed to make his dynamic insight more conscious and able to be translated into action. The use of homework (Stricker, in press-b) is a valuable addition to psychodynamic psychotherapy in that it gives the patient clear responsibility for the outcome, yet it requires the foundation of a sound positive transference to be effective. I asked Saul not to take things personally, and he felt that he gained immensely by keeping this in mind. He often would pause before responding to realize that some slight he had received was not about him, and he could go forward without recalling the deep sense of inadequacy that he carried with him. I also asked him not to expect people to be what they were not. In his dealings with Eli (and with Sharon), he constantly found himself disappointed that they were not more responsive to his feelings and needs, but persisted in expecting more from them, so that he then felt hurt and rejected when they behaved as they always had. Much of treatment held his feelings and reactions up to this awareness of the need not to take things personally and not to expect people to change.

The depression that brought Saul to treatment lifted very rapidly, as soon as Saul began to take more responsibility for himself and to realize that he could do so. He also began to deal more constructively with his father, standing up for himself and not caving in to the pressure to make a deal that would not be in his best interests. Even when an initial deal fell through, because Eli backed out, Saul did not become depressed, but instead recognized that his father had been at fault rather than he, and he was able to move forward in a productive manner.

Although Saul was functioning in better ways, he initially questioned whether we were getting anywhere, an example of continuing negative transference alongside the very positive feelings that were dominant. He continued to work hard and to try to make connections between his early experiences, his current predicament, and the therapeutic relationship. He saw these connections as being expressed in his social relations as well as the familial ones, and began to be a little more assertive, and with that, more comfortable in situations he previously had avoided. Gradually he came to accept the need for patience while working toward change, and was determined to be true to himself, act with integrity, and be pleased whatever the outcome.

Saul began one session by saying that no catastrophes happened during the week, and that he was trying to preplan what he does so that he doesn't get caught in uncomfortable situations. He then gave an example, I began to comment positively, and he explained what he had meant. I remarked on how he had become defensive before I finished and he noted that I had just gotten a glimpse of the real Saul. We then spoke about his discomfort with the praise he craved but never received, and that his discomfort was because it always had been the other way. He saw the self-fulfilling prophesy aspect of his view of praise and the world, and how he expected to be an old man by himself, just like his grandfather, and was acting in a way to ensure that it would happen. By my demonstrating this pattern in the context of the transference, and by providing a corrective emotional experience, Saul was able to make significant progress in this area.

I asked Saul for permission to write up this case, partly for ethical reasons and partly to show him the respect he deserved. His immediate response was that it would be alright with him, but he didn't want to read it because he didn't need to be reminded of all his problems. I asked him whether he realized that I also would be including something about how much I liked and respected him, and how decent and competent he is. He said he realized that, but always focused on the negative. However, in the next session he said that he would like to read the report, and to show it to Sharon so that she would realize some of his good qualities. Again, I had acted in a different way than he had come to expect from others, and he gradually came to appreciate and grow from this. However, the need to do this repeatedly is an example of working through, and how a single interpretation never is sufficient.

SUMMARY

Parataxic distortion is an omnipresent event in human interaction. When it occurs in the therapy room, it is referred to as transference and is central to the conduct of effective therapy. In a mild and positive form, transference is the basis for the therapeutic alliance and lays the groundwork for a corrective emotional experience. As transference becomes more intense or more negative, it can serve as an impediment to psychotherapy and must be dealt with in order for treatment to proceed. The interpretation of transference, therefore, is most necessary with intense negative affect and can be bypassed with mild positive affect. The more experience near the transference, the more likely it is that an interpretation will be successful. Transference can be accentuated by frequent sessions and by minimal therapist input, and will be less likely to occur in more directive treatments with an active therapist. If transference is to be addressed, it is important to keep the interpretive triangle in mind, relating in-session transference to current life events and past occurrences.

REFERENCES

Alexander, F., & French, T. (1946). *Psychoanalytic therapy*. New York: Ronald Press.

Beutler, L. E., & Harwood, T. M. (2000). *Prescriptive psychotherapy: A practical guide to systematic treatment selection*. New York: Oxford University Press.

Binder, J. L., Strupp, H. H., & Henry, W. P. (1995). Psychodynamic therapies in practice: Time-limited dynamic psychotherapy. In B. Bongar & L. E. Beutler (Eds.). *Comprehensive textbook of psychotherapy: Theory and practice* (pp. 48–63). New York: Oxford University Press.

Blatt, S. J. (1992). The differential effect of psychotherapy and psychoanalysis with anaclitic and introjective patients: The Menninger Psychotherapy Research Project revisited. *Journal of the American Psychoanalytic Association, 40,* 691–724.

Breuer, J., & Freud, S. (1961). Studies on hysteria. In J. Strachey (Ed.). *The standard edition of the complete psychological works of Sigmund Freud* (vol. 2). London: Hogarth Press. [Originally published 1895.]

Buirski, P., & Haglund, P. (2001). *Making sense together: The intersubjective approach to psychotherapy*. Northvale, NJ: Jason Aronson.

Cooper, A. M. (1987). Changes in psychoanalytic ideas: Transference interpretation. *Journal of the American Psychoanalytic Association, 35,* 77–98.

Freud, S. (1961). The dynamics of transference. In J. Strachey (Ed.). *The standard edition of the complete psychological works of Sigmund Freud* (vol. 12, pp. 99–108). London: Hogarth Press. [Originally published 1912.]

Gabbard, G. O. (2000). *Psychodynamic psychiatry in clinical practice* (3rd ed.). Washington, DC: American Psychiatric Press.

Gold, J., & Stricker, G. (2001). Relational psychoanalysis as a foundation of assimilative integration. *Journal of Psychotherapy Integration, 11,* 43–58.

Greenson, R. R. (1967). *The technique and practice of psychoanalysis* (vol. I). New York: International Universities Press.

Haley, J. (1973). *Uncommon therapy*. New York: Norton.

Hoffman, I. Z. (1983). The patient as interpreter of the analysis experience. *Contemporary Psychoanalysis, 19,* 389–422.

Kohut, H. (1977). *The restoration of the self*. New York: International Universities Press.

Menninger, K., & Holzman, P. S. (1973). *Theory of psychoanalytic technique*. New York: Basic Books.

Mitchell, S. (1993). *Hope and dread in psychoanalysis*. New York: Basic Books.

Singer, E. (1970). *Key concepts in psychotherapy*. New York: Basic Books.

Stricker, G. (in press-a). Assimilative psychodynamic psychotherapy integration: The case of Saul. In G. Stricker & J. Gold (Eds.). *A casebook in psychotherapy integration*. Washington, DC: American Psychological Association. (still in press)

Stricker, G. (in press-b). Using homework in psychodynamic psychotherapy. *Journal of Psychotherapy Integration*. (still in press)

Stricker, G., & Gold, J. R. (2002). An assimilative approach to integrative psychodynamic psychotherapy. In J. Lebow (Ed.). Comprehensive handbook of psychotheraphy: *Integrative/eclectic* (vol. 4, pp. 295–315). New York: Wiley.

Sullivan, H. S. (1953). *The interpersonal theory of psychiatry*. New York: WW Norton.

Weiner, I. B. (1998). *Principles of psychotherapy* (2nd ed.). New York: John Wiley & Sons.

Wolitzky, D. L. (2003). The theory and practice of traditional psychoanalytic treatment. In A. S. Gurman & S. B. Messer (Eds.). *Essential psychotherapies: Theory and practice* (2nd ed., pp. 24–68). New York: Guilford.

8

THE TEMPORAL STRUCTURE OF THERAPY: KEY QUESTIONS OFTEN ASSOCIATED WITH DIFFERENT PHASES OF SESSIONS AND TREATMENTS (PLUS TWENTY-ONE HELPFUL HINTS)

MICHAEL F. HOYT

Kaiser Permanente Medical Center
San Rafael, California

There is a season for everything, a time for every occupation under heaven.
— Ecclesiastes 3:1

Organizing is what you do before you do something, so that when you do it, it's not all mixed up.
— Christopher Robin in *The Complete Tales of Winnie-the-Pooh* (Milne, 1926)

Mastery involves a superior level of performance across a variety of situations. Patients come to our offices with a wide variety of issues and complaints. We need to have skills, both conceptual and technical, to

---

Portions of this chapter, including Figures 1 and 2, are adapted from M. F. Hoyt, *Some Stories Are Better Than Others* (Philadelphia: Brunner/Mazel, 2000); and M. F. Hoyt, *The Present Is a Gift* (New York: iUniverse.com, 2004). Copyright 2000, 2004, M. F. Hoyt. Used with permission. Figure 3, which originally appeared in *The New Yorker* (March 1, 2004, p. 8), is used with permission of *The New Yorker*.

reconnoiter and traverse successfully the clinical terrain of anxiety, loneliness, depression, interpersonal conflicts, eating disorders, parent–child problems, marital discord, sexual dysfunctions, and so on. Although every case is unique, guidelines and thinking structures can be helpful. Indeed, without them, how would we know where to begin or how to proceed?

As described in *The First Session in Brief Therapy* (Budman, Hoyt, & Friedman, 1992, p. 347), there are a series of tasks to accomplish in an initial meeting:

1. Establish rapport.
2. Define the purpose of the meeting, orienting the patient (and therapist) on how to use therapy.
3. Establish an opportunity for the patient to express thoughts, feelings, and behaviors.
4. Assess the patient's problems, strengths, motivations, expectations, and goals.
5. Evaluate possible psychiatric complaints when indicated, including biological/medical factors, suicide/homocide risk, and alcohol/drug abuse when appropriate.
6. Mutually formulate a treatment focus.
7. Make initial treatment interventions and assess their effects.
8. Suggest "homework" (sometimes called *tasks, directives, practice opportunities*, and so on).
9. Define treatment parameters (such as who will attend sessions and possibly estimating length of treatment, or at least implying time sensitivity by suggesting "only as long as needed").
10. Make future appointments as needed.
11. Handle fees, payments, cancellation policies, and so forth.

There are also a number of "universal elements" shared by most therapies that deliberately set out to be brief or time sensitive (Budman et al., 1992). These generic components include:

1. Rapid and generally positive working alliance between therapist and patient
2. Focality, the clear specification of achievable treatment goals
3. Clear definition of patient and therapist responsibilities
4. Expectation of change, the belief that improvement is within the patient's grasp
5. Here-and-now (and next) orientation, a primary therapeutic focus on the present and near future rather than on the distant past
6. The introduction of novelty, getting the client to have new experiences
7. Time sensitivity, an awareness that "the present is a gift" (Hoyt, 2004), the understanding that life is limited and that all problems cannot be solved,

but that some important changes can be made now; as well as the idea that pieces of therapy may be done on an intermittent, serial basis (Budman, 1990; Cummings & Sayama, 1995; Hoyt, 1995; 2000, 2004).

THE TEMPORAL STRUCTURE
OF THERAPY

There is a basic structure or model that helps organize my thinking and therapeutic responses when I need to figure out where the client and I are and what we need to do. Of course, this is only a general schema or guideline, one that needs adaptation and application in particular situations, which is the art and craft of doing therapy.

At the risk of oversimplification—remember, these are just guidelines— I would like to suggest that the course of each therapy session can be conceptualized as having five phases or stages, as seen in Figure 8.1. They tend to be pyramidal or epigenetic—that is, they tend to occur in sequence and each flows from the preceding so that successful work in one preconditions the next. The client elects therapy before forming an alliance; the therapeutic alliance establishes the ground for defining goals; goal setting leads to focusing on specific change strategies; goal attainment leads to discussion about homework, relapse prevention, and leave taking; and termination points toward continued growth and possible return to treatment.

As seen in Figure 8.2, there is also often a microcosm–macrocosm parallelism—that is, the structure of each therapy session tends to mirror or parallel the overall course of treatment. Issues typically involved in the first portions of treatment are similar to those involved in the first portions of each session; the middle of treatment resembles the middle of each session; the issues that characterize the later portions of the course of therapy tend also to characterize the later portions of each session. As biologists might

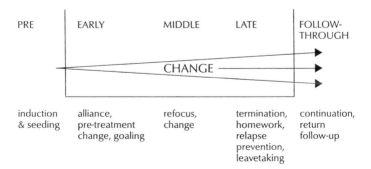

FIGURE 8.1   The temporal structure of therapy.

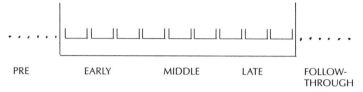

| PRE | EARLY | MIDDLE | LATE | FOLLOW-THROUGH |

FIGURE 8.2 Therapy as a temporally structured sequence of sessions, each with a temporally structured sequence.

say, "Ontogeny recapitulates phylogeny—the development of the individual mirrors the development of the species"; crystallographers and chaos theorists may prefer to think about how a fragment replicates the whole. Recognizing the respective phases of treatment and their requisite tasks, both in each session and in the overall course of treatment, can help to make therapy more effective and efficient.

SOME QUESTIONS TO CONSIDER AT DIFFERENT JUNCTURES IN THERAPY

Drawing from a variety of theoretical perspectives, especially those approaches—such as solution focused, narrative, redecision, and strategic—that go under the general rubric of "constructive therapies" (Hoyt, 1994, 1996, 1998; also see Goldberg, 1998; Hubble, Duncan, & Miller, 1999; and Ziegler & Hiller, 2001), here are some often useful questions organized around the dimension of time.

PRETREATMENT

Change begins even before contact with the client. He/she/they have decided there is a problem and would like assistance to resolve the difficulty. Here are some questions to ask—by therapist or triage screener, on the telephone or by questionnaire—while making an initial appointment:

- What's the problem? Why have you called now?
- How do you see or understand the situation?
- What do you think will help?
- How have you tried to solve the problem so far? How did that work?
- When the problem isn't present (or isn't so bad), what is going on differently?
- Please notice between now and when we meet, so that you can describe it to me, when the problem isn't so bad (when you and your spouse are

getting along, when you're not feeling depressed, when you don't drink too much, and so on), what are you doing differently then? This may give us some clues regarding what you need to do more of—identifying exceptions to the problem that led you to call will focus on solutions that may be useful to you. OK?

EARLY IN TREATMENT AND EARLY IN EACH SESSION

As we begin a session and a therapy, we should especially attend to forming a good alliance, inquiring about possible changes since our last contact, and establishing goals for the session and the therapy. Some useful questions might include:

- Since we last spoke (or, since you made the appointment), what have you noticed that may be a bit better or different? How did that happen? What did you do?
- When is the problem not a problem?
- What do you call the problem? What name do you have for it?
- When (and how) does (the problem) influence you, and when (and how) do you influence it?
- What's your idea or theory about what will help?
- How can I be most useful to you?
- If we were only going to meet once or a few times, what problem would you want to focus on solving first?
- What needs to happen here today so that when you leave you can feel this visit was worthwhile?
- What are you willing to change today?
- Given all that you've been through, how have you managed to cope as well as you have?
- If we work hard together, what will be the first small indications that we're going in the right direction?
- On a scale of one to ten, where is the problem now? Where would it need to be for you to decide that you didn't need to continue coming here?
- Suppose tonight, while you're sleeping, a miracle happens, and the problem that led you here is resolved. When you awaken tomorrow, how will you first notice the miracle has happened? What will be the first sign that things are better? And the next? And the next?

IN THE MIDDLE OF TREATMENT AND THE MIDDLE
OF EACH SESSION

We need to keep track of the client's goals, whether we have a good working alliance and whether we are going in the right direction or if some course "corrections" need to be made. Possible refocusing is directed by the client's response to questions such as these:

- How did that work? What did you do to help it happen?
- Is this being helpful to you? What would make it more so?
- Do you have any questions you'd like to ask me?
- Are we working on what you want to work on?
- I seem to have missed something you said. What can I do to be more helpful to you now?

LATE IN TREATMENT AND LATE IN EACH SESSION

Termination, which may be nicely defined as "extracting the therapist from the equation of the successful relationship" (Gustafson, 1986, p. 279; also see Hoyt, 2000, especially pp. 237–261), becomes central. There are a number of issues to be addressed, as the following guideline questions suggest:

Goal Attainment/Homework/Post-Session Tasks

- Has this been helpful to you? How so?
- Which of the helpful things that you've been doing do you think you should continue to do? How can you do this?
- Between now and the next time we meet (or, to keep things going in the right direction), would you be willing to (do this)?
- Before we stop in a couple minutes, when I'll walk you back to the waiting room, let's discuss what's next.
- Who can be helpful to you in doing _____? What might interfere, and how can you prepare to deal with those challenges?

Goal Maintenance and Relapse Prevention

- What would be a signal that the problems you were having might be returning? How can you respond if you see that developing?
- Suppose you wanted to go back to all the problems you were having when you first came in. What would you need to do to make this happen, if you wanted to sabotage yourself?
- How might (the problem) try to trick you into letting it take over again?
- What will you need to do to increase the odds that things will work out OK even if you weren't to come in for awhile?
- Who will be glad to hear about your progress? Who in your present or past (family, friends, colleagues) would support your efforts?
- Do you sometimes find yourself thinking about the things we discuss here?

Leave Taking

- Would you like to make another appointment now, or wait and see how things go and call me as needed?

- Would you like to make our appointment for three weeks, six weeks, or wait a bit longer?
- What is the longest you can imagine handling things on your own?

A FEW OTHER HINTS

1. I often, but not always, find that the harder I listen, the smarter the client gets. Do not underestimate clients' strengths. Let them do most of the work. Remember that, ultimately, the power is in the patient. We don't really change patients, we create contexts in which they can change themselves. Emphasize client choice and responsibility (see Schneider & May, 1995).

2. While recently devouring Bob Dylan's autobiography, *Chronicles* (2004, p. 20), I nodded with agreement when I read

> I told him about my grandma on my mom's side who lived with us. She was filled with nobility and goodness, told me once that happiness isn't on the road to anything. That happiness is the road. Had also instructed me to be kind because everyone you'll ever meet is fighting a hard battle.

3. Have a focus for sessions and treatments. If you're too well rounded, you're not pointed in any direction. Remember, "It's a long day on the golf course if you don't know where the hole is. Have a specific goal and be purposeful on every stroke" (Hoyt, 2000, p. 6). Consider "Why now?" has the patient sought therapy (Budman & Gurman, 1998). What is their theory about how they are stuck, when aren't they stuck, and what might be needed now to help them to get unstuck? While remaining open to moment-by-moment discovery (see Hoyt, 2001), develop an agenda and manage the session, as needed. Avoid unnecessary detours.

4. Clarify and cultivate the client's motivation (as suggested by Goulding & Goulding, 1979; Burns, 1989; and others) by exploring responses to items such as

- What's the problem?
- Is it a problem for you?
- Do you want to work on it?
- How hard/much are you willing to work?

5. During a predoctoral supervision session in 1974, Leigh Roberts, MD, told me: "If they're into the facts, go for the feelings; if they're into the feelings, go for the facts." I still find this useful.

6. What's in a name: *patient* or *client?* Some prefer to call the people we meet in our offices by the former appellation, whereas others prefer the latter. The first highlights the idea that there is suffering to be relieved and evokes the medical model (and perhaps the idea that the people have to be

patient and await our attention), whereas the latter highlights a more egalitarian connection and evokes more of a business relationship. It is important to recognize, whichever term is used, what it may imply about the roles of those involved, who has what powers, and what are the expected underlying mechanisms of change (see Hoyt, 1995, especially pp. 205–207 and 209–211).

7. Pay close attention to the client–therapist relationship. Client responses may be more usefully thought of as feedback for what works rather than as *resistance.* Quickly surveying the client's perception of the therapeutic relationship and possible progress at the end of a session—using easy-to-administer instruments such as those provided by Johnson (1995, pp. 47–48) or the Institute for the Study of Therapeutic Change (www.talkingcure.com; also, see Lambert, 2005)—may give clues to what therapists need to do differently to be more effective.

Drawing from solution-focused therapy, consider whether the client is relating as a *customer, complainant,* or *visitor* (de Shazer, 1985, 1988):

> Here the distinction between customer, complainant, and visitor-type relationships offers guidelines for therapeutic cooperation or "fit" (Berg & Miller, 1992; de Shazer, 1988). If the relationship involves a *visitor* with whom the therapist cannot define a clear complaint or goal, cooperation involves nothing more than sympathy, politeness, and compliments for whatever the clients are successfully doing (with no tasks or requests for change). In a *complainant* relationship, where clients present a complaint but appear unwilling to take action or want someone else to change, the therapist cooperates by accepting their views, giving compliments, and sometimes prescribing observational tasks (e.g., to notice exceptions to the complaint pattern). Finally, with *customers* who want to do something about a complaint, the principle of fit allows the therapist to be more direct in guiding them toward solutions.... [T]he customer–complainant–visitor categories represent dynamic, changing attributes of the therapist–client relationship, not static characteristics of the clients themselves. Visitors and complainants can become customers and vice versa. In fact, one of the main reasons to cooperate with clients in this way is to increase possibilities for customership. (Shoham, Rohrbaugh & Patterson, 1995, p. 153; italics added)

Combining solution-focused therapy with Prochaska's (1999; Norcross & Beutler, 1997) transtheoretical model of stages of change can suggest some differential intervention strategies (Hoyt & Miller, 2000, p. 212; also see Hubble et al., 1999; and Miller, Donahey, & Hubble, 2004; Miller, Dunean, & Hubble, 1997):

Precontemplation: Suggest that the client "think about it" and provide information and education.

Contemplation: Encourage thinking, recommend an observation task in which the client is asked to notice something (such as what happens to make things better or worse), and use a "Go slow!" directive to join with the client's not yet being ready for action.

Preparation: Offer treatment options; invite the client to choose from viable alternatives.

Action: Amplify what works; get details of success and reinforce.

Maintenance: Support success, predict setbacks, and make contingency plans.

Termination: Wish well, say goodbye, leave an open door for possible return as needed.

8. Recognition leads to explanation; experience leads to change. Understanding and "insight" are seldom (if ever) enough. Help the client experience something new. This can be accomplished through a variety of ways:

- Education (e.g., providing information about different types of anxiety disorders and treatments)
- A well-timed psychodynamic transference interpretation (e.g. "When you hesitated, I thought you might be expecting me to respond the way you said your parents used to respond. Does that fit your experience?")
- Reframing (e.g., asking "Have you considered that when he acts that way, even though it seems controlling and bothersome, maybe that's his way of trying to show concern and be helpful?")
- Inquiring about exceptions to the problem, times when the presenting problem is not present (e.g., "What did you do differently the time when you felt somewhat nervous but didn't have a full-blown panic attack?")
- Mental imagery methods, visualizing desired outcomes
- In-session practice and role-playing (e.g., teaching relaxation skills or having a couple turn to one another and practice effective communication)

9. Work with biology. The mind lives inside the brain, and the brain is a physical organism. Mood and energy predispositions ("temperment") are somewhat inborn and need to be appreciated. Medical factors are also important. Medications can be very useful, but be alert to side effects. A couple of quick examples: (1) Heart and blood pressure medications cause depression in a significant portion of patients. Is the person depressed because their recently diagnosed hypertension or cardiac event has put them in touch with mortality and the finitude of life, or because their medication has iatrogenic effects, or both? Consultation with their doctor may result in a switch to another medication. (2) Psychiatric medications, including antidepressants, can be useful for improving mood and thinking, and for helping to restoring the person's "restorying" capacity (Hoyt, 2000). The most common antidepressants, however, cause sexual side effects for many people, probably more than the drug companies report. When someone's marriage isn't going well, they may get depressed (and/or depression may contribute to the marital problem). If a selective serotonin reuptake inhibitor

is prescribed and it knocks their libido down (or out), the subsquent diminuation in sexual activity and pleasure bonding isn't likely to help the marriage recover. Again, consultation with the prescribing physician is in order.

10. Emphasize strengths and abilities, not weaknesses and deficits. This is consistent with the recent call for a *positive psychology*: "[O]ur message is to remind our field that psychology is not just the study of pathology, weakness, and damage; it is also the study of strength and virtue. Treatment is not just fixing what is broken; it is nurturing what is best" (Seligman & Csikszentmihalyi, 2000, p. 7). I think this is also what Milton Erickson (1980, p. 540; also see Haley, 1973) had in mind when he emphasized the idea of *utilization*:

> The fullest possible utilization of the functional capacities and abilities and the experiential and acquisitional learnings of the patient...should take precedence over the teaching of new ways in living which are developed from the therapist's possibly incomplete understanding of what may be right and serviceable to the individual concerned.

11. Sometimes helping people recall and access forgotten or submerged abilities is enough, but other times—especially if they are relating as *customers* (de Shazer, 1985, 1988; Hoyt, 2004)—they will appreciate and benefit from learning new ways to improve their parenting, their emotional self-regulation, their interpersonal communication, their sex lives, and so forth. The above quoted remarks of Milton Erickson notwithstanding, teach skills when appropriate. If considering homework, make sure that what is being discussed is realistic and that the client is willing to do it. Whenever possible, have clients design the specifics, and establish when during the week they will have time to do it.

12. Treat a human being, not a diagnosis. I agree with Yalom (2002, p. 4) when he writes:

> Though diagnosis is unquestionably critical in treatment considerations for many severe conditions with a biological substate (for example, schizophrenia, bipolar disorders, major affective disorders, temporal lobe epilepsy, drug toxicity, organic or brain disease from toxins, degenerative causes, or infectious agents), diagnosis is often *counterproductive* in the everyday psychotherapy of less severely impaired patients.

A supervisor once told me I'd better diagnose the patient quickly, before I got to know too much about the person! Again, Erickson (quoted in Zeig, 1980): "And I do wish that all Rogerian therapists, Gestalt therapists, transactional therapists, group analysts, and all the other offspring of various theories would recognize that not one of them really recognizes that psychotherapy for person #1 is not psychotherapy for person #2."

13. Also be careful about "normal." "Neurosis," "psychosis," and "normosis" are all diseases. We may all be "more human than otherwise," as Harry

Stack Sullivan said, but we're not all the same—and don't need to be. Moreover, much of what psychology teaches about "normal development" and "normal family structure" is based on studies of white Europeans and their descendants, a still largely invisible ethnocentric monoculturalism (see Sue, 2004; Guthrie, 1997). Healthy solutions may be different for different people.

14. Some things cannot be changed. Acceptance (good reality testing) does not mean defeat. How you recall and relate to past events is malleable, but unless you're younger than 18 years old, your childhood isn't going to change. There's a lot of wisdom in the famous A. A. Serenity Prayer (Hazelden Foundation, 1987, p. 129):

> God grant me the serenity
> To accept the things I cannot change,
> The courage to change the things I can,
> And the wisdom to know the difference.

15. If a client is not making progress toward his or her goal, consider whether any of the following needs to be addressed:

- Wrong goal; not attainable
- Misalliance; client is not ready/therapist may be pushing too hard
- Missed diagnosis (e.g., depression, alcohol and/or drug abuse, obsessive-compulsive disorder).

16. Extending an idea from Gustafson (1992, p. 76), I find that marital (and other committed relationship) conflicts usually have to do with one (or more) of the following four themes: in/out, top/bottom, close/far, hot/cold. We're not (necessarily) talking about sex here. The four respective themes are commitment, power or control, intimacy, and passion. When couples get together, they tend to cut a deal, consciously or unconsciously, along these four dimensions. Sooner or later, one partner or the other wants something different, maybe a change in who makes which decisions or how they are made (*power and control*); or one person wants more time together or more time apart (*intimacy*); or one person wants sex more often or less often (*passion*). Challenges on one dimension may raise issues on others ("Does this mean you don't want to be committed to this relationship?") If the couple is not able to negotiate these changes on their own, they may seek our professional services.

17. Have a sense of humor. In archaic times, humor was a moisture or vapor. In old physiology, humor was a fluid or juice that circulated within the body, influencing one's disposition, mood, or state of mind. We now think of humor not in physiological terms, but as a caprice, a whim, a fancy, as something that appeals to the comical or absurdly incongruous. In psychotherapy, having fun can be a lubricant, a balm, a restorative. It can be both the medium and the message. It can be an attitude and an antidote, both where we come from and how we get there.

It's best when humor emerges naturally, not as a technique. It can provide comfort and relaxation and help build the therapeutic alliance. Humor can also operate in a deconstructive mode, addressing how you hold things, helping to shift frames. I recall one of my teachers, Carl Whitaker (see Whitaker, 1989), saying: "Humor is a way to get around the corner without tearing down the building." With the right timing and tact, it can convey, "This is serious, but there are other ways to look at this, and some might even give you pleasure rather than all the pain you're currently having." A couple who were struggling with the burdens of marriage were able to make a useful shift when I handed them the cartoon shown in Figure 8.3 (from *The New Yorker*, 2004, March 1, p. 8).

18. Pay attention to what you pay attention to. How we make sense of our worlds—the stories we tell ourselves and each other—does much to determine what we experience, our actions, and our destinies. Some stories are better than others because they are more enlivening and encouraging, helping people to get more of what they want. They carry wisdom and hope. They open people's hearts and touch their feelings. They speak to the person's truth or dream. They tap into our strengths and resources. They invigorate us, making us feel more alive and more deeply human. As discussed at length in *Some Stories Are Better Than Others* (Hoyt, 2000) and

"Gays and lesbians getting married—haven't they suffered enough?"

FIGURE 8.3   ©The New Yorker Collection 2004 Michael Shaw from cartoonbank.com. All Rights Reserved.

The Present Is a Gift (Hoyt, 2004), how we look influences what we see, and what we see influences what we do, 'round and 'round. What you focus on tends to grow, so be mindful of your language and what you choose to emphasize.

19. When you're stuck (and we all get stuck), don't blame the patient. Consult. First, see if the client has any ideas about what is needed to go forward. If this doesn't break the impasse, try discussing the situation with a colleague. Although it's usually tempting to consult with someone of similar orientation and background, in my experience it is often helpful to talk with someone who has a different theory and different training. They may be able to see something that my "lenses" don't see. Depth perception is better with binocular vision.

20. To avoid burnout, burn in. Follow your passion, be emotionally involved, and stay curious.

21. Use good clinical judgment. Be smart. As Jay Haley (quoted in Crenshaw, 2004, p. 46) said when asked how he knew to use a certain intervention at a certain time: "You wouldn't use it on someone it wouldn't work on!"

REFERENCES

Berg, I. K., & Miller, S. D. (1992) *Working with the problem drinker: A solution-focused approach*. New York: Norton.

Budman, S. H. (1990). The myth of termination in brief therapy: Or, it ain't over until it's over. In J. K. Zeig & S. G. Gilligan (Eds.). *Brief therapy: Myths, methods, and metaphors* (pp. 206–218). New York: Brunner/Mazel.

Budman, S. H., & Gurman, A. S. (1988). *Theory and practice of brief therapy*. New York: Guilford Press.

Budman, S. H., Hoyt, M. F., & Friedman, S. (Eds.). (1992). *The first session in brief therapy*. New York: Guilford Press.

Burns, D. D. (1989). *The feeling good handbook: Using the new mood therapy in everyday life*. New York: William Morrow.

Crenshaw, W. (2004). *Treating families and children in the child protective system*. New York: Brunner-Routledge.

Cummings, N. A., & Sayama, M. (1995). *Focused psychotherapy: A casebook of brief, intermittent psychotherapy throughout the life cycle*. Philadelphia: Brunner/Mazel.

de Shazer, S. (1985). *Keys to solution in brief therapy*. New York: Norton.

de Shazer, S. (1988). *Clues: Investigating solutions in brief therapy*. New York: Norton.

Dylan, B. (2004). *Chronicles* (vol. 1). New York: Simon & Schuster.

Erickson, M. H. (1980). *Collected papers* (vol. 1). New York: Irvington.

Goldberg, M. C. (1998). *The art of the question: A guide to short-term question-centered therapy*. New York: Wiley.

Goulding, M. M., & Goulding, R. L. (1979). *Changing lives through redecision therapy*. New York: Grove Press.

Gustafson, J. P. (1986). *The complex secret of brief psychotherapy*. New York: Norton.

Gustafson, J. P. (1992). *Self-delight in a harsh world: The main stories of individual, marital and family psychotherapy.* New York: Norton.

Guthrie, R. V. (1997). *Even the rat was white: A historical view of psychology* (2nd ed.). New York: Harper & Row.

Haley, J. (1973). *Uncommon therapy: The psychiatric techniques of Milton H. Erickson, M.D.* New York: Norton.

Hazelden Foundation. (1987). *The twelve steps of Alcoholics Anonymous.* New York: Harper/ Hazelden.

Hoyt, M. F. (Ed.). (1994). *Constructive therapies.* New York: Guilford Press.

Hoyt, M. F. (1995). *Brief therapy and managed care: Readings for contemporary practice.* San Francisco: Jossey-Bass.

Hoyt, M. F. (Ed.). (1996). *Constructive therapies* (vol. 2). New York: Guilford Press.

Hoyt, M. F. (Ed.). (1998). *The handbook of constructive therapies.* San Francisco: Jossey-Bass.

Hoyt, M. F. (2000). *Some stories are better than others: Doing what works in brief therapy and managed care.* Philadelphia: Brunner/Mazel.

Hoyt, M. F. (2001). Direction and discovery: A conversation about power and politics in narrative therapy with Michael White and Jeff Zimmerman. In M. F. Hoyt. *Interviews with brief therapy experts* (pp. 265–293). New York: Brunner-Routledge.

Hoyt, M. F. (2004) *The present is a gift: Mo' better stories from the world of brief therapy.* New York: iUniverse.com.

Hoyt, M. F., & Miller, S. D. (2000). Stage-appropriate change-oriented brief therapy strategies. In M. F. Hoyt. *Some stories are better than others* (pp. 207–235). Philadelphia: Brunner/ Mazel.

Hubble, M. A., Duncan, B. L., & Miller, S. D. (Eds.). (1999). *The heart and soul of change: What works in therapy.* Washington, DC: American Psychological Association.

Johnson, L. D. (1995). *Psychotherapy in the age of accountability.* New York: Norton.

Lambert, M. J. (Ed.). (2005). Enhancing psychotherapy outcome through feedback. *Journal of Clinical Psychology/In Session, 61,* 141–217. [whole issue].

Miller, S. D., Donahey, K. M., & Hubble, M. A. (2004). Getting "in the mood" (for a change): Stage-appropriate clinical work for sexual problems. In S. Green & D. Flemons (Eds.). *Quickies: The handbook of brief sex therapy* (pp. 26–44). New York: Norton.

Miller, S. D., Duncan, B. L., & Hubble, M. A. (1997). *Escape from Babel: Toward a unifying language for psychotherapy practice.* New York: Norton.

Milne, A. A. (1926). *The complete tales of Winnie-the-Pooh.* New York: Dutton.

Norcross, J. C., & Beutler, L. E. (1997). Determining the therapeutic relationship of choice in brief therapy. In J. N. Butcher (Ed.). *Personality assessment in managed health care: A practitioner's guide.* New York: Oxford University Press.

Prochaska, J. O. (1999). How do people change and how can we change to help many more people? In M. A. Hubble, B. L. Duncan, & S. D. Miller (Eds.). *The heart and soul of change: What works in therapy.* Washington, DC: American Psychological Association.

Schneider, K. J., & May, R. (1995). *The psychology of existence: An integrative, clinical perspective.* New York: McGraw-Hill.

Seligman, M. E. P., & Csikszentmihalyi, M. (2000). Positive psychology: An introduction. *American Psychologist, 55,* 5–14.

Shoham, V., Rohrbaugh, M., & Patterson, J. (1995). Problem- and solution-focused couple therapies: The MRI and Milwaukee models. In N. S. Jacobson & A. S. Gurman (Eds.). *Clinical handbook of couple therapy* (2nd ed., pp. 142–163). New York: Guilford Press.

Sue, D. W. (2004). Whiteness and ethnocentric monoculturalism: Making the "invisible" visible. *American Psychologist, 59,* 761–769.

Whitaker, C. A. (1989). *Midnight musings of a family therapist.* New York: Norton.

Yalom, I. D. (2002). *The gift of therapy: An open letter to a new generation of therapists and their patients.* New York: HarperCollins.

Zeig, J. K. (Ed.). (1980). *A teaching seminar with Milton H. Erickson.* New York: Brunner/ Mazel.

Ziegler, P., & Hiller, T. (2001). *Recreating partnership: A solution-oriented, collaborative approach to couples therapy.* New York: Norton.

9

RESISTANCE AS AN ALLY IN PSYCHOTHERAPY

NICHOLAS A. CUMMINGS

Cummings Foundation for Behavioral Health
Reno, NV and Scottsdale, AZ

To the weary psychotherapist struggling to overcome the patient's resistance, the suggestion that resistance can be a therapeutic ally that could be useful in accelerating progress would seem absurd. Frustrated and often stymied by it, the psychotherapist understandably sees resistance as an enemy to be challenged and overcome. This notion has been canonized throughout more than a century of psychological thought, beginning with Morton Prince (1903), who attempted to overcome it with hypnosis, and Sigmund Freud (1933), who saw insight painstakingly fostered by prolonged psychoanalysis as the solution. Whatever the modality of the therapist, resistance is seen as something to be defeated in one way or another, with notable exceptions being radical behaviorists who have not yet discovered it, or postmodernists who believe resistance *is* the solution. The position taken in this chapter is a patient-centered one in which resistance is both understandable and potentially an ally.

A DEFINITION: PATIENTS HAVE A RIGHT TO THEIR RESISTANCE

Patients cling to faulty or outmoded behaviors because, knowing no other way, they are terrified to let go. Even though their way of life has gotten them into emotional trouble, they imagine that any change constitutes an unknown that could be worse. Picture a hiker clinging to a ledge to which he has fallen and is now facing the deep chasm below. Rescuers are urging him to jump to another ledge, from which a dangling helicopter rope ladder would be accessible. Unsure of his ability to make the jump successfully, the stranded hiker sees only falling into the abyss. He is frightened on the ledge, but terrified of jumping. He is helpless and emotionally paralyzed. This simple analogy is not unlike our patients. As therapists we cannot ask the patient to do something terrifying until we can demonstrate assurance that the "jump" (i.e., change) is safe and worthwhile. This defines resistance as terror, and the task of overcoming the resistance is overcoming the terror.

In our definition, resistance does not include the innumerable instances when the psychotherapist has misjudged the patient's actual intent in coming to psychotherapy, resulting in patient and therapist striving toward incompatible goals. Unfortunately in such situations, the therapist erroneously attributes the struggle to resistance rather than her own misreading of the patient. At times the resistance will seem manipulative or even malingering, especially with borderline and other personality disordered patients. Unless the patient is deliberately deceitful, as is often the case with sociopaths, in the majority of instances even the most far-fetched resistance is offered by the patient with belief and sincerity. The therapist should never take these manifestations lightly, seeking rather to understand the patient's fear of change and enlisting the resistance as an ally.

WHO IS PRESENTING WHAT, AND WHY?

People have distinct characteristics, attributes, and personalities aside from their psychological problems, and these styles are not infinite. They can be identified as constituting distinct groups, with considerable overlap of course. By understanding group characteristics, the psychotherapist has a heads-up regarding what kind of resistance can generally be expected from a member of that group. In the early and mid 20th century, the approach to understanding the patient was psychoanalytical, with its overemphasis on psychopathology. Everything had to be understood in terms of childhood psychosexual development, an approach that fortunately ran its course. Then came the cognitive revolution that ignored the characteristics of the person, but addressed the condition, proffering the interventions of skills training and cognitive restructuring. Finally there are the deconstructionists and their subsequent normalizing of all behavior, no matter how aberrant. In all of this we lost the uniqueness of the person who is presenting. In moving away from Freud's overemphasis on the person's psychopathology, we threw the baby out with the bathwater. The expectation that a smoking cessation program will bring the same response whether the smoker is a sociopath, an obsessive, a borderline personality, or an alcoholic is sheer folly. The same can be said of all blanket interventions. And if mere information or education were sufficient, the American people would have quit smoking 40 years ago when the Surgeon General's warning was first put on cigarette packs.

A potent, if not amusing, example will illustrate. Almost 50 years ago, an administrative social worker who was seeing me in treatment conceived of the notion that if prostitutes were trained in an occupational skill, they would have a better way of earning a living and would give up prostitution. She persuaded the state of California to fund such a project in San Francisco, a city that at the time was awash in street walkers. These women were rounded up and given the choice of jail or skills training. Understandably most accepted the training, which in this case led to becoming a skilled masseuse. They graduated, and within months, O'Farrell Street no longer had street walkers, but a row of sleazy massage parlors. The skills training had given them a way of moving prostitution indoors and to masquerade as legitimate businesses. The new industry spread from the West Coast across America, so now every city has such sleazy massage parlors. So much for skills training that does not take into account the personality characteristics of the trainees.

By understanding who is presenting, then discerning what is expected (the what) of treatment, and finally why the patient is presenting now, the psychotherapist can anticipate the resistance and make it a beneficial, accelerating force in psychotherapy.

INITIAL STRATEGIES FOR WORKING WITH RESISTANCE

All the strategies for understanding and dealing with resistance cut across the length of the therapeutic process, but for purposes of convenience they can be divided into initial and ongoing strategies, with the understanding that initial strategies may be used at any time and thus also be ongoing. A complete exposition is not within the scope of this chapter, and for more information the reader is referred to comprehensive textbooks (Cummings & Sayama, 1995; Cummings & Cummings, 2000a).

NEVER STRONG-ARM THE RESISTANCE: AN INTRODUCTION TO PSYCHOJUDO

No matter how gently or accurately the therapist engages the resistance, it will always be viewed as strong-arming by the frightened patient. The following case illustrates this common problem, complicated by the usual therapist's response.

Peggy was a young woman living with a man who was contributing nothing to the relationship. She worked to support both of them, and she did all the cooking and house cleaning. He spent his days smoking pot and pretending he was writing poetry. She came to treatment ostensibly for help to leave Earl. In three previous attempts she quit in the second session with therapists who set out to help her liberate herself from this man. In seeing me, she repeated her plea that there must be something she could do better to make this man love her enough to clean up his act. I assigned as homework that she should do three loving things she had never done before that would make him love her. She returned the following week with homework completed, but complained he had not changed. I was unrelenting, stating she had not yet done enough, and assigned homework to do three additional loving things she had never done before. She returned the third session complaining her love still was not effective. Stubbornly, I insisted there must be something she missed, and again assigned the same homework. On the fourth session she returned announcing she had left Earl because he is worthless and hopeless, and it had never been her fault. All along Peggy was terrified that Earl was the best she deserved, and without him she would have no one. Now that the resistance had been put aside, therapy could address the issue of her low self-esteem. The previous therapists had tried from the onset to bolster her self-esteem so she could leave Earl, and the resistance (fear) resulted only in her bolting treatment.

Not strong-arming the resistance has been called *psychojudo*, referring to the art of moving the patient to health by taking advantage of her own momentum. Peggy was helped to leave Earl only after the fourth therapist correctly used her momentum that she should do something more loving. The result was her realization that it was Earl, not her, who was at fault. Think of it as turning around an ocean liner, a vessel that cannot turn abruptly as an automobile. The pilot must go in the direction the ship is going and turn it around slowly until it is going in the opposite direction. With our patients, psychojudo takes time, skill, and patience. By going with the resistance, the patient eventually turns around and then therapy moves rapidly without the fear of change.

Paradoxical intention is a useful technique in psychojudo (see also Zeig's Chapter 14 on incongruent interventions in this volume). A note of caution is indicated. Most psychotherapists begin a paradoxical intervention appropriately, but end it prematurely, thus negating the benefit. In the case of Peggy, terminating the paradox in the second or third session, when she was strongly complaining she had exhausted all loving ways, would have resulted in a strengthening of the resistance.

PRESCRIBING THE RESISTANCE

Prescribing the resistance is a variation of psychojudo. By directing the patient to continue behavior that seems antitherapeutic, the therapist surprises the patient's defenses, engages the patient in a positive working relationship, and forces oppositional patients to adopt the position of the therapist. Consider the case of Patricia, the overprotective cotherapist.

Ten-year-old Billy was referred by a beleaguered school system that was unable to cope with the boy's attacks on other students, his abusiveness toward his teachers, and his truancy. The therapist appropriately discerned that at the root of the problem was an overprotective mother, and that treating Billy without treating his mother would be futile. Patricia, Billy's mother, refused to be seen in therapy, and refused permission for the social worker to see Billy without her being present. The therapy was at a standstill. The therapist's supervisor saw the mother along with the therapist. He had read a case presentation of Billy written by the mother that was surprisingly complete and insightful. He complimented Patricia, said she knew more about Billy than anyone, and invited her to become the social worker's cotherapist in treating Billy. Patricia accepted, and overnight became positive, participated in the sessions, and honestly and fearlessly addressed both Billy's defiant behavior and her own overprotectiveness. As a result, she asked for individual sessions for herself, and treatment for both mother and son progressed rapidly and successfully.

More simple examples of prescribing the resistance would include the prescription for a man with erectile dysfunction not to have an erection during love making. Relieved of his performance anxiety, and if the paradox is continued sufficiently, the man begins to have erections.

HUMORING THE RESISTANCE

Although generally useful in establishing rapport and disarming the resistance, humor is especially useful with borderline personalities and other axis II patients. It can also be used as a variant of psychojudo. This must be skillfully crafted so that the patient does not feel mocked or ridiculed, and the process results in a therapeutic outcome. It is useful with adolescents and those adults who are still behaving as adolescents.

Brooke was a 19-year-old woman from New Jersey who was attending college in San Francisco, an arrangement made financially possible by her wealthy grandmother. The grandmother was concerned that such a young woman in a large, distant city would get into trouble, and she stipulated, and Brooke accepted, that she would have weekly sessions with a psychotherapist as a condition of receiving a monthly check. The patient announced to me she would keep her weekly appointments as specified, but she had no intention of participating in psychotherapy. This disclosure resulted in a previous psychologist refusing to see her unless she became a patient. A second previous psychologist agreed to see her as she demanded, but she had to promise that she would keep an open mind about the possibility of engaging in therapy at some future time. Both psychologists had inadvertently strong-armed her resistance, and she never returned. Brooke then saw me, and I agreed to go along with her plan on one condition. I did not want to look ridiculous at some point because Brooke was not participating in treatment—a fact that would be revealed if and when she got into trouble. She would be required to write a letter each week to her grandmother detailing her insights in the last session. She would first read the letter to the therapist, who would listen for contradictions or discrepancies, and ultimately the letter would have to be plausible and believable. The patient thought this was a splendid plan, and she heartily laughed about it. In making the letters plausible, Brooke (without realizing it) was confronting real problems within herself, and in ostensibly helping her make the letters consistent, the therapist was guiding her toward real solutions. During the sixth session Brooke laughingly acknowledged that in spite of herself she was really in treatment, she found it surprisingly helpful and planned to continue, and the charade could be ended. As with most successful paradoxes, the patient was not angry with the psychotherapist and rather complimented him on helping her do the right thing in spite of herself.

DENYING TREATMENT

For someone who is determined to be there for nontherapeutic reasons, the most therapeutic thing the therapist can do is to deny treatment. If this denial is done skillfully, a patient who presents with no legitimate intent may return at a later time for legitimate reasons. One such patient remarked, "Well, there was one message that came through: 'If I'm here to bullshit you, I may as well not come in at all'." By planting a seed that will blossom later into new-found motivation, denial of treatment can be a useful form of psychojudo. There are several purposes in denying treatment, each with its own techniques.

Denial of Treatment to Motivate Treatment Now

The patient's seeking treatment may be a phony way of perpetuating unacceptable behavior, and in some cases this can be moved toward an honest reason by denying treatment. A man with a history of more than ten years of marital infidelity presented with insincere contrition and a phony desire for help. It was apparent that he wanted to convince his wife that she should forgive him, making her believe he was sincere and would never have another affair. The therapist complimented the man for his uncanny ability to con his wife over several affairs in the last ten years. He told the patient he had successfully conned his wife for a decade and, learning from his last mistake, he could continue to con her for another ten years. This was only a temporary setback, and he did not need the psychotherapist. The man's demeanor changed drastically. He acknowledged that his wife (who had kicked him out of the house) really meant it this time, and he finally has come to his senses. He demanded to be seen. The therapist agreed only if the patient refrained from extramarital encounters and even flirting with other women for the duration of the treatment. The slightest violation would result in the termination of therapy. The patient agreed, and settled into a surprisingly intense and productive therapy.

Denial of Treatment Designed to Bring the Patient Back at a Later Time

With some persons it is apparent, in spite of verbalizations to the contrary, they are flatly resistant to treatment, and any attempt to motivate them would result in endless game playing with no therapeutic resolution. The therapeutic thing to do is to deny treatment, candidly state why, and offer to refer her to any number of colleagues who might be fooled into thinking she has serious intent. A middle-age inveterate shoplifter was referred for psychotherapy after being caught attempting to steal a surprising amount of expensive clothing. This was her eighth arrest and her seventh referral for psychotherapy by a crowded and indulgent justice system that had accepted her diagnosis of kleptomania. She had previously attended therapy sessions only for the length of her probationary period, after which she resumed her shoplifting behavior. It would be only a matter of two or three years before she was caught again. I refused to see her, candidly described her past manipulative behavior, and then described the characteristics of the kind of shoplifter with whom I would be happy to work. I wished her well in her continued game playing with the indulgent court, and hoped she tired of the charade before the court did, finally—in exasperation—remanding her to a jail sentence. She left angry, began regular sessions with another psychologist on the court panel, and saw him for several months before she terminated her sessions with her and returned to me, now with serious intent.

Denying Treatment to Addicts

Denying treatment is especially effective when engaging an addict who is in denial. Addicts characteristically present with seeming determination to quit drinking or drugging, especially if they are in serious difficulty with the police, the court, an employer, a spouse, or other important institutions or figures in their lives. In actuality, however, every addict harbors the secret conviction that he can, with a modicum of help and the passing of the current crisis, become a controlled user. There are sufficient numbers of cognitive therapists that earnestly believe controlled drinking or drug using in a confirmed addict is possible, and more than likely the patient has already been in one, two, or three episodes of such treatment or, even more seriously, in one or more inpatient rehabilitation centers. You do not have to participate in this revolving door. A skilled therapist can candidly state the patient is not ready for abstinence, may not really be addicted, and then describe the attitudes, behaviors, and deceit of the true addict. Actually, the patient is already there and the description fits like a well-tailored glove. This challenge is complicated, and requires considerable skill. Cummings and Cummings (2000b) have compiled a textbook of skills, with research that demonstrates how at a future time, the addict returns to the therapist that understood him and denied treatment pending serious intent.

IMPERATIVE STRATEGIES FOR
WORKING WITH RESISTANCE

Embedded in the resistance are the real reasons the patient is coming in now and the real expectations from psychotherapy. Patients want to be good patients, so they say what will present them in the best light. This includes saying what they believe the therapist wants to hear. Most may be sincere in what they offer, whereas others are more or less aware of their manipulations. These manifest reasons should never be accepted at face value; rather, the psychotherapist must strive to render an operational diagnosis (why now) and elicit the implicit contract (for what).

MAKE AN OPERATIONAL DIAGNOSIS: WHY IS THE
PATIENT HERE NOW?

The operational diagnosis (Op Dx in the following lists) reveals why the patient is really here *now* instead of last year, last week, or next month. This is imperative to understanding and dealing with the resistance because it zeros in on the patient's actual intent and motivation. Saying "I am an alcoholic" does not answer the question, because he has been an alcoholic for more than ten years and has not come in until today. The operational diagnosis is not readily apparent, and often seems far-fetched, but it is a window on the resistance. In the case of Peggy and Earl, the ostensible reason why she was there (for help to leave shiftless Earl) hid the fact that she was terrified he was going to leave her. Earl had shown a casual interest in another woman, and Peggy's low self-esteem told her she would be left with no one. By discerning the operational diagnosis, I ignored the verbalized reason why she was there and focused on reducing her fear of abandonment as a prelude to addressing her relationship with Earl.

Until the psychotherapist is certain of the operational diagnosis, he moves forward with peril. Peggy had unsuccessfully seen two previous well-intentioned therapists who had made interventions based on the erroneous belief she was there for help to leave her boyfriend, and thus they frightened her away. The operational diagnosis is elusive because the patient is unwilling to confront the actual problem, or is hoping for an outcome other than one that would be the therapeutic one. The operational diagnosis and the presenting reason may be slightly off focus or markedly disparate. Here are some examples:

Patient 1 : I am a sex addict.
Op Dx   : His wife caught him cheating on her for the third time.
Patient 2 : I am a kleptomaniac who needs help.
Op Dx   : This is her fourth arrest for shoplifting.
Patient 3 : I am an alcoholic and want to quit.

Op Dx   :   The boss just fired him for missing too many days from work.
Patient 4 :   I am hooked on cocaine and need help to quit.
Op Dx   :   He has been dealing cocaine at work and has been caught.
Patient 5 :   I am having severe panic attacks.
Op Dx   :   She is pregnant and her religion forbids an abortion.
Patient 6 :   I recently became a conscientious objector.
Op Dx   :   His reserve unit has been called up for deployment to Iraq.
Patient 7 :   My husband says he doesn't love me any more.
Op Dx   :   This happened only after she gained 80 lb.
Patient 8 :   My children are neglecting their elderly father and I can't sleep nights.
Op Dx   :   Twenty years ago he abandoned his family and now he wants them back.
Patient 9 :   The children are driving me nuts and I have a constant headache.
Op Dx   :   She is too self-centered to bother with the children.
Patient 10: I am deeply depressed over my husband's death. He was only 52.
Op Dx   :   Her depression is repressed anger that he left no life insurance.

As seen from the foregoing, the therapist cannot be content that the presenting complaint resembles the operational diagnosis. It can be just fuzzy or totally mask the resistance, and leads away from confronting the real problem. If the operational diagnosis has come too readily, the therapist should be skeptical and probe deeper, for if it is in error, the most skilled therapeutic interventions are likely to fail.

ELICIT THE IMPLICIT CONTRACT: WHAT DOES THE PATIENT REALLY WANT?

Determining what the patient really wants from psychotherapy is the other half of the resistance equation. When coupled with the operational diagnosis, the therapist knows why the patient is coming in and for what. The patient will always present an explicit contract that embodies the ostensibly hoped for outcome. The therapist must listen, but not buy into this explicit contract. Somewhere in the early part of the first session, every patient will reveal the implicit contract—what is really wanted out of treatment. This will always be thrown out as an aside or even as a tangent. Psychotherapists tend to listen intently to the main points the patient is making and are not attuned to hearing something that is seemingly trivial. As with the operational diagnosis, when the implicit contract is elicited it must be discussed openly with the patient and a legitimate goal must replace it. The therapist should do this with understanding and empathy, because in most cases the patient is not consciously manipulating, but is sincere in his resistance.

Such was the case in which Don came to treatment for marital counseling to "save my marriage" (explicit contract). He described his wife, whom he claimed he loved deeply, and his girlfriend of several years from whom he could not break away even though he knew he should. He wanted treatment to help him resolve this dilemma. As an aside, he mentioned he and the two women in his life realized this may take time. The psychotherapist followed this lead and probing revealed the girlfriend had grown tired of waiting for Don to leave his wife, called the latter on the phone, told her of the longstanding affair, and this precipitated the crisis. Don was in danger of losing both women. He conceived a brilliant plan: long-term psychotherapy during which time both women would agree to wait patiently for the psychotherapeutic process to resolve the issue for Don. This was the implicit contract; psychotherapy would allow Don to continue with both his wife and mistress indefinitely. After this implicit contract was openly discussed and acknowledged by the patient, Don was full of sincerity, saying he had thought this to be the best way to go. Without being judgmental, the therapist required Don to make a choice between his marriage and his mistress, a defined goal that could be addressed in treatment. When confronted with this reality, the resistance evaporated, and Don chose to save his marriage. Instead of the phony long-term therapy, this became a goal he realized in only five sessions.

If there has been no aside revealing the implicit contract, it is because the therapist has not learned to listen for it and to hear it. Every patient in every first session will throw this out because this permits a belief that the therapist was told and accepted the implicit contract as the goal of treatment. No wonder there are so many instances in which patient and therapist are working toward incongruent goals. The patient is not consciously deceiving the therapist; thus is the nature of resistance.

Looking at the operational diagnoses of the ten patients listed earlier, let us look at the explicit and implicit contracts for each, elicited after first hearing the aside that led to its revelation.

Patient 1: I want to be cured of my sexual addiction.
Aside   : With your help, my wife will realize I'm addicted and can't help it.
Implicit : She will forgive this and future indiscretions.
Patient 2: Please cure my kleptomania.
Aside   : The courts recognize this is a disease.
Implicit : Help convince the judge not to throw the book at me this fourth time.
Patient 3: Diagnose and cure my alcoholism
Aside   : The boss needs reassurance I will get better.

Implicit   :   Convince my boss to rehire me and then make me a social drinker.
Patient 4 :   Help me break free of my addiction; I am desperate.
Aside   :   I only sell to support my habit.
Implicit   :   Convince the police I'm a victim and not the big dealer I really am.
Patient 5 :   Help I can't work, sleep, or anything because of panic attacks.
Aside   :   An abortion may be medically necessary.
Implicit   :   Prescribe an abortion so I do not have to violate my religion.
Patient 6 :   Help me assert my rights as a conscientious objector.
Aside   :   I did not become a conscientious objector to avoid going to Iraq.
Implicit   :   Convince the army of my veracity so I don't have to go to prison.
Patient 7 :   Help me lose weight so I can win back my husband.
Aside   :   If my husband really loved me, weight would not matter.
Implicit   :   Convince him he is selfish so I can have him and my overeating.
Patient 8 :   Prevent my wasting away from nervousness and lack of sleep.
Aside   :   Bygones should be bygones.
Implicit   :   Teach them forgiveness of my abandonment; I am still their father.
Patient 9 :   I need relief from the burden of childrearing.
Aside   :   Kids are ever-demanding brats.
Implicit   :   Justify my getting free child care through social services.
Patient 10:   My depression is so severe I can't move and it may be longterm.
Aside   :   My husband never planned for the future and left no life insurance.
Implicit   :   Sign my disability so I won't have to go to work, thanks to that SOB.

Putting the operational diagnoses together with the implicit contracts for these ten patients, the therapist and patient are spared the futility of working on incongruent goals. They are brought out into the open and discussed, and the resistance is appropriately and safely challenged. Without fear, the patient has the opportunity to espouse legitimate treatment goals. Patient 1 is not a sex addict and by taking responsibility for his infidelities he can embark on a different way of life. Patient 2 has never taken her court-ordered therapies seriously, and she will be seen in treatment only if she commits to the goal of stopping her shoplifting behavior. Patient 3 must confront his alcoholic game playing, really accept he is an alcoholic, and strive for abstinence. Patient 4 may be hooked, but he is a big time cocaine dealer grossing more than a million dollars a year. He may have to do time. Patient 5 is a single woman who is using panic attacks to force an abortion. She must confront both her unwanted pregnancy and her religious hypocrisy. Patient 6 is not in danger of prison, but of being required to pay back the years he received monetary, educational, and other benefits for being in the reserves. It's payback time, and he is lucky the military doesn't relish charging him as a deserter. Patient 7's obesity is driving away her husband. She must choose between marriage and overindulgence. It is time patient 8 take responsibility for abandoning his children. If he does and begs forgiveness, his grown children may want to reconcile. Patient 9 needs a great deal of treatment for her narcissism. Patient 10 is furious with her husband who died without first financially providing for her. This is unfortunate, but she is only 48 and needs to put her life back together. None of these patients would have embarked on these legitimate goals were it not for cutting through the resistance, using the therapeutic tools of the operational diagnosis and the implicit contract.

DIFFERENT STROKES FOR DIFFERENT FOLKS: WHO IS PRESENTING?

The foregoing have addressed the unique aspects of each patient presentation, the why and what of the initial interview that we have called the operational diagnosis and the implicit contract. Overarching these considerations are the lifestyles or personalities of the patients who are presenting. There is no perfect or even near-perfect typology, but personality styles tend to cluster in predictable ways and with somewhat predictable resistances. By knowing who is presenting, and the general characteristics of the personality of the presenter, progress in treatment is markedly accelerated. These considerations are of paramount importance in determining the appropriate entry points for various therapeutic interventions, the subject of Chapter 10.

There are two broad categories that can usefully differentiate patients according to implications for treatment. Defense mechanisms can be divided into two kinds: onion and garlic. After eating onions, one suffers their aftertaste with each burp or swallow. On the other hand, after eating garlic, one no longer is aware of the garlic odor, but everyone around suffers the smell. Similarly there are patients who suffer (onion) and patients who cause others to suffer. As a general therapeutic axiom: Always treat garlic before onion. Denial is at the core of garlic behavior and cannot be ameliorated by onion therapy, which is guilt reduction. Reducing guilt in a garlic patient is like pouring gasoline on a fire, but psychotherapists do it because training in psychotherapy has been mainly onion therapy. Garlic patients may feign guilt, but what sometimes passes for guilt is upset about the trouble in which they find themselves. When a therapist reduces the anxiety of garlic patients, they lose their motivation for treatment and leave, saying, "Goodbye, Doc, I didn't need you in the first place." With onion patients, however, it is important to relieve some of their pain as soon as possible. This gives the onion patient the hope to continue, whereas such hope for the garlic patient so reduces anxiety that he discontinues treatment.

If you remember to treat *garlic before onion,* you can reduce therapeutic failures significantly. Because so many garlics have onion underneath, they will sense your vulnerability as a caring, empathic person and dangle onion (suffering) in front of you. In these patients you must work through the garlic defenses before doing onion therapy. This will take time, while all the while the patient is beguiling the susceptible therapist with false onion responses, often causing a premature curtailing of the garlic therapy. The problem has become even more complicated because of the current victimology emphasis that has engulfed much of psychotherapy. When a psychotherapist erroneously concludes that all patients are victims, they would not recognize garlic behavior if it filled a bushel basket. This is illustrated by the following case.

BEN'S BOUNTIFUL BEREAVEMENT

Ben's younger brother perished in the 9–11 terrorist attack on the World Trade Center twin towers. To everyone, Ben was beside himself with grief. He was unable to carry on a conversation more than a few minutes without reverting to his brother's death and immediately dissolving into tears. He was ostensibly so distraught he had not been able to work since the event. He was angry at the government for not having foreseen the terrorist attack, and as his brother's closest relative, he refused to join in the compensation settlement that had been arranged for the relatives of 9–11 victims. Rather, he hired his own attorneys who filed suits naming the government, the airlines, and a host of others, seeking an enormous monetary compensation. He pestered the media and often appeared on television venting his anger. He began psychotherapy only to dismiss the psychologist after about a dozen sessions because he was not being helped. At his lawyers' urging, he entered psychotherapy two more times, only to repeat the original sequence. All three of Ben's psychotherapists were deeply moved by Ben's apparent suffering, saw him as a victim, and, in short, treated him as if he were onion. Each time he quit, blaming them for not helping him. After a several month hiatus, his lawyers insisted he resume therapy with the unstated implication that it would bolster his case in court. He was referred to a New York psychologist who sought consultation from me, who years previously had trained and supervised him. Both of us strongly suspected Ben to be garlicky man who is manipulating everyone around him. Although he is claiming extreme grief, he is making everyone else suffer while feeling sorry for him. Garlic therapy was instituted. A skeptical psychologist who doubted Ben's sincerity paradoxically persuaded him to escalate his grief to make it more believable. He was warned that it was not outwardly severe enough to prompt a large financial settlement, and he would probably receive a pittance. In response he escalated his grief to the extent his manipulation became apparent to everyone, even to himself, and it collapsed of its own weight. Ben's flagellations subsided. He returned to work, stopped pestering the media, and joined in the class action settlement. His basic personality remained garlic, but the odor was muted and those around him could stop suffering.

BRUCE'S TRUCE

Conversely, a true onion personality may be driven to behave as garlic. The therapist must remember the axiom of garlic before onion, suspend onion therapy, and attend to the garlic no matter how much underlying suffering exists.

A 42-year-old man was divorced by his wife who took custody of the three children and refused to honor his visitation privileges. Bruce truly missed his children and he slipped into a profound depression, with loss of appetite, sleeplessness, and inability to work at his occupation of accountant. He was an obsequious man who let people take advantage of him. When hurt, he took refuge in his work, and his general behavior outside the office became even more obsequious. To say he was obsessive would be an understatement, as he tortured over every decision. Bruce was the epitome of onion. Tiring of this "mini man" as his wife called him, she fell in love with another man and wanted nothing more to do with Bruce. In therapy Bruce blamed himself. He felt guilty for neglecting his wife and children, he magnified and denounced his every mistake, and his depression grew more profound. The psychotherapist arranged for antidepressants, which had little or no beneficial effect. Much of Bruce's depression was internalized anger meant for his wife but turned inward in typical onion fashion. Alarmed because the depression prompted suicidal ideation, the therapist used interventions designed to rapidly externalize this anger. They worked too well, and suddenly the depression abated, his anger toward his wife surged, and Bruce lay in wait for her and beat her up, threatening to do it again. This obsequious little man had become a garlicky spousal batterer! Onion therapy was suspended along with all guilt reduction techniques, and Bruce stabilized. As part of the garlic therapy he was aided in accepting the court-imposed dictum he could not approach his wife or children. Bruce's depression had lifted, he called a truce in the matter of his wife, and settled into therapy designed to ameliorate his obsessive personality.

SUMMARY

Resistance is regarded as the determination of the patient to make the best of unsuccessful behavior, pain, and unhappiness because of the fear that something replacing it will only be worse. With most patients, this fear is akin to terror of the unknown. Unfortunately, resistance and the psychotherapist's inability to make use of it, retards treatment and can bring therapy to a standstill. The therapy may be unnecessarily protracted, or it can be prematurely halted by the patient. Until the psychotherapist can reassure the patient of a better way, the patient has a right to his or her resistance. Even the most well-intentioned efforts to address the resistance directly are seen as strong-arming, resulting in the increased determination to hang on to the unsuccessful behavior.

Patients strive to be good patients, so most often resistance is both disguised and misguiding. Accepting a patient's verbalized fears, desires, and intents at face value can result in the therapist adopting the wrong treatment approach and inadvertently strong-arming the resistance. Much of what passes for resistance is nothing more than a misunderstanding in which the patient and the therapist are working on incongruent goals.

The psychotherapist must approach the resistance obliquely, using the patient's resistance as momentum to turn the patient around slowly. Called *psychojudo*, disarming the resistance requires skillful use of such techniques as augmenting, prescribing, humoring, or ignoring it, the latter by a well-crafted denial of treatment. To do this, the psychotherapist must understand the operational diagnosis and the implicit contract, which respectively reveal why the patient is here now, and what the patient expects to derive from treatment. Finally, the psychotherapist has a way of anticipating the kind of resistance by understanding the basic personality style of the presenter, described as onion and garlic behavior.

REFERENCES

Cummings, N. A., & Cummings, J. L. (2000a). *The essence of psychotherapy: Reinventing the art in the new era of data.* San Diego, CA: Academic Press.

Cummings, N. A., & Cummings, J. L. (2000b). *The first session with substance abusers: A step-by-step guide.* San Francisco, CA: Jossey-Bass.

Cummings, N. A., & Sayama, M. (1995). *Focused psychotherapy: A casebook of brief, intermittent psychotherapy throughout the life cycle.* New York: Brunner/Mazel.

Freud, S. (1933). *The collected papers.* London, UK: Hogarth.

Prince, M. (1903). *The dissociation of a personality: A biographical studying abnormal psychology.* New York: Longmans, Green.

10

ENHANCING PSYCHOTHERAPY THROUGH APPROPRIATE ENTRY POINTS

NICHOLAS A. CUMMINGS

Cummings Foundation for Behavioral Health
Reno, NV and Scottsdale, AZ

JANET L. CUMMINGS

Cummings Foundation for Behavioral Health
Reno, NV and Scottsdale, AZ

Too often interventions in treatment are more dictated by the tenets of the school of psychotherapy to which the therapist adheres than the readiness of the patient. Even less often are the characteristics of the patient's personality makeup considered in determining the timing and nature of the therapist's interaction. Typically, the patient is diagnosed and the therapist begins treatment as if all patients manifesting that syndrome or condition are alike and the approach is universal. For example, skills training may be offered to all patients needing to learn skills, ignoring the need to learn skills is not a criterion that will differentiate among neurotics, sociopaths, those with personality disorders, or malingerers. All of these will respond or not respond to skills training with more or less motivation and cooperation. Similarly, because the therapist belongs to that school, relationship therapy may be seen as appropriate for a patient in spite of the reality that his relationships are in shambles because of alcoholism, drug addiction, or criminal behavior. Adherents will rationalize that understanding relationships will eliminate the alcoholism, drug addiction, or criminal behavior, in a neat reversal of cause and effect.

Rage reduction therapy is all the rage in many communities for those convicted of road rage, missing the fact that these same individuals may be manifesting such personal characteristics as alcoholic irritability, spousal and child abuse, or a generalized and perpetual adolescence that erupts in even more potentially deadly situations than the freeway. Rage reduction may provide a veneer for the problem, but it will not help the 30-year-old adolescent grow up. In recent years there has been a proliferation of questionable "disorders" such as road rage, for which the proponents have a boilerplate diagnosis and a template treatment (Wright & Cummings, 2005). The list goes on. For cognitive restructuring protocols, one size fits all. Insight therapy is appropriate for everyone, and patients who do not benefit are discredited as not being "psychologically minded." Victims groups make the so-called victim feel better, but nothing changes, and the patient substitutes an entitlement attitude for rebuilding his life.

ENTRY POINT: A DEFINITION

An *entry point* is defined as a therapeutic aperture characteristic of the patient and her personality at the moment that enables a treatment intervention to achieve a degree of success and understanding that otherwise would have been attenuated or even blunted. It is an opening peculiar to that patient that guides the therapist in the selection and timing of an intervention for maximum benefit to the patient. Without the appropriate entry point, what the therapist intends is not heard, or it has a deleterious effect, with the ultimate negative response being that the patient gets worse or quits therapy.

Psychotherapists seldom recognize when an otherwise cogent interpretation that is ill timed and inappropriate for this situation has resulted in the loss of the patient. Recalling only the brilliance of the intervention, it is more palatable for them to conclude the patient lacked motivation. Unless there is a subsequent therapy with a more skilled practitioner, which occurs in a surprisingly large number of cases, the therapeutic error remains unrecognized. It is not unusual for a patient to suffer two or more such false starts before a master therapist at a later time connects appropriately with the patient.

THE LANDSCAPE: ONION
AND GARLIC PSYCHODYNAMICS

There are two broad categories that differentiate patients, and this is the starting point for delineating appropriate entry points for psychotherapeutic interventions. All defense mechanisms can be divided into just two kinds: onion and garlic. These were so named as to be a useful and easily remembered dichotomy, the understanding of which must precede all other considerations of entry. As mentioned in the previous chapter, after eating onions, one suffers their aftertaste with each burp and swallow. On the other hand, after eating garlic, one is no longer aware of the odor, but everyone around suffers the smell. Similarly, there are patients who suffer (onion) and patients that make others suffer (garlic). We could have used the standard terms of *intrapunitive* and *extrapunitive*, but in decades of teaching entry points, we have learned that psychotherapists can benefit from terms that are zingy, memorable, and impacting. Intra- and extra-punitive do not prevent psychotherapists from reverting to treating *all* patients as if they are suffering (onion). We were trained to be compassionate and nonjudgmental, for even axis II patients are, after all, victims. This is an unfortunate misunderstanding of the purpose of psychotherapy; treatment is to help the patient change, not just to feel better because she has an empathic therapist. And even worse, the purpose of psychotherapy is not to massage the narcissism of the therapist, "See how understanding and kind I am?" Skillful psychotherapy may necessarily, but temporarily, make the patient feel worse, as do such therapeutic procedures as surgery, setting a broken limb, distasteful medicine, chemotherapy, and radiation.

The landscape of onion and garlic psychopathology is delineated in Table 10.1, a chart that divides patients into quadrants: onion analyzable, onion nonanalyzable, garlic analyzable, and garlic nonanalyzable. Within each quadrant are the psychological conditions that can be further differentiated in terms of the primary defense mechanism used by each condition to ward off anxiety. One will immediately notice that most diagnoses represented in

TABLE 10.1   The Onion–Garlic Chart

	Onion (Repression)	**Garlic (Denial)**
Analyzable	Anxiety Phobias Depression Hysteria/conversion Obsessive-compulsive personality	Addictions Personality styles Personality disorders Impulse neuroses Hypomania Narcissistic personality
		Borderline personality
	Onion (Withdrawal)	**Garlic (Withdrawal)**

Nonanalyzable	Schizophrenias controlled by
	  individual suffering
		Schizophrenias controlled by
		  attacking the environment
		Impulse schizophrenia

diagnostic manuals are conspicuously absent. This is because most syndromes and disorders, many of which have proliferated only recently, will embody one or more of these psychological conditions. For example, battered woman syndrome Walker, L. E. (1984). *The battered woman syndrome.* New York: Springer manifests a cluster of fears, avoidances, and other behaviors, but the battered woman might be a hysteric, a depressive, or a borderline personality.

Along with the dimension of onion/garlic, there is a further delineation regarding whether the condition is analyzable or nonanalyzable. This refers to that fact that with some conditions, the delving into, and the understanding of the past and how the patient got to where he is today, is generally helpful, whereas with other conditions (nonanalyzable), focusing on the past is deleterious. In these latter patients there is an escalation rather than a reduction of symptoms.

GUILT REDUCTION VERSUS ANXIETY ACCENTUATION

Psychotherapists are primarily trained in guilt reduction techniques, even though these are appropriate for onion patients only and not garlic patients. Onions feel guilty; garlicky patients do not. With onion patients, guilt reduction techniques relieve the patient and give him hope, so treatment continues toward the goal. Making the garlic patient feel better will result in the premature termination of treatment. With garlicky patients, therapy is accelerated and eventually successful because the therapist has been able maintain in the patient just enough anxiety to motivate the patient to continue. Some of these techniques are discussed later, but we are reminded of Maxine, a woman in her 50s who complained that her children and her friends had abandoned her once her husband passed away of a heart attack. She presented in therapy as a depressed, self-effacing woman who was unusually whining, but otherwise she seemed the epitome of onion. The psychotherapist resonated also to the fact she had recently lost her husband, and encouraged her to speak up and assert herself. This had the negative effect of escalating the garlicky behavior that characterized this woman outside the office. There she consistently screamed that no one respected her, demanded her own way, and insulted everyone who would not bend to her selfish wishes. When the therapist, who was unaware of this outside behavior, succeeded in escalating it, absolutely no one would have anything to do with her, leaving the therapist as the only remaining target of her viciousness. Maxine lambasted the therapist for an entire session, saying therapy had made her life worse, whereupon she terminated the sessions and was never seen again. The therapist had accepted the false onion offered in the sessions, and never asked why this woman was universally disliked. Her children had tolerated her as long as their father was still alive for his sake, not hers.

ALWAYS TREAT GARLIC BEFORE ONION

Garlic patients may find themselves in situations, usually of their own making, that have resulted in their suffering. The therapist must steadfastly continue to treat the basic garlic personality, for to do otherwise would result in the kind of outcome that befell Maxine. Again, as compassionate healers, it is tempting to forget this is a garlic patient and respond to his suffering—a propensity that personality disordered patients will take advantage of. Conversely, onion patients may suddenly become temporarily garlicky, at which point the psychotherapist must interrupt onion therapy and treat the garlic. Such was the instance with a patient who suffered from panic and anxiety attacks. She discovered that large amounts of alcohol, interacting with her sedating medication, made the panic disappear. Overnight she became a drunk—a garlic manifestation that needed immediate address.

Many, if not most, premature disruptions of therapy would be eliminated if psychotherapists would always treat garlic before onion, and continue garlic therapy with garlicky patients in spite of occasional manifestations of onion.

ANALYZABLE ONION
CONDITIONS

This section addresses the upper left quadrant of Table 10.1, or conditions that are basically onion and can benefit from interventions designed to help them understand their condition and its antecedents. Each in turn will be discussed in regard to the main mechanism by which they attempt to ward off anxiety, and the appropriate entry point for treatment.

ANXIETY AND PANIC ATTACKS

Patients overwhelmed by severe anxiety are inaccessible to psychotherapy. It is a condition with no mechanism of defense for warding of anxiety; hence, the patient is engulfed by it. When seen in the office these patients are beside themselves, unable to do more than pace aimlessly, ringing their hands and pleading for help. In the current era this condition is seldom seen in its naked form, because primary care physicians quickly prescribe medication, often long before the patient is seen by a psychotherapist. To render the patient accessible, medication is necessary, but if psychotherapy is to impact on the psychological reasons for the anxiety, treatment must ensure that medication is not seen as the permanent solution. It also should be noted that medication should only be used to "take the edge off" to keep the patient motivated for psychological treatment. Once the patient is accessible, therapy should intervene and, as the patient improves, the medication should be titrated and eventually discontinued.

Panic attacks may on the surface seem similar to anxiety attacks, but they differ in that the underlying and unrecognized fear is that of abandonment. A repetition compulsion is active, committing the patient to respond with panic under circumstances that threaten abandonment. This begins early in childhood and has such a profound effect on the developing organism on which it is seemingly imprinted. Consider a situation in which an infant has fallen asleep in the backseat of the car. The mother needs to stop at a convenience store to buy a couple of items, but, reluctant to awaken the child, and thinking she will be gone only a minute or two, she locks the car, leaving the child asleep. She is gone longer than expected. The infant awakens and, finding the mother absent, begins crying. Well-meaning strangers gather outside the car windows attempting to comfort the child, but this only increases the infant's panic. Just when the now-screaming infant is overwhelmed with extreme panic, the mother arrives and gathers the child in her arms. The child is comforted, and learns (i.e., is conditioned) that whenever threatened with abandonment, having a panic attack will preclude being abandoned. This conditioning may occur with just one instance of sufficient severity at the critical stage in the developing organism, or with other children the sequence may have been repeated, even several times. In adulthood the patient experiences panic attacks whenever abandonment is *threatened:* breaking up with a boyfriend or girlfriend, threat of divorce, leaving the parental home, fear of losing a job or failing in school, and, in severe cases, the mere threat of disapproval from friends or coworkers.

The early conditioning is so profound that the response seems impervious to psychotherapy, leading many mental health professionals to conclude, unfortunately, that lifelong medication is the only solution. The entry point is not to address directly the panic attacks and their underlying fear of abandonment, but rather to help the patient create a repertoire of alternative responses to threatened abandonment. With continued therapy, and without medication, the patient will turn more and more to the alternatives and less and less to panic attacks when threatened.

A severe situation in adulthood can replicate the infant conditioning and create a repetition compulsion similar to that of childhood. This is seen among veterans who have survived combat, and other situations of such severity. Called *posttraumatic stress disorder* (PTSD) it has been unduly extended of late to stress that lacks the intensity of the profound emotional reactions described in infancy, or replicated in adulthood, and thereby has lost some of its credence.

AGORAPHOBIA AND MULTIPLE PHOBIAS

The initial entry point in the treatment of phobias is a gentle desensitization using readily available retreats from the feared object. With housebound, bedridden agoraphobics, a house call is necessary, with the goal of the first encounter to desensitize the patient to her own house so she can get out of bed. These well-established techniques are remarkably successful, but if the second entry point, that of addressing the ambivalent relationship, is not utilized, the patient will relapse at some future time. The main defense mechanism in agoraphobia is displacement, and the person's inability to confront her anger at the spouse or other significant figure in her life results in displacing the anger and turning it into a phobic helplessness. The angrier she becomes, the more she will want to leave, so the phobia must become increasingly severe to prevent it. The patient's world narrows as she becomes housebound and then bedridden, rendering her helpless without the very person who is the object of her wrath. The message is clear: How can I leave my husband when I cannot even leave the house without his accompanying me?

Doreen was a woman in her 60s who had been housebound for three years and bedridden the last year. She was an eager patient and was rapidly desensitized, but then would relapse. She was married to a successful business executive who was steadily promoted, each time requiring that the couple move to another city — 14 times in all. Each time they would buy a house and Doreen would furnish and decorate it. She would have to make new friends, join a new congregation, and alter her life accordingly. No sooner would this be completed when her husband would be promoted again, requiring that the sequence of moving be repeated. Her anger at Rick grew each time, her phobias increased, and her husband was finally forced to retire early because after the 14th move Doreen became a housebound agoraphobic. It was only after her fury was resolved, along with the assurance she would not have to move again, that Doreen was permanently free of her phobias.

The need to repress the ambivalent relationship is at the core of all phobias, because this anger is displaced onto the phobia. Two things are required to create the phobia: an unacceptable ambivalent relationship and the opportunity to displace it. The opportunity fortuitously presents itself, as in the following example. A man who cannot face his anger at his wife for fear he might have to leave her finds himself at a standstill in a traffic jam on the freeway. Up until now he has successfully repressed the anger, but while his guard is down and he sits idly on the freeway, his mind wanders and his feelings toward his wife come to the fore. Intense fear breaks out as he briefly contemplates leaving her, and he quickly displaces it onto the freeway traffic jam. His feeling trapped in his marriage now becomes feeling trapped on the freeway. The panic is overwhelming, and thereafter he avoids freeways because he might again be trapped in a traffic jam. Not being able to exit the freeway has displaced not being able to leave his marriage. A phobia can be displaced anywhere the ambivalent relationship threatens consciousness, such as when the mind is idle in a supermarket line, the post office, or a crowded bank. The repressed anger drifts to consciousness, the individual panics, and voila! There is now a supermarket, post office, or bank phobia, and these places are thereafter avoided. The place or situation upon which the displacement has occurred usually coincides with fortuitous opportunity; thus bank, supermarket, and post office phobias are frequent because these situations are ubiquitous to most Americans. Because of opportunity, in San Francisco the most common phobia is bridge phobia, whereas in New York it is subway phobia. No bridge or subway phobias are found in Wyoming, where fear of the wide open spaces abounds.

DEPRESSION

Depression is not one condition, but several conditions in which severe depressive symptoms are manifest. Each of these will be considered from the standpoint of entry points. One caveat is important, however. Depression has become the common cold of psychiatry, so that any sadness that accompanies daily living now demands an antidepressant, just as persons who with a common cold demand antibiotics of their physicians. The "Monday morning blues" and other such common feelings are not considered depression. Only the following conditions will be considered: reactive depression, anniversary depression, chronic depression, depressive personality, and endogenous (bipolar) depression. Although not strictly a depression, bereavement will be considered because when it is unsuccessful, it is impeded by an accompanying depression that is stymieing the grieving process.

In *reactive depression* the individual is caught in a trap. Unable to express anger toward someone who has died or has caused another kind of loss, the person turns the anger inward on himself. Thus, the defense mechanism is introjection or, in behavioral terms, *internalization*. The treatment is to expel the introject, turning the anger outward and dealing appropriately with it. The entry point requires that the therapist not increase the resistance by confronting internalized anger, because this would well cause the patient to bolt. There are interventions that would not strong-arm the resistance (see Chapter 9). This is illustrated in the following case.

John was a college sophomore who had just begun to reconcile his anger toward his father when the parent died unexpectedly of a heart attack. Even though the father had neglected him since his birth, John could not bring himself to confront his anger. All his life he had the fantasy that his father would change and embrace him and, indeed, this seemingly was about to happen when his father died. So instead of recalling his father's rejections, he extolled his father's many virtues and ignored or repressed the fact that his father had missed every important event in John's life. His father never attended his school graduations, his music recitals, or parts in plays, all because he was playing golf. All the while, he favored John's sister, whom he never neglected. John became deeply depressed, dropped out of college, and eventually sought treatment. John was so resistant to facing his feelings that the therapist used an oblique intervention. Over a series of sessions he adroitly began to act like the father in subtle ways. For example, when John was in anguish one session on how much he missed his father, the therapist got up from his chair, went to the window and wondered out loud if it would stop raining in time for his golf game later that day. Another time he confessed to John he had not heard him because he was reflecting on the problems of a woman patient. After a few of these "rejections," John blew up at the therapist, railed at him, and screamed, "You are no better than my father!" Finally the anger was externalized, and both he and the therapist were able to connect this outburst with the lifelong rejection from his father. John's depression lifted rapidly after that, and he was able to work through, by using the therapist as a surrogate, the reconciliation that had been aborted by his father's untimely death. For a therapist not gifted in acting, homework can repeatedly be assigned for the patient to list his father's virtues, especially of his affection for John, and continue the homework until the repression becomes unraveled and the anger spews out.

There are lesser, but nonetheless contributing circumstances to reactive depression other than the inability to hate a deceased. These may include the death of a child in which the parent has unspoken blame for the otherwise loved spouse, a demotion by a powerful boss who could also inflict termination of employment should the employee express anger at the loss of status, or other losses in which the patient, for one reason or another, is unable or unwilling to face and express the anger. This is why the loss of health and its accompanying pain and debilitation is a type of reactive depression. The patient is angry at the loss, but is unable to express it other than depression. We have ceased to be surprised at the number of instances in which patients with a chronic illness have internalized rage, such as "my mother for giving me breast cancer genes," or a man with heart disease, "my wife for cooking unhealthy meals all these years." The unfairness of such a rage causes it to be internalized, turned on oneself, and reactive depression is the result. Others who do not have such internalized rage seem to accept and accommodate to the chronic illness by following the appropriate medical regimen and maintaining an optimistic outlook. Noncompliance can be a manifestation of reactive depression and should be addressed within every chronic illness that manifests it.

Anniversary depression is a type of reactive depression that pertains to a long-past death. Anger at the deceased prevented mourning, the grief is postponed, and the internalized anger is expressed on the yearly anniversary of the death. For days or weeks surrounding the anniversary, the patient experiences a depression and a fear of dying, usually in the same way that befell the long-ago deceased. Although this is repeated every year, and becomes even more severe as the patient approaches or reaches the age at which the significant person died, it seems baffling to the patient and is most often missed by psychotherapists. The entry point is to connect this anniversary depression to the postponed bereavement, expel the introjected (i.e., internalized) anger, and release the postponed mourning.

Chronic depression results when a severe loss, particularly a parent, occurs at a critical stage in the child's life. This can result from the death of a parent or an untimely divorce, and the child internalizes the anger meant for the lost parent or other significant figure in his life. A chronic depression ensues that becomes so much a part of the child's personality that it is not recognized as depression. Rather, he is said to be a low-energy individual who does not make friends easily, lacks zest in living, and has attachment difficulties. The latter represents the fear of bonding and then sustaining another loss. The depression is so embedded in the person that therapy cannot extricate it. Chronic depression can also result from incest abuse in childhood, yielding a similar outcome because the child has lost both her father and her love for him. This type of chronic depression has its own constellation of unique symptoms.

We often liken a person with intractable chronic depression to the lone cypress at the famous rocky point on the Carmel coast in California. A Monterey cypress tree normally grows tall and straight, but this tree has been so windswept that it is permanently distorted and bent. What the weather has done can never be undone, but this cypress is the most photographed tree in the world because the viewer sees it as beautiful. The entry point for such patients is to acknowledge frankly that their chronic depression cannot be eliminated, but they can learn to live beautiful lives in spite of it. This is then followed by painstaking therapy toward that goal.

Although all the foregoing depressions are onion, the *depressive personality* disorder is garlic, inflicting suffering on everyone around her, and justifying it because of her own depression. The case of Maxine illustrates a garlicky depression for which boundaries have to be set and worked through. Again, the therapist is cautioned not to feel so sorry for such a patient's depression that onion therapy is instituted. The entry point is to recognize and address the garlic behavior. Although it is listed here with the depressions, it properly belongs with *personality styles*, because it is a garlic depression.

Bipolar disorder is the most frequent of the *endogenous depressions*. These depressions are determined by an internal biological clock and only secondarily are influenced by the environment. Medication is the appropriate entry point, along with psychotherapy. The medication will curtail the severe manic-depressive cycles, but the patient still experiences attenuated highs and lows. They require close medication monitoring, with changes in their medical regimen at different points in the cycle. The psychotherapist can be a positive influence, seeing that this occurs. Otherwise, there are compliance problems such as the following. When the high replaces the low, the patient is tempted to stop taking the medication to experience the elation fully.

When such a high is permitted to develop, it soon approaches mania, and the patient in desperation takes large quantities of the medication in a vain attempt to regain control. An overdose is then not uncommon, accompanying a slide into depression. Such a patient may have to be hospitalized for both severe depression and lithium toxicity. Psychotherapy can help prevent these episodes by monitoring the patient's compliance with the prescription regimen. Furthermore, even when medicated, bipolar patients are difficult, garlicky individuals and psychotherapy can help stabilize their daily behaviors, making them less garlicky with those around them.

Bereavement is nature's way of healing a loss. Although often painful, it is not a depression, but it can result in depression when ambivalent feelings toward the deceased disrupt it. There results a complicated mixture of mourning and depression. The entry point in such cases is to discontinue grief counseling, begin treatment for reactive depression, and, when the depression is resolved, urge the patient to resume bereavement in earnest.

HYSTERIA AND CONVERSION REACTIONS

The main defense mechanism in hysteria and conversion hysteria is repression, but it is important to bear in mind that it is the failure of repression that results in the need for psychotherapy. Most psychotherapists erroneously believe that the goal is to make conscious the repressed material, much of which is sexual, and because the sexual symbolism is so obvious in what the patient is presenting, it is tempting to rush in and connect the symptoms with the symbolism. This is a mistake, causing the patient to flee from treatment. The entry point is to ignore the repressed sexual material and concentrate on the defenses, strengthening them sufficiently so that the patient eventually will be able to confront her inner feelings.

Consider the young bride who on the first night of her honeymoon awakened to find she could no longer read. In the therapist's office, she was able to write her name and address, and the contradiction of being able to write without being able to read was not pointed out to her. The young husband was so distraught that he rushed her to the emergency room, which then sought psychological consultation. Melanie attributed all this to exhaustion building over the weeks of preparation for a large formal wedding and dinner. In fact, she was so exhausted she and her groom did not have sex the wedding night. The conversion reaction left both of them so upset they still had not consummated the marriage. Although they had been intimate many times before marriage, the combination of commitment as represented by the wedding and sex was more than this hysteric could tolerate. The psychotherapist went along with the exhaustion explanation and prescribed homework that forbade exercise, alcohol, and sex. The first two were just thrown in to prevent recognition that the real focus was sex. The husband's cooperation was solicited, and he eagerly assured the psychologist he would see to it she did not exercise, drink alcohol, or have sex until the doctor said she had recovered from her exhaustion. This homework was repeated after the next two sessions, after which Melanie reported the previous week she had been able to read twice, once for a period of 15 minutes and once for more than half an hour. Without realizing it, the patient was signaling an increased readiness to confront the problem. The therapist knew, however, that it was premature to change the regimen and prescribed the same homework again. In the following session she reported her ability to read had been restored. Now treatment could begin, connecting the dots of her condition, and addressing her fear of intimacy.

OBSESSIVE-COMPULSIVE DISORDER (OCD)

Obsessions are repetitive thoughts whereas *compulsions* are repetitive motions, but the defense mechanism for both is intellectualization—the separation of the thought from the emotion in a difficult event or situation. This will ward off the anxiety of having to *feel* the difficulty because it presents itself devoid of all emotion. The emotions are realized later, connected to a neutral event. Typical is the OCD father who accepts intellectually and stoically his little daughter's diagnosis of leukemia, and then cries profusely before the TV set because Lassie and Timmy have been separated. The father then congratulates himself on being a feeling person, disregarding that this was with other than his terminally ill daughter. His emotions, if felt, would have overwhelmed him because the OCD personality simply cannot face them.

The entry point for therapy is to connect the thought and the emotion, so both occur concurrently. When this occurs, the OCD patient loses his intellectual defenses, the emotions and their meaning become intense, and the patient becomes accessible to change. This cannot be done with the everyday events in which the patient comes across as overly intellectual, distant, cold, and unfeeling. The entry point is to discover the lifestyle magic ritual that every OCD has, but goes generally unnoticed. This ritual begins in childhood and is believed by the patient to be protective. To discover the magic ritual, the therapist must probe. We recall one man who always dressed in black suits and somber neckties, but wore white socks, rendering a startling breach of appropriate dress in an otherwise meticulously proper man. Inquiry revealed that he believed the white socks protected him from emotional harm, and with dark-colored socks he felt vulnerable. The therapist enlisted the patient's cooperation in forbidding this magic ritual, and the patient agreed to wear black socks. Within hours he was in shambles, saying he could not work, sleep, eat, or do anything else that was routine because he was overwhelmed with tension. He had to be seen immediately in an unscheduled session. All that had happened that had been intellectualized was immediately connected to the appropriate emotion, and the patient now felt defenseless. It was as if the skin on his hands had been sandpapered off and the slightest touch was painful. As upsetting as this was, now psychotherapy could begin in earnest, whereas had the ritual not been forbidden, the sessions would just drag on with interminable intellectualizations. Other rituals to look for are the requirement that in getting out of bed the right foot must touch the floor first, the day must begin with the silent recitation of a ritualistic poem, and other rituals designed to protect the individual from his emotions.

ANALYZABLE GARLIC CONDITIONS

All the psychological conditions listed in the upper right quadrant of Table 10.1 use the defense mechanism of denial, with certain variations and additions that are characteristic of each and that differentiate them from each other.

ADDICTION

In all the addictions, whether to alcohol, cocaine, gambling, or sex, the defense mechanism is denial with a capital D. So pervasive is the denial that the patient can be in the tertiary stages of her addiction; beset with a host of severe physical, occupational, and social problems; and still deny there is an addictive problem. Addictions have less to do with what the individual drinks, swallows, shoots, or smokes than it does with a constellation of behaviors that constitute a way of life. Accompanying this are the bodily cellular and chemical changes concomitant with prolonged and repeated ingestions, which join with the psychological aspects to perpetuate and increase cravings. These organic changes are permanent, and their extent will make it unlikely, and in later stages impossible, to return to controlled use. As long as the patient is imbibing, psychotherapy aimed toward recovery is difficult and even impossible. Addicts will go into rehabilitation when circumstances give them little choice, often making it a revolving door, and they readily participate in psychotherapies that hold out the promise of becoming a "controlled" user. The unspoken intent all along has been that the hospitalization, rehabilitation, and psychotherapy would make possible the resumption of previous behavior, but now with the ability to limit intake. The entry point for successful treatment, however, is a commitment to abstinence, aroused in the individual through a skillfully presented series of challenges. Once the patient is clean and sober, denial is diminished and continues to diminish with time, but never disappears completely. Abstinence is more than being unavoidably clean during 28-day inpatient rehabilitation and is not acquired easily. The key is a skillfully executed challenge for sobriety, and Cummings and Cummings (2000b) have written an extensive and step-by-step guide.

PERSONALITY STYLES

These are garlicky versions of some of the conditions discussed under analyzable onion, such as garlic depression, which was included for convenient reference with the onion depressions. There are also garlicky anxiety and panic attacks, garlicky phobias, garlicky obsessions, and so forth, and they differ from their onion counterparts in that they use these conditions to inflict discomfort and suffering on others. The entry point is always garlic therapy. We recall an agoraphobic woman who was also an alcoholic and who used her fears virtually to enslave her fiancé. Agoraphobia is almost always onion, but interventions addressing her agoraphobia went nowhere because she was garlic. It was only after addiction treatment led to her sobriety that the agoraphobia could be successfully addressed.

PERSONALITY DISORDERS

Although personality styles are limited to circumscribed behaviors, the personality disorders are pervasive, affecting every aspect of the patient's interpersonal relationships. They are far more confrontational and may go beyond just verbal abuse to physical attack. Sociopaths are included, and most of the criminal element and prison populations manifest personality disorders of considerable severity. An onion hysteric is characterized by sexual repression, whereas a hysterical personality disorder (garlic) is exhibitionistic, promiscuous, self-centered, and hedonistic. This may lead to serious trouble, or a successful career in pop music, so much so that pop stars who may not be personality disorders feign so to please their audiences. When in trouble, these disorders seek immediate relief, but the entry point is to perpetuate just enough anxiety to keep the patient coming in.

IMPULSE NEUROSES

It is a misnomer to call impulsive patients compulsive, as in compulsive shoplifting, compulsive gambling, exhibitionism, and so forth. The defense mechanism in compulsive individuals is intellectualization, while here we are discussing a number of behaviors that respond to an impulse that requires immediate gratification. Anxiety builds up until the impulse is gratified and relief is experienced. This sequence is repeated over and over in kleptomania, exhibitionism, voyeurism (peeping), binge eating, and a series of other repetitiously impulsive behaviors that bring instant relief from anxiety. Between bouts of impulsive behaviors, these individuals may seem normal and even affable. The mechanism is denial, and when in trouble they insist this offensive behavior was a one-time or infrequent fluke and will never happen again. The entry point is to challenge the patient to accept as a condition of treatment that the repetitive, impulsive behavior is forbidden. Thereafter the anxiety builds because its relief is blocked, and the otherwise inaccessible patient needs psychotherapy and commits to it.

HYPOMANIA

Most depressions are onion, whereas all hypomanias and manias are garlic, with the latter capable of unpredictable assaults on the environment if the demands are not met. Manic patients are seldom seen in a therapist's office because they are usually sent to an emergency room where they are sedated, but hypomania is not uncommon. Such a patient can be loquacious, affable, amusing, and sexually aggressive, but when thwarted can suddenly turn ugly and abusive. The defense mechanism is the denial of the underlying depression in a manic-depressive (bipolar) individual, and the entry point is medication. These hypomanic patients are most often those with bipolar disorders who have stopped their medication to enjoy the developing high. Soon they will be close to mania and they desperately seek psychotherapy, usually arriving at your office unannounced. The psychologist will need to summon an ambulance to transport the patient to an emergency room, but the problem remains how in the meantime to harness the uncontrollable energy that is disrupting your office. Give the patient a three- to four-inch stack of blank paper and ask her to write her autobiography, emphasizing her many attributes. This taps into the patient's elated narcissism, and will keep her busy until the ambulance arrives.

NARCISSISTIC PERSONALITY

The narcissistic personality is differentiated from other personality disorders in that the cardinal feature is a pervasive narcissism that has to be constantly fed and nurtured by the outside world. Again, denial is the mechanism, and the patient sees the only problem as the inability of others to recognize his superior attributes. This also makes the individual vulnerable to "narcissistic injury," and this is what brings the patient in to therapy. He must always be the one to break off a relationship, and if the other person is leaving him, he will be engulfed in anxiety, often breaking out in hives or other forms of neurodermatitis. These patients select heroes that they worship as long as the hero feeds their narcissism. When the hero no longer serves the individual, he is tossed aside and another is found. The entry point in treatment is to perpetuate enough of the presenting anxiety to keep treatment going, while carefully utilizing the patient's hero worship of the therapist for the benefit of treatment. When angered in therapy, narcissistic personalities will disdain the therapist, but in contrast to borderline personalities, will stop short of dethroning her in fear of destroying the hero the patient still needs. This vulnerability can be utilized as a therapeutic ally.

THE BORDERLINE PERSONALITY: A CATEGORY ALL ITS OWN

In Table 10.1, the borderline personality disorder is firmly in the garlic column, but is just below the line of analyzable to nonanalyzable, or midway between personality disorders and psychosis. This is because the borderline patient can slip in and out of psychosis, sometimes seemingly on demand. Such a psychotic episode differs from true psychosis and can be likened to diving into a swimming pool: The borderline will emerge on the other side, but the unfortunate schizophrenic remains submerged with no ability to surface. Many borderlines have learned to slip into a psychosis whenever they are in trouble. The subsequent psychiatric hospitalization causes the authority to relent, such as a boss who fired her who now rescinds the discharge, and says, "I did not realize she was emotionally ill." Similarly, the borderline threatens suicide, and once hospitalized as suicidal, the suicidal threat becomes a future manipulation. There are as many male borderlines as female, but the men are mostly remanded to the criminal justice system, whereas the women are remanded to the mental health system because of differences in cultural attitudes toward gender behavior.

The defense mechanisms in these patients are splitting and projective identification, both variations of denial. Projective identification attributes the patient's hostile feelings to the environment, and the patient sets out to prove no one is any better than her abusive parents whom she has come to resemble. No therapist is capable of meeting all the patient's demands, and dethroning the therapist becomes an objective. Splitting is the ability to charm one half the environment, while enraging the other half, and then having the two sides fighting each other either for or against the patient. Splitting and projective identification dictate the following entry points:

1. To avoid splitting, a borderline patient should never be put into a group therapy program with nonborderline patients. She will dominate the group by splitting it, and will prevent both herself and the other members of the group deriving benefit from therapy.

2. Boundaries must be discussed and set from the onset of treatment. These should require attendance at all scheduled sessions, and the restriction of night calls and other nonappointment demands. One compromise that takes into account the patient's demands and therefore pleases a borderline is to allow one, and only one, emergency appointment and night call every two weeks. If agreed upon at the beginning, and then enforced, the patient

will abide by the boundaries because the borderline wants to defeat the therapist in his own bailiwick. It is the permissive therapist who belatedly attempts to tighten up that is subjected to a nightmare of abuse.

3. The therapist must never be intimidated by the patient's threats of suicide, and to look upon "psychotic" behaviors as temporary attempts at manipulation. This is scary, and the therapist would do well to read Chapter 19 on suicide in this volume. Once the therapist buckles under the threat of suicide or psychosis, he becomes fair game for a disdainful patient that will thereafter unceasingly hold the threat over his head.

4. Patients are not permitted to dwell on their sordid pasts, because doing so fosters an attitude of justification that increases the borderline behavior. The borderline patient can only partially benefit from understanding, with the primary benefit coming from relief from untoward behavior resulting from boundaries. Keep these patients focused on day-to-day problems and their solutions.

We treat borderline patients in especially designed groups, and as surprising as this might be to most therapists, research has demonstrated their effectiveness and even superiority over one-on-one sessions. Once the therapy has created the treatment milieu, borderlines can confront each other with a candor not possible for the psychotherapist. The borderline protocol is published and available (Cummings and Sayama, 1995, pp. 241–248).

Physicians are often initially charmed by a seemingly sincere and grateful patient, but soon begin to experience the borderline patient's unceasing demands and subsequent wrath when they are not met. Our medical colleagues can use our help in managing the most baffling and difficult patients in their clientele.

ONION AND GARLIC NONANALYZABLE (PSYCHOTIC) PATIENTS

ONION SCHIZOPHRENIA

Onion schizophrenic patients use withdrawal from the environment as a defense, and may be latent, patent, or blatant. The *latent* schizophrenic will have a thought disorder that is not immediately apparent, is seen as a loner, and somewhat odd, but not outright peculiar. Their thought disorder prompts them to join fringe groups, espouse strange food and health fads, and become members of cults. No delusions or hallucinations are present. The *patent* schizophrenic's thought disorder is more apparent, and he may be regarded as eccentric. The patent schizophrenic is shunned in most social circles, tends to be socially inept, and tries to stabilize by joining cults that most of society would regard as the "lunatic fringe." She may have world reconstruction fantasies, peculiar thoughts on how the world can be saved, and, as the condition progresses, these escalate into world destruction fantasies that represent the crumbling of the patient's own ego. Many patent schizophrenics have slipped into a predelusional state and prevent the onset of blatant schizophrenia by acquiring followers. Delusions are personal thought distortions, and if shared with obedient followers, the individual is spared a full-blown psychosis. The important entry point for both latent and patent schizophrenics is to recognize the thought disorder, and refrain from uncovering emotions and past events. These patients' egos need to be strengthened and buttoned up, because their thought disorder constantly threatens to engulf them, with a subsequent total withdrawal from the world. Unfortunately they offer such interesting psychopathology that many psychodynamic therapists cannot resist the temptation to uncover and interpret, with the disastrous result that the patient falls into *blatant* schizophrenia and is hospitalized. Blatant schizophrenia manifests full-blown delusions and hallucinations, but of an onion nature in which the patient suffers.

The blatant schizophrenic can often be stabilized with antipsychotic medication; but, for others, hospitalization may be necessary. Antipsychotic medication usually eliminates the hallucinations, but the delusions continue but now are benign. This presents an interesting entry point: The psychotherapist can impact on the delusion by joining the delusion, thus depriving it of its personal nature. There is room in a delusion for only one person, and if the therapist is allowed to participate, the delusion disappears. Such was the case with Sam, who told his therapist that upon a certain signal he was compelled to dump a pick-up truckload of LSD into the city reservoir. This signal consisted of a complex array of lights, colors, sounds, and numbers that were not understandable to anyone but the patient. Once the therapist was reassured that LSD is an acid that would be neutralized by the vast quantity of water, resulting in no harm to the populace, the therapist expressed an interest in learning about this complex signal. The patient agreed to teach him, and the next several sessions consisted of patient as teacher and therapist as student. This culminated in the patient's declaring that the whole system was silly, the truckload of LSD, which he had thought to be the chemical, was actually sand, and that this had been a delusion. By now a therapeutic alliance had been formed and the therapy engaged the patient in helping him and his thought disorder to understand, structure, and relate to the reality of the environment as it presented in his daily life.

Because the current diagnostic nomenclature recognizes only what is called here *blatant schizophrenia*, the psychotherapist must learn to recognize the thought disorder found in latent and patent schizophrenics. This will alert the therapist to antipsychotic rather than antidepressant medication, and prevent other therapeutic errors that inevitably will cause a worsening of the condition into blatant schizophrenia. Some onion patients may become garlic due to poor treatment (uncovering psychotherapy or antidepressant and anxiolytic medication). Proper antipsychotic medication and appropriate psychotherapy can return them to onion. Others, as in the following section, are always garlic.

GARLIC SCHIZOPHRENIA

These are latent, patent, and blatant schizophrenics who harness their thought disorder by attacking the environment. Whereas the onion catatonic becomes mute and immobile to disarm his hostility, the garlic catatonic unleashes his fury, often killing many (garlic impulse schizophrenia). Others are serial killers, whose ritualistic selection of victims is often a futile attempt to control and limit their killings (e.g., I can only kill blue-eyed blonde schoolteachers during a full moon). Others, like the infamous serial killer Ted Bundy, occasionally have one appointment with a psychotherapist never to return. The patient will come across as one of the most charming, self-assured, and likable patients the therapist had ever interviewed, but he is left baffled as to why this very healthy man came in and why he never returned. Years ago, by using this baffling presentation as a possible indication of a serial murderer, the senior author reported a man he had just seen, who was indeed wanted and was later convicted of several killings. Other than this, there is no possible entry point or known successful treatment for what might be termed a *schizophrenic sociopath* other than removal from society, either in a mental hospital or prison.

TURNING UP THE HEAT WITH GARLIC PATIENTS

This chapter would be remiss if it did not discuss the usually high recidivism rate with court-ordered patients and how this can be improved. The courts are overwhelmed and our jails are crowded, so often judges will order a person to receive psychotherapy as a function of probation and as an alternative to jail. This relieves an overworked system and makes the court think it has done something positive. The patient perfunctorily keeps his appointments until the end of the probationary period, the therapist is paid, but seldom has this been therapeutic. The authors have, for years, successfully seen court-ordered referrals using a system that works: (1) The court and the patient agree there will be a monthly report and if the patient was not actually engaged in serious, productive therapy, during the period of the report, the sessions would be terminated, whereupon (2) the court will remand the patient to spend the remainder of the probationary period in jail (Cummings & Cummings, 2000a, 2000b).

Patients will not have much choice, but the courts are reluctant to enter into such an agreement in the beginning. Once they have seen the remarkable results of this arrangement, they are eager to participate in this meaningful three-way partnership of the patient, the court, and the psychotherapist. The revolving door is finally shut. We have even been able to conclude successful therapy with shoplifters and—the most revolving door patients of all— exhibitionists who expose themselves to young schoolgirls. Judges are reluctant to use precious jail space for such troublesome recidivists as shoplifters and exhibitionists, but an insistent merchant or an outraged parent requires the court to do something. Most judges are cynically aware of the limitations of the psychotherapy under these circumstances, but they must do something. The arrangement described transports a charade into treatment with demonstrable results, as follow-ups have shown.

SUMMARY

This chapter concentrated on techniques for enhancing psychotherapy through utilizing appropriate entry points, and has not discussed theory or research. However, it must be emphasized that these techniques are evidence based, at times using randomized clinical trials with large populations, which are then refined in large mental health delivery systems. The results reflect literally hundreds of thousands of episodes (see, for example, Cummings, Cummings, & Johnson, 1997; Cummings, Dorken, Pallak, & Henke, 1993; Cummings, O'Donohue, & Ferguson, 2002; Cummings & Wiggins, 2001; Wiggins & Cummings, 1998). These are part of the Biodyne model of focused, intermittent psychotherapy throughout the life cycle, with its roots in the 1950s at Kaiser Permanente, proceeding through the Hawaii Medicaid/Federal Employees Study of the 1980s, and American Biodyne nationally from the early 1980s through the early 1990s.

By utilizing the opportunity provided by natural entry points for various psychological conditions, avoiding treating garlic patients as onions, knowing when and when not to use medication, and using the momentum provided by the patient's circumstances or predicament, psychotherapy is an effective and efficient system for patients manifesting a wide variety of problematic behaviors.

REFERENCES

Cummings, N. A., & Cummings, J. L. (2002a). *The essence of psychotherapy: Reinventing the art in the new era of data.* San Diego, CA: Acdemic Press.

Cummings, N. A., & Cummings, J. L. (2002b). *The first session with substance abusers: A step-by-step guide.* San Francisco, CA: Jossey-Bass.

Cummings, N. A., Cummings, J. L., & Johnson, J. N. (1997). *Behavioral health in primary care: A guide for clinical integration.* Madison, CT: Psychosocial Press.

Cummings, N. A., Dorken, H., Pallak, M. S., & Henke, C. J. (1993). The impact of psychological intervention on health care costs and utilization: The Hawaii Medicaid Project. In N. A. Cummings & M. S. Pallak (Eds.). *Medicaid, managed behavioral and and implications for public policy. Vol. 2. Healthcare and utilization series* (pp. 3–23). South San Francisco, CA: Foundation for Behavioral Health.

Cummings, N. A., O'Donohue, W. T., & Ferguson, K. E. (2002). *The impact of medical cost offset on practice and research: Making it work for you. Vol. 5. Foundation for Behavioral Health utilization and cost series.* Reno, NV: Context Press.

Cummings, N. A., & Sayama, M. (1995). *Focused psychotherapy: A casebook of brief, intermittent psychotherapy throughout the life cycle.* New York: Brunner/Mazel.

Cummings, N. A., & Wiggins, J. G. (1997). A collaborative primary care/behavioral health model for the use of psychotropic medication with children and adolescents. *Issues in Interdisciplinary Care, 3,* 121–128.

Walker, L. E. (1984). *The battered woman syndrome.* New York: Springer.

Wiggins, J. G., & Cummings, N. A. (1998). National study of the experience of psychologists with psychotropic medication and psychotherapy. *Professional Psychology: Research and Practice, 29,* 549–552.

Wright, R. H., & Cummings, N. A. (in press). *Destructive trends in mental health.* New York: Brunner/Routledge (Taylor and Francis).

11

DEALING WITH FEELINGS
OF DEPRESSION

ALVIN R. MAHRER

School of Psychology
University of Ottawa
Ottawa, Canada

Picture a fellow who can't get that recent scene out of his mind. In a voice that is removed, dead, drained of feeling, he slowly tells about what happened yesterday. It is Sunday morning. He is sitting by himself in the neighborhood restaurant that he owns with his older brother. There are a few customers and the two waitresses who had worked there for years. He is in his usual state of being pulled in, withdrawn, lonely, but this time it seems deeper, blacker, with awful feelings of just giving up, what's the use, why try, failure, apathy, meaninglessness, emptiness, lifelessness, despair, gloom, depression.

The purpose of this chapter is to show how you can start with this painful scene, and end the session with the person achieving two magnificent, extraordinary changes. First, the person who began the session can undergo a radical, wholesale change into becoming a transformed, qualitatively new and different person that the person is capable of becoming. Second, the person who enters the session can leave the session as a qualitatively new person—an altogether new person who is essentially free of the painful scene and the painful feelings that were front and center for the person who entered the session. These are extraordinary changes. They call for extraordinary methods.

DEFINITIONS

DEFINING WHO THIS CHAPTER IS FOR

This chapter is for those with a glow of interest in becoming master practitioners. This includes both students, beginning and seasoned practitioners, and those with a spark of interest in undergoing their own experiential sessions (Mahrer, 2002).

DEFINING THE LOGISTICS OF AN EXPERIENTIAL SESSION

Picture an office that is soundproof, with two large chairs very close to each other, both pointing in the same direction, both with armrests and footrests. Both people can lean back, close their eyes throughout the session, which ends when they both agree that work is done, usually after an hour and a half or so.

DEFINING EACH SESSION AS ITS OWN "MINI THERAPY"

Instead of the common picture of psychotherapy starting with an initial session, proceeding through a series of sessions, and ending with the final session, each experiential session is its own "mini therapy" in that (1) the work of this session begins with the person deciding what is to be front and center in starting this session, the focus of the work for this session; (2) the session unfolds over the same sequence of steps as virtually every other session; and (3) each session can be judged as successful or unsuccessful independent of other sessions. Did the session achieve the sequence of steps? Based on this session's picture of what the person can become, did the person achieve this magnificent transformation? Based on what the person identified as front and center in the beginning of this session, is the qualitatively new person essentially free of the identified painful scene and accompanying painful feelings?

DEFINING THE THERAPIST AS TEACHER–GUIDE OF THE PERSON WHO CARRIES OUT THE WORK

Throughout the session, the role of the therapist is that of teacher–guide who shows the person what to do next, how to do it, and why to do it, and who joins with the person in undergoing each step and substep, and in undergoing the changes right along with the person. The uncommon aims and goals of each experiential session can help account for such a serious departure from the ordinary role of most therapists.

The other person is the one who mainly undertakes and carries out the concrete work of the session. The therapist shows what to do and how to do it, and the person is the active agent in moving through the session, in determining what pace to follow, in determining one's own readiness to undertake the next substep or not, or in determining whether to try again or to pause for a while. Although the therapist is mainly the teacher–guide, the other person does not readily fit the usual meanings of "client" or "patient" so much as the other person almost fits the meaning of "practitioner," or the one who undertakes the work of an experiential session.

EXPERIENTIAL SESSIONS CAN OFFER AN ALTERNATIVE TO THE DIAGNOSIS AND TREATMENT OF DEPRESSION

The Experiential Alternative

Rather than conflicting or competing with the diagnosis and treatment of depression, the experiential alternative comes from a mind-set that differs in at least three ways: (1) The focus of attention is this particular person's particular cluster of painful bad feelings which, in this particular situation, can be described using words such as meaninglessness despair, depression, pulled in, withdrawn, lonely, giving up, what's the use, why try, failure, apathy, emptiness, lifelessness, gloom. In this mind-set, there is a person, in a given situation, and having a painful package or cluster of his own particular bad feelings. In this mind-set, there is no diagnostic entity called depression.

(2) Instead of diagnosing and treating depression, one aim is to explore down into this particular person's particular cluster of painful feelings in this particular situation, to discover what lies deeper, and to use that to enable the person to become the qualitatively new person that the person can become. The aim is deep-seated transformation. (3) Instead of diagnosing and treating depression, the other aim is for the qualitatively new person to have a world essentially free of those painful scenes, and to be a person essentially free of that former cluster of painful feelings in those painful scenes.

Identifying What the Session is to Work on

In the beginning of each session, the therapist shows the person how to select a scene of strong feeling that the session can work on—some time, some situation, in which the person had a feeling that was relatively strong, full, saturating, notable. The therapist shows how to do it; the person identifies the "scene of strong feeling" for this session.

The person is quite free to find (1) a scene from rather recently, from some time ago, from quite long ago; (2) a powerful, big, dramatic scene or one that is more mundane and everyday; or (3) a scene from real life or from a dream. The feeling can be painful and hurtful, or pleasant and thoroughly enjoyable. The "scene of strong feeling" can be similar to one worked on in previous sessions or one that is relatively fresh and new. The scene of strong feeling may be exceedingly front and center for the person, the target of the person's attention, or the person can identify several possible scenes of strong feeling and choose one on which to work.

He has a powerful, painful scene of strong feeling that is compellingly front and center on his mind. A few days ago, Sunday morning, as usual, he is sitting alone with his newspaper and coffee, in the neighborhood restaurant that his father, brother, and he had owned for decades. In his usual state of distanced withdrawal, deadness, and emptiness, this time things became worse. Much worse. Even the waitress was compelled by

his sinking into a frightening state of utter detachment, withdrawal, emptiness, nothingness, numbness, meaninglessness, apathy, despair, gloom,
depression.

He had not only identified where to start, he was already living and being
in his scene of strong feeling.

THEORY AND
CONCEPTUALIZATION

For those interested in a relatively full exposition of the experiential
picture of human beings, there is a resource (Mahrer, 1989). The experiential
conceptual model of psychotherapy is given in two other resources (Mahrer,
1996/2004, 2002). For those interested in becoming master psychotherapists,
the aim is to provide a sufficient overview of the theory and conceptualization of the clinical strategies.

WHAT HELPS TO ACCOUNT FOR FEELINGS
OF DEPRESSION?

First, in the experiential system, "personality" is pictured as made up of
the kinds of "experiencings" this person is capable of undergoing. These are
called *potentials for experiencing*, and each person can have virtually distinctive potentials for experiencing, such as an experiencing of tenderness,
gentleness, softness; playfulness, silliness, whimsy; strength, firmness, tough-
ness; wickedness, devilishness, adventurousness; docility, compliance, giving
in; ripeness, fruition, creativity; rebelliousness, defiance, opposition; dominance, power, control. Some potentials for experiencing can be more on the
surface and some can be deeper inside the personality. One cause includes
a relatively surface experiencing, in this person, of utter detachment,
withdrawal, emptiness, nothingness, numbness, meaninglessness, apathy,
despair, gloom, depression.

Second, potentials for experiencing relate to one another in ways that can
be described as (1) good, positive, friendly, welcoming, accepting, loving,
integrative; or (2) bad, negative, unfriendly, hateful, distancing, disintegrative. A second cause is that relationships are exceedingly disintegrative with
this person's potential for experiencing utter detachment, withdrawal, emptiness, nothingness, numbness, worthlessness, meaninglessness, apathy, despair, gloom, depression.

Third, to experience what it is important for a person to experience, a person
creates a personal world, appropriate situations, to enable the person to
undergo what it is important for the person to undergo. This particular person
builds, creates, finds, establishes, constructs scenes that are appropriate for the
experiencing of this person's experiencing of utter detachment, withdrawal,

emptiness, nothingness, numbness, meaninglessness, apathy, despair, gloom, depression. The final cause is the person's constructing, building, using a situation or scene that is appropriate for undergoing the feelings of depression.

HOW CAN A PERSON BECOME FREE OF FEELINGS OF DEPRESSION?

In an experiential session, there are two ways that work with one another.

Relationships between Potentials for Experiencing Shift from Painful to Welcoming

When relationships are painful, hateful, negative, a potential for experiencing can occur as a painful, hurtful pushiness, dominance. When relationships shift to welcoming, loving, positive, that potential for experiencing can occur as a good sense of leadership, guiding. A potential for experiencing painful aloneness, solitariness can become a pleasurable experiencing of independence, autonomy. In the same way, a painful potential for experiencing depression, gloom, despair can become what it can become when relationships shift to magnificent relationships of welcoming, accepting, loving, positive relationships.

A 'Deeper Potential for Experiencing' Becomes an Integral New Part of a Qualitatively New Person

On the surface, a person may have the potential for experiencing a painful sense of depression, emptiness, worthlessness, despair, gloom. In the experiential way of thinking, there are inner, deeper potentials for experiencing that underlie the more surface potentials for experiencing.

The work of an experiential session is (1) to probe deeper inside, to discover the deeper potential for experiencing underlying the experiencing of painful depression; and then (2) to help bring about a dramatic shift in which the deeper potential for experiencing becomes an integral new part of the qualitatively new person. The magnificent consequence is that the painful experiencing of depression can be set aside, extinguished, replaced by the former deeper potential for experiencing. The qualitatively new person is thereby freed of the painful feelings of depression.

CASE FORMULATION

CASE FORMULATION IN MANY THERAPIES

Many therapies consist of a series or program of treatment sessions, and it is relatively standard to arrive at a formulation prior to or early in treatment. Generally, this formulation remains relatively stable over and sets the direction for change in the beginning, middle, and later phases of treatment. Typically, the case formulation tells about the client's presenting complaints, symptoms, the nature and severity of the mental disorder, motivation for treatment, prior treatments, mental status, current life situation, medical history, vocational history, sexual history, family history, personality structure, personality strengths and weaknesses, and so on.

CASE FORMULATION IN EXPERIENTIAL SESSIONS

Because each experiential session is its own mini therapy, there is no standard pretreatment evaluation or assessment. Furthermore, to determine on what the immediate session is to work and to have as its goals, each session identifies the "scene of strong feeling" and the "deeper potential for experiencing" that are the focus of the session. Accordingly, the therapist's notes or case formulation consist of the scenes of strong feeling and the deeper potentials for experiencing identified in each of the experiential sessions.

CLINICAL STRATEGIES

Each experiential session is to proceed through the same four steps as indicated in the following list, regardless of whether this is the initial session or a subsequent session. The clinical strategies consist of the four steps and the substeps under each of the steps. When the session is completed, the therapist and the person can decide if they want to have a subsequent session, and each subsequent session again proceeds through the same four steps.

Picture the therapist and the person, if the person is ready, as leaning back in large comfortable chairs, their feet on large footrests, both chairs quite close to one another, facing in the same direction. Both the therapist and the person have their eyes closed throughout the entire session.

The therapist is largely in the role of the teacher or guide who (1) shows the person what to do and how to do it, in proceeding through each substep; and (2) joins with and accompanies the person in proceeding through each step of the session. The person is mainly the one who carries out each working substep, provided the person is ready and willing. Accordingly, the therapist continually sees if the person is ready and willing, and the person is quite free to go ahead or to pause for a while, or even to decline and bring the session to a close at any point during the session.

Step 1: Discover the deeper potential for experiencing

- Get into state of readiness for change.
- Find scene of strong feeling.

- Live and be in scene of strong feeling.
- Discover moment of peak feeling in scene of strong feeling.
- Discover the deeper potential for experiencing in the moment of peak feeling.

Step 2: Welcome and accept deeper potential for experiencing

- Name and describe deeper potential.
- Give positive and negative reactions to deeper potential for experiencing.
- Use other methods of welcoming and accepting deeper potential.

Step 3: Being the deeper potential for experiencing in past scenes

- Find past scenes.
- Be deeper potential for experiencing in past scenes.

Step 4: Being the qualitatively new person in the qualitatively new world

- Find and create unrealistic postsession scenes.
- Be qualitatively new person in unrealistic postsession scenes, including initial painful scene.
- Find and create realistic postsession scenes.
- Be qualitatively new person in realistic postsession scenes.
- Modify and rehearse being qualitatively new person in postsession scenes.
- Be ready and committed to being qualitatively new person in qualitatively new world.
- Be qualitatively new person in qualitatively new world.

In most therapies, there is a client and a therapist, and their attention is mainly on one another. In an experiential session, the person's attention is mainly on a third thing (i.e., on whatever is front and center for the person, on some scene or center of attention). The therapist "listens" by also attending mainly to whatever the person is attending to, by seeing what the person is seeing.

As the person talks, the therapist is positioned so that the person's words are coming in and through and from the therapist, as if both the person and the therapist are saying the words, in the same way, with their attention mainly on the third thing out there. It is as if the therapist were inside the person, or a part of the person, or as if the outer boundary of the person were enlarged to include the therapist. In effect, the therapist generally sees and feels and undergoes what the person is seeing and feeling and undergoing.

When the therapist talks, it is, as always, with attention mainly out there, on whatever the person is attending to, seeing and feeling and undergoing along with the person. This means there is little or no room for what most therapists rely on as a stream of private thoughts and inferences. The therapist is "programmed" to know and follow the steps of the session.

The session ends when work is over, when they finish the four steps. Typically this takes an hour or two. After the session, they open their eyes and decide when the next session is to be. Occasionally the session ends when the person is not especially ready to do the immediate substep, and that can occur at any point. When the session proceeds through the four steps, the session genuinely ends when the person leaves the session as the new person and is this new person in the postsession new world.

STEP 1: DISCOVER THE DEEPER POTENTIAL
FOR EXPERIENCING

Get into a State of Readiness for Change

The therapist explains that the aim is to unlock and to be free of the usual controls that lock the person into being the ordinary person. If the person is ready and willing, both therapist and the person will spend the next minute or two taking deep breaths and blasting out the exhalations with the utmost power and strength, volume and noise. There are shrieks and bellows, high-pitched laughter and roars, hissings and gruntings, blasts and explosions, yelps and whelps, groans and moans, shouts and screams. Throughout the balance of the session, both therapist and person are to talk with loud voices, and the person is to have no pauses, no silences, if the person is ready and willing.

Find a Scene of Strong Feeling

The therapist shows the person how to find a time, some situation or scene, when the feeling was relatively strong. The feeling may be of any kind, good and pleasant or bad and unpleasant. The scene or the feeling may be relatively new or it may be from a previous session or sessions.

The person may already have a scene that is front and center, or it can take some looking around to find a scene, or perhaps two to three possibilities from which the person can select one on which to work. The scene and its feeling may be one that the person is willing to put on the table, or the scene of strong feeling is one the person is reluctant to put forward—is embarrassed, guilty, fearful of and about. It may come from real life or from a dream, may be dramatic or quite mundane, may be recent or from some time ago, may have been manifest and public or private and unexpressed, may have been fleeting or persistent for some time. In any case, the work culminates with a scene of strong feeling. "That's it! That's the time when feeling was strong. Oh yes."

Live and Be in Scene of Strong Feeling

Once the person selects a scene of strong feeling, the person is to live and be in that scene fully, rather than mainly being in the office, talking about the scene. The therapist shows the person what to do so that the person is wholly living and being in the alive, real, immediate, current scene.

Discover the Moment of Peak Feeling in the Scene of Strong Feeling

As the person is living and being in the scene of strong feeling, the person is to (1) slow the scene down, freeze the scene; dilate the scene; then the person (2) actively searches here and there in the scene, looking for the precise instant when the feeling peaks, and for precisely what is occurring in the precise moment of peak feeling. Finding the precise moment of peak feeling is almost always a genuine discovery, the culminating payoff of exploration, complete with a sense of surprise at finding something new, something unknown, something hidden. Until it is actually found, the person rarely knows that precise moment of peak feeling.

Discover the Deeper Potential for Experiencing in the Moment of Peak Feeling

By living and being in the moment of peak feeling, by holding this moment still and dilating it, the person is at the doorway to the inner, deeper hidden world of deeper potentials for experiencing. They are close by, within breathing distance, and the person can discover the deeper potential for experiencing by using one of the following useful methods until there is a sudden shift in what the person is feeling and experiencing:

1. When the moment of peak feeling is sketchy, incomplete, missing a key or critical piece of the circumstances, finding and filling in the critical missing piece can let the person shift to touching or being touched by the deeper potential for experiencing.

2. Regardless of the nature of the experiencing, in the moment of peak feeling, keep intensifying the experiencing until there is a sudden shift to the person touching or being touched by a new, different deeper potential for experiencing.

3. When the experiencing, in the moment of peak feeling, is painful, hurtful, awful, keep penetrating deeper and deeper down into the awful feeling until the very heart or core is reached, penetrated, opened up, released. In the sudden shift, the painful feeling is replaced with one that is much less painful, or can even be pleasurable, and the person touches or is touched by the deeper potential for experiencing.

4. When the moment of peak feeling includes a special other person or thing that is compelling, important, playing a central role, the person can literally

assume the identity of that special other person or thing, undergo that special other person's feeling or experiencing until the sudden shift occurs, and the person touches or is touched by the deeper potential for experiencing.

5. In the moment of peak feeling, when the feeling is unpleasant, bothersome, bad, replace the bad feeling with feelings that are determinedly pleasant, happy, buoyant, enjoyable, and undergo these pleasant feelings until a sudden shift occurs and the person touches or is touched by a qualitatively new experiencing; this is the deeper potential for experiencing.

STEP 2: WELCOME AND ACCEPT DEEPER POTENTIAL FOR EXPERIENCING

This step enables the person to welcome and accept, to feel good about, to love and embrace, the deeper potential that had been deeper inside, without the person even knowing that it had been sealed off, hidden, feared and hated—the deeper potential that had been discovered in step 1.

Name and Describe Deeper Potential

In step 1, for a moment or so, the deeper potential for experiencing was right here, present, sensed, touched, felt. Both therapist and the person can name and describe what it was, with special value on the words of the person. They arrive at a joint description of the experiencing: "Free, liberated, free of confinement, cut loose, no more constraints!"

Give Positive and Negative Reactions to Deeper Potential for Experiencing

Both therapist and the person can enter into a context that is fun, playful, exaggerated, perhaps accurate or wholesomely inaccurate, open, exuberant as they work together in celebrating all sorts of positive and negative reactions to the deeper potential for experiencing as a wonderful gift, and as a loathsome quality that ought to be cauterized.

Use Other Methods of Welcoming and Accepting Deeper Potential

Following no special order, the therapist shows the person how to use other methods such as the following:

1. Identify how the kind of person the person is, and the kind of personal world the person lives in block, hide, deny, and disprove that there is such a potential for experiencing in the person.

2. Assemble evidence sufficient for the person to admit that there can be such a deep-seated quality hidden deep inside.

3. Challenge the person to find unfitting, uncharacteristic, and exceptional occasions, recently or long ago, when the person actually enjoyed undergoing that deeper potential for experiencing.

4. Invite the person to confess proudly to sealing off effectively this deeper potential for experiencing, keeping it hidden.

5. Challenge the person to say out loud, or to sit still and hear the therapist say out loud, what the deeper potential can jump up and down, point its finger at, and say to the person who effectively imprisons and seals off the deeper potential for experiencing.

6. Identify people in the person's past and current life whom the person dislikes and criticizes, or envies and enjoys, because they embody the delightful, pleasant form of the person's own deeper potential for experiencing.

STEP 3: BEING THE DEEPER POTENTIAL FOR EXPERIENCING IN PAST SCENES

The purpose of step 3 is for the person literally to "be" the radical new person who is the deeper potential for experiencing. For perhaps the first time in one's life, the person is to undergo a complete metamorphosis, a complete transformation, a shift out of the person the person has been and into the wholesale, altogether new, and radically different deeper potential for experiencing. The shift is qualitative, radical, like a leap into the abyss. It is a complete disengagement out of the person one has been and is, and is a switch into being the whole new person. Indeed, what is now present is the alive, vibrant deeper potential for experiencing, with full-scale immediacy and presence. The magical, magnificent transformation has occurred, and the person is being the deeper potential for experiencing.

Find Past Scenes

Look for some past scene, incident, time that can serve as a context for the person switching into being the deeper potential for experiencing. Almost any past scene or situation can do. It doesn't have to be some special scene. The scene can be from recently or from a while ago or from long ago or from early in childhood. You can find a scene by seeing what past scene comes to mind when you recite the general contours of the scene of strong feeling (e.g., you are all by yourself, outdoors, and just walking along a path) or by starting with the deeper potential for experiencing and seeing what past scene comes to mind (e.g., you're feeling a sense of riskiness, new territory, excitement of something new, what's going to happen).

Once you actually undergo the switch into being the deeper potential for experiencing, look for a number (e.g., four to eight or so) of past scenes for being the deeper experiencing. These can include past times when the person began to be the deeper experiencing or started to, or when the person could or should have been the deeper experiencing, or when it would have been absolutely out of place to be the deeper experiencing, or past scenes and incidents that stand out as important in the person's past.

Be Deeper Potential for Experiencing in Past Scenes

Here are some guidelines for how to be the deeper potential for experiencing in the past scene:

- Be quite clear about the specific nature and content of the deeper potential for experiencing, and of the explicit past scene.
- The person who is the deeper potential for experiencing is not you. You are to step aside, be replaced with a whole new agency, person, who is the exaggerated pure form of the deeper potential for experiencing.
- The replacement of you with the whole new person-who-is-the-deeper-potential-for-experiencing is to occur in a flash, an instantaneous switch. "Three! Two! One! Go!"
- The context is sheer unreality, wholesale fantasy, utmost absurdity, silly, ridiculous, comedic, slapstick, burlesque, zany, outrageous.
- The voice is to be the exaggerated voice of the deeper potential for experiencing, and not at all recognizable as your voice.
- The experiencing is to be powerful, all the way, pumped up, saturating.
- Keep going until the experiencing is quite real, until you are actually undergoing and being the deeper potential for experiencing.
- The experiencing is to be accompanied with feelings of sheer joy, buoyancy, excitement, happiness.
- Once the switch occurs, the whole new person is to remain throughout all the past scenes in step 3, and is to be here when step 3 ends.

STEP 4: BEING THE QUALITATIVELY NEW PERSON IN THE QUALITATIVELY NEW WORLD

In step 3, the person undertook the magnificent shift into being the deeper potential for experiencing, and continued as this new person throughout scenes from the past. In step 4, the radically new person continues being present; the scenes of the past are replaced by scenes from after the session, from tomorrow and beyond; and what had been a deeper potential for experiencing is now an integral part of a transformed, qualitatively whole new person who leaves the session and lives and exists as the qualitatively whole new person in what can be a qualitatively whole new personal world.

Find and Create Unrealistic Postsession Scenes

The therapist and the new person and the person leave the office, walking into the new personal world of the rest of the day, tonight, tomorrow, and beyond. Just as in step 3, the context is wholesale unreality, absurd, playful, whimsical, foolish, fanciful, fantasy filled, outlandish, outrageous, silly, zany, cartoonlike, slapstick, comedic, make believe, ridiculous. There are no constraints or restraints.

The scenes can be fitting, appropriate, and ideal for being the whole new person. The scenes can include the general contours of the former person's world, or the scenes can boldly and refreshingly depart from the former person's world. The scenes can be mundane, from the little things of everyday life, or the scenes can be highly dramatic, novel, big ones.

Be the Qualitatively New Person in Unrealistic Postsession Scenes, Including the Initial Painful Scene

Once the postsession scenes are identified, the radically new person is to live and be in each scene, and to do so all the way, with wholesomely unconstrained enthusiasm and buoyant exuberance and joy. The context continues to be one of utmost fantasy and unreality, playfulness and zaniness, and it is the qualitatively new person who is alive and present.

Go from one scene to another, living and being in perhaps three to seven of these postsession scenes, including the postsession occurrence of the initial painful scene that may have been front and center for the former person in the beginning of the session. The magnificent difference is that it is the qualitatively new person who is now living and being in what had been the initial painful scene, which now is almost certainly far from being painful

Find and Create Realistic Postsession Scenes

As the qualitatively new person is increasingly alive and present, find and create new postsession scenes that are injected with high doses of reality, that can actually be found and created in the postsession world. These can be whole new scenes in which the qualitatively new person would revel, love to be in, scenes that are custom fit for the whole new person. These can be scenes that arise out of or that are exceedingly bold departures from the former person's world. These can be scenes that are relatively small and safe, or they can be big, challenging, risky. They can be mundane, such as the way the person walks and talks, or they can be dramatic, such as where the person lives, people the whole new person is with.

The realistic new scenes are present from when the session ends and the transformed new person leaves the session and enters into the qualitatively new world, from the rest of the day, from tonight and tomorrow, and the next tomorrows.

Be Qualitatively New Person in Realistic Postsession Scenes

The person continues as this qualitatively whole new person, but the postsession scenes are somewhat less fantasy and wholesale unreality, and somewhat more what it can be like for this transformed person to live and be in these postsession opportunities to live and be as the transformed person.

1. After living and being in the postsession scene, the therapist shows the person how to check the bodily felt sensations, to describe where they are located in the body, and what they are like. Are the bodily felt sensations all over the body or in some particular part? Good and pleasant, or bad and unpleasant? Vibrant and alive or muted, numb, dead? Peaceful and harmonious or disjointed and in pieces?

2. Give the former person, and other parts of the person, plenty of opportunity to voice their reactions to the radically new person being this radical new way in the postsession scenes. "Who do you think you are? You can't be that way! You are dangerous, bad, alien, wrong, sick, evil. You will upset my life, ruin everything, get into big trouble!"

3. Allow for the real possibility that the whole new person will evaporate, be replaced by the former person who started the session. Allow for the alternative real possibility that the deeper potentiality that was discovered in step 1 can become an integral new part of a whole new person, a radical and qualitative new person, an utterly transformed new person. Allow for the alternative real possibility that the painful scene can no longer exist, can no longer be painful, can no longer include painful feelings, in the qualitatively new world of the qualitatively new person.

Modify and Rehearse Being Qualitatively New Person in Postsession Scenes

It is try-out time. The aim is to try being the qualitatively new person in selected postsession scenes, to keep modifying and rehearsing what happens. Use the bodily felt sensations as helpful gauges, tracking guides. Try it out; check the bodily felt sensations. Keep going until the bodily felt sensations are delightfully pleasant, and over much or most of the body.

If the bodily felt sensations are quite good ones, over much or most of the body, the person is ready to be the qualitatively new person in the postsession scenes. If the bodily felt sensations are unpleasant, bad, or even neutral or equivocal, the mission can be aborted.

Be Ready and Committed to Being Qualitatively New Person in Qualitatively New World

The whole new person is given an opportunity to sign the contract of remaining alive and present, of full-scale readiness and commitment to remain being the qualitatively new person (1) when eyes open and the transformed new person ends the session, leaves the session, and enters into the immediate postsession, qualitatively new world; and (2) when the qualitatively new person lives and exists in the rehearsed postsession scene.

Alternatively, the qualitatively whole new person is exceedingly free to slide away, to exist no longer, to be unready and uncommitted to remain, and instead to be replaced by the continuing former person who began the session.

Be Qualitatively New Person in Qualitatively New World

The experiential therapist's work is over when both people open their eyes and the person leaves the session. The session is over, and the work of the session is completed, when the qualitatively whole new person leaves the session, enters into a qualitatively whole new world, and continues as the qualitatively whole new person in the selected postsession scene or scenes.

KEY MISTAKES AND
MISCOMPREHENSIONS

EXPERIENTIAL SESSIONS CAN BE FOR VIRTUALLY ANY PERSON, BUT ONLY FOR SELECTED THERAPISTS

Judging from actual experience, there can be some restrictions on who seems to be able to go through experiential sessions:

- These sessions seem out of place with young children.
- The person should not be in a state of being mind drugged, high on drugs.
- The main consideration seems to be if the person is quite ready and willing to undertake each substep in proceeding through the session, and this apparently has little or nothing to do with many issues that are generally considered relevant by most other therapists. For example, almost anyone can go through a session, even if the person is in what is called a state of poor health, medically ill, frail, in a wheelchair, handicapped, unable to see; even if the person is described as being mentally ill, psychotic, in poor contact with reality, having a severe, deep-seated depression, even if the person is judged as lacking psychological mindedness.

The Therapist's Way of Thinking Must be Friendly to What Happens in an Experiential Session

It is almost certain that a therapist has some outlook, perspective, way of thinking about such things as what people are like—personality structure—how people can change, the limits and possibilities of change, how and why a person has feelings such as depression, and so on. Rather than trying to compare the therapist's way of thinking about depression with the experiential way of thinking, it seems to be more practically important that the therapist can see what happens in an experiential session as reasonably friendly, cordial, sensible, understandable, and not especially in grating opposition to what the therapist believes.

The Therapist Must Cherish the Two Goals of an Experiential Session

It seems essential that the therapist take for granted that each session can achieve (1) a wholesale transformation so that the qualitatively new person who comes alive in the session, and who leaves the session, can be the whole new person that the person can become; and (2) a qualitative change so that the new person is essentially free of the painful scene, and the painful feelings in the scene, that was front and center for the person who began the session. These two goals can be a significant departure from most goals of most approaches—for example, to treat the client's mental disorder of depression, or the depressive symptoms of the mental disorder.

THE THERAPIST MUST ACHIEVE A HIGH LEVEL OF PROFICIENCY IN THE METHODS

It usually takes a rather long period of explicit skill learning, of gradual and slow practice, training, and skill development, for the therapist to achieve a sufficiently high level of proficiency in the methods used in the experiential session. It can be an error to believe that a therapist can achieve a successful session by getting the general idea of the methods or by trying them out a few times.

THE EXPERIENTIAL THERAPIST AND THE PERSON ATTEND MAINLY TO THE THIRD THING, RATHER THAN MAINLY TO ONE ANOTHER

Throughout the session, both the therapist and the person have their eyes closed. Throughout the session, the person's attention is mainly "out there," on living and being in the scene, on the third thing. Similarly, the therapist's attention is continuously and mainly "out there", on living and being in that scene, on that third thing. This holds even when they say something to one another. It is a mistake, an error for their attention to be mainly on one another.

THE EXPERIENTIAL THERAPIST IS THE TEACHER– GUIDE, RATHER THAN THE ONE WHO APPLIES TREATMENT METHODS

In each substep, the therapist is the teacher who shows the person what to do and how to do it, on the firm understanding that the person is the one who carries out the method, and on the firm condition that the person is ready and willing to carry out the method. It is a mistake for the therapist to be in the relatively common role of the one who applies the treatment methods.

The experiential therapist is the guide who goes through each substep as and together with the person. In each substep, what the person is undertaking, so too is the therapist, and the therapist does so with full readiness, willingness, exuberance, and commitment to undergoing the changes that are the gift of each substep and step. When the therapist is the teacher–guide, the session can be a success. If the therapist is in the common role of the applier of the interventions, the session almost certainly fails.

CASE STUDY

This is a session with a fellow who seems to be in his late 30s or early 40s. He had called a week or so ago for an appointment, and the telephone conversation was mainly around the arrangements for when and where, for the length being open ended, and our working one session at a time.

STEP 1: DISCOVERING THE DEEPER POTENTIAL FOR EXPERIENCING

With eyes closed, he accepts the invitation to get into the right state by joining with the therapist in taking deep breaths, inhaling explosively, and yelling, shrieking, howling, blasting, hissing, screaming, for a few minutes of unbuckling the usual controls.

When we search for scenes of strong feeling, there is a dramatic recent scene that is already front and center. He and his older brother own a neighborhood restaurant. It is Sunday morning, there are a few customers, the usual two waitresses, and he is sitting alone at his usual booth, with the newspaper and his mug of black coffee. There are thoughts about arranging for his aging parents to move to a smaller, one-floor house to accommodate his father's worsening state of multiple sclerosis, thoughts about steering the budding tennis career of his 13-year-old daughter, thoughts about expanding the restaurant, getting a liquor license, thoughts about taking over the restaurant from his disinterested older brother, thoughts about no sex with his wife for the last six months or so.

He is in his usual state of feeling gloomy, unhappy, lonely, withdrawn, numb, despairing, apathetic, empty, meaningless, failure, what's the use, depressed. But this time it is much worse. He retreats even further inside himself, sounds and voices recede, the black gloominess engulfs him, awareness diminishes. Cold. Emptiness. Nothingness. Suddenly he is jolted into hearing the waitress, her face close to his. She is scared, stunned, staring at the mug of hot coffee that he poured onto the table, and is in little puddles on the floor. He barely registers what is happening. It is like watching something alien, something from a distance, something not happening to him.

When he slows down and dilates the scene of strong feeling, the precise moment of peak feeling is when he slowly, gradually, bit by bit, empties the full mug of black coffee on the table. He is staring fixedly at the white mug, and the exact moment is when a mechanical "I did it" is present as he finally empties the last little bit of coffee. Freezing and dilating that moment of peak feeling, attention targeted on the empty mug, the therapist's selected method is in the words, "Pump it up! Say it again and again, louder and louder!"

As he says "I did it" louder and louder, the depressed pain becomes increasingly saturating, enveloping, powerful, implosive, breaks all bounds. There is a sudden switch and a vibrant, giggly new voice proclaims, "I emptied it. Just let it go!" We are both touched by the deeper potential for experiencing.

STEP 2: WELCOMING AND ACCEPTING THE DEEPER POTENTIAL FOR EXPERIENCING

The methods begin with trying to find the right words to describe the deeper potential for experiencing, including his own words: peacefulness, free, just letting it go, emptying out, no more having to, no more trying, utter peacefulness.

Another method looked for times when he had felt this. "Never! Nothing like that. Maybe the closest was when I first got drunk, but not that same feeling of just letting things go, being so peaceful, not driven."

Would he love to feel this way? "Wow! Yes!"

We punctuate how being this way would surely destroy whole chunks of his current life.

Could he even imagine being this whole new way? Yes he could, and it could be just wonderful!

Has he ever known anyone who embodies this way of being? He remembers the frail old priest whom everyone revered. He and a few other kids sat with the old priest in the church garden, and he was struck by the old priest's radiant inner peacefulness, freedom from any striving, just letting things be. The deeper potential for experiencing was welcomed, accepted, loved, cherished.

STEP 3: BEING THE DEEPER POTENTIAL FOR EXPERIENCING IN PAST SCENES

If he is ready, if he wants to, would he be willing to see what it can be like to detach, disengage, set aside, who and what he is, and to throw himself fully and completely into literally being this deeper potential for experiencing? He can always stop, whenever he wants to. "Sure. Why not? Yeah, I'll give it a try."

He and the therapist find a few scenes from the past. One was roughly similar to the original scene from the session, only it was when he was a very little boy and he accidentally knocked over his glass of milk. Using this past scene as the point of entry, the guidelines are simple, and agreed upon: First, he is to live and be in that early scene, all the way, completely. Second, He is to dive headlong into being the radically, qualitatively, altogether different little boy who is the full embodiment of the experiencing of sheer peacefulness, freedom, letting be, letting things go, freedom from having to, striving after. Third, he is to be this whole new person all the way, full scale, completely, with saturated forcefulness and strength. Fourth, the accompanying feelings are to be utterly pleasant, wonderful, satisfying. Fifth, the context is to be complete fantasy, unreality, slapstick, make believe, absurdity, silliness, playfulness.

In a theatrical voice, he begins: "Just let it be ... Milk will spill ... It is the grand nature of the world ... Deep breath ... Slowly exhale ... Feel the peacefulness ... The glass is free, empty ... So too is the milk ... Free, let go, emptied ... Let them be ... They come and go ... Notice how I am all peace, and I am slowly lifting up, rising ... Above my chair ... I bestow upon you my inner peace ... See the cucumber on the table ... Just let it be ... Be one with the cucumber ... Yes ... "

If he is ready, if he is willing, he can and does remain being this transformed whole new person as he moves from one past scene to another, including the initial scene in his restaurant with the careful slow pouring of the coffee on the table.

STEP 4: BEING THE QUALITATIVELY NEW PERSON IN THE QUALITATIVELY NEW WORLD

He remains being the altogether new person, the qualitatively new person. And the context remains that of playful unreality, absurdly silly fantasy. The difference is that the scenes from the past are replaced with the transformed new fellow ending the session and walking into the qualitatively new post-session world of the rest of the day, of tonight and tomorrow. "So what can you do when you leave here, walk toward your car, and it is all absolutely unrealistic, all silly fantasy. What would you love to do?" The fellow who is quietly giggling is the transformed embodiment of utter peacefulness, letting things be, freedom from striving after, liberation from having to, from efforts after.

"I walk down the sidewalk, just follow the smells, whatever I see. I follow the path. Oh hello car! What would you like to do? You can drive yourself. Take me wherever you want. Look at that little boy with the ice cream cone!"

He casually wanders over to the meeting tonight: "At our place ... to decide about mom and dad moving to a smaller place ... and I am the prime mover, the chair of the meeting, the one they are to follow ... How silly! ... I am dancing with my older brother ... Dum de dum, round and round ... Anyone want to chair? I'm rolling on the floor, eating jelly beans. Mom, your eyes are so pretty. You can do whatever you want. ... "

Soon he comes across his wife, at home, after he leaves the session. "Hello. Here's the special ice cream you like ... I saw a little boy ... We're supposed to plan the agenda for the family meeting tonight? Let it go! It's not all that important? No, I'm not high on something... Let's take a walk and see where it takes us. How about floating in the air like two balloons holding hands?... I am floating. Here and there. Who knows where we are going?... Oops, look down. See the restaurant? Enlarge it? Contractors? Liquor license? Julie's the older waitress, been there before dad left it to us... Hey Julie, you decide! The restaurant is yours... How about coming to the family meeting? Be the chair." He is quietly giggling. Everything has been in the context of playful unreality.

We shift to the final stage of step 4, and the context is now friendly reality. So what is this qualitatively new fellow ready to do after the session? Anything? Nothing? He is ready to go home, to be with his wife: "I think I just woke up, and I'm not sure what's going to happen, but I've spent my whole life... trying, striving, pushing like a big gloomy force and it seems, well, over with, kind of silly. I'm ready to let it go." He rehearses being with her, talking with her, almost for the first time, until the bodily sensations are friendly and ready.

The therapist speaks with the voice of other parts of the former fellow: "She'll think you lost your mind, flipped. Back to the hospital, you depressed lunatic!" "The whole family depends on you, and the meeting is tonight, at your place!" "What about the restaurant, all the plans, the expansion, the liquor license, everything?" "Your daughter's tennis will suffer! Think about the effects on her!" "Enough of this nonsense! You got a bad depression! You'll be your old self as soon as you walk out of here! Start taking the pills!" This qualitatively whole new person is quietly giggling, peaceful, happy: "Those sure are big worries... It's OK, the world can go on... Maybe it's not all that important... Let it go for a while... It can pass... Push push push; you sure have a lot of energy... Let's slowly empty some cups of coffee...".

The session is over. This qualitatively new fellow is ready to head home to be with his wife in what seems to be a qualitatively new personal world.

WHAT HAPPENED AFTER THE SESSION?

There can be at least two ways of seeing what happened after the session. One is to see who shows up for the next session. Is it the qualitatively new person or more of the person who was there at the beginning of the last session? A second way is to see if looking for scenes of strong feeling in the subsequent session can shed any light on what happened after the session. He began with what happened when he arrived home. The whole family was there, waiting for his chairing the expected heavy meeting, which never happened because the new fellow who showed up was playful, twinkling, easy, letting things be, especially as he and his wife left the place, went on a walk together, and fell in love again. By the time they returned, everyone had left, and there was a note on the dining room table: "Best time we ever had. Thanks! You two look like you want to be alone."

When they woke up in the morning, in each other's arms, what radiated from both of them was his new-felt peacefulness, freedom from strivings, from having to, a sense of quiet liberation. It was delicious. But the other scene of strong feeling, in the next session, was the long and serious talk his 13-year-old daughter negotiated with him, the next day, about her "daddy-driven" professional career, his pleasantly playful nodding at each point she made, his letting go of his 13-year career as the depressed, heavy force propelling his daughter toward winning tournaments for him, and the quiet appreciation of the wonderful qualities he saw in the daughter he saw for the first time.

From then on, what seemed to have been left behind were the awful, painful, frightening feelings of utter despair, gloom, loneliness, withdrawal, numbness, emptiness, failure, black depression. Many sessions later he offhandedly mentioned that he and his brother had sold the restaurant, and the only treasured remembrance of the place was a white coffee mug there on the mantelpiece, in between trophies his daughter had won when she used to play tennis.

SUMMARY

If you want to enable a person to become the qualitatively new person that the person can become, and to be free of the painful depressed scene and the person's own particular painful feelings of depression in that scene, then consider learning how to carry out an experiential session that is expressly developed and designed to achieve those two magnificent goals.

At the end of the session, if you both want to have a subsequent session, then that subsequent session can enable the person to start with whatever scene of strong feeling is front and center for the person, to discover what is deeper, to become whatever that deeper potential for experiencing enables the person to become and, if the scene was one of painful feelings, to become free of that painful scene of painful feelings.

REFERENCES

Mahrer, A. R. (1989). *Experiencing: A humanistic theory of psychology and psychiatry*. Ottawa: University of Ottawa Press.

Mahrer, A. R. (2002). *Becoming the person you can become: The complete guide to self-transformation*. Boulder, CO: Bull.

Mahrer, A. R. (2004). *The complete guide to experiential psychotherapy*. Boulder, CO: Bull. [Originally published 1996.]

12

DESIGNING AND ASSIGNING EFFECTIVE HOMEWORK

RICHARD KAMINS

Magellan Health Services
Greenwood Village, Colorado

DEFINITION AND HISTORY OF HOMEWORK IN PSYCHOTHERAPY

More than 70 years ago, behavioral therapists recognized the value and power of utilizing extratherapeutic time to enhance the outcome of therapy sessions. Later, taking advantage of the time between sessions, homework[1] became a cornerstone to cognitive–behavioral therapies, consistent with its emphasis on skills building. However, homework is often used currently by practitioners with many other theoretical orientations. Brief forms of psychodynamic therapy (Badgio, Halperin, & Barber, 1999), marital and family therapies (Dattilo, 2002), and solution-focused approaches (Beyebach, Morejon, Palenzuela, & Rodriguez–Arias, 1996) frequently utilize homework assignments. Of more than 500 outcome studies published in the mid to late 1970s, Shelton and Levy (1981) found that 68% included self-help assignments. Similarly, in a survey by Kazantzis and Deane (1999), 98% of psychologists stated they gave homework assignments in an average of 57% of therapy sessions. Thus, homework is considered by most psychotherapists as an integral part of the change process.

---

[1] In this chapter, the term *homework* or *homework assignment* will refer to any out-of-session task given to a client. The assignment may be a behavioral task, self-monitoring, exercise, observation, taping of an out-of-session interaction, reading, or other undertaking.

Not only is homework administered frequently, a meta-analysis of 32 studies revealed therapy involving homework produces a better treatment outcome than therapy without homework (Kazantzis, Dean, & Ronan, 2000). Based on the positive mean effective size from the meta-analysis, 68% of clients would be expected to improve when therapy involved homework, compared with only 32% when it did not (Kazantzis & Lampropoulus, 2002). As reported by Tompkins (2003), "Empirical evidence suggests that homework may assist clients to become well faster and remain well longer and that homework compliance may be an important predictor of a positive treatment outcome" (p. 49). Thus, therapists who can design, implement, and motivate clients to complete homework assignments will be more successful than those who do not.

Given homework's effectiveness, the next step for a practitioner is to decide what type of assignment to provide. A good start is to be familiar with manuals for empirically supported treatments (ESTs), which describe homework assignments that are effective for particular disorders (see Woody and Sanderson, 1998, for a list of EST manuals) or workbooks that match homework assignments to presenting problems (Schultheis, 1998). Be this as it may, adherence to completing homework (and thus improved outcome) can be increased by understanding the impact of individual client variables and "common factors" in therapy. As a result, master therapists not only know effective interventions for various psychological problems, but attend to therapeutic alliance and the concept of client fit to deliver and select the proper homework assignment. This chapter discusses how to design, assign, and review homework assignments to maximize client acceptance and treatment outcome. Case examples will be used to illustrate concepts.

THEORY AND CONCEPTUALIZATION: THE PURPOSE OF HOMEWORK

Utilizing extratherapeutic time, homework, as discussed in this section, may enhance the outcome of therapy in a multitude of ways (Freeman & Rosenfield, 2002; Garland & Scott, 2002).

CHANCE TO PRACTICE SKILLS

In the therapy session, the client and therapist are able to talk about and understand certain issues, but homework promotes learning at an experiential level and helps generalize learning from therapy into real life. For example, the client may learn about the relationships of cognitions and feelings in therapy, but the practice of disputing maladaptive thinking in a problematic situation allows change to occur more readily.

EXTEND THERAPY INFLUENCE

Issues covered during the therapy session can be sufficiently complex that clients may forget some key points. However, homework can reinforce learning and keep it fresh in the client's mind. Out-of-session tasks enable clients to take therapy home with them.

GAUGE CLIENTS' LEVEL OF MOTIVATION AND READINESS TO CHANGE

A client may say one thing to the therapist and act another way outside the session. Homework assignments help the therapist learn the actual level of client motivation. For example, a client may state an interest in changing, but when required to practice this change through homework assignments, may not be willing to do it. When this is revealed in the next session, the therapist can adjust interventions based on the client's behavior, thereby optimizing therapeutic time.

HELP PREVENT RELAPSE

Clients who successfully use assigned homework to overcome problems will likely continue to practice or work on issues after therapy, thereby reducing the chance of relapse after therapy ends.

INVOLVE SIGNIFICANT OTHERS

Involving significant others in therapy often can improve outcomes. Homework assignments, such as psychoeducational reading, can help teach family members about certain aspects of the client's illness or effective support strategies. Involving significant others also allows the therapist to assess the level of social support and determine whether these individuals are working toward the same goals as the client.

HOMEWORK AS EXPERIMENT

If the therapist is not sure of the causes of the presenting problem, homework assignments may help differentiate among different possibilities. Similarly, if a client is not convinced that a suggested new behavior would be helpful, an assignment may help him learn what is effective.

SELF-EFFICACY

Assigning homework is a collaborative message and communicates to clients their critical role in the process of change. As Cummings and Sayama (1995) stated, "Homework is at the heart of targeted, focused psychotherapy. It is the critical feature that convinces patients that they are truly partners in their own treatment" (p. 97). The therapist can teach, but the client learns that he must implement. When therapy ends, the client will be more able to attribute improvement to his efforts rather than exclusively to the therapist.

CLINICAL STRATEGIES

THE IMPORTANCE OF THERAPEUTIC ALLIANCE

Although psychotherapy in general has been shown to be effective, certain therapists are more effective than others (for a review, see Lambert and Ogles, 2004). The difference among therapists is minimally to modestly related to discipline, age, theoretical orientation, or experience (Beutler, Malik, Alimohamed, et al., 2004); however, therapeutic alliance has been shown to play a significant role in treatment outcome (Keijsers, Schaap, & Hoogduin, 2000). For instance, Burns and Nolen–Hoekseman (1992) studied therapists who followed a structured cognitive–behavioral approach for treating depression. Therapists perceived as the most empathic had better success with both completed homework assignments and treatment outcomes.

According to Bordin (1979), the therapeutic alliance is comprised of the therapeutic bond, agreement by the client and therapist on goals for therapy, and agreement on therapy tasks. Master therapists understand that homework assignments should only be created and delivered after these conditions are achieved; noncompliance often follows when these criteria are not met. The "best" interventions are worthless if not acceptable to the client. Thus, the master therapist attends, as described here, to these aspects of alliance in preparation to assigning homework.

Therapeutic Bond or Rapport

Homework assignments should not be given until the client has successfully bonded with the therapist. If the bond is not strong, then the therapist should try to determine the cause (e.g., the client has not felt supported or understood) and try to repair the relationship. Only after the bond is solid should the therapist consider assigning homework.

Goal Setting and Agreement

After establishing a rapport, therapeutically relevant goals must be set. Then the process of developing specific homework assignments can be undertaken. After goals have been established, specific homework assignments then are intimately tied to the agreed-upon goals. Because the homework assignments are based on goals, the more therapeutically relevant the goals are, the more helpful the assignments will be.

Goals can be based on any theoretical orientation, but they should relate directly to the reason the client is in therapy, allow progress to be measured, and, as a result, permit the client and therapist to know when therapy is finished. Useful goals are *salient* to the client; *concrete* and *specific*; and *behavioral, realistic,* and *achievable.*

Salient goals ensure that clients are invested in achieving these goals. Clients are more likely to do homework when the therapist matches the assignment to the client's view of the problem (Conoley, Padula, Payton, & Daniels, 1994).

Goals that are concrete, specific, and behavioral are objective, and therefore measurable. The client and therapist should work as a team to operationalize general, vague, or subjective goals, such as increasing self-esteem or reducing depression. For example, reducing depression is usefully defined as sleeping through the night, gaining five pounds, engaging in pastimes, or other measurable indicators of progress.

Lastly, goals should be realistic and achievable. Two clients may have the same problem, but because of differences of internal and external strengths and weaknesses, appropriate therapy goals may vary. Furthermore, large goals should be addressed in stages. If the client wants to go from "A" to "D," the therapist should help the client focus on getting to "B" and "C" first. If a client suggests goals that are unachievable, the therapist needs to negotiate more realistic goals collaboratively.

Agreed-upon Task

Many different types of homework assignments based on therapy goals are possible. All types should be designed collaboratively between the client and therapist. The following three models demonstrate various factors to consider in homework formation.

Heuristic Model for Adherence

Detweiler and Whisman (1999) proposed that the characteristics of the task, the therapist, the client, and the interrelationships of all three impact whether a client will complete an assignment. The model can be graphically illustrated (Figure 12.1).

According to this model, attending to task, therapist, and client variables will influence adherence. Even if the therapist chooses a "therapeutically appropriate" assignment topic, task factors such as difficulty and time will affect client acceptance. Similarly, therapist factors such as delivery, confidence, and rapport will impact adherence. Lastly, client

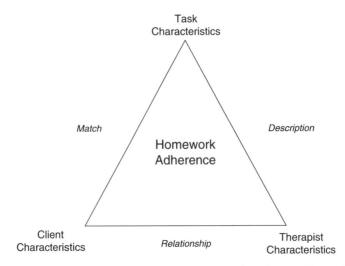

FIGURE 12.1   Heuristic model for understanding homework adherence. Source: Detweiler, J. B., & Whisman, M. A. (1999). The role of homework assignment in cognitive therapy for depression: Potential methods for enhancing adherence. *Clinical Psychology: Science and Practice, 6*, p. 274. By permission of Oxford University.

variables such as motivation and intelligence need to be taken into account in designing appropriate tasks. The most successful assignments consider all these aspects.

Stages of Change Model

A key element in designing effective homework is making it consistent with the client's level of readiness for change. Prochaska, DiClemente, and Norcross (1992) identified five stages of motivation during therapy: precontemplation, contemplation, preparation, action, and maintenance.

Effectiveness of homework depends on readiness stage. Behavioral assignments tend to be successful for clients at the action stage, but routinely fail for clients at the precontemplation or contemplation stages (Prochaska et al., 1992). On the other hand, precontemplation clients respond well to motivational interviewing strategies such as reflective listening, summarizing, and affirmation (DiClemente & Velasquez, 2002). Similarly, for ambivalent clients at the contemplation stage, self-monitoring or observational assignments are more likely to be effective than behavioral ones. Only at the preparation stage and beyond would behavioral assignments typically fit with the client's readiness to change. Correct judgment of a client's readiness stage and collaborative development of an appropriate assignment will increase adherence to the treatment plan, reduce dropout, and improve outcome. Choosing the right type of assignment helps the client move to the next level of readiness for change.

An example of matching homework to the client's stage of readiness is illustrated by the case of a 50-year-old single woman experiencing increased feelings of depression following her mother's sudden death two years previously. Her father, deceased for eight years, had been an abusive alcoholic. The client's two other siblings disengaged from the family, but the client let the mother move in with her. On the evening of her mother's death, the client heard a noise coming from her mother's room but did not immediately investigate; by the time she did, her mother had passed away. The client felt guilt over her mother's death, even though she was reassured by her friends and family doctor that she was not responsible. Although she was tired of feeling depressed, she retained an underlying belief that she deserved to suffer. The therapist assessed that she was not ready to let go of her guilt (thus, at the contemplation stage of change as reflected by strong ambivalence). He believed if he gave her cognitive–behavioral assignments about disputing her "irrational thoughts" or other assignments for clients at the preparation or action stage that she would become more entrenched in her guilt. Instead, he acknowledged her feelings of responsibility and her desire to punish herself for her part in her mother's death. Consequently, as a homework assignment, he asked her to think through what length "sentence" she should serve for her "crime" based on what percent culpability she felt she deserved and what percent others deserved. She came back the next week reporting that she was 20% responsible. She assigned 50% blame to her father for his constant abuse of her mother, 20% to her mother for putting up with the abuse, and 10% to her siblings for not being willing to take care of her mother. The client decided two years was a long enough sentence and she was ready to move on with her life. Because the therapist validated the client's feelings of guilt and acknowledged her right to suffer rather than advocating for her to change, this allowed the client to look objectively at her role and response. Rather than assuming the client was at the preparation or action stage and prematurely encouraging change, this master therapist gauged his client's level of readiness and geared the homework appropriately.

Clients' Presentation of Problem

The last model points out the importance of fitting the homework to the client's presentation style. Brown–Stanbridge (1989) describes a $2 \times 2 \times 2$ matrix for determining homework type. The three dimensions are direct versus nondirect, behavioral versus nonbehavioral, and paradoxical versus nonparadoxical (Fig. 12.2).

Understanding the client's placement on each dimension, based on how the problem is articulated, helps the therapist know how to design the homework to increase acceptance by the client. Eight separate types

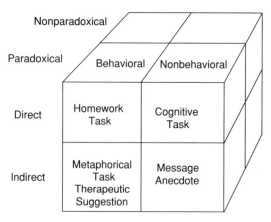

FIGURE 12.2 Therapy task construction paradigm. Source: Brown–Standridge, M. D. (1989.) A paradigm for construction of family therapy tasks. *Family Process, 28*, 477. By permission of Blackwell Publishing Ltd.

of homework assignments are considered, depending on where the client falls on each of the three dimensions. For example, a couple who has trouble discussing a marital problem (nondirect), in enough emotional pain to take action (behavioral), and responds cooperatively to therapy would likely profit from a metaphorical task or indirect suggestion.

All three models demonstrate methods to fit homework optimally to clients' needs. Homework assignments solely based on diagnosis generally assume "one size fits all," clients are at the preparation or action stage, and clients are ready to change. Ideally, the uniqueness of every client should be recognized so that each homework assignment is tailored for that client, taking into account not only motivational level, but educational and socioeconomic levels, ethnicity, religious beliefs, cognitions about their problems, support of significant others, personal strengths, and so forth. Even using the term *homework* to describe out-of-office assignments may need to be changed for clients who viewed school in a negative light. Instead, the therapist may want to refer to homework as *tasks* or *exercises* to increase acceptability.

HOMEWORK DESIGN

Although successful homework assignments are unique for each individual, they have certain characteristics in common. Tompkins (2002) outlined key features of homework that maximize adherence. These features make the homework "well formed" and include the clinical strategies previously mentioned.

Meaningful

Clients are more likely to comply with assignments when they are relevant to the central goals of therapy, salient to the focus of the session, agreeable to therapist and client, and appropriate to the client's sociocultural context.

Doable

Assignments should be concrete, specific, and geared to the client's current skill level. Concrete and specific assignments are more likely to be completed than general or vague assignments (Shelton & Levy, 1981). Similarly, assignments that utilize clients' personal strengths are more often completed (Conoley et al., 1994). Doable assignments include specifics on when, where, with whom, how, and for how long. For example, a well-formed homework assignment for a client learning to relax would be stated as: "Listen to side 1 of the relaxation tape for 15 minutes every other evening in bed right before bedtime and use the response sheet to record experiences of your practice sessions." A vague and less helpful assignment would be: "When you have time, practice some of your relaxation exercises."

Begin Small

As a general rule, it is best to start with smaller assignments. This increases the odds the client is successful (Conoley et al., 1994), which in turn increases confidence the client has in therapy, the therapist, and with himself. Simultaneously, goals should also be viewed as challenging. This latter principle helps clients feel a sense of accomplishment.

Have a Clear Rationale

Not only do clients complete assignments more readily when they agree with the rationale, but they are more likely to improve faster and are more likely to have successful outcomes (Addis & Jacobson, 2000). The therapist should attempt to design the homework task so it is not only consistent with the client's view of the problem but with his view of the solution. Until the therapist is certain the client agrees with the rationale for assignments, he or she can ask the client, "Does the reason I'm recommending this homework assignment make sense to you?"

Include a Backup Plan

The therapist should discuss with the client potential obstacles to doing the homework assignment and suggest a plan for dealing with them. If necessary, the therapist and client can rehearse ways during the session to get around obstacles.

ASSIGNING HOMEWORK

After the therapist has conceptualized the appropriate homework assignment based on the client's problem, belief system, presentation style, and other relevant factors, the homework is then presented to the client.

Framing Homework

Prior to giving the initial assignment to the client, the therapist should explain how homework (or whatever term the therapist believes will be most acceptable to the client) plays a role in therapy. To a college graduate who did well in the classroom, the therapist could say, "Just as you succeeded in school because you studied what you learned in class, I was wondering how you'd feel if I gave you some things to practice at home based on what we talk about in here?" To someone who didn't like school or may have done poorly, relating the assignment to a successful aspect of the client's life is helpful. If the client is successful in sports, for example, the therapist can discuss how practicing free throws is essential to shooting well during a game. Or if the client is an excellent cook, the therapist and client can discuss how reading a recipe is not sufficient to be a good cook. It is essential to experiment, practice, and do real cooking. When the client has a positive attitude and understanding for the purpose of homework, then the therapist may progress and offer the assignment.

Presentation of Homework

After the therapist is certain the client appreciates the value of homework, then the therapist can explain what the specific assignment entails. To start, the therapist should confirm that he and the client agree on the primary goal for therapy. The therapist should then explain how the homework ties in to this goal. The specific assignment should be consistent with both the client's stage of readiness and preferences for learning. Thus, someone who dislikes reading should not be given a reading assignment. Conversely, a person who enjoys aerobics may be given "an exercise" to do. Because people prefer choices, when possible, variations of an assignment should be offered. Similarly, after presenting the homework, the therapist can ask if the assignment "fits" and ask the client for suggestions to modify it. One effective strategy to ascertain whether the client is likely to complete the assignment is to ask the client based on a numeric scale (e.g., 1–100) how likely he is to do the assignment (Freeman & Rosenfield, 2002). If the client responds with a number reflecting a low likelihood of completion, the therapist can ask about barriers and help find ways to overcome them. Alternatively, rather than trying to overcome the barriers, the therapist may instead want to modify the assignment until the client is confident he will complete it.

For several reasons, the therapist is urged to write down homework assignments and give a copy to the client. For one, the client is less likely to forget the specifics of the assignment or misunderstand it. Second, the therapist is giving a message of the importance of the assignment by writing it down. Finally, the client is less likely to forget to do the assignment altogether. Research has demonstrated that clients are more likely to complete assignments that are given to them in writing rather than verbally (Cox, Tisdelle, & Culbert, 1988). Older adults may also need a reminder call during the week to do assignments (Coon & Gallagher–Thompson, 2002). If the therapist is so inclined, he can let the client know to contact him if he has any questions about the homework. After the client has succeeded at easier assignments, the therapist may want to consider more complex ones. As a rule of thumb, the assignment should be hard enough so the client feels he has accomplished something important, but not so complex that he does not have a good chance of succeeding. If an assignment by nature is complex, the therapist should strongly consider having the client practice it during the session so the therapist can verify the client is able to do it.

When to Present Assignments

Typically, homework assignments are given near the end of the session. Enough time should be left so that the client is able to ask questions and understand fully the assignment.

The following is a short vignette to illustrate presentation and selection of a first-session homework assignment. A middle-age man in a science-related profession comes to see a therapist because he is losing his temper more frequently. After doing a diagnostic assessment, the therapist believes his outbursts are directly related to his excessive drinking, which is also getting worse. When the therapist questions the client about his anger being related to his drinking, the client does not deny it outright, but is extremely ambivalent about any connection. At the end of the first session, after building a good rapport through reflective listening and support, the therapist proposes a homework assignment:

Therapist: So, basically you feel you have a problem with your anger and it is getting worse.

Client : Yes, that is right. I seem to get angry out of the blue and then say or do things that I regret.

Therapist: And you can't seem to put your finger on why you get angry and feel you need to know the reason before you can learn to control it.

Client : Yes, exactly.

Therapist: You mentioned you are a meteorologist. I was wondering if you would be willing to do an experiment.

Client : Sure (laughing), if it will help.

Therapist: Okay, good. Let me describe what I am suggesting and you tell me if you think it will be helpful. Every time you get angry, I would like you to write down on a piece of paper, what was happening at the time. It is impossible to be aware of everything, so in particular I would like you to note the day, time, who you are with, where you are, what you are drinking or eating if anything, and barometric pressure. Hopefully, after a few weeks of monitoring you will be able to detect a pattern. Does this sound like a good idea?

Client   : Yes, I hadn't thought of tracking what might be connected to my outbursts, but I'd like to add one more thing. When you said barometric pressure, it reminded me that I may be sensitive to other climatic conditions, like if it is cloudy or sunny, so I am going to note that as well.

Therapist: That makes sense. Also write down anything else that you think may be relevant.

In this vignette, the therapist links the assignment to the goal of therapy (i.e., finding a reason for the anger) and designs the task consistent with the client's belief system. He does not force his theory that the client's anger is related to drinking, which might be viewed as disrespectful, confrontive, and possibly inaccurate. If so, it could result in the client dropping out of treatment. Instead, he proposes an experiment consistent with the client's scientific background, maintaining collaboration and minimizing resistance. The intervention is consistent with client's stage of readiness (contemplation) by being an observational, not behavioral, task. Finally, the therapist does not propose the homework until a good bond with the client is established. Only then may the therapist focus the homework on the client's goal of wanting to understand why he gets angry, an important antecedent of change. The therapist succeeded in proposing a task agreeable to the client that allows the client to discover a connection with what is causing his outbursts.

Reviewing Homework

Unless there is a strong clinical reason not to, homework that is assigned in a previous session should be reviewed at the beginning of the next session. It shows the client that the therapist takes the homework assignment seriously and considers it important to successful outcome in therapy. The therapist summarizes the assignment and asks how it went. Several outcomes are possible. The client may have completed the assignment, partially done it, not done it, or modified it.

When the client completes the assignment, the therapist should not rate the client's success like a test, but rather express support and curiosity. The therapist should ask questions such as: How did it go? What did you learn? Clients should also be given praise for doing the assignment. If the client believes the assignment was helpful, the next assignment should build on the success. If the client thinks it was not helpful, the therapist should elicit more data. The therapist should view the homework as an experiment in which information is always obtained, regardless of whether the assignment was successful. What wasn't helpful? What could be done to make it more useful?

When the client partially completes the assignment, the therapist should question the client to determine in what ways the assignment was only partially done. Did the client not practice as often as was requested? Did he do just part of the assignment and not another part? Before exploring why the assignment was only partially completed, the therapist should reinforce and compliment what the client *did* do. Assignments should not be a source of contention between the therapist and client, but a vehicle for change. Only after the therapist gives encouragement should the therapist explore with the client the reasons why the client did not finish. This often is a fruitful discussion because there are many possible reasons for noncompletion. These include practical barriers (lack of transportation), attitudinal barriers (perfectionism), or the homework may not have been a good fit. The client may have completed part of the assignment while modifying another part, and thus reports that he only did part of it. Based on the reason for the modification, the therapist and client can talk about the obstacles for completion and improvements for the next assignment.

When the client modifies the assignment, which happens quite frequently, it may be because the client misunderstood it. If this is the reason, the therapist should see why it was misunderstood. Did the therapist fail to write down the assignment? Was it too complicated for the client? More frequently, the client deliberately changed the assignment. When there is good therapeutic alliance, the change is usually for the better. The client realized he could learn more by altering it. The therapist should always think about the intention of the assignment rather than the specifics. With modifications, the client should be given the benefit of the doubt. On occasion, the client may modify the assignment because of avoidance. He may be fearful of failure or may actually fear having the problem improve. If this is the case, the therapist must explore these issues with the client.

Lastly, the client may have not done the assignment at all. Although there are varied reasons for this, inquiring usually determines the cause. Often it relates to therapeutic alliance issues, such as lack of rapport, lack of match with the therapy goals, or lack of agreement with task construction. Or the therapist may have miscalculated the client's stage of readiness. If the therapist is having difficulty determining the cause of partial or complete nonadherence, he may want to consider administering the Homework Rating Scale (Kazantzis, Deane, & Ronan, 2004), a 12-item questionnaire, designed to help assess reasons for noncompliance.

KEY MISTAKES AND
MISCOMPREHENSIONS

Ineffective or neophyte therapists tend to choose homework assignments arbitrarily and do not collaborate with their clients. They are not aware which homework assignments have a high chance of succeeding for certain problems. Furthermore, they determine what goals, methods, and homework tasks are best for clients instead of discussing and negotiating. Similarly, they will suggest homework before a strong bond is formed, not tie homework directly to the reasons the client came into treatment, and form a bad match between the client and the homework task.

Good therapists may learn what empirically supported approaches and interventions are supported by research, but master therapists know the importance of helping people change, rather than treating disorders. Master therapists customize homework to fit the individual client.

To illustrate this principle, a therapist was working with a college-age woman who had a fear of choking and as a result had a problem swallowing her food (Connor–Greene, 1993). Because the patient had several traumatic experiences earlier in her life related to choking and because behavioral approaches have been shown to be an effective approach to phobias (McNally, 1986), the therapist opted to teach the client relaxation procedures. During the course of treatment, the client inconsistently did the homework. She did not believe the cause of her choking problems was related to anxiety. Her condition worsened as she limited her intake of foods to ones that had a soft consistency. Noting that the client was Catholic, the therapist asked her if she ever had her throat blessed. The therapist knew the religious story of the young boy who was healed by St. Blaise after a fish bone lodged in his throat. She speculated that the client may have been traumatized by such a "dramatic and potentially frightening experience for a young child" (p. 379). The client did not know and said she would ask her mother. Her mother stated the client, in fact, had her throat blessed several times as a young child. Even though the client had no recollection of it, she trusted her mother's memory. In addition, she had just taken a course on Freud and repression, and believed this explained her problems. Immediately, she began eating solid foods and no longer had a fear of choking. The therapist rightfully concluded that the client did not believe in the therapist's initial theory on why she had a problem with swallowing and thus did not actively participate in therapy. The client eventually improved when the therapist suggested a cause consistent with the client's belief system.

This case shows several important points. First, empirically supported interventions are not always therapeutic and should be abandoned when they are not effective or when it is clear the client rejects the premise for doing them. Second, it is important to take into account the client's view of the problem and gain agreement before offering homework. And third, the therapist should not initially assume the worst for a client's nonadherence (e.g., lack motivation, secondary gains for being dysfunctional, or not suitable for therapy). Instead, the therapist first should look for lack of agreement on goals, tasks, or some practical obstacle to explain nonadherence.

CASE STUDIES

SPEAKING THE CLIENT'S LANGUAGE

In a case seen by the author, a father came in with his 16-year-old son because of repeated contentious arguments between the two of them. It was clear from observing them in session that although there was a strong bond between the two, both had a tendency, when hurt by the other, to counter with inflammatory comments, which quickly escalated into shouting matches. They acknowledged it would be better not to blurt out the first thing that came to their minds, but they didn't know how not to respond impulsively. When calm and in the presence of the therapist, they could clumsily tell the other person their feelings; however, they were not able to maintain this in everyday situations.

Looking for exceptions to the problem, the therapist asked them about times they got along well. Both agreed they could discuss sports and even disagree without insulting comments or loud arguing. In response, the therapist gave them each a yellow handkerchief. He suggested they bring the handkerchiefs home with them and keep them in their back pockets. When they felt the other person made a comment that "pissed them off," they were authorized to "throw the flag." Both father and son laughed, understanding the sports connection. Seeing that the clients liked this idea, the therapist continued. The flag meant a penalty and they were to take a five-minute timeout. No talking was allowed during this time (as if in a penalty box) and they were to use the time to think of what they wanted to say that would help the situation, rather than expressing their hurt feelings through anger. To confirm understanding of the assignment, the therapist had the clients practice in the session. The assignment was effective in diffusing explosive outbursts and improving communication between father and son.

Because of their lack of psychological sophistication and for other specific reasons, the therapist believed it would either take a long time or it would be ineffective to teach them communication skills such as "I" statements, reflective listening, and other strategies typically used for conflict management. Instead, knowing that one of the few areas they both enjoyed together was sports, the therapist found an assignment consistent with their goal that made sense to them. Rather than trying to teach them a brand new skill, the problem resolution was based on an existing strength.

CONNECTING HOMEWORK TO THE
CASE FORMULATION

This client was seen by Nick Cummings, PhD, and is notable not because the homework assignment per se was unusual, but because how he arrived at it reflects the skill of a master therapist.

The client was a middle-age woman who decided to fulfill a lifelong dream to go back to school and become a nurse. She took all her coursework, but failed her licensing exam after studying many months. She planned to it take again. While at nursing school her husband became interested in the profession and also studied to become a nurse. He planned to take the exam at the same time she was to take the second exam. While they studied together, it became obvious to her that he was doing better than she was. She became afraid she would not pass. The night before the exam, she became suicidal. Her husband took her to the emergency room and both missed the exam. After spending a few days in the hospital, she saw an outpatient therapist for several sessions without improvement. The therapist requested Dr. Cummings to see the client for a session. After talking with the client, his operational diagnosis (see Cummings and Sayama, 1995, for a complete description of this concept) was that the client was angry at her husband for succeeding at her dream. She felt it was not fair that she might not become a nurse and he would. At a subconscious level, the suicide attempt was to get back at him for usurping her dream and to make sure he wouldn't steal it from her, although her stated reason for being suicidal was because she felt scared she would fail again. Cummings wanted to help her express her anger in a constructive manner, so she could work out an acceptable solution with her husband.

After building a rapport with the client, by respecting her view of the problem and not directly challenging it, Cummings stated that he could understand completely how she, or anyone, might be angry at her husband. He further stated that because of her sensitive nature it was probably hard for her to acknowledge this anger. After telling her a story about a child who was mad at his mother, then kicked a wall with his foot thinking he would get back at her, but instead just hurt his foot, the client tacitly agreed that her suicidal behavior was self-defeating and not an effective way to express her anger. Seeing how reluctant she was to acknowledge or express anger, Cummings knew that a standard approach to teach her how to act assertively would require many sessions. As an expert in brief therapy, he devised a strategic intervention. He suggested that one way she might show her anger was to set her husband's bed on fire while he was asleep. Surprising the primary therapist (who was behind a one-way mirror), but not Cummings, the client laughed. He gave a few more extreme forms of expressing anger that also evoked more laughter from her. She then started adding a few of her own absurd examples. Finally, Cummings suggested she write down all the ways she could express her anger and then discuss these ideas with her therapist the following week. She thought it was a great idea. Next to Cummings was a stack of computer printer paper. He gave her a few pages to write her responses. She said she would need more than a few pages. As Cummings handed her a ream, she chuckled. As she was putting it in her purse and noticed how heavy it was she said with a smile, "I think I will tell my husband I am too tired to carry my purse and I will have him carry it for me."

The client came in depressed with suppressed rage and left laughing. Interestingly, she didn't end up doing the assigned homework, but instead told her husband that she was mad that he was going to become a nurse instead of her. He didn't realize she felt that way and he told her he would help her pass the test and he would only take the test after she passed.

Cummings found a way, through normalizing and then amplifying her emotions, to help her appropriately express her feelings. The homework was effective because it followed the principles outlined in this chapter. It was only offered after rapport was established, related specifically to the reason the client entered therapy, was salient to the focus of the session, agreeable to the therapist and client, doable, and had a clear rationale. It was also tailored specifically to this client. Cummings gave outrageous examples of expressing anger as a prelude to the assignment. Through contrast, he gave permission to the client to acknowledge and express more appropriate forms of anger. He would never have said what he did to a client who had a history or tendency toward aggressive or violent behavior, a thought disorder, or even someone able to express anger appropriately. This example shows how master therapists use homework to speed up the course of therapy and how it is tied into a deep understanding of clients' dynamics, reasons for entering therapy, and presentation style.

SUMMARY

Research has shown that therapy that includes homework improves outcome. This is likely because homework takes advantage of time available between therapy sessions, allows the client to practice concepts learned in therapy, and helps the client be an active participant in the change process. Unfortunately, approximately one third of clients do not complete homework assignments (Hansen and Warner, 1994). Because increasing adherence improves outcome, methods that increase adherence are extremely important. How and when homework is presented, framed, and reviewed impact adherence. The following are the main considerations for designing and assigning effective homework:

- Form a strong bond with the client through effective use of reflective listening, empathy, and genuineness.
- Understand the client's view of the problem and aim one's approach to be consistent with the client's understanding.
- Achieve goal consensus with the client.
- Respect the client's level for readiness to change. Gear interventions to the client's stage of readiness.
- Learn empirically supported treatments, yet tailor assignments to the specific client.
- Achieve task consensus.
- Make assignments small and relatively simple at first.
- Build assignments on clients' strengths.
- Confirm the client understands, has the ability to complete, and has confidence he can accomplish the assignment.
- Make assignments "well formed."
- If necessary, practice the homework in session and write down specifics for the client.

In conclusion, master therapists not only know the literature on what homework assignments are likely to work with specific problems, they attend to client characteristics and beliefs, and tailor interventions to fit uniquely for that person.

REFERENCES

Addis, M. E., & Jacobson, N. S. (2000). A closer look at the treatment rationale and homework compliance in cognitive–behavioral therapy for depression. *Cognitive Therapy and Research, 24,* 313–326.

Badgio, P. C., Halperin, G. A., & Barber, J. P. (1999). Acquisition of adaptive skills: Psychotherapeutic change in cognitive and dynamic therapies. *Clinical Psychology Review, 19,* 721–737.

Beutler, L. E., Malik, M., Alimohamed, S., Harwood, T. M., Talebi, H., Noble, S., & Wong, E. (2004). *Therapist variables.* In M. L. Lambert (Ed.). *Bergin and Garfield's handbook of psychotherapy and behavior change* (5th ed., pp. 227–306). New York: Wiley.

Beyebach, M., Morejon, A. R., Palenzuela, D. L., & Rodriguez–Arias, J. L. (1996). Research on the process of solution-focused therapy. In S. D. Miller, M. A. Hubble, & B. L. Duncan (Eds.). *Handbook of solution-focused brief therapy* (pp. 299–334). San Francisco: Jossey-Bass.

Bordin, E. S. (1979). The generalizability of the psychoanalytic concept of the working alliance. *Psychotherapy: Theory, Research, and Practice, 16,* 252–260.

Brown–Standridge, M. D. (1989). A paradigm for construction of family therapy tasks. *Family Process, 28,* 471–489.

Burns, D. D., & Nolen–Hoekseman, S. (1992). Therapeutic empathy and recovery from depression in cognitive–behavioral therapy: A structural equation model. *Journal of Consulting and Clinical Psychology, 60,* 441–449.

Connor–Greene, P. A. (1993). The therapeutic context: Preconditions for change in psychotherapy. *Psychotherapy, 30,* 375–382.

Conoley, C. W., Padula, M. A., Payton, D. S., & Daniels, J. A. (1994). Predictors of client implementation of counselor recommendations: Match with problem, difficulty level, and building on client strengths. *Journal of Counseling Psychology, 41*, 3–7.

Coon, D. W., & Gallagher–Thompson, D. (2002). Encouraging homework completion among older adults in therapy. *Journal of Clinical Psychology, 58*, 549–563.

Cox, D. J., Tisdelle, D. A., & Culbert, J. P. (1988). Increasing adherence to behavioral homework assignments. *Journal of Behavioral Medicine, 11*, 519–522.

Cummings, N., & Sayama, M. (1995). *Focused psychotherapy: A casebook of brief, intermittent psychotherapy throughout the life cycle.* New York: Brunner/Mazel.

Dattilo, F. M. (2002). Homework assignments in couple and family therapy. *Journal of Clinical Psychology, 58*, 535–547.

Detweiler, J. B., & Whisman, M. A. (1999). The role of homework assignment in cognitive therapy for depression: Potential methods for enhancing adherence. *Clinical Psychology: Science and Practice, 6*, 267–282.

DiClemente, C. C., & Velasquez, M. M. (2002). In W. R. Miller & S. Rollnick (Eds.). *Motivational interviewing: Preparing people for change* (2nd ed., pp. 201–216). New York: Guilford Press.

Freeman, A., & Rosenfield, B. (2002). Modifying therapeutic homework for patients with personality disorders. *Journal of Clinical Psychology, 58*, 513–524.

Garland, A., & Scott, J. (2002). Using homework in therapy for depression. *Journal of Clinical Psychology, 58*, 489–498.

Hansen, D. J., & Warner, J. E. (1994). Treatment adherence of maltreating families: A survey of professionals regarding prevalence and enhancement strategies. *Journal of Family Violence, 9*, 1–19.

Kazantzis, N., & Deane, F. P. (1999). Psychologists' use of homework assignments in clinical practice. *Professional Psychology: Research and Practice, 30*, 581–585.

Kazantzis, N., Deane, F. P., & Ronan, K. R. (2000). Homework assignments in cognitive and behavioral therapy: A meta-analysis. *Clinical Psychology: Science and Practice, 7*, 189–202.

Kazantzis, N., Deane, F. P., & Ronan, K. R. (2004). Assessing compliance with homework assignment: Review and recommendations for clinical practice. *Journal of Clinical Psychology, 60*, 627–641.

Kazantzis, N., & Lampropoulos, G. L. (2002). Using homework assignments in psychotherapy. *Journal of Clinical Psychology, 58*, 487–585.

Keijsers, G. P., Schaap, C. P., & Hoogduin, C. A. (2000). The impact of interpersonal patient and therapist behavior on outcome in cognitive–behavior therapy. *Behavior Modification, 24*, 264–297.

Lambert, M. L., & Ogles, B. M. (2004). The efficacy and effectiveness of psychotherapy. In M. L. Lambert (Ed.). (2004). *Bergin and Garfield's handbook of psychotherapy and behavior change* (5th ed., pp. 139–193). New York: Wiley.

McNally, R. J. (1986). Behavioral treatment of a choking phobia. *Journal of Behavior Therapy and Experimental Psychiatry, 17*, 185–188.

Prochaska, J. O., DiClemente, C. C., & Norcross, J. C. (1992). In search of how people change. *American Psychologist, 47*, 1102–1114.

Schultheis, G. M. (1998). *Brief therapy homework planner.* New York: Wiley.

Shelton, J. L., & Levy, R. L. (1981). *Behavioral assignments and treatment compliance.* Champaign, IL: Research Press.

Tompkins, M. A. (2002). Guidelines for enhancing homework compliance. *Psychotherapy in Practice, 58*, 565–576.

Tompkins, M. A. (2003). Effective homework. In R. L. Leahy (Ed.). *Roadblocks in cognitive–behavioral therapy* (pp. 49–66). New York: Guilford Press.

Woody, S. R., & Sanderson, W. C. (1998). Manuals for empirically supported treatments: 1998 update. *The Clinical Psychologist, 51*, 17–21.

13

SKILLS TRAINING: HOW THE MASTER CLINICIAN UNDERSTANDS AND TEACHES COMPETENCIES

WILLIAM O'DONOHUE

Department of Psychology
University of Nevada
Reno, Nevada

The philosopher Immanual Kant (1957) has stated that "Ought implies can." This is a claim that states that it is wrong, and even nonsensical, to request that someone ought to do something when in fact they simply cannot do that behavior. It is the thesis of this chapter that following this precept is of utmost importance in psychotherapy. Thus, therapists need to understand accurately what in fact a client can or cannot do as both life and therapists ask clients to perform behaviors. We, as therapists, can either underestimate our client's abilities and potential, leading to one set of problematic therapy outcomes, or overestimate our clients' abilities, leading to another set of undesirable outcomes. In the case of skill deficits, therapists may need to respond appropriately to them, sometimes by teaching clients how to avoid situations that call for these skills (difficult but not impossible), or, in the usual case, by teaching clients the requisite skills so they can be more successful emotionally and instrumentally in these situations. It is the thesis of this chapter that a master psychotherapist never violates Kant's dictum and is indeed quite skilled in recognizing skills deficits and competencies, and in remediating key deficits.

One of the clearest cases of skill deficits, but by no means the only case, is with the developmentally disabled. Autistic children often do not possess a range of basic skills, including the skill of making eye contact, of interactive play, or even of naming objects (Lovaas, 2003). The same can be said of the mentally retarded (Rush & Frances, 2000). In one example of a therapist who was clearly not a master, I saw a group of developmentally delayed adults in "group therapy" who were being chastised by the group's therapist for contributing too little to the group discussion. I had had contact with most of the group's participants and knew that, unfortunately, many were non-verbal and the rest did not have the more advanced verbal skills to participate in group therapy. This was clearly a case of a therapist not understanding their clients' skill level and not responding appropriately with skill training. The therapist was simply trying to fit his preferred modality, group therapy, to a client population he found in his caseload. However, this example also reflects an important lesson: Perhaps when we are becoming frustrated with our clients it is because we are asking them to do something they in fact cannot do. We have inadvertently violated the Kantian dictum.

Another important lesson is that skills deficits are idiosyncratic. We may have the skills to respond effectively to one problem but not to another, even when the problems or the skills are seemingly closely related. We may have the ability to start conversations with individuals of the same sex but not with individuals of the opposite sex, for example. Or we may have the ability to talk to the opposite sex but not to ask them out for a date or to initiate and maintain conversations in this context. In addition, skill deficits are idiosyncratic in that individuals who belong to one diagnostic group can vary tremendously in their skill level. The moderately mentally retarded, for example, may not have occupational skills, or may have high levels of them. Individual assessment of both clients' skill sets and of environmental demands is imperative.

However, I do not want to construct a misconception. I am not claiming that skills training is only relevant to the developmentally disabled. Paul (1974), for example, has constructed an extremely effective program for schizophrenics that relies on skills training. The chronically mentally ill, even after medication, often have what are called *negative symptoms*, which, in part, consist of a variety of skills deficits including those relevant to social interactions, grooming, employment, recreation, and so forth. Paul's (1974) program targets these skills deficits directly and has very positive outcomes.

Another highly systematic and successful population has been juvenile delinquents (often given the diagnoses of conduct disorder or oppositional defiant disorder). Goldstein and McGinnis (1997) in his innovative and evidenced-based *Skillstreaming the Adolescent* teaches adolescents, including adolescents who have had problems with the law, skills such as opening and maintaining conversations, empathy, conflict resolution, and even talking to the police. In fact developmental theorists (Marini, 1984; Moore & Carey,

2005) have discussed that as one progresses through life one has different tasks that need to be performed. A key clinical issue it the extent to which the client has these skills. Clients may have skills for one set of developmental tasks (parenting), but not another (handling retirement). Table 13.1 gives a rough idea of what some of these developmental tasks may be.

TABLE 13.1   Developmental Tasks

Life Stage	Developmental Task
Infancy (birth–2 y)	Social attachment Maturation of sensory, perceptual, and motor functions Sensorimotor intelligence and primitive causality Understanding the nature of objects and creating categories
Toddlerhood (2–4 y)	Improved locomotion Language development Self-control
Early school age (4–6 y)	Sex role identification Early moral development Self-esteem Group play
Middle school age (6–12 y)	Friendship Concrete operations Variety of functional skill learning Self-evaluation Team play
Early adolescence (12–18 y)	Formal operations Emotional development Membership in the peer group Sexual relationships
Later adolescence (18–22 y)	Autonomy from parents Sex role identity Internalized morality Career choice
Early adulthood (22–34 y)	Marriage Child bearing Work
Middle adulthood (34–60 y)	Nurturing the marriage relationship Management of household Parenting Management of a career
Later adulthood (60–75 y)	Promoting intellectual vigor Redirecting energy to new roles and activities Adopting one's life Developing a point of view about death
Very old age (75 y until death)	Coping with physical changes of aging Developing a psychohistorical perspective

Other examples of skill training approaches include

1. *Parent training*—teaching parents (including parents of children with attention deficit disorder [ADD]) how to use positive attention, time in and time out, reward systems, and so on, to increase their ability to manage the behavior of their children

2. *Marital and couples' skills*—teaching couples how to listen, validate, reflect, call "timeouts," resolve conflicts, and so on

3. *Assertion training*—teaching individuals to stand up for their rights without violating the rights of others by teaching assertive statements, appropriate escalation, and anger control

4. *Problem-solving skills*—teaching clients how to see life challenges as problems, make constructive problem statements, brainstorm solutions, choose among solutions generated, implement one possible solution, evaluate the progress on the problem, and perhaps go through the cycle again

5. *Social skills training*—teaching a wide range of individuals (the shy, the socially anxious, those having problems dating, ADD children, and so on) how to initiate, maintain, and close conversations; how to resolve conflict; how to find and engage in common interests, and so forth

6. *Academic skills*—teaching students the organizational, note-taking, test-taking, problem-solving skills necessary to succeed at school

7. *Vocational skills training*—teaching, especially the developmentally delayed, the skills necessary for successful employment

8. *Stress management skills*—teaching individuals how to cope and respond to stress by using techniques such as deep breathing, progressive muscle relaxation, coping statements, and seeking social support

9. *Recreational skills*—teaching individuals how to enjoy life through hobbies, downtime, and so forth, which can be particularly important for workaholics and type A individuals

These are just a few examples. O'Donohue and Krasner (1995) have compiled a extensive collection of skills-based interventions.

BACKGROUND: WHY ARE SKILLS NECESSARY?

The most general answer to this question is that life itself presents a series of problems and these problems need skillful responses for the person to survive. This view is consistent with evolutionary epistemology of leading thinkers such as the social psychologist Donald Campbell (1974), the analytical philosopher Wilford Van Orman Quine (1994), the learning researcher B. F. Skinner (1953), and the philosopher of science Karl Popper (1999) (see O'Donohue, Lloyd, and Ferguson, 2005, for a further explication of evolutionary epistemology). The central idea is that survival and reproduction are problems, and they give rise to numerous subproblems that some solve and some do not. Life's problems require skillful performance for their resolution. Life typically throws a large number and a diverse set of problems at us and typically, to navigate life successfully, we need a wide range of competencies. When we don't have them, we can feel depressed, anxious, and be dysfunctional in some context. Skills training can potentially remediate these problems.

More specifically, a skill-based approach to therapy is based on the following considerations:

1. Situations and problems arise regularly in which, to achieve some end (e.g., solve the problem, realize some personal goal), an individual must be able to respond in a competent, skilled manner.

2. Situations and problems create diverse demands (e.g., need to communicate, need to solve some problem, need to relax, need to interact successfully with others).

3. These diverse demands require diverse skills and capacities (e.g., communication skills, social skills, relaxation skills, problem-solving skills) for this resolution. Life has its "hidden curriculum" (Chan & Rueda, 1979).

4. Individuals vary in their abilities to execute various skills. All individuals have a range of potential abilities, although, as a result of certain conditions (e.g., genetic, physiological, or environmental/learning problems), individuals can have restricted potentials or restricted levels of achievement within a given potentiality.

5. Some individuals, at certain times and in certain situations, are deficient in skills necessary to meet some demand or achieve some end. The qualifiers in the previous sentence are there to indicate the situational specificity of performance deficits.

6. When situational demands arise that exceed the individual's skills, states of affairs may arise that may be variously described as lack of success, frustration, or even depression; psychophysiological illnesses; and the like. The manner in which these consequences are described has important implications concerning what appears to be a reasonable way to improve these states of affairs.

7. These individuals can often profit from an educational (psychoeducational) experience in which skill and performance deficits are directly addressed and remediated.

8. Remediation itself involves skills. Understanding that one has a problem involves the skill of being appropriately self-critical (O'Donohue & Lloyd, 2005), being motivated to attempt to change it also involves skills (Miller & Rollnick, 2003); and even successfully participating in therapy involves skills (Linehan, 2000).

Another issue is that diagnosing some performance as evidence of a "skills deficits" involves a value judgment. This value judgment is complex. McFall (1982) has stated:

> When a behavior is called competent, this involves a value-based judgment by an observer concerning the effectiveness of an individual's performance in a specific task. Three aspects of this definition need to be stressed: First, competence is a judgment about behavior and not a judgment about some enduring characteristic of the performer; second, the judgment is based on an episode of behavior within a context, not merely on a single, isolated molecular act; and third, the judge who evaluates the competence of a performance does so on the basis of certain implicit or explicit values. (p. 23).

It is important to note that there is typically a distinction between possession of a skill set and competent performance. Someone may or may not possess a skill set, and this may be the reason for a problematic performance in some situations. On the other hand, someone may have the requisite skill set but have interfering factors (such as intoxication, anxiety, depression, fatigue) interfere with competent performance. The master clinician must also keep this hypothesis in mind during assessment.

The master therapist needs to make these judgments well; prioritize what are the key skill deficits, particularly judging what are key performance demands for this particular client (possibly among many skills deficits and performance demands); and understand the kind and validity of judgments of skills being made by key individuals in the client's environment.

POTENTIAL ADVANTAGES OF A
SKILLS TRAINING APPROACH

It may be useful to understand some of the advantages of attempting to understand at least a part of the client's problems resulting from skill deficits. O'Donohue and Krasner (1995) have suggested that these are the following:

1. Psychological skills training relies on the mechanism of "learning" that is relatively well researched, clear, and understood; instead of on less well-researched, clear, and understood mechanisms such as cathartic insight or authentic living.

2. Psychological skills training relies on the notion of continua of skill abilities and competencies, as well as of situational demands determining what abilities are necessary to produce what ends. Therefore, by eschewing categorical pejorative judgments such as those found in the Diagnostic and Statistical Manual of Mental Disorders (DSM-IV-TR), psychological skills training construes problems in living in which a way as to decrease stigma associated with psychological difficulties. Reducing stigma is important because it can be an iatrogenic cost to help-seeking behavior.

3. Psychological skills training potentially decreases power differentials (and thereby potential abuses) between trainer and client in several ways. By stressing that the trainer relies on and can improve on the same skill as the client, the trainer avoids creating a potentially invidious dichotomy in which the healthy (or rational) is helping the sick (or irrational). Clearly, explication of goals gives the client a better basis for independently determining his or her own progress and status. Finally, explicating the content of training (e.g., assertion skills) puts the client in a better position to understand therapy.

4. Psychological skills training directly implies a course of remediation, unlike problems encountered when conceptualizing problems along the lines of the diagnoses found in the *Diagnostic and Statistical Manual of Mental Disorders,* third edition, revised (American Psychiatric Association, 1987), which have notorious problems in predicting what treatment will be recommended.

5. A psychological skills training model provides clear, testable hypotheses concerning the origin of psychological problems (e.g., deficiencies in exposure to skilled models at certain developmental periods). Skills deficits may represent a potentially important source of proximate causes of psychological problems. For example, social skills and problem-solving deficits may be an important proximate cause of depression (Becker, Heimberg, & Bellack, 1987; Lewinsohn, Mischel, Chaplin & Barton, 1980); deficits in relaxation skills may lead to anxiety (Wolpe, 1958). McFall (1976) suggests that skills deficits themselves may arise from "lack of experience or opportunity to learn, faulty learning as a result of unrepresentative or faulty experiences, obsolescence of a previously adaptive response, learning disabilities resulting from biological dysfunctions, or traumatic events, such as injuries or diseases, that nullify prior learning or obstruct new learning" (p. 6). Thus, the etiological chain could be as follows: one of McFall's factors → competency deficit → psychological sequelae (e.g., depression). This model would predict and therefore could be tested by the existence of a direct relationship between increased competency and decreased psychological problems. In fact, DeNelsky and Boat (1986) have recently advanced a model of psychological diagnosis and treatment in which problems are analyzed in terms of skill deficits rather than in terms of symptoms or pathologies.

6. Skills training may be an important method for the prevention of problems. For example, early training in basic competencies and application of certain skills at key developmental periods may lessen the degree of problems in adulthood. Building competence in skills may serve to buffer or obviate the negative effects of stress, conflict, and problems. Egan (1984) recounts an interesting fable relevant to this issue:

> A person walking beside a river sees someone drowning. This person jumps in, pulls the victim out, and begins artificial respiration. Then another drowning person calls for help. The rescuer jumps into the water again, and pulls the second victim out. This process repeats itself several times until finally, much to the amazement of the

bystanders who have gathered to watch this drama, the rescuer, even though the screams of yet another victim can be clearly heard from the river, gets up from administering artificial respiration and begins to walk upstream. One of the by-standers calls out, "Where are you going? Can't you hear the cries of the latest victim?" The rescuer replies, "You take care of him. I'm going upstream to find out who's pushing all these people in and see whether I can stop it." He might have added, "I'm also going to find out why all these people can't swim and see whether I can teach them how." (p. 23)

Competencies in skills may reduce the threat of stress and psychological diatheses. For example, Liberman, DeRisi, and Mueser (1989) have suggested that skills training, especially social skills training, can improve psychosocial functioning and decrease the relapse rate among schizophrenics. Finally, to the extent that there are predictable developmental problems and tasks (Erikson, 1956; Havighurst, 1953), psychological skills training can be used across the life span to enable individuals to handle these developmental tasks better.

7. Problems are seen as arising from a discrepancy between an individual's capabilities and environmental demands. This interactive model is consistent with the literature (Mischel, 1976), which shows that the greatest portion of variance is accounted for by this interaction.

8. Psychological skills training avoids what may be called the *irrationalist's inconsistency* of certain models, in which therapists are rational scientist–practitioners who weigh evidence in coming to their conclusions, but whose conclusions are that human behavior is controlled by irrational (e.g., unconscious sex and aggressive) forces. Helping professionals, as part of their specialized role, should be especially competent at problem-solving skills in domains relevant to their professional work, as well as at scientific thinking skills (Kuhn, Amsel & O'Loughlin, 1988).

9. Psychological skills training in providing clearly specified and focused topics and training goals is more amenable to scientific evaluation than more artful forms of psychotherapy that rely on less replicable and more idiosyncratic modes of therapeutic interaction. Replication is a key to the scientific study of a phenomenon.

10. Although consistent with a deficit model of intervention, psychological skills training also is consistent with a personal growth model in which individuals who are performing relatively competently strive for further improvement in various skill areas.

11. Goldstein, Gershaw, and Sprafkin (1985) have argued that traditional psychotherapy, with its emphasis on verbal abilities, insight, and middle class values, is often inappropriate with lower socioeconomic status clients, and that psychological skills training has advantages (e.g., it is shorter term, more concrete, and more directive) that are particularly useful for this population.

12. To the extent that similar component skills are necessary for topographically dissimilar tasks (e.g., pain management is necessary for both maintaining an exercise regimen and coping with chronic headaches), an independent measure of this component skill should allow more accurate prediction of behavior across similar (e.g., different episodes of headache coping) as well as dissimilar (e.g., headache coping, maintaining a jogging regimen) tasks. As Schlundt and McFall (1985) have pointed out, prediction based on an assessment of component skills and task demands is potentially more useful than other models of behavioral assessment, which predict that similar behaviors will occur in similar situations.

13. Psychological skills training, to the extent that it teaches general skills such as problems solving, may enable the client to be in a better position to solve diverse problems and not only the problem that may have precipitated professional contact. As Larson (1984) has stated, "to treat [in traditional therapy] is to give a person a fish, to train [in skills] is to teach a person how to fish" (p. 9).

14. Larson (1984) has suggested that "the replicability, accessibility, portability, brevity, and efficiency of skills training approaches make them ideal vehicles for extending training in helping skills beyond the circumscribed traditional population of mental health workers" (p. 9). Kiesler (1980) has suggested that, given recent epidemiological data (Regier, Goldberg, & Taube, 1978), current supplies of professional helpers cannot meet current needs:

> If the nation used the whole 65 million hours of service delivery potentially available to it through licensed psychologists and psychiatrists, a total pool of approximately three hours per person needing treatment per year would be involved, for the most optimistic estimates of need. This would vary downward to 40 minutes per person per year at the most pessimistic estimate. (p. 1070).

Larson (1984) argues for the use of paraprofessionals, health care workers, self-help groups, parents, teachers, and other lay helpers as additional sources of trainers in psychological skills. This is in direct contrast to psychoanalytical models of professional helpers in which extensive training and perhaps years of individual psychotherapy are required before a position is ready to provide help to others.

15. Some recent research reveals that some problems in depression may be successfully remediated by teaching a basic set of skills, including regular exercise and behavioral activation (basically teaching clients that they have to work each day to program response-contingent reinforcement into their lives). These basic skills can also have positive effects on other problems (such as weight control, blood pressure, and so on) and therefore may have very widespread, fundamental benefits.

THE MAJOR CLINICAL
QUESTIONS IN SKILLS TRAINING

Once the clinician has adopted a skills training perspective, there are several choice points that the master psychotherapist must make well. These include

1. *Whom to teach?* This decision involves two questions: Who is going to be the trainer and who will be the participants?

2. *What to teach?* This requires a careful assessment of the needs of the individuals to be taught. If Rude and Rehm (1991) are correct, for the treatment of depression it requires a careful assessment of the individual's strengths. A clear identification of goals is important both for the trainer and the participant.

3. *Reasons for teaching?* Why is it desirable for the participants to achieve a certain level of particular skills?

4. *Where and when to teach?* Should such skills be taught early, in an attempt at primary prevention? Are they so crucial that they should be taught in an important institutional setting, such as schools?

5. *How to teach?* What means and methods are available for achieving the desired ends? Considerations include beginning at a point already reached by the participant; working at an appropriate pace for the participant; arriving at clear, reasonable goals to which the client gives informed consent; setting shorter term goals; evaluating progress; and providing feedback and reward.

6. *What to evaluate?* Davis and Butchner (1985) have correctly pointed out that, just as feedback is essential in training, so is feedback essential for the course designer and trainer. This is particularly important because feedback is essential in improving the intervention. Given the critical nature of feedback, Davis and Butchner (1985) have recommended that it be viewed as a vital and integral part of the course.

Larson (1984) has suggested that psychological skills training is characterized by the following:

- They all involve the active participation of clients and trainees in the process.
- There is a focus on specific behaviors (internal and external) and the mastery and maintenance of these behaviors.
- The programs are based on established learning principles of observing, discriminating, reinforcing, and generalizing
- Each program includes both didactic and experiential emphases.
- The programs are highly structured.
- Goals are clear.

- Progress is monitored.
- Mystification is minimized.

Schlundt and McFall (1985) also have proposed that tasks are useful units of analysis. According to McFall (1982):

> One must understand these important features of [a] task: its purpose, its constraints, its setting, the rules governing task performance, the criteria for distinguishing between successful and unsuccessful performance and how the task relates to other aspects of the person's life system (p. 15).

McFall (1982) has provided a useful conceptual framework for skills training: (1) identifying and prioritizing relevant and critical life tasks for the individual or group, (2) providing a behavioral analysis of each task, (3) obtaining a representative sample of each individual's performance on each task, (4) establishing task-specific criteria of competent performance for each task, (5) evaluating performance samples, and (6) providing summarizations, integrations, and interpretations of the evaluation results.

Schlundt and McFall (1985) have also suggested that the concept for life space is useful for the assessment in psychological skills training. An individual's life space is the totality of tasks that structure the individual's day-to-day activities. Similar individuals have similar life spaces. For example, all students are involved in academic and social tasks, among other tasks.

Some important questions to ask to identify skills deficits include

1. What sort of skills deficits might be responsible for the clinical presentation (self-control and exercise among the obese, activation skills among the depressed, and so on?)

2. Is there any evidence that the client has ever performed in that manner required by this task? If not, perhaps there is a skill deficit; if so, perhaps a factor such as anxiety may be interfering with competent performance.

3. Can I create an analogous situation (e.g., role-play) to determine whether the client can perform the task competently?

4. Is the skill a common deficit that aligns with the clinical presentation (such as heterosocial skills among adolescents, parenting skills among recent parents, relaxation skills among the high achieving) that might be reasonable to have at least a moderate index of suspicion?

5. When I interact with this patient what sort of strengths and weaknesses do I sense?

TECHNOLOGY, DISSEMINATION, AND SKILLS TRAINING

The task can seem daunting, but there are a variety of evidence-based resources that are quite useful in skills training. A number of self-help books have been written to teach skills that can either be used by the clients alone or as adjuncts in therapy. Becker's (1971) *Parents Are Teachers* or Patterson's (1977) *Living with Children* teach parenting skills. Robin, Kent, O'Leary, Foster, and Prinz (1977) teach problem and communication skills with adolescents. *A Couple's Guide to Communication* (Gottman, Notarius, Markman, & Gonso, 1990) teaches reflective listening, validation, compromise, and problem solving skills. Nezues and Nezu's (1989) *Clinical Decision Making in Behavior Therapy: A Problem Solving Perspective* teaches basic problem-solving skills. Sbraga–Penix's and O'Donohue's *The Sex Addiction Workbook* (2004) teaches self-control and relapse prevention skills to those who have a sexual control problem. Often these books are based on evidenced-based principles and have been evaluated with positive results.

Carol Webster–Stratton (2003) has made a very nice series of videotapes that teaches a wide variety of child management skills to parents. This is an important but somewhat neglected medium in our profession. We know that individuals can learn from modeling (Bandura, 2004), and Webster–Stratton (2003) does a very nice of job of using coping models, not just mastery models. We also know that some individuals have verbal problems that make talk therapy more difficult for them. Video is a nice medium for these individuals. With the emergence of the Web and streaming technology, therapy development should look to Web-based skills training. This can be of particular importance in making this approach more affordable, less stigmatizing, and more accessible to many neglected populations.

SUMMARY AND CONCLUSIONS

Life has its "hidden curriculum". Good functioning requires a wide variety of competencies. Individuals vary considerably in their skill sets and in their actual performances of these skills. A master psychotherapist understands the skills sets and performances that are needed for good functioning in the client's particular environment. Some of these competencies are hard to come by for many (e.g., heterosocial skills for adolescent males); some hard to come by because of underlying problems (work skills for the developmentally disabled); some inhibited due to other problems (fluent speaking by the speech anxious); some a bit "strange" sounding (e.g., effectively interacting with police so that the adolescent can avoid arrest) and with all of these there can be important questions about the level of competency, the consistency, and other nuances that can have a large impact on how competent the behavior actuall is. A master therapist never asks or allows the client to keep operating in an environment in which the client simply cannot perform the requisite skills. Instead the master therapist understands the the "hidden curriculum" necessary for the client to function, and teaches or disinhibits skills so that the client has important success experiences.

REFERENCES

American Psychiatric Association. (1987). *Diagnostic and statistical manual — III.* Washington D.C.: American Psychiatric Association.

Bandura, A. (2004). Swimming against the mainstream: The early years from chilly tributary to transformative mainstream. *Behavior Research & Therapy 42,* 613–630.

Becker, W. C. (1971). *Parents are teachers: A child management program.* Chicago: Research Press.

Becker, R. E., Heimberg, R. G., & Bellack, A. S. (1987). *Social skills training treatment for depression.* New York: Pergamon Press.

Campbell, D. T. (1974). Evolutionary epistemology. In P. A. Schilpp (Ed.). *The philosophy of Karl Popper* (pp. 47–89). La Salle, IL: Open Court.

Chan, K. S., & Rueda, R. (1979). Poverty and culture in education: Separate but equal. *Exceptional Children 45,* 422–428.

Davis, H., & Butchner, P. (1985). Sharing psychological skills. *British Journal of Medical Psychology 58,* 207–216.

DeNelsky, G. Y., & Boat, B. W. (1986). A coping skills model of psychological diagnosis and treatment. *Professional Psychology: Research and Practice 17,* 322–330.

Egan, G. (1984). People in systems: A comprehensive model for psychosocial education and training. In D. Larson (Ed.). *Teaching psychological skills: Models for giving psychology away* (p. 21–43). Monterey, CA: Brooks/Cole.

Erikson, E. H. (1956). Growth and crises of the "healthy personality." In C. Kluckhohn & H. A. Murray (Eds.). *Personality in nature, society and culture* (2nd ed). New York: Knopf.

Goldstein A. P. & McGinnis, E. (1997). Skills training the adolescent: New strategies and Perspectives for teaching prosocial skills. 2nd ed. Chicago, IL: Research Press.

Goldstein, A. P., Gershaw, N. J., & Sprafkin, R. P. (1985). Structured learning: Research and practice in psychological skill training. In L. L'Abate & M. A. Milan (Eds.). *Handbook of social skills training and research* (pp. 284–302). New York: Wiley.

Gottman, J. M., Notarius, C., Markman, H., & Gonso, J. (1990). *A couple's guide to communication.* Chicago: Research Press Company.

Havighurst, R. J. (1953). *Human development and education.* New York: Longmans, Green.

Kant, I. (1957). *The critique of judgment.* Oxford: Claredon Press.

Kiesler, C. A. (1980). Mental health policy as a field of inquiry for psychology. *American Psychologist 35,* 1066–1080.

Kuhn, D., Amsel, E., & O'Loughlin, M. (1988). *The development of scientific thinking skills.* San Diego: Academic Press.

Larson, D. (1984). *Teaching psychological skills: Models for giving psychology away.* Monterey, CA: Brooks/Cole.

Lewinsohn, P. M., Mischel, W., Chaplin, W., & Barton, R. (1980). Social competence and depression: The role of illusory self-perceptions. *Journal of Abnormal Psychology, 89,* 203–212.

Liberman, R. P., DeRisi, W. J., & Mueser, K. T. (1989). *Social skills training for psychiatric patients.* New York: Pergamon Press.

Linehan, M. M. (2000). Commentary on innovations with dialectical behavior therapy. *Cognitive & Behavioral Practice 7,* 478–481.

Lovaas, O. I. (2003). *Teaching individuals with developmental delays: Basic intervention techniques.* Austin, TX: PRO-ED.

Marini, M. M. (1984). The order of events in the transition to adulthood. *Sociology of Education 57,* 63–84.

McFall, R. M. (1976). *Behavioral training: A skill-acquisition approach to clinical problems.* Morristown, NJ: General Learning Press.

McFall, R. M. (1982). A review and reformulation of the concept of social skills. *Behavioral Assessment 4*, 1–33.

Miller, W. R., & Rollnick, S. (2003). Motivational interviewing: Preparing people to change. *Journal of Forensic Psychology 21*, 83–85.

Mischel, W. (1976). *Introduction to personality* (2nd ed). New York: Holt, Rinehart & Winston.

Moore, T., & Carey, L. (2005). Friendship formation in adults with learning disorders: Peer-mediated approaches to social skills development. *British Journal of Learning Disabilities 33*, 23–26.

Nezu, A. M., & Nezu, C. M. (1989). *Clinical decision making in behavior therapy: A problem solving perspective.* Chicago: Research Press.

O'Donohue, W. T., & Krasner, L. (Eds.). (1995). *Theories in behavior therapy.* Washington DC: American Psychological Association Books.

O'Donohue, W., & Lloyd, A. (2005). Philosophical problems in psychology. In W. Craighead & C. Nemeroff (Eds.). *Encyclopedia of psychology and neuroscience.* John Wiley & Sons, 112–115.

O'Donohue, W., Lloyd, A., & Ferguson, K. E. (In preparation). *Evolutionary epistemology: An account of knowledge for contemporary psychology.*

Patterson, G. R. (1977). *Living with children: New methods for parents and teachers.* Chicago: Research Press.

Paul, G. L. (1974). Experimental–behavioral approaches to schizophrenia. In R. Cancro & N. Fox (Eds.). *Strategic intervention in schizophrenia: Current developments in treatment.* Pasadena, CA: Behavioral Publications, 63–84.

Popper, K. R. (1999). *All life is problem solving.* New York: Routledge.

Quine, W. V. O. (1994). Epistemology naturalized. In H. Kornblith (Ed.). *Naturalizing epistemology.* MIT Press: Cambridge, MA, 22–36.

Regier, D. A., Goldberg, I. D., & Taube, C. A. (1978). The de facto U.S. mental health services system. *Archives of General Psychiatry 35*, 685–693.

Robin, A. L., Kent, R. N., O'Leary, K. D., Foster, S., & Prinz, R. (1977). Teaching parents and adolescents problem solving communication skills. *Behavior Therapy 8*, 887–897.

Rude, S. S., & Rehm, L. P. (1991). Response to treatments for depression: The role of initial status on targeted cognitive and behavioral skills. *Clinical Psychology Review 11*, 493–514.

Rush, A. J., & Frances, A. (2000). Expert consensus guideline series: Treatment of psychiatric and behavioral problems in mental retardation. *American Journal on Mental Retardation 105*, 159–228.

Sbraga–Penix, T., & O'Donohue, W. (2004). *The sex addiction workbook.* Oakland, CA: New Harbinger.

Schlundt, D. G., & McFall, R. M. (1985). New directions in the assessment of social competence and social skills. In L. L'Abate & M. A. Milan (Eds.). *Handbook of social skills training and research* (pp. 22–49). New York: Wiley.

Skinner, B. F. (1953). *Science and human behavior.* New York: Macmillan.

Webster–Stratton, C. (2003). *The incredible years: Parents, teachers, and children training series.* Boulder, CO: Center for the Study and Prevention of Violence, Institute of Behavioral Science, University of Colorado at Boulder.

Wolpe, J. (1958). *Psychotherapy by reciprocal inhibition.* Stanford, CA: Stanford University Press.

14

USING TASKS IN ERICKSONIAN PSYCHOTHERAPY

JEFFREY K. ZEIG

The Milton Erickson Foundation Phoenix, Arizona
www.erickson-foundation.org

The first consideration in psychotherapy should be determining desired outcomes and goals. Patient goals and therapist goals often coincide, but sometimes they do not. The patient may not know specifically what to accomplish; the therapist may want to work on a different level of experience than the patient anticipates. Still the clinician must think; What is that I want to communicate to the patient that will promote change? Therapist goals are derived from answering this imperative question.

SETTING GOALS IN THERAPY

Different schools of psychotherapy have divergent ideas about determining goals. In psychoanalytical models therapist goals may entail working through transference issues. In somatic therapy goals focus on changing a patient's body armor based on the philosophy that the problem is housed in the body, not just in the psyche. Goals within systemic, family-oriented practice may focus on rearranging structural aspects of the system, recognizing that systemic change leads to individual change. In humanistic approaches, having an "I–Thou" relationship may be the desired outcome.

SETTING GOALS IN
ERICKSONIAN THERAPY

In teaching Ericksonian therapy I emphasize eliciting phenomenological goals and subgoals. The approach is derived from the philosophy that change in therapy is the process of the reassociation of internal life. Internal resources must be experientially rearranged and contextualized. I will outline this complex process and describe six aspects of goal setting.

Goals in Ericksonian therapy are created by dividing problems into their component subphenomenology, the social and interpersonal "tactics" that the person uses eventually to tab themselves "depressed," "anxious," or "insecure." From the perspective of a biological psychiatrist, depression is a brain disorder. From a social construction, "depression" is merely a construct of convenience, a label used to describe a phenomenological complex.

An Ericksonian can create a phenomenological "map" of how a patient "does" depression. Conceive depression as a series of intrapsychic and social actions: One could "do" depression by being internal versus external in focus of attention, inactive versus active socially, temporally living in the past rather than the present, becoming absorbed in tactile sensations, enhancing the negative in the world, and engaging in exaggerated self-blame. In this model, the clinician maps "depression" as a phenomenology, a set of describable components.

In Ericksonian therapy, a second aspect of goal setting is to emphasize the positive. This is done by helping patients discover inner strengths and orienting them toward a constructive future. The solution "state" has its own phenomenology, and a map can be created for it, including social and psychological components.

A third aspect of goal setting in Ericksonian therapy is fostering self-determination as soon as possible. Jay Haley (1976) sagely explained that psychotherapy is a problem, not a solution. The problem is to get patients out of therapy and back into mainstream life, independent of therapy, as soon as possible.

A fourth goal consideration is, whenever possible, to work with structures that exist in the present. By working with "what is," one is not focused on past influences that led to the problem. Ericksonians actively help modify the psychological, physiological, and sociological structures that currently keep patients stuck in their problem state.

A fifth goal orientation in Ericksonian therapy is to use techniques that are systemic and interactional. The therapist should seek solutions that involve others. Patients live and develop problems within a social matrix; change, therefore, should constructively engage a social matrix. The therapist should not merely be directed to intrapsychic change.

A sixth goal area in Ericksonian therapy is to access constructive associations that exist, but currently are dormant in the patient. For example, every smoker knows how to be comfortable without a cigarette, every anxious person knows how to relax, and every depressed person knows how to change his/her mood. The job of Ericksonian therapy is to help identify and recontextualize the patient's resources so that they can be constructively accessed.

Once a clinician understands how the patient "does" the problem, the clinician can better delineate directions for change. In summary, and in simplified form, when establishing therapeutic direction in an Ericksonian approach, the therapist can map a problem phenomenology and "flip" it. Again, use depression as an example. If a patient experiences himself being internally-oriented, find a way to help him become absorbed in the external word. To counteract absorption in the past, involve the patient in the present. Withdrawn individuals can become socially engaged. Each patient has the requisite (flipped) skill set in their history that they need to access experientially. The therapist's job is to help the patient experientially realize and consolidate the skill set that comprises the solution state.

A problem in therapy is that patients may know what to do, but they might not *realize* what they know. How, then, can therapists facilitate experiential realization? An answer lies in "gift wrapping" goals or therapeutic ideas. Therapeutic tasks gift wrap ideas in a way that a patient can better realize dormant potentials.

GIFT WRAPPING

Ericksonian therapy recognizes that the patient really "cures" himself. The therapist simply directs the patient to find and use his own inner resources. Assigning tasks is an excellent method to foster therapeutic realizations.

An underlying philosophy is that techniques in therapy do not cure; they are experiential methods of helping patients to realize dormant potentials. Hypnosis, a common gift-wrapping technique used in Ericksonian therapy, doesn't cure anybody. Just like the use of metaphors, fantasy rehearsal, parallel communication, anecdotes, or the interspersal technique, hypnosis experientially "gift wraps" ideas (goals or subphenomenology) to the patient. Tasks are merely another way to "gift wrap" goals to the patient.

As an analogy, consider making sugar candy. Placed before you is a large pot with water and sugar that creates, as it boils, a supersaturated solution. To make the candy, the desired outcome must be crystallized out of the supersaturated solution that threatens to make a mess if not treated properly. A thread, therefore, is put into the solution. This thread becomes the catalyst around which the crystals will form, thus creating the desired outcome. The crystals were inherently there, but unless the thread is introduced, the crystallization process doesn't happen and a mess ensues.

Experiential gift wrapping by using tasks is like the thread that gives the patient's resources something around which to crystallize. The resources were always there, but the experiential catalyst, placing the thread in the sugar water, was missing. Tasks are gift-wrapping forms that provide an experiential catalyst. To understand the gamut of therapeutic tasks, we can look at a taxonomy of tasks.

A TAXONOMY OF TASKS

There are two categories of tasks that can be given to a patient: direct or congruent tasks and indirect or incongruent tasks. Then, tasks can be given as homework or within the session, as illustrated in Table 14.1.

There is an additional dimension: There are tasks for the patient to follow and tasks to reject.

First I describe some congruent homework assignments.

TABLE 14.1   Zeig using tasks in psychotherapy to gift-wrap ideas

DIRECT—CONGRUENT (Homework)	INCONGRUENT (Homework)
• Exercise	• Paradoxical Intention (Frankl)
• Relaxation training/mediation/self-hypnosis	• Symptom Prescription (Weeks & L'Abate, Zeig)
• Assertiveness training	• Ambiguous Function (Lankton & Lankton)
• Reflective listening (with couples)	
• Writing: Lists/Autobiography/Social History/Journals	• Symbolic (Erickson)
	• Rituals (Gilligan; van der Hart)
• Bibliotherapy	• Absurd (Keeney)
• Volunteer work	• Ordeals (Haley)
• Social activities	
• Support groups	
• Exceptions (de Shazer)	
• Miracle Question (de Shazer)	
DIRECT—CONGRUENT (In Session)	**INCONGRUENT (In Session)**
• Miracle Question (de Shazer)	• Hypnotic Symptom Prescription
• Fantasy Rehearsal	• Symbolic Tasks
• Hypnosis	• Sculpting
• (and any of the congruent homework assignments listed above)	

Also: There are tasks to do, and tasks given with the purpose of promoting behavioral resistance, but which will guide constructive associations

CONGRUENT HOMEWORK TASKS

Congruent homework tasks are easy to conceptualize because they are direct and straightforward. In the example of depression, a congruent task would be to tell the patient to *exercise*, which in itself could be enough to break the depression. An anxious patient can be taught *relaxation exercises* and *self-hypnosis*. Relational problems may respond to the task of assigning *assertiveness training*. With couples experiencing communication problems, an example of a congruent task would be assigning *reflective listening*. Indecisive persons can benefit from the congruent task of *list making*. *Writing assignments* could include journaling or writing a social history. *Bibliotherapy*, assigning self-help or inspirational books to read, also qualifies as a congruent task. A withdrawn person can be assigned a *social task* of volunteering at a hospice. Sending patients to *social and support groups* such as Parents Without Partners or Alcoholics Anonymous are examples of congruent tasks.

Congruent tasks can be used in infinite ways. A patient lacking in self-care could be told to dress up for the therapy. I recently gave an obese patient the task of carrying a digital recorder and commenting any time she was eating. She would send me the digital files so that I would "accompany" her at each meal.

Congruent tasks start the patient on a train of activity that allows them to experience themselves differently. Cognitive dissonance can lead to constructive changes in self-concept.

A problem with congruent tasks is that often the patient has already tried them unsuccessfully. If traditional direct tasks do not elicit change, there is a unique class of congruent tasks that can be found in the solution-focused approach of Steve de Shazer (1985).

Solution-Focused Congruent Tasks

One congruent task in solution-focused therapy is to direct the patient to *look for exceptions.* In the example of depression, a patient would be told to list times when he is not depressed no matter how small or seemingly insignificant. Generalizing often maintains a problem: A depressed person can believe that he is depressed "all the time." By assigning the task of listing exceptions, he can discover that there are many times when he is not depressed. The task of listing exceptions creates a proper perspective. Accessing and organizing strengths promotes cognitive dissonance, and works on the level of changing attitudes, self-attributions, and even identity. Once a "depressive" realizes there are many times in which he is not depressed, self-concept can change.

A related congruent task is keeping a log of positive events and successes that are written in a *"victory journal,"* a method that also focuses on exceptions and strenghts.

The use of the *miracle question* in solution-focused therapy is also a congruent task. The miracle question is as follows: "If a miracle happened overnight and suddenly your problem was taken away, what would you do first? How would you act?" Patients are encouraged to act *as if* the miracle already has happened. Acting *as if* can lead to enduring change. If one wants to realize how to be, he can realize it through action. Behavior change can lead to changes in self-concept.

In-Session Use of Congruent Tasks

Assigning congruent tasks may not work with many patients, but I commonly begin with them. If resistance occurs, I can change direction, perhaps giving a congruent task in session. An in-session congruent task can be better monitored by the clinician. Many of the congruent homework tasks can be used in session, including reading to the patient or journaling successes.

A *fantasy rehearsal* could be used to practice in imagination a skill needed in the future. Traditional *hypnosis* can be thought of as an in-session congruent task. A phobic, for example, could be hypnotized and offered direct suggestions, "You will be comfortable in an airplane." Making a *hypnosis tape* would be categorized as a homework task.

A therapeutic consideration is to maintain flexibility; if one approach fails, rather than doing more of the same, the clinician has options for presenting goals. And if congruent homework or in-session tasks fail, another approach is to use incongruent tasks.

INCONGRUENT TASKS

Some patients better respond to indirect or incongruent tasks. A principle is that the amount of indirection to apply is directly proportional to the perceived resistance (Zeig, 1980). The more resistance I encounter, the more I will use indirect and incongruent methods.

Incongruent tasks are often symbolic and paradoxical in nature. On the surface, incongruent tasks appear illogical, and even manipulative. But, problems are illogical (and socially manipulative). The therapist can meet illogic with constructive "illogic." Incongruent task are best when they are way of gift wrapping solutions, not ways of manipulating. They are methods to help patients realize dormant potentials. Curiously, there have been experts who have specialized in specific incongruent tasks.

Paradoxical intention was a technique championed in the work of Victor Frankl (1963), the author of the beautiful and inspiring book *Man's Search for Meaning*. Frankl (1963) invented paradoxical intention as a way of addressing anticipatory anxiety. Anxiety problems, he realized, were often complicated by the anticipation that preceded them. He divided the anxiety into the problem itself—the anxiety—and into the anticipation of the problem—that's the anticipatory anxiety. He realized that if he did something about the anticipation part, it could change the problem itself. Paradoxical intention should be directed to this level of human experience, the precursor that triggers and maintains the problem.

To demonstrate paradoxical intention, take the example of a man with a social phobia. Frankl could tell the man to imagine being invited to a party and to construct the following scenario beforehand: "Get two champagne glasses, filled to the brim, and then approach the most attractive woman in the room," Frankl would whimsically instruct the man. "You're walking to that woman with trepidation, so much so that you're spilling and shaking the champagne all over yourself. Then you trip as you reach the woman, and you pour the champagne all over your evening clothes."

The idea is to construct a "worst case" scenario so absurd that the patient is forced to imagine his worst fear. "Better a moment of horror than horror without end," Frankl might chide. The tone of the therapist is to stimulate humor in the patient. This is an example of a task that the patient is to resist, not actually do. He wasn't actually to go to the party and do these embarrassing things, or to perform this task. The idea was to disrupt ("infect") the anticipatory anxiety with humor. The purpose of paradoxical intention was to be a "computer virus" that would contaminate the anticipatory anxiety.

A related technique, and another incongruent task, is *symptom prescription*. Symptom prescription and its uses in different schools of psychotherapy are well described by Gerald Weeks and Luciano L'Abate (1982). The technique entails directing the patient to have on request some aspect of his symptoms. (For more information on symptom prescription also see Zeig, 1980.)

A therapist could tell a patient, "It seems you've had this troubling problem with depression for a number of years, and you don't fully understand it. There may be something valuable you can learn from it; we often learn from our adversaries. So, after breakfast each morning, I would like you to go to the smallest room in your house with a notebook, and sit there and behave depressed for 30 minutes. During that time, really act as depressed as you can. Make some notes about what it is that you learn, keeping in mind that often pearls are discovered in the mud. Then, do something with the notes you created before you leave the room. Then help your spouse with some small clean-up task."

Creating a well-formed symptom prescription is an art. There are a number of approaches that can increase effectiveness:

1. Do not address the entire problem. Choose an element of the symptom complex to prescribe, such as behavior or attitude. (See Zeig, 1980a, for examples.)

2. Carefully chose a context, a time and place, for the task to be carried out.

3. Look for an interactional solution. Give a task that constructively engages others.

4. Create a task that is benign. Never prescribe anything that could be dangerous.

5. Follow up on the task in a subsequent session. Do not leave "hanging threads."

6. A three-step process can be applied: *set up, intervene*, and *follow through*. The *setup* appears as the initial empathy and instructions. The *intervention* is the task. (In the case of symptom prescription, it is the instruction to go into the room with the notebook and behave depressed.) Finally there is the *follow-through*, which could be the reason to follow the assignment, including indications about what might be accomplished. To increase effectiveness, all therapeutic tasks should be presented temporally within the three-step process.

7. When using this technique, the therapist can additionally improve the response by making a distinction between defiant and compliant people, which "tailors" the approach depending on the style of the individual. A defiant person's need to be defiant can paradox them out of the symptom; their need to defy may eclipse their "need" for the symptom. They will not do what they are told, and if they are told to have some of their symptomatic behavior, they may rebel into more functional patterns. A compliant person will follow the instruction and get control out of a situation that was previously out of control. Additional forms of tailoring would include assessing the patient and giving tasks that the patient is likely to do, and fitting the task to the patient's unique values.

8. *Be* the best therapist for the patient, taking your personal style into account. Therapist attitude alone can determine the effect of the task. For some patients the therapist will do well to "flavor" the task with a subtle sense of irony. In the example of symptom prescription, consider the irony of doing the task in the smallest room of the house and disposing of the list after leaving it. Frankl's charismatic, whimsical humor carried the paradoxical intention so that they patient would not feel discounted in any way. Therapists must use tasks that fit their personality, and they should only use tasks if they are comfortable if, in their own personal therapy, they would enjoy their therapist prescribing such a task.

It should be stressed that techniques in and of themselves are limited by the ability of the therapist to target the goal, chose a relevant gift-wrapping method, tailor to the individual, establish a process of change, and *be* the best therapist for the patient.

Another incongruent task to consider is the use of *ambiguous function assignments*. Building on the work of Milton Erickson, who seems to have been the inventor of the method, in their book *The Answer Within*, Stephen and Carol Lankton (1983) first describe the use of what they called *ambiguous function assignments*. In using this technique, the therapist gives benign assignments to a patient, sometimes not even knowing the specifics of why he gave that assignment. For example, a therapist can tell a patient to go home and light a candle at dinnertime each night for the following week, then return and explain why that assignment was given. Interesting results often follow. The patient may report, "That was incredible. By lighting this candle I realized that we don't have enough illumination in our family life. We've lost track of our family history, and our substance and meaning. We've lost touch with our family rituals. How did you know to give us such an assignment to help us realize something so important?" And the answer, of course, is that the therapist didn't know. Patients best learn, however, when they do something, and we can trust in the basic, health-seeking motivations of patients to turn an ambiguous assignment into a therapeutic step.

Other ambiguous assignments are to ask a patient to carry around a sheet of white paper or a particular book for one week, or the patient could be instructed to purchase and carry a timer, but never turn it on. The patient would be instructed to return and explain why he was asked to do the task.

Ambiguous assignments should be respectful and benign. The idea is not to trick the patient out of his problem. The design is to insert a little thread into the psychosocial mix so that a resource can crystallize from it. Remember the example of the sugar candy. The ambiguous assignment acts as the thread that is put into the supersaturated solution, allowing crystallization to take place. Ambiguous function assignments work by stimulating activation. Inertia maintains problems; action promotes change.

Symbolic tasks are an evolution of ambiguous function assignment. Milton Erickson provides one such example in *A Teaching Seminar with Milton Erickson* (Zeig, 1980). A psychiatrist from Pennsylvania and his wife came to Erickson for marital therapy. After listening to their problem for just a short while he told the husband to go, the following morning, to the Botanical Gardens, a beautiful outdoor attraction in Phoenix. He then told the wife to climb a popular mountain area known as Squaw Peak, at the same time. The husband returned and said, "The Gardens were outstanding. Did you know that 50% of all the varieties of cacti in the world are housed there?" The wife, on the other hand, said bitterly to Erickson, "I climbed that goddamn mountain. It was hot, it was difficult, and I cursed you every step of the way up. I turned the air blue cursing you. When I reached the top I felt a moment of triumph, but I cursed you every step of the way down."

Erickson told the husband on the following day to climb Squaw Peak and the wife to go to the Botanical Gardens. The husband came back and said, "I climbed Squaw Peak and it was amazing. I never knew the desert was so beautiful. What a view!" The wife reported, "Ugly cactus. It was horrid, boring, ridiculous." Erickson then told the couple, "Tomorrow, choose your own assignment and come back and tell me what you discovered." The husband came back and said he had gone back to the Botanical Gardens, and once more he raved about its beauty. The wife came back and said sheepishly, "I don't know why, but I climbed that goddamn mountain again."

Erickson said to the couple, "Your marital therapy is complete. You can return home." When they got home the wife immediately filed for divorce. The husband called Erickson and said, "Now what should I do?" Erickson refused to discuss divorce over the phone. Instead, Erickson asked what had happened on the trip back home. The husband said that the wife had wanted to know why they had been given such boring assignments. The husband thought that they had had some interesting experiences. Divorce ensued and both made satisfactory adjustments. This couple previously had had years of unsuccessful psychoanalysis and marital counseling. Erickson merely gave them assignments.

He commented that the wife had been climbing the barren mountain of marital discord day after day, feeling only a momentary sense of triumph. So he gave her an assignment that was isomorphic with her marital situation.

The genius in the therapy was in the third assignment. The couple could have chosen to go climbing together, gone to the Botanical Gardens together, gone roller-skating together, but they didn't. The marriage was over, but they were not admitting it to themselves consciously. Through the use of symbolic assignments the couple could unconsciously recognize themselves. Erickson said that the couple did well, and both sent patients to him.

Another example of symbolic therapy from Milton Erickson (Zeig, 1980) was a woman who was depressed because she was childless. Erickson investigated her problem with a physician and found that if she was very careful she could conceive and carry a child. The woman became pregnant and had a daughter. Subsequently the child died at age six months from sudden infant death syndrome. This time, the physician had said the woman could not bear more children. The woman returned to Erickson suicidally depressed. "How dare you," Erickson chided the woman, "want to destroy those beautiful memories of your daughter?" He then assigned a task. He told her to plant a fast-growing tree in her backyard and name it Cynthia, after her daughter. He told her he would come and visit her and they would sit underneath the shade of Cynthia. When he did return to visit, she had made a satisfactory adjustment. In this case, the symbolic assignment was given to absorb some of the grief the woman was feeling.

The use of symbolic tasks can provide interesting data for the therapist. A woman who was a nurse came to me complaining of many physical symptoms. I thought she was depressed, but she could only talk about her somatic symptoms. I told her to find a black rock (symbolic of depression) and carry it around for ten days then return and report why she had been given the assignment. Being compliant, the patient carried the rock around. When I asked where she had put the rock after the ten-day period, she said that she hadn't known what to do with it, so she put it in her husband's library. I surmised, through the use of the symbolic assignment, that she was telling me her problem was marital, not depression as I had initially postulated. The assignment allowed me to discover something about her that she was previously unclear about. I suggested that her husband come to the next session with her, and we commenced marital therapy.

Another use of a symbolic and incongruent task would be the use of *rituals*. Steven Gilligan (1986) describes the use of rituals in his work. Onno van der Hart (1983) also wrote cogently about rituals in therapy. Rituals are complex congruent and symbolic tasks. A complex ritual assignment can be given to a patient as a means for overcoming grief or for self-discovery.

Human beings are trained from a very early age to respond to rituals. Religious rituals, holiday rituals, dinnertime rituals all add substance and meaning to life. Therapeutic rituals merely build on a cornerstone of life experience.

Bradford Keeney (1991) describes the use of *absurd assignments* in his work *Improvisational Therapy*. An absurd assignment, in the case of a fearful person, might be the following: The therapist instructs the patient, "I want you to go to the park on Saturday morning and bring a box of Wheaties. (This American breakfast cereal is known as "the breakfast of champions." On each cereal box, a picture of a popular stellar athlete is featured. In other words, if you get your picture on the box of Wheaties, it's national news.) The therapist continues, "Face the sun holding your box of Wheaties. Reach into the box and get a handful of cereal in your right hand, get another handful in your left hand, hold your arms out to the sun, close your eyes, and now visualize your fears and demons. Really take hold of them and collect them and squeeze them into the Wheaties that you're holding in your hands. Then take off your shoes. Put your right handful of Wheaties into your left shoe, and the left handful of Wheaties into the right shoe. Walk around the park for 15 minutes further compressing your fears into the Wheaties. Then take a napkin, remove your shoes and put your fear-soaked Wheaties into a napkin and tie them into a fear bomb. Throw the fear bomb into the garbage can in the park, lob it into the air, or throw it into the pond." This, of course, is a completely absurd task. Now when the patient thinks about the fear, he thinks about the Wheaties and the fear bomb in the park, hopefully, with a chuckle. Again, this is *not* an assignment that the therapist necessarily wants the patient to do; it is an assignment that the patient can reject. But, in rejecting it, the patient may mentally add humor to his situation, contaminating the anxiety. Again, this procedure is like a "computer virus" that can disrupt the integrity of the problem. Also, it requires a sensitive therapist who can present the task in such a way that the patient feels supported and respected. I do not use absurd assignments in my practice because they do not fit my personal style.

A final example of an incongruent task is *ordeal therapy*, as outlined in the book by the same name by Jay Haley (1984). To my knowledge, Milton Erickson was the first person to use ordeals in therapy.

An ordeal can make it harder for the patient to retain the symptom. The classic example is a patient with insomnia (Haley, 1973). Erickson asked the man a few questions and determined that the man absolutely hated polishing his wooden floors. Erickson instructed the man to put on his bedclothes at the normal bedtime hour and spend the night polishing the floors. He was to polish the floors four nights in a row. Because the man had only been sleeping two hours a night, Erickson told him that he was only losing eight hours of sleep: The first night, he would lose two hours of sleep, the second night four hours, and so on. The man returned to the subsequent session and reported that for the first three nights, he polished the floors. By the fourth night, he decided to "rest his eyes" for a few minutes before he began polishing. He then slept for eight hours. The man placed a can of floor polish on his fireplace mantel, knowing that he would polish floors if he had insomnia. Erickson said that the man would do anything to avoid polishing floors, even sleep.

One of Erickson's daughters, who also suffered from transient insomnia after working a stressful evening shift, used this method on herself. She told herself that if she couldn't sleep, she would have to run up and down the stairs in her house ten times. Rather than go through this ordeal, she learned to sleep. Again, the purpose of the ordeal task is not to trick the person; it's to get them in touch with their own resources and capabilities.

A variation is to play one problem against the other. A compulsive person who is socially withdrawn could be told that any time he engages in his compulsion three times, he is "compelled" to write down the ritual and atone for it by giving a stranger a compliment.

IN-SESSION TASKS

The tasks that have been outlined thus far are used as homework, oriented as therapy outside the session. However, as I have evolved in my practice, I increasingly use more in-session tasks. This allows more collaboration between the therapist and the patient. I use congruent in-session tasks, such as having the patient make lists, reading a passage of literature to them, or asking the miracle question and practicing the miracle in session. But, as I have evolved as a therapist, I use less congruent tasks and more incongruent in-session tasks such as *hypnotic symptom prescription*.

In the case of a phobia about flying in an airplane, a patient could be put into a trance and demonstrate the phobia in the session, instead of in the actual situation that triggers the phobia. (See an example of Erickson in Zeig, 1980.) The patient is then having the symptom in the session, not in the airplane. This moves the symptom out of the context of the situation and into the office, and that change might be significant to change the entire problem. Any change, not matter how small, can be built on.

Puzzles can often be used as in-session *symbolic tasks*. To show a patient that some problems are best solved unconsciously, I give him a puzzle that is best solved with the hands, without thinking. I have at least a dozen puzzles in my office, each of which illustrates a unique human rigidity and, when solved, an accessible flexibility.

Another in-session task I now use extensively is therapist role-playing, or *therapist sculpting*. I "sculpt" into a form that represents an aspect of the patient's problem (or solution). The patient is asked to tell me how to mold myself into a sculpture that resembles his problem, be it anxiety, aggression, or depression. By taking the problem and making it physical, I discover the opportunities to empathize and intervene. Sometimes I ask the patient to slightly exaggerate the sculpture inorder to create an image that could 'contaminate' the problem state. Because a picture is worth a thousand words, the patient gets a new view of an aspect of himself, which in itself may be palliative.

ADDITIONAL CONSIDERATIONS

Patients also can assign themselves tasks. One patient, a professional athlete who worked in sales, was very competitive. He set himself an ordeal. He and a coworker found an old weather-beaten can on a walk in the desert. They made a deal that whoever had the least growth in sales for that week would have to keep the rusty can on his desk for that period of time. The patient, being competitive, didn't want that can on his desk. By using his competitiveness as an asset, he set up a task that promoted his success.

The therapist, moreover, can give himself tasks. A family once came to me with a child who was pulling out her own hair, a condition known as *trichotillomania*. (This derives from a French word that means "frenzied hair pulling.") This child had been through psychotherapy, medication, and so forth, but nothing had helped. Being a middle class, church-going family, the girl's parents and younger sister thought this condition was very weird. I asked them to come as a family and began to communicate in parallel. I started the session using a common principle, that of starting on the periphery. In family therapy I commence with the individual typically farthest "out" in the emotional field. In this case I started with the father, talking about his habits, and how the family could help him modify habits. The father wanted to eat less junk food. Then I discovered that the mother wanted to eat fewer chips; the younger daughter wanted to drink fewer diet sodas. Then I asked the identitied patient, the girl with trichotillomania, what she wanted to change, thinking that she would offer the trichotillomania. She decided, however, that she wanted to drink fewer diet sodas.

I had previously determined that the two daughters did not receive an allowance, so I made an agreement with the parents to give the children an allowance, with a provision for a reverse allowance. Each member of the family would have to be in compliance with keeping the new habit, or else they would have to put money back into the family fund. I also joined into the agreement and said that if I consumed more than one diet soda per day, I would put the required amount into the family fund. I gave myself a task and joined the family in the effort of making changes.

In the second session I devised several creative tasks, one of which was to have the parents buy a wig that they were to name "Ilga." They were to establish a relationship with the wig. The father was to say when leaving the home, "Bye, Ilga, I'm going to work. see you later." The mother would say, "Ilga, I'm going to the store. Can I get you anything?" The younger daughter would tell the wig when she left for school and when she got home. After some time of establishing the relationship, the job of the patient would be to pull the hair out of the wig. The parents were to ask the daughter questions during 30-minute sessions of pulling Ilga's hair, including asking voyeuristic questions about the mechanics of the hair pulling, in order to make the daughter overly conscious of the details of pulling out hair.

I then asked the patient the question, "How do you know you can get over this problem?" She responded with many intelligent answers, including that her parents loved her, she had support, she could pray about it, and so on. I prompted her, "You can get over this because you've gotten over other habits before, like sleeping with the night-light on, and biting your nails." Right there I stopped and looked at her nails. They were bitten to the quick. So were her sister's nails, and her mother's and her father's. I then realize I had made a mistake; I violated one of the first rules in Ericksonian therapy, which is to be observant of the patient.

Here was a hypocritical situation in which the parents thought the child's hair pulling was weird, yet they were all biting their nails. I told the parents they would have to stop biting their nails to counsel their daughter adequately. The mother stopped, but the father would not. This was an interesting case in that I assigned myself a task that should have worked well, but I lost power because of the nail-biting issue. I concluded that someone would get cured in this therapy, and if not them, it might as well be me. To this day I have never had more than one diet soda a day.

SUMMARY

Tasks are a way of gift wrapping ideas to foster experiential realization. There are a number of considerations to keep in mind when providing a well-formed task.

When a therapist gives a task, he should remember to follow up and ascertain the results. Not checking up on homework is a common error.

In the use of tasks, it is well to remember that there are some tasks that you would like the patient to do and some tasks you would like the patient to reject. Paradoxical intention and absurd tasks are commonly used to change patient thinking, not to have the patient perform them.

Again, a therapist should only give the kind of task he would be willing to get. If the clinician is uncomfortable with the task in any way, he should not prescribe it. Certainly, no task should be prescribed that could be harmful to the patient in any way.

In giving tasks, what the therapist does before, during, and after is what makes the task come alive. It's not just the task itself. The setup and follow-though are the art that makes the intervention effective.

A well-formed task has a number of criteria. There should be a specific focus, an interactional component that promotes change within the social matrix and takes into consideration the systemic function of the problem; a dramatic process should be created to make the invention come alive; the task should be individualized to the unique values of the patient; and the clinician should have the flexibility and compassion to *be* the therapist needed at the moment.

The clinician can consider which level of human experience he wants to address before giving the task. What level of human experience should the therapist address? For example, paradoxical attention addresses the pro-dromal phase of the symptom complex. Rituals appeal to the constructive history dormant in the patient. A symbolic task may change the associational net that maintains the symptom. Looking for exceptions addresses the human tendency to generalize.

The purpose of the tasks is to gift wrap a phenomenological goal. The therapist uses tasks as a context to help the patient elicit previously dormant resources. A task is really just a way of "gift wrapping" ideas and possibilities. At their best, tasks put patients in situations in which they can experientially realize their innate capabilities. The field of physical medicine is designed to cure people. The techniques of psychotherapy are not designed as cures; but, rather, they are catalysts to elicit resources so that patients can crystallize the cure within.

REFERENCES

De Shazer, S. (1985) *Keys to Solution in Brief Therapy*. New York: Norton

Frankl, Viktor E., *Man's Search for Meaning. An Introduction to Logotherapy*. Beacon Press, Boston, 1963–2000. (A revised edition of *From Death-Camp to Existentialism*). ISBN 0-8070-1426-5.

Gilligan, S. G. (1986). *Therapeutic trances: The cooperation principle in Ericksonian hypnotherapy*. New York: Brunner/Mazel (now Taylor & Francis).

Haley, J. (1973). *Uncommon therapy: The psychiatric techniques of Milton H. Erickson, M.D.* New York: W. W. Norton.

Haley, J. (1976). Problem solving therapy. San Francisco: Jossey-Bass. (now Wiley)

Haley, J. (1984). *Ordeal Therapy: Unusual Ways to Change Behavior*. San Francisco: Jossey – Bass. (now Wiley)

Keeney, B.P. (1991) *Improvisational Therapy: A Practical Guide for Creative Clinical Strategies*. New York: Guilford Publications.

Lankton, S., & Lankton, C. (1983). *The answer within: A clinical framework of Ericksonian hypnotherapy*. New York: Brunner/Mazel. (now Taylor & Francis)

Van Der Hart, O. (1983). *Rituals in Psychotherapy: Transition and Continuity*. New York: Irvington.

Watzlawick, P., Weakland, J., & Fisch, R. (1974). *Change: Principles of problem formation and problem resolution*. New York: Norton.

Weeks, G.R. & L'Abate, L. (1982) *Paradoxical psychotherapy: theory and practice with individuals, couples, and families*. New York : *Brunner/Mazel*. (now Taylor & Francis)

Zeig, J.K. (Ed. and Commentary) (1980b). *A Teaching Seminar with Milton H, Erickson*. New York: Brunner/Mazel (now Taylor & Francis).

15

USING ACCEPTANCE
IN INTEGRATIVE
BEHAVIORAL COUPLE
THERAPY

CHRISTOPHER R. MARTELL

Private Practice
University of Washington
Seattle, WA

DAVID ATKINS

Fuller Graduate School of Psychology
Pasadena, CA

Several new behavior therapies include acceptance components as the main thrust of the treatment, as in acceptance and commitment therapy (Hayes, Strosahl, & Wilson, 1999) and DBT (Linehan, 1993), which emphasizes radical acceptance of oneself and the world as it is. Other behavior therapies include acceptance in an implicit fashion, such as in behavioral activation treatment for depression (Martell, Addis, & Jacobson, 2001) when clients are asked to act according to a goal or plan, rather than according to a feeling of the moment. All these individual therapies emphasize to varying degrees the need to allow emotional experience rather than avoid it, to manage emotional and behavioral impulses, and not to act according to mood, but rather according to a plan or value. This chapter looks at acceptance techniques as they pertain to integrative behavioral couple therapy (IBCT) (Christensen, Atkins, Berns, Wheeler, Baucom, & Simpson, 2004; Jacobson & Christensen, 1996), which focuses on helping couples to give up their agenda to change one another and interact in such a way—both in therapy sessions and at home—to build greater intimacy through acceptance.

Clinical Strategies for
Becoming a Master Psychotherapist

DEFINITIONS

The word *acceptance* conjures positive and negative images. Most people desire to be accepted for who they are, and thus acceptance could be defined as loving someone or taking them at face value. On the other hand, acceptance is easily confused with helpless reserve. People who have been beaten down throughout their lives may come to accept their lot as one of inferiority and disappointment, discontinuing attempts at developing a life worth living. Acceptance in psychotherapy refers to neither of these concepts. Moreover, the term differs depending on the type of therapy to which one refers. In individual therapy, acceptance can be defined as the opposite of avoidance. Acceptance is being present with one's own psychological reactions, rather than attempting to blunt them or change them. When working with couples, the term is more akin to understanding a partner as they are and accepting them for who they are, while acknowledging differences as opportunities for greater intimacy, rather than fodder for a battle. As Jacobson and Christensen (1996) state in their work on IBCT: "Sometimes people want a voice more than they want a resolution. Sometimes people can experience intimacy not when they have achieved change from the other, but when they have given up the battle to change the other" (p. xiii).

In IBCT, acceptance is dyadic. The goal is to structure sessions so that couples are talking differently to one another in a way that fosters acceptance and motivates change. In individual therapies such as behavioral activation (Martell et al., 2001), acceptance pertains to approaching situations or engaging in behaviors despite the negative feelings associated with them. In essence, acceptance in some forms of individual behavior therapy is a variation of exposure, blocking avoidance of fears, sadness, and other emotions that the individual experiences as negative.

Working with couples provides a unique situation in which to understand the lack of acceptance between two people. The very fact that the couple typically comes to therapy with a wish that something will change in the relationship inherently demonstrates nonacceptance. However, it is essential to differentiate between not accepting problems in the relationship (e.g., "I can't continue to live in this loveless situation") with not accepting the other person (e.g., "She is a lazy slob"). The IBCT therapist would seek to change the former through acceptance of the latter. In other words, the overall quality of the relationship will be improved as the two people in the couple stop blaming one another and regain a collaborative set (Jacobson & Margolin, 1979) in resolving problems in the relationship.

At the start of therapy, couples often blame one another and ascribe their difficulties to their partner's character defects. Acceptance transforms these into a mutual problem that they can work together to resolve. For example, instead of one partner complaining that the other is unassertive in public, a discussion around both partners' backgrounds may reveal that the complaining partner was raised in a family that valued argument, and had a sense of the right and necessity to make needs known, whereas the offending partner may have been raised to "be seen and not heard," or may have carried a family shame (e.g., Dad was the town philanderer) that makes it painful to speak out and feel like the center of attention. The acceptance goal would be to soften the complaining partner's criticism through understanding the context in which the offending partner's behavior is embedded. The assessment process focuses on uncovering these types of themes, vulnerabilities, and conflicts.

DETECTION AND OTHER ASSESSMENT ISSUES

IBCT therapists use standard assessment measures such as the Dyadic Adjustment Scale (DAS) (Spanier, 1976) and the Marital Satisfaction Inventory (MSI) (Snyder, 1979). When working with same-sex couples, the MSI is less desirable because it has forms for "husband" and "wife," but the DAS is gender neutral. The Conflict Tactics Scales (CTS) (Straus, 1979) is a good assessment tool for domestic violence. A final tool, currently under development, is the Frequency and Acceptability of Partner Behavior Scale (FAPB) (Christensen & Jacobson, 1997), which measures areas of concern to each partner, and how acceptable (or not) the behavior is to the partner, as well as frequency of occurrence. The assessment phase covers four sessions, wherein the couple is interviewed together, each partner is interviewed individually, and the therapist provides feedback and a case formulation to the couple.

The assessment should answer six questions (Jacobson & Christensen, 1996):

1. How distressed is the couple?
2. How committed are they to the relationship?
3. What are the issues that divide them?
4. Why are these issues such a problem?
5. What are the strengths holding them together?
6. How can therapy help?

The therapist should be able to answer these questions easily using the formal assessment tools and doing comprehensive interviews with the couple.

THEORY AND
CONCEPTUALIZATION

This therapy approach is broadly based on the philosophy of contextualism (Pepper, 1942) and specifically on a functional analysis of behavior. Contextualists and behaviorists look to factors external to the organism that influence behavior, including peoples' histories, cultural practices, and social systems (Jacobson, 1994). From this perspective, all behavior "makes sense." All behavior may not be morally sound (as determined by cultural factors and social agreement) or personally healthy (as determined by the problems it may cause for an individual or society), but it all makes sense given the individual and his or her history of interacting in the environment. The heart of acceptance is to experience emotion as something that just *is*—not as something to run away from—and to experience one's partner as someone behaving as best as he or she can in negotiating his or her environment.

Acceptance has two components: (1) to help partners translate conflict into opportunity for intimacy and (2) to help partners let go of attempts to change one another (Jacobson & Christensen, 1996). Jacobson and Christensen (1996) identify five factors that determine how incompatibilities in couples get managed:

1. Level of the couple's incompatibilities
2. Their mutual attractions
3. Individual behavioral repertoires
4. Conflict resolution skills
5. Stressful events that are impacting the relationship

These five factors represent individual learning histories that have reinforced certain behaviors, attractions, and behavioral repertoires, and environmental events that impact each member of the couple. Acceptance involves giving up the struggle to make changes happen. The irony is that giving up the struggle to do away with negative feelings and interactions often is a curative factor leading to increased positive regard.

IMPACT ON CASE FORMULATION

According to Jacobson and Christensen (1996) the formulation is the "single most important organizing principle in [IBCT]...the overarching goal...is to get the couples to adopt our formulation..." (p. 41). It is essential that the client understands and agrees with the formulation, because the client's adoption of the case conceptualization has been shown to predict positive outcome regardless of the type of therapy (Addis & Carpenter, 2000).

There are three components to the formulation: the *theme,* the *polarization process,* and the *mutual trap.* During the joint and individual interviews, the therapist listens for the theme or themes that predominate in the couple's conflicts. Themes are usually stated in terms of opposites. For example, if one partner likes to entertain, go out to events, and expresses feelings freely whereas the other partner enjoys quiet evenings at home and only expresses feelings after having contemplated a problem and coming up with a possible solution before speaking, the theme might be stated as "outward/inward." Jacobson and Christensen (1996) identified several common themes such as closeness/distance, control/responsibility, artist/scientist, conventionality/ unconventionality, and "You don't love me" "Yes I do; it is *You* who doesn't love *me.*" Therapists are advised not to try to fit couples into any one of these particular themes. There may be an entirely different theme identified for any couple, and the therapist can be creative in trying to name the theme. Most important, the therapist needs to hypothesize the controlling variables and consequences that maintain the function of the couple's behavior. The theme should make sense to the couple. When a couple says "yes, that sounds like us," they are more likely to work collaboratively with the therapist in reviewing how the themes come up in many conflict situations.

The polarization process occurs as partners become more entrenched in each of their positions on a recurrent problem issue, or as they become set in their ways. When differences are less tolerated, and are reified by each partner as deficiencies in the other, they become more polarized. As Jacobson and Christensen (1996) describe it, polarization goes hand in hand with the mutual trap. "People know about and experience their own sense of entrapment daily, but they usually do not know that their partner feels trapped as well" (p. 54). Acceptance involves helping couples to recognize when they are polarized, and to generate empathy and compassion for one another's feelings of being trapped.

CLINICAL STRATEGIES

IBCT is a practical therapy that is relatively straightforward to conduct. The overall goal of treatment is to optimize client access to natural reinforcement either in a relationship or in life in general. The treatment does not make much use of arbitrary reinforcers, such as social praise or people giving themselves treats. Although IBCT therapists may use techniques like behavior exchange (Jacobson & Margolin, 1979) that do utilize arbitrary reinforcement in the form of assigning partners to do nice things for one another, such techniques are used sparingly. IBCT uses change strategies always in the context of acceptance. The specific techniques used in the treatment are described briefly next.

IBCT CHANGE TECHNIQUES

IBCT evolved from traditional behavioral couple therapy. Thus, the change techniques that are specified in texts such as Jacobson and Margolin (1979) and Baucom and Epstein (1990) are used in the context of the therapy. There is a difference in the way such techniques are applied, however. The therapist maintains flexibility throughout the therapy, rather than emphasizing behavior exchange or communication training, and does not require that the couple rigidly adhere to an agenda of homework and practice exercises. There also is no formal cognitive restructuring involved, although it could be argued that cognitive reappraisals occur frequently in the therapy as the partners begin to discuss their problems with one another in a different way than they have prior to therapy. A complete description of the techniques is beyond the scope of this chapter, and interested readers can find more comprehensive descriptions in Jacobson and Margolin (1979).

Behavior Exchange

This strategy is used in cases when couples have lost a collaborative set and have become increasingly polarized. There are several varieties of behavior exchange exercises. A common strategy is to have couples write a list of small things that he or she could do to please his or her partner. Although no particular behavior on the list needs to be undertaken, both partners agree either to set aside a special day when they will concentrate on doing things on the lists, or they can agree to doing one or two things each day. In some cases partners may be so polarized that they can only engage in the assignment for an hour or so out of an entire week. This is fine as a way of shaping new behavior and helping the couple to break standoffs. The difference between IBCT and traditional behavioral couple therapy in the behavior exchange work is that the therapist always takes the stance of acceptance and will use the acceptance techniques (described next) in conjunction with these change strategies.

Communication Training

Active listening is a common intervention in traditional behavioral couple therapy but is used sparingly in IBCT. Teaching clients to be specific in what they are saying and to paraphrase what the partner has said is good practice for slowing couples down in their communication and making sure that they listen to one another. The IBCT therapist has the added task of bringing the couple back to the formulation and the themes identified in the feedback session. These themes run throughout the therapy, and the therapist actively points out when particular discussions or arguments center on themes and how they are understandable given the context in which each partner acts.

Problem solving

Although acceptance is the overriding goal of IBCT, and is assumed in the theory to lead to more permanent change, couples are still encouraged to engage in problem solving. It is accomplished slightly differently in IBCT than in traditional behavioral couple therapy. In the latter, couples would identify a specific problem, brainstorm solutions, discuss the pros and cons of each solution, agree to a solution to try, and set a specific time to examine the outcome. A typical problem-solving session may go something like this in traditional behavioral couple therapy:

Partner 1:   I just can't stand that he doesn't respect me enough to call when he is going to be late coming home, even though he knows that I worry and it is so inconsiderate of him!

Therapist: Let me interrupt you for a minute, before he paraphrases what you have said. Can you remember the rules to be concrete and behavioral in your definition of the problem? If you are remaining neutral and not negative, is there a different way that you would state the problem?

Partner 1:   Well, perhaps I wouldn't say that it is inconsiderate.

Therapist: I agree. I also wonder if saying that he doesn't respect you or that he knows that you worry are behaviors that you observe in him or if you are making assumptions.

Partner 1:   I see, I guess they are assumptions.

Therapist: So, can you try to state the problem again? Remember, you can state the problem in terms of the X, Y, Z formula "when you do X, in Y circumstance, I feel Z."

Partner 1:   When you don't call me when you are going to be late coming home, I feel very worried and it makes me angry.

The partner would then paraphrase. Once they agreed on the problem definition, they would generate a solution list and agree on a possible solution. In IBCT, the exchange may look something like this:

Partner 1:   I just can't stand that he doesn't respect me enough to call when he is going to be late coming home, even though he knows that I worry and it is so inconsiderate of him!

Partner 2:   What do you think I'm doing, running away to Mexico? I'm not a little kid you know, and I don't know why you should get so worried!

Therapist: This problem sounds like one that you've had in several different ways. I think there is a theme in this, do you see it?

Both
Partners :   Yes, responsibility and control.

Therapist: I think so. [To partner 1], this situation reminds me of the story you told about your father coming home drunk nearly every day and you being frightened when you were young.

Partner 1	:	Well, I don't think that he is out getting drunk. Not at all.
Therapist	:	Of course not. I wonder though, does the feeling of waiting for him feel familiar to you at all, when you are at home and he hasn't called?
Partner 1	:	Yes, slightly. I just get antsy. I can't explain it, and I know that worrying is silly. I know he hasn't gone off to Mexico. I just feel worried.
Therapist	:	A bit like a little kid does when she or he is uncertain of the condition that Daddy will be in when he comes home?
Partner 1 (tearfully)	:	A little, yes. It's stupid, but I have the same feelings like when I was a little kid. Waiting for someone just feels bad to me.
Therapist [to Partner 2]:		Have you known this before?
Partner 2	:	Well, I knew about the alcoholism history, but I didn't know that my being late caused this kind of distress. I just saw it as a control issue.
Therapist	:	Yes, and "control issues" really bother you don't they?
Partner 2	:	You got it. My ex was on my butt all the time, "Don't look at that person; don't say this at a party; come home at this time." I vowed I'd never do that again!
Therapist	:	So, being required to call home if you're late feels like the control thing again. What are you usually thinking when you are late?
Partner 2	:	Well, I'm usually upset because I know there's going to be a fight when I get home. I just don't want to get caught in that trap of feeling like I'm tethered to a telephone so that I don't get yelled at. So usually I'm anxious and by the time I get home I am already frustrated.
Therapist [to partner 1]:		And have you been aware that this is his experience when he's late?
Partner 1	:	I know he's always frustrated when he comes home. That's obvious. I just don't see how my wanting him to call if he's late is like his ex wanting to control his every move!
Therapist	:	Do you think that just like you know you're not waiting for a mean drunk to come home, but you still feel worried and anxious when you wait, that he may know you are not going to get on his case for every little thing, but still even the smallest obligation, like needing to call when he is late, can feel like the same thing?
Partner 1	:	Well, when you put it like that I guess I'd say yes, I can see that.

Therapist   :   So both of you end up feeling anxious and frustrated. I think that is the problem that we need to talk about, because it shows up in more situations than just when one of you arrives home.

The difference in these two exchanges shows both the different therapeutic stance as well as the different philosophy behind the two therapies. In traditional behavioral couple therapy, the therapist is acting primarily as a skill instructor. The therapist will teach the clients how to do behavior exchange and communication/problem solving, and then shape the couple's attempts at doing them in session through correction and repeated practice. The IBCT therapist also takes a didactic approach, but is not as interested in teaching a skill. The focus on concrete skills and observable behaviors brings the focus of traditional behavioral couple therapy to derivative problems.

IBCT therapists attempt to uncover the controlling variables behind the problems (Jacobson & Christensen, 1996), and herein lies a philosophical difference with traditional behavioral couple therapy. Because many of the controlling variables are to be found in the clients' learning histories, IBCT attempts to turn problems into possibilities for increased intimacy through reminding the couple of the various contexts from which they have come. History can provide a reasonable hypothesis about what controls various behaviors. Thus, in the previous example, partner 2 is not coming home late without calling because he is an insensitive lout, but because he has been conditioned to resist control by a partner. Partner 1 is not a "control freak," but has a conditioned emotional reaction to waiting for someone to come home. Note that the therapist pointed out these connections between current behavior and past history. Could the therapist have been wrong? Yes, but it does not matter that he or she is right; rather, the shift is to increase the partners' empathy for one another and to stop vilifying each other for bad behavior. This is the hallmark of IBCT and the acceptance techniques therein.

IBCT ACCEPTANCE TECHNIQUES

There are two primary acceptance techniques in IBCT and four tolerance techniques. They are used in a hierarchical fashion. The hierarchy depends on the ability of the couple to gain acceptance as these techniques are applied. If the first technique does not work, the therapist tries the second, and then moves to the various tolerance techniques as adjunctive tools when acceptance seems unlikely. The hierarchy follows logically because the acceptance techniques of empathic joining and unified detachment are attempts at creating understanding and acceptance in the couple, and second, if that does not occur, to help them to see the problem as something outside either person that they can solve together. Admittedly, some problems cannot be solved, and some behaviors cannot be accepted. IBCT there-fore also makes use of tolerance exercises that decrease the negativity and volatility in a couple by decreasing the aversive effect of certain partner behaviors that are resistant to change. Tolerance techniques are pointing out the positive side of negative behaviors, role-playing negative behavior in the session, faking negative behavior at home, and learning greater acceptance through self-care.

Empathic Joining

This technique is used frequently in IBCT. The goal of empathic joining is to get partners to see the softer side to problems. Because IBCT is a contextual therapy, in some situations the softer response may actually be a behavior that looks hard. Moreover, this is not an attempt to make couples into "bleeding hearts" or to have all exchanges be "feel good" moments. Having completed the interviews and developed the formulation, typical IBCT sessions consist of the couple debriefing problems that occurred during the week. This provides the opportunity for empathic joining. The IBCT therapist does not come to the session with a preconceived agenda to teach a specific skill or to address any particular problem.[1] The couple is asked to talk about any problems that came up between therapy sessions, and the therapist listens carefully to identify the themes, polarization process, mutual traps, and other components of the formulation that are indicated in the problem under discussion. IBCT therapists must remain alert and flexible, being aware of the context in the session and willing to change course at any time. The therapist shifts attention back and forth from one partner to the other. An outside observer may think that IBCT is a series of microtherapy sessions with each individual partner. The therapist attempts to get each partner to talk about their behavior in a situation in such a fashion as to soften the other toward them.

For example, Rea and Seth got into frequent fights about how much time Seth, a jazz musician, spent in activities that did not bring in money. Rea worked as an accountant and felt that she carried the burden of the financial stability. There was a theme of responsibility and control, but more import-ant, a theme of closeness/distance. Rea enjoyed talking about her day, relieving stress by watching a movie with Seth or playing board games. Seth was a bit of a loner. He liked watching movies at home as well, but preferred to be eating dinner in front of a video than at the table talking with Rea. Rea brought up the following problem in therapy and the therapist used an empathic joining intervention.

Rea   :   Seth and I had a big fight last week. Do you want to tell her about it?

---

[1] Certain behaviors, such as substance abuse or domestic violence need to be attended to, but the IBCT therapist always maintains the stance that the most important thing in the session is a partners most recent remark, and this defines the agenda. In the case of battering, couple therapy may, in fact, be contraindicated (Bograd & Mederos, 1999), and IBCT is not recom-mended in such circumstances. This needs to be assessed during the evaluation phase.

Seth   : No. You brought it up, and I knew we'd talk about this in here so you go right ahead.

Therapist: It looks like there is a bit of feeling around this topic already, so it probably is a good thing for us to discuss. Rea?

Rea   : Well, Seth knows that I have been working really hard lately with tax time coming up. This is also the time of year when I make most of my money. That is important since the club only pays Seth a pittance, and his other band is barely getting shows. Anyway, Monday was going to be a night to just stay home because I'm working late the rest of the week, and he has to work at the club over the weekend. Well, he knew this was important to me, and on Sunday, Jared called him to ask if he wanted to play a gig at a charity auction because one of the trumpeters was sick. Because it was charity, they weren't getting paid. Seth said yes without even asking me.

Seth   : Right, you didn't want me to do charity work. Because I don't make enough money, I can't do a good deed.

Rea   : Oh, right, a good deed. That is such crap. You did it because you wanted to play with Jared's band. You would play with that band for a whole week without money just so you can play with them.

Therapist: Can I jump in here for a minute? Both of you are getting very angry quickly around this and I wonder if you each know why the other is so upset?

Seth   : She's upset because I don't earn enough money, like always.

Rea   : Wrong again. You just don't get it do you?

Therapist: Well that's what we're doing here is trying to get it. [To Rea] Can you say a little bit about what was important to you about Monday night?

Rea   : It was going to be a time for us to be together. I am really stressed at work, and it was going to just be a nice night in.

Seth   : Yes, and you said you took a hot bath and had a nice relaxing night anyway.

Rea   : That's not the point. I was by myself and that was not what we had planned.

Therapist: So, was it the fact that you were by yourself or that the plan had been changed that troubled you most?

Rea   : Both, but mostly that I was by myself. Although I was counting on us spending the night together.

Seth   : But what was the big deal?

Therapist: Seth, I would guess that you would really enjoy spending the night alone if you were stressed.

Seth   : Absolutely.

Therapist: So, does it make sense to you that Rea really wanted to spend the time with you even though she is stressed at work?

Seth   : Sort of, but I don't see why it mattered. She needed some time to unwind because she is working late all week

Therapist: So, you knew that it was important for her to unwind, but you thought it would be fine for her to do so by herself?

Seth   : I actually thought it would be preferable.

Therapist: Because it would be for you?

Seth   : Not all the time, but certainly when I've been stressed out I just want to be alone.

Therapist: So, is this the closeness/distance thing rearing its head again?

Seth   : I guess.

Therapist
[to Rea] : Were you thinking that Seth didn't realize how important it was that you spend Monday evening together?

Rea   : I told him enough times. It really bothers me that he didn't know.

Therapist: But, do you know that, for him, being alone is relaxing and he assumed you would also relax alone?

Rea   : I see his point, but he should know me by now. It feels like he doesn't know who I am.

Therapist: I would think that if you really believe he doesn't know who you really are that must be a pretty lonely feeling.

Rea   : It is lonely.

Seth
(inter-
rupting) : Oh, come on, I am not some out-to-lunch jerk. What do you mean I don't know who you are? That's crap.

Therapist: Seth, hold on a second. [To Rea] Can you help me to understand what is different when you are spending time with Seth rather than relaxing alone?

Rea   : When I'm alone I can't shut my mind off. I just think about everything I have to do at work. Yes, I took a hot bath, and kind of dozed off, but mostly I was just sad and depressed Monday night because Seth was at that stupid charity thing. I like spending time with Seth. When I'm really stressed, he makes me laugh or we talk about engaging things. He's very smart and he's very entertaining. I'm not saying I want him to entertain me, but I feel safe from all the cares of the world when we just hang out together.

Therapist: That sounds very important that you feel safe when you and Seth are hanging out. [To Seth] Is this the first you are hearing about this?

Seth   : About the safe part yes. I never thought Rea felt unsafe. She's the most competent person I know, and I'm always feeling like I'm the deadbeat.

Therapist: So, when she is stressed about work, do you feel a little guilty?

Seth   : Yes.

Therapist: So, here we seem to have a dilemma, Rea feels overwhelmed at work and needs Seth to hang out with and make her feel safe, but because Rea is so overwhelmed, Seth feels guilty because he thinks Rea thinks of him as a deadbeat.

Rea
[to Seth] : I don't think you are a deadbeat. I'd like you to make more money, but that's what I get for marrying a musician. You work as hard as I do. I just wanted to spend time with you because [becoming teary] I've been feeling really scared that all this work is not going to get done and some client is going to blast me or I'll get into trouble.

Seth   : But you never do, and you go through this every year.

Rea   : Yes, but I need you to tell me things like that. That makes me feel stronger.

Seth   : Oh, I didn't know that you cared about my opinion.

Rea   : It's not your opinion. It's your experience of living with me. You have a clearer head and are more mellow. I needed an evening of your mellowness.

Seth   : I'm sorry. If I'd known that, I probably would have stayed.

Therapist: So, is this conversation a little different than ones you've had at home about this topic?

Both   : Yes.

Note in the previous exchange that the therapist does not insist that each partner take turns in the conversation, as would happen in traditional communication training. Rather, she let the couple get into the same argument they did at home. By probing for the softer feelings—Rea feeling scared, Seth feeling guilty—she brought the conversation around to what was really at work: Rea's experience of feeling comforted by reaching out to others and Seth's experience of getting comfort by being alone. This difference between the two was getting in the way of their full understanding of the problem at hand, and got them stuck in the situational argument over Monday night. By the end of the conversation, the couple is interacting with one another in a more loving and sympathetic fashion. This is the goal of empathic joining.

Unified Detachment

Therapists try to create unified detachment in a couple by helping them to see problems as something that the partners can join together to solve, rather than a means to vilify and blame each other. The therapist can do this in several ways. When a couple states a problem, especially a "he does this" or "she does that" kind of problem, the therapist should get both sides of the story. It is a good idea to listen for mutual traps, dilemmas, or joint vulnerabilities. For example, Alison says, "Kate is a terrible housekeeper. I come home and she has not done anything even though she gets home two hours earlier than I. She is not keeping her side of the deal." The therapist solicits Kate's perspective and Kate says "Yes, I come home two hours earlier, but Alison works at a desk all day and is stressed, but I climb telephone poles all day and am exhausted when I get home. I literally need an hour nap, and then I get up and start making dinner." The therapist can respond with "so, it sounds to me like there is a dilemma here in that you, Alison, are very stressed and don't want to take all the domestic responsibilities, and you, Kate, are physically exhausted at the end of the day and need to sleep until it is time to make dinner." If the couple agrees to this, the therapist can then point out that Kate's domestic chore of fixing dinner may make even more mess, and then Alison has more to clean in the kitchen. If Alison and Kate can begin to view the problem as something like "we both work really hard and find it challenging to keep up with housework," they are more likely to collaborate on a solution than if the problem remains "Kate is a slob and Alison is a nag."

Other techniques that are helpful in promoting unified detachment are naming the problem. Sometimes, simply giving a recurring problem a name helps the couple work together to resolve it. In the Alison and Kate example, the problem might be named "the housework monster." Humor is also useful in this regard, helping couples to get distance from the emotional distress of the problem. The therapist can also go over the sequence of a problem, identifying triggers and comparing and contrasting incidents when things escalated or did not, thus objectifying the problem for the couple. Ultimately, unified detachment leads to good problem solving, rather than vilification and hopelessness.

IBCT TOLERANCE TECHNIQUE

As stated earlier, there are some behaviors that are just not susceptible to change. Partners need to learn to tolerate some of the things that they cannot change in one another. There may be circumstances when one partner wants to make a relationship work with someone whose behavior is dysfunctional or destructive, and therapists should never try to help people tolerate the intolerable. The problem is that what is intolerable to one person is tolerable to another. This is where the FAPB measure (Christensen & Jacobson, 1997) can be useful, because it requires partners to identify problem behaviors and rate the acceptability of those behaviors. Therapists need to keep their own values of what is acceptable or tolerable out of the session. Most often the things that require tolerance techniques are personality factors such as how outgoing partners are, their ability to express emotion, and so on, that are incompatible between the partners. There are four key tolerance exercises in which clients can engage and the therapist can use when acceptance or change is not forthcoming.

Finding the Positive in Negative Behavior

This idea may at first sound like a Pollyanna notion, but it makes sense in many instances. When the therapist has done a careful formulation with a couple, he or she will understand the controlling variables of a given behavior. Several behaviors that, over time and through the polarization process, feel negative or annoying to a couple may have a positive side. For example, one husband complained that his wife was too outgoing and quick to make social plans for them without consulting him. Even when she agreed to consult him, her social needs were more than his and he continued to feel like there was too much planned. However, he had complained of feeling lonely and was troubled by excessive shyness. In this situation the therapist could point out how the wife's social planning provided an impetus for the husband to break out of himself and socialize despite his shyness. He agreed, and although he didn't like that his wife wanted to make social plans, he was better able to tolerate the behavior.

Role-Playing the Negative Behavior in Session

This intervention functions as a form of exposure or desensitization. Seeing the behavior acted out in session allows observation by the sensitive partner and, again, may provide objectivity that is missing at home. It can also work paradoxically when a partner may recognize the aversive nature of his or her behavior or be embarrassed about acting out the behavior in front of the therapist. When such insight or embarrassment occurs, the partner is more likely to change a behavior that he or she now sees as problematic. If this paradoxical effect does not happen, role-playing allows the therapist to see each partner's reaction as the couple experiences similar feelings in the role-play as they do in real life. In addition, it allows practice of a negative behavior in a situation that is not as emotionally charged.

Faking Negative Behavior at Home

This technique also can serve to desensitize partners, but its primary function is to help the offending partner observe his or her partner's response to a negative behavior. When problem behaviors have been identified for each member of the couple, they are then assigned the faking negative behavior homework. The task is to fake a behavior at a time when there is no emotional involvement, and then observe their partner's response. In this way, the partners have an opportunity to see the impact their behavior has without the personal investment of their own feelings or agenda getting in the way. Jack was a somewhat impulsive 28-year-old, and Julie, his wife, was timid and worried about their financial and domestic stability. Jack would frequently come up with a plan and as soon as Julie heard him say anything like, "I've got an idea," she would get worried and respond with hostility. Because he was impulsive, it was nearly impossible for Jack to stop coming up with ideas and plans and telling Julie about them. Luckily he had decreased the times that he actually acted on the plan without getting her feedback. The conversation, however, made Julie highly anxious and irritated. Jack's assignment was to say enthusiastically to Julie "Hey, I've been thinking, and I have a great idea" and to observe Julie's reaction. In all faking negative behavior assignments, the couple is to allow the "fake" to continue for only three or four minutes, and then disclose that this was an example of the homework. Julie had a tendency to roll her eyes at Jack when he said something that she thought was ridiculous. Jack got furious at this and felt completely discounted. Julie's fake behavior was to roll her eyes during a time when she actually had no negative feelings at all toward something Jack said. The couple then talks about their observations in the next therapy session. Many couples also get a paradoxical benefit from this assignment, because they are less reactive even when the partner does the behavior in reality, because they are waiting to hear if it is a faking behavior and have an easier time tolerating the behavior.

Building Tolerance through Self-Care

This tolerance exercise is necessary when there are situations that will not change. For example, if one partner acquires a serious illness or disability and is no longer able to provide the emotional or physical connection that he or she once did, the healthy partner may need to seek other friends in whom to confide, plan respite stays outside the home, get involved in activities that will provide intellectual stimulation, or a variety of other self-care behaviors.

KEY MISTAKES AND MISCOMPREHENSIONS

The first and foremost mistake that any therapist can make when trying to promote acceptance in therapy is to try to force or command acceptance. When acceptance becomes the sole agenda of the therapist, the treatment can go awry. Because of this, the concept of acceptance is openly discussed very little in IBCT. Therapists need also to take an acceptance stance; thus, it would be contradictory for the therapist to demand that the couple accept one another. The most common acceptance response on the part of the therapist should simply be that each partner's behavior is understandable given the context in which it occurs. That is not to say that the behavior does not need to be changed, but rather that the person is not fundamentally flawed because of misbehavior.

Another misconception is that IBCT is all about acceptance, when, in fact, it is about balancing acceptance and change in couple therapy. The theory would suggest that lasting change is more likely to happen when acceptance is achieved, because the treatment works on the controlling variables of behavior, rather than the derivative problems. Nevertheless, focusing too much on acceptance can lead to too little help with problem solving when a couple may require it. For example, when John and Linda recognized that they could not agree on whether it was a good time to have children, the therapist could easily make a mistake by bringing them back to whatever theme had been identified in the formulation or helping each to understand the other's position. It is likely that they both understood quite well, but would disagree in their desires nonetheless. Such a conflict is fertile ground for teaching the couple to identify the problem, brainstorm solutions, and come up with one solution to try. In this case it might be more helpful for the couple to list pros and cons of having a child now or in the future, and to agree on some method for getting further information about how children would affect their lives, such as volunteering to be a big brother or big sister for six months, before having a discussion again. In such a standstill, accepting the other's position will not further the couple's progress in resolving the difference.

Acceptance in couple therapy should not be interpreted as a means for maintaining the status quo. *This cannot be overemphasized.* This would not only be antitherapeutic, but in many ways it would be a misogynistic notion, because it is not uncommon for males in heterosexual couples to be satisfied with the status quo whereas females are seeking change so that their relationship will better meet their needs. Partners *never* need to accept unacceptable behavior. Being cursed at, slapped, demeaned, intimidated, bullied, ignored, and so on, is never acceptable. While being accepting of the person, the IBCT therapist would work to have the offending partner see his or her negative impact on the loved one. This can be accomplished, particularly through empathic joining or through several of the tolerance exercises. Thus, the person is accepted as a person, but the offensive behavior is not accepted.

CASE EXAMPLE

Jason was a 47-year-old attorney and Ella was a 50-year-old former school teacher. They had been married for 17 years and had a 16-year-old daughter and two adopted children, a son age 9 and a daughter age 5. At the start of therapy, their MSI ratings showed moderate distress in a number of areas for both partners. Although both of them had thought about ending the relationship, neither had sought the advice of an attorney. Their DAS scores—75 points for Ella and 88 points for Jason—both indicated significant marital distress, although Ella reported more distress with their communication patterns than Jason. The CTS revealed no significant violence or potential for domestic abuse, and both clients denied any physical altercations or intimidation in the individual interviews. The FAPB revealed that Jason found two of Ella's behaviors highly frequent and unacceptable: (1) not earning money for the family and (2) being too tired for or disinterested in sexual contact. Ella found four behaviors of Jason's to be frequent and unacceptable: (1) yelling at her and calling her names, (2) demanding that his rules be the rules of the house, (3) being too strict with the children, and (4) neglecting his share of yard chores at home. They had become particularly polarized on the issues of Ella returning to the workforce and intimacy.

Ella did not want to return to teaching until her youngest child was completely through elementary school. Ella's parents had been loving, but totally uninvolved in her school activities. They did not believe it was their place because neither had completed school past grade nine. Consequently, Ella felt that her participation in arts and crafts, and later in sports and theater, were unappreciated by her parents. When she had children she wanted to be able to help with school and be involved, especially in the early years. She was unable to do so for their eldest daughter, because Ella returned to full-time work when she was four. This left Ella with a great sense of guilt because her daughter, now 16, was having trouble with teachers at school and refused to come home for family dinner more nights of the week than not.

Jason's parents had both been hard working, but very poor. His father worked in lumber mills in the Pacific Northwest, and his mother worked as a nurse's aid in convalescent centers. Jason and his two brothers started working at age 12 with paper routes, and Jason continued to support himself through college and law school. He and Ella struggled in the initial years of their marriage when he was just completing his law degree, and Jason was grateful for Ella's teaching income. He had strong ideas about the need for everyone to "carry their weight," and felt that he had agreed to the adoption of the younger children at Ella's request, on the condition that she would return to work as soon as the youngest child was in nursery school. He was angry and disappointed that she was still not working. The theme that was identified here was responsibility and control. A related theme could be referred to as "The nurturer and the pragmatist," which were nonpejorative descriptors for Ella and Jason's respective philosophies and experiences of life.

When Ella and Jason debriefed arguments about her returning to work, the therapist used empathic joining by pointing out the relevant theme and eliciting the emotional content that each partner experienced around this issue that was rooted in their learning histories, which changed the way that they discussed the issue. For example, previously Jason would get angry and say "I'm not going to be the workhorse forever. You care more about those kids than me!" Ella would respond by saying, "You're as cold as ice with the kids. Look at what we've done to Alya [the 16-year-old]! I work. I work hard with this family. So don't flatter yourself just because your work brings income!" The therapist intervened in the following manner:

Therapist: Both of the themes that we talked about in our feedback session seem to be working here. Jason, you don't want to have the sole responsibility for earning money, and this makes sense given that in your family one person earning an income was a foreign concept.

Jason   :   That's right, we all pitched in. I don't know why Alya isn't working, she just wants to spend time on the phone or out with friends.

Ella   :   She works around the house. God. Can't you understand that there is work that doesn't bring income? You make a huge salary, more than we ever thought you would!

Therapist: Yes, both of you have good points. [To Jason] I wonder, though, how secure you feel with your current income?

Jason   :   Well, we're very comfortable. I have to work very hard for this though, and I have to drum up a lot of work for my firm.

Therapist: Do you ever worry that the work won't come?

Jason   :   All the time. It is a constant worry. It is also a constant worry that the firm will spend thousands of dollars on cases that we lose and not get money from it. That can affect my income, and my standing in the practice!

Therapist: So, you worry that this can all be taken away.

Jason   :   Unless everyone pitches in and defers the responsibility, it could. There's little cushion.

Therapist
[To Ella] :   Have you and Jason discussed this concern of his before?

Ella   :   No, but it seems ridiculous to me. We have nothing to worry about financially.

Therapist: And for you it is very important that the children receive all the attention they can get, rather than just have financial needs met.

Ella   :   Well, I certainly want financial needs met, but we can afford way beyond the basics. The children's need for a mom that is involved in their lives is more important. Alya has suffered from my not being there. She's so distant.

Therapist: And you don't want that distance to develop with the other children.

Ella   :   Right. It is too hard to bear. I don't want my children to resent me the way I resent my own family.

Therapist: So, here is a dilemma. Jason, you don't want to suffer financially like your family suffered, even though there is no evidence of that happening. And Ella, you don't want your children to feel neglected and become resentful, even though there is no evidence of that. So the result is that you are at loggerheads about this issue.

As Jason and Ella began to see one another's perspective, they were better able to discuss the problem. It remained a problem, however, and needed a solution. The therapist helped them work out a solution that was acceptable to both. They agreed that Ella would sign up as a substitute teacher, taking work only when she knew it would not interfere with volunteering at the children's schools or attending after-school activities. Jason agreed that he was resenting Ella not working, and needed to take more time with the kids and do more work around the house. He agreed to leave work early one night a week and make that his night to cook dinner and enlist the kids' help with fixing dessert. He also took bedtime duty on that night.

There were other problems that were discussed over the course of therapy. In this case, empathic joining and unified detachment led to the partners' responding to one another more favorably. They worked together in a collaborative fashion to come up with solutions to their differences. Jason was not able to stop worrying about money, and Ella was not able to stop fretting about attention to the children. This led to the only tolerance exercise, during which Jason would fake the behavior of saying, "How much did you spend on that?" when he was actually not concerned, and Ella would fake by saying, "I can't do that. I have to do such and such with one of the children" when she had no such engagement. This became a running joke between them, and the situation that once caused distress now provided a source of humor.

SUMMARY

Adding acceptance to behavioral couple therapy has emerged from the use of the functional analysis of couples' problems. Therapists maintain dialectic between acceptance and change, shifting therapeutic stance when necessary. Ironically, change often occurs when couples discontinue their change agenda. IBCT therapists strive to create a therapeutic environment in which a couple's differences and problems become opportunities for empathy and understanding. Often partners accepting one another as struggling human beings—each with his or her own sorrows, traps, and desires—is the most basic change that therapy can initiate.

REFERENCES

Addis, M. E., & Carpenter, K. M. (2000).The treatment rationale in cognitive–behavioral therapy: Psychological mechanisms and clinical guidelines. *Cognitive and Behavioral Practice, 7,* 147–156.

Baucom, D. H., & Epstein, N. (1990). *Cognitive–behavioral marital therapy.* New York: Brunner/Mazel.

Bograd, M., & Mederos, F. (1999). Battering and couples therapy: Universal screening and selection of treatment modality. *Journal of Marital and Family Therapy, 25,* 291–312.

Christensen, A., Atkins, D. C., Berns, S., Wheeler, J., Baucom, D. H., & Simpson, L. E. (2004). Traditional versus integrative behavioral couple therapy for significantly and chronically distressed married couples. *Journal of Consulting and Clinical Psychology, 72,* 176–191.

Christensen, A., & Jacobson, N. S. (1997). *Frequency and Acceptability of Partner Behaviors Scale.* Unpublished questionnaire. Los Angeles: University of California.

Hayes, S. C., Strosahl, K. D., & Wilson, K. G. (1999). *Acceptance and commitment therapy: An experiential approach to behavior change.* New York: Guilford.

Jacobson, N. S. (1994). Contextualism is dead: Long live contextualism. *Family Process, 33,* 97–100.

Jacobson, N. S., & Christensen, A. (1996). *Integrative couple therapy: Promoting acceptance and change.* New York: WW Norton.

Jacobson, N. S., & Margolin, G. (1979). *Marital therapy: Strategies basedon social learning and behavior exchange principles.* New York: Bruner/Mazel.

Linehan, M. M. (1993), *Cognitive-behavioral treatment of borderline personality disorder.* New York: Guilford.

Pepper, S. C. (1942). *World hypotheses.* Berkeley: University of California Press.

Snyder, D. K. (1979). Multidimensional assessment of marital satisfaction. *Journal of Marriage and the Family, 41,* 813–823.

Spanier, G. B. (1976). Measuring dyadic adjustment: New scales for assessing the quality of marriage and similar dyads. *Journal of Marriage and the Family, 38,* 15–28.

Straus M. A. (1979). Measuring intrafamily conflict and violence: The Conflict Tactics (CT) Scales. *Journal of Marriage and the Family, 41,* 75–88.

16

SHORT-TERM DYNAMIC PSYCHOTHERAPY GOES TO HOLLYWOOD: THE TREATMENT OF PERFORMANCE ANXIETY IN CINEMA

LEIGH MCCULLOUGH

Harvard Medical School
Dedham, Massachusetts

KRISTIN A. R. OSBORN

Cambridge, Massachusetts

Performance anxiety is rampant in our culture and is one of the most prevalent forms of anxiety. Jerry Seinfeld once joked that at a funeral, "Most people would rather be in the casket than giving the eulogy!" In fact, there are abundant examples of anxiety disorders in popular films *(e.g., Engstrom, 2004)* that can illustrate how to use short-term dynamic psychotherapy (STDP).

In the British comedy Four Weddings and a Funeral, Father Gerald is a priest with performance anxiety who must present bridal vows before a large wedding party. He enters the church licking his lips and gulping for air. Possibly hoping to appear pious, Father Gerald backs against the wall of the church, and pretends to read his Bible. In fact, he is beside himself with terror.

When he finally arrives at the altar, he forgets the bride and groom's names. He refers to the holy ghost as the holy goat, and asks the groom to take the bride to be his awful wedded wife. He ends the ceremony reciting, "The Father, the Son, and the Holy Spiggot...uh, Spirit." Father Gerald has performance anxiety. And it's bad!

Broadcast News is another film that vividly portrays performance anxiety. During a live broadcast, the news announcer drips with sweat, turns pale, and smacks his lips. He asks, *"Just how noticeable is this?"* A colleague responds, *"This is more than Nixon ever sweated!"* During a commercial, the crew rushes the news set, aiming a hair dryer at his hair and pushing fresh shirts at him. In his final report he refers to the death of 22 people and— while still on camera—mutters to himself, *"I wish I were one of them!"*

Finally, the master of anxiety, Woody Allen, gives us a classic example as an anxious suitor in Play It Again, Sam! He is besieged with anxiety before his first blind date after a divorce. As his mutual friend greets his date at the door, he tells himself to embody his idol, Humphrey Bogart: *"I am an absolute master."* Not quite. He frantically struggles to put on his coat and, in frustration, flings it across the room, with the sound of glass breaking in its path. He wrings his hands and babbles senselessly. His friend whispers protectively, *"Alan is a trifle tense."* The date replies, "Is he on something?"

Such examples of performance anxiety are common presenting problems in therapy. How could Father Gerald be helped to become poised? What would transform the news anchor into a confident announcer? What does the anxious suitor need to become calm and self-assured? How would a therapist using STDP treat this all-too-common problem? In this chapter we first describe the basic concepts of STDP, then we use the film characters presented here to illustrate how performance anxiety is treated in STDP.

SHORT-TERM DYNAMIC
PSYCHOTHERAPY

The STDP therapist conducts an in-depth diagnostic and historical evaluation to determine a hypothesis for treatment and to evaluate whether STDP is appropriate for the patient with a GAF off 55 or above (Endicott, J., Spitzer, R.L., Fleiss, J.L. & Cohen, J. 1976). Questions include: Are there other existing axis I and axis II diagnoses? What is the intensity and duration of the overwhelming anxiety? What are the symptoms of physiological arousal? Is the person's functioning sufficiently compromised for medication to be considered? How old was the patient when the first signs of performance anxiety emerged? Was there a precipitating event? And so on. In STDP, the initial evaluation is often two to three sessions in length to permit an in-depth exploration of these matters and to determine whether the patient can tolerate the rapid uncovering of feeling—the hallmark of this affect-focused treatment.

Specific to STDP is the understanding of several concepts:

- Affect phobia
- The Two Triangles
- Restructuring defenses, affects, and attachments

Affect phobia refers to what feeling is avoided. The Two Triangles describe how the avoidance of feeling happens and with whom. Restructuring refers to the exposure and response prevention mechanisms that are used to desensitize the affect-phobic individual.

AFFECT PHOBIA

Most people are familiar with external phobias—the fear and avoidance of such things as bridges, spiders, elevators, blood, open spaces, social situations, or heights. In contrast, affect phobias are less well-known internal phobias in which people are afraid of the experience of a specific feeling. Prominent examples are being ashamed to cry, afraid to stand up and be assertive, in too much pain to be close or tender with someone, or too guilty or undeserving to feel adequate self-esteem.

Performance anxiety might seem like an external phobia—the fear of standing up in front of other people. But like so many external phobias, performance anxiety has a related, internal affect-based component: an inability to access the emotional experience necessary to give a performance comfortably. STDP theory posits that affects are our basic motivational system and that phobias about affects are the most basic impairment and the origin of many, if not most, behavior problems. Although maladaptive cognitions also play a fundamental role in pathology, we believe that affective impairment is even more basic.

Thus, an STDP therapist focuses on the inner emotional conflict about performance, the core conflict or affect phobia. The question becomes: What core affect or affects are conflicted and thus being avoided? The STDP therapist begins observing the avoidant or anxious behaviors and wonders what underlying phobic feeling was being warded off that the patient needed to access to be able not to be anxious about performance.

In this chapter we generate hypotheses about affect phobias and defensive patterns used by each of the film characters. But first, we describe the Two Triangle schema that puts these affect phobias in context.

TWO TRIANGLES

David Malan (1979), one of the pioneers of STDP, developed a conceptual schema (based on Freudian conflict theory) called the Two Triangles—The

Triangle of Conflict and the Triangle of Person—which organize and operationalize what happens, and with whom, when intrapsychic conflict develops and phobic affects result.

As shown in Figure 16.1, the Triangle of Conflict guides the therapist in identifying behaviors that represent defenses (D), anxieties (A), and underlying adaptive feeling (F).

The defense pole (D) represents the defenses that block or avoid the conflicted feelings. Defenses are many and varied, and can take the form of behaviors (avoiding bridges or social events), thoughts ("I'm no good"), and feelings (trembling rather than speaking).

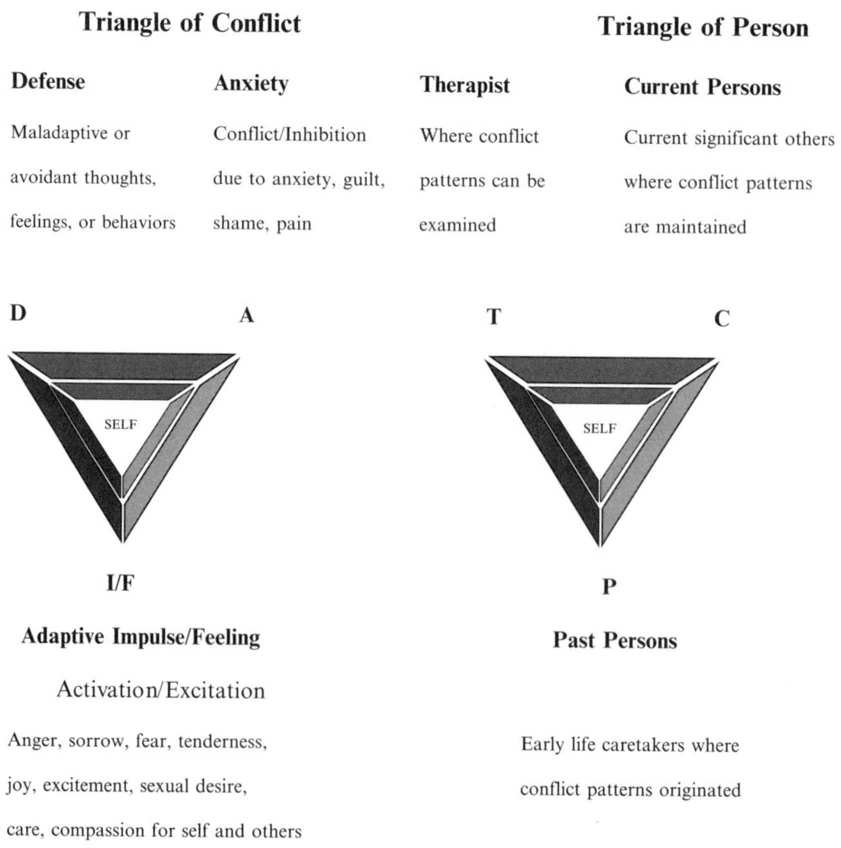

Triangle of Conflict   Triangle of Person

Defense	**Anxiety**	**Therapist**	**Current Persons**
Maladaptive or	Conflict/Inhibition	Where conflict	Current significant others
avoidant thoughts,	due to anxiety, guilt,	patterns can be	where conflict patterns
feelings, or behaviors	shame, pain	examined	are maintained

D   A   T   C

I/F   P

Adaptive Impulse/Feeling   **Past Persons**

Activation/Excitation

Anger, sorrow, fear, tenderness,	Early life caretakers where
joy, excitement, sexual desire,	conflict patterns originated
care, compassion for self and others	

FIGURE 16.1   An adaptation of Malan's two triangles for treating affect phobias

Such defenses may have been adaptive and useful at some time, but they become destructive when they result in maladaptive behaviors. The STDP therapist is vigilant in pointing out how these defensive patterns are serving to avoid feelings.

The anxiety pole (A) represents the four main categories of inhibitory feelings: anxiety, shame/guilt, emotional pain, and contempt/disgust. These inhibitory feelings signal us to stop, slow down, or be on guard about ourselves or others. They are adaptive in moderate doses; however, too little inhibition can result in sociopathy or psychopathy. Too much inhibition can be crippling, as in the film characters such as the news announcer's withdrawal when feeling anger and the anxious suitor's feeling ashamed and acting foolish. It is the task of the STDP therapist to identify to the patient how and why they are using inhibitory feelings.

The feeling pole (F) represents the activating feelings that motivate adaptive behavior, such as grief, anger, closeness, sexual desire, excitement, and positive feelings toward the self. These are feelings endowed at birth to help us navigate through life. These healthy action tendencies become phobically avoided because they have become associated with something negative. The STDP therapist helps the patient understand what underlying adaptive affects are being avoided.

The Triangle of Person guides the therapist to identify the relationships in which these conflict patterns began. As shown in Figure 16.1, these patterns can originate in past relationships (P), continue in current relationships (C), and can be played out in the relationship with the therapist (T).

Indeed, affect phobias are typically learned in early childhood from caretakers and are then practiced with others into adulthood. Children develop fears of feeling as a result of a frightening, shameful, or painful event. For example, a child may learn that sadness or anger is bad: "Big girls don't cry! Never question what Mommy says!" When natural, healthy responses are not permitted, the child may become anxious, withdrawn, or put on a happy face instead. The STDP therapist must help the patient see the origins of these feared feelings to assist in the desensitization of the affect phobias. For example (using the Two Triangle schema):

Therapist   : Father Gerald, can you see that your anxious behavior in church (D) as well as with me (T) is similar to how you responded last week to the bishop (C)? This pattern seems to have come from how hard you tried as a boy to please your father (P).

Father Gerald: It's true. He set incredibly high standards for me, and I always was anxious about falling short of them. I can see I am still doing that.

RESTRUCTURING DEFENSIVE
AND AFFECTIVE PATTERNS

STDP methods are designed to desensitize the affect phobia. These methods entail defense restructuring (decrease use of maladaptive defenses), affect restructuring (exposure to the "true" but phobic feeling), self/other restructuring (improve sense of self and relationship with others), and anxiety regulation (decrease anxiety, shame, or pain associated with that feeling). Barlow (1988, 1993) and colleagues value the use of exposure to resolve emotional and behavioral conflict. Barlow (1988) writes:

> The overwhelming evidence from emotion theory is that an essential step in the modification of emotional disorders is the direct alteration of associated action tendencies. . . . prevention of behavioral responses . . . associated with fear and anxiety, and the substitution of action tendencies associated with alternative emotions, may account for the effectiveness of this technique. (p. 312)

In STDP theory, we see the major change agent as the substitution of action tendencies with more adaptive forms of affective responding. Six major objectives guide treatment interventions.

The first two objectives concern two obstacles that need resolution to restructure defenses properly. The patient has to be able to recognize and understand their defensive patterns, and be motivated to give them up. It is the task of the STDP therapist to point out the defensive behaviors and educate the patient about the costs of what is being done, to encourage change.

In the film examples, Father Gerald, the news anchor, and the anxious suitor are not using traditional defenses to avoid their painful situations. Rather, each man is struggling mightily to perform, even though he is overwhelmed with anxiety, shame, and pain. In such cases, the flooding of anxiety or shame or pain blocks an effective emotional response, so the anxiety response itself serves as the defense or avoidance mechanism. The whole top of the triangle can be seen as defensive. The same question then arises: What feeling or feelings are needed that are not being accessed?

Thus, the second two objectives concern the experiencing and expression of appropriate feelings. However, before one can desensitize the affect phobia, it has to be correctly identified. Sometimes the true feeling is obvious and easy to determine, but other times, especially when it is unconscious, it can be difficult and confusing. It is helpful to remember that the choices are few. Still, many therapists become confused at this point, thinking that the "phobic feeling" that is being avoided is shame or anxiety, because, of course, no one likes these negative experiences.

The definitive question is: Does this person need more anxiety or shame to get better? Certainly not. These inhibitory feelings are causing the trouble because they are overdone. What must be identified are the activating feelings that motivate adaptive behavior but have become conflicted because of their association with anxiety, guilt, shame, or pain. Thus, the challenge for the

STDP therapist is to listen to the patient's story and identify the natural, healthy feelings that would help the patient behave effectively and feel better.

CASE ILLUSTRATIONS

What might we hypothesize are the true feelings that our film characters need to access to resolve their performance anxiety? What feelings would help Father Gerald overcome his performance anxiety at the wedding? What feelings does the news anchor need to stop his terror of live performance? What does the anxious suitor need to feel that would help him enjoy his date and be the confidant, warm, open man that he aspires to be?

Is there one feeling? Or several? Are all three men's needs the same or are they different? The STDP therapist explores this by eliciting further information from the patients. Close attention is paid to the nonverbal and verbal responses toward feelings. The therapist and patient begin to link the anxieties and defenses, moving closer to uncovering the actual blocked feeling and its origins. Next we hypothesize about the film characters, but use our clinical experience with actual patients to develop their stories.

FATHER GERALD'S AFFECT PHOBIA

Let's imagine that Father Gerald contacted an STDP therapist, concerned that he has done poorly in previous ceremonies and is getting increasingly anxious, which is making things worse. In addition, he is deeply disappointed in himself that he is not the inspiring priest he had hoped to be. Further discussion might uncover that he feels guilty about his hubris of wanting to be inspiring, and thus not entitled to his grief about his loss of self-image. Through a process of trial and error, the therapist makes various suggestions to be corroborated, or not, with Father Gerald.

Father Gerald: I never liked public speaking, but I used to do OK. Then one time I fumbled and was so upset over it that now I'm a nervous wreck before every service.

Therapist   :   So maybe you're being too demanding on yourself and keeping those overly high standards like your father did.

It appears that Father Gerald needs to be less demanding or more compassionate about his mistakes.

THE NEWS ANCHOR'S AFFECT PHOBIA

The news anchor tells the therapist that he has been furious because he has been unable to negotiate a satisfactory contract with his station. He is overworked and underpaid compared with another announcer. Therefore, he is well aware that he feels jealous, angry, and devalued, but is still unable to negotiate a better contract. The dialogue might go something like this:

News Anchor: I seem to do OK in the beginning negotiations, but I always choke up at the end and lose my initiative.

Therapist   :   I wonder if you're struggling with more than a block toward anger?

At this point the therapist would explore whether the news anchor feels he is not entitled to succeed, not really good enough. He might be devaluing himself as well. During the discussion the following emerges.

News Anchor: No, I've never felt adequate. I always feel like I am not good enough and am faking it and am going to be found out.

This would indicate to the therapist that the patient needs desensitization of anger/assertion, but that there is also shame or guilt about his sense of self (his entitlement to have negative feelings) that needs to be dealt with.

ANXIOUS SUITOR'S AFFECT PHOBIA

The STDP therapist might hypothesize that the anxious suitor lacks self-confidence or sufficient self-esteem with women. Discussion reveals several factors. He has always felt inadequate or unattractive. His family was not warm or affectionate and never praised the children. To make things worse, he had been cruelly teased by his sisters while growing up, and never wants to let himself be seen for who he is.

What emotions does he need to access to master this situation? Obviously he needs to develop a healthy self-esteem and self-confidence. He also may need to feel more comfortable with feelings of closeness to others because his family was cool and unexpressive. In addition, he probably would need to face his angry feelings toward his family, and grieve what he did not get as a child so that he could proceed in the future to respond differently and more adaptively.

When some hypotheses about feelings have been identified, the final question is: Why have the feelings been so avoided? What is the specific anxiety, shame, or pain that inhibits the natural, healthy response? Patients are encouraged to explore the emerging anxieties so they can develop an awareness of the fears associated with moving closer to experiencing true feelings — and learning to master them. Here are some examples from the film characters:

Therapist
[to Father Gerald]:   What is the most shameful thing about not perfectly performing vows?

Therapist
[to the news anchor]:   Can we look at what it is about public performance that is the most terrifying for you?

Therapist
[to the anxious Suitor]: What is the most painful part of being rejected by a woman? (He might possibly also need to grieve the loss of closeness in his early life but feels too afraid and ashamed. Some patients have more than one of these inhibitory feeling working in concert that thwart adaptive feeling or action. Some have only one or two. The anxious suitor seems to have a good number of them.)

Exploring the maladaptive cognitions and then disputing their logic is a popular and effective intervention in cognitive therapy. It is used in STDP to give the patient some perspective (developing an observing ego) to help them better cope with their fears.

Although these film characters are fictitious, their behaviors and our interpretations of their underlying problems follow typical problems in treatment that STDP conceptualizes using the Two Triangle schema. Father Gerald appears to have a mild phobia (A) about self-presentation (F). The news anchor feels shame (A) about anger or assertion (F), but also a fair amount of unworthiness (A, shame) instead of self-esteem (F), because he feels like a fake (D), and is also unentitled (A) to fight hard (F) for what he wants in his contract. He would need to build a strong self-esteem and self-image (F, positive feelings associated with the self) and become comfortable with appropriate expressions of anger/assertion (F).

The anxious suitor shows the most impairment to the self, with a great amount of shame and feelings of being unattractive, unlovable, and worthless (D, self-attack). He also mentions anxiety (A) about closeness (F) since childhood. The anxious suitor would need to become confident and positive (F) about himself, unafraid to be close (F) to others, and probably also have to feel grief (F) and anger (F) to early life figures (P) until he could feel better about himself (F) and put his family in perspective.

The STDP therapist would then encourage these patients to explore the hypotheses (interpretations) and revise them if necessary. In this collaborative process, the patient begins to understand his defensive behavior, his inhibitory anxieties, and the underlying avoided feeling.

The hypothesis about the affect phobia is always a work in progress, an educational tool constantly being reshaped and expanded throughout the treatment by both the patient and the therapist. We can never know if the hypotheses are correct or historically accurate. We can only hope the hypothesis rings true and that it is effective in guiding interventions that result in behavior change.

Despite the careful identification of the defensive patterns, awareness or insight is rarely sufficient for change to occur. Most often, the patient must be exposed to the avoided affect and learn how to experience true feeling without the negative intrusion of excessive inhibitory anxieties and defensive behaviors.

At this point, the STDP therapist (armed with the core conflict formulation to guide the interventions) and our film character patients (ideally with defenses sufficiently restructured to have acquired enough insight and motivation to bear the process) move to affect restructuring to desensitize their respective affect phobias.

There is abundant research that demonstrates that the most effective treatment for a phobia is exposure and response prevention. STDP treatment follows similar premises. Effective treatment involves exposure to the phobic feelings to reduce the inhibitory feeling that prevent these feelings from being properly expressed.

Similar to a behavior therapist helping a bridge-phobic patient approach a bridge, the STDP therapist must assist affect-phobic patients in approaching, bearing, and incrementally working through the bodily experience of anger, sorrow, tenderness, or pride that has become conflicted and warded off. Similar to behavior therapy, the STDP process is initially conducted in imagery to desensitize the inner experience of feeling, and then in vivo to desensitize the outer or interpersonal expression of feeling. The therapist is also vigilant for the avoidant defensive responses and helps alert the patient to prevent those responses.

There are three main components for the process of desensitization of affects. First is to prevent the defensive responses by pointing out avoidance and to refocus the patient. Second is to expose the patient to the phobic affect, guiding the patient to experience the feeling on a visceral level for behavior to change. Gestalt techniques are very useful here. And third, reduce the associated inhibitory affects (anxiety, guilt, shame, pain). Cognitive techniques work well for this.

Gestalt techniques and guided imagery are excellent methods for exposing patients to the experience of a feeling that they once learned not to have. Desensitization is achieved through repeatedly exposing the patient to the feeling until whatever anxiety, guilt, shame, or pain that has become associated with it is lessened. The STDP therapist is vigilant for signs of adaptive responding and encourages the patient to make behavioral ratings of improvement every few weeks.

The STDP therapist will help Father Gerald face that he is not yet as inspiring in his performance as he would have hoped. This should elicit some sorrow on his behalf and help him bear that he will make mistakes sometimes. Father Gerald needs to see the high standards he sets for himself (defense of perfectionism), and become more accepting and compassionate (F) toward himself.

Therapist   :   What do you think the congregation is thinking of you when you mix up your words?

Father Gerald: : They probably think I am a fool and incompetent to do my job.

Therapist : Is that what you would feel if you saw a young priest in your shoes?

Father Gerald: No. I would feel sympathetic toward him and know he was nervous.

Therapist : Well, isn't it sad that you feel sympathetic toward this imaginary person, but not for yourself? And you worry that your congregation would think so badly of you, but when you imagine yourself in the congregation, you feel sympathetic. Don't you think you're being pretty hard on yourself?

Father Gerald: Yes, I can see that. And it's just what my father did.

Therapist : I wonder if you can let yourself feel gentler toward yourself?

The subsequent exposure to self-acceptance reduces a good deal of the anxiety and shame about performance, and takes some of the burden off his performance anxiety. Father Gerald has some areas where he feels self-worth, so that he can readily accept that he does not always have to be a perfect performer. The acceptance of his imperfections as a speaker calms him, and he is now able to reassure and calm himself as he begins the services. Although this is a fictitious example, his absence of severe impairment to the self, and the rapid resolution of his anxiety, follow some well-trodden pathways of cases that are classic short-term treatments that might last five to ten sessions.

In the case of the news announcer who is blocked in standing up for himself, the therapist must desensitize the experience of feeling appropriately angry or assertive. This will enable him to set limits or ask for his needs to be met. He also needs help with restructuring his impairment to his sense of self so that he feels worthwhile and entitled to stand up for himself.

Exposure to the avoided feeling must be felt on a physiological level to be effective, and may begin with small and tolerable doses. The process starts by the patient describing a specific problematic incident in vivid detail, as if it were really happening in the moment, to help the patient to access and experience the emotions associated with the scene.

The process might involve interactions like this:

Therapist : You mentioned how difficult it is for you to negotiate for yourself. Could you imagine being back in the boss' office when you were going over the contract? What were you feeling toward the boss at that moment?

News Anchor: Not much toward him. I was just tied in knots. I guess I was angry at him, but couldn't say so.

Therapist   : Could you go back and try to feel some of that anger now? As though you are face to face with him? Of course, we never intend to explode in anger at anyone. We are just exploring these feelings so that you can become comfortable with them.

The therapist listens and watches, asking the patient to describe bodily responses associated with the emerging feelings (e.g., tension in hands due to feelings of anger). This use of imagery creates the "exposure" to feeling.

Therapist   : What would you do if you put that angry energy out on your boss? Can you let yourself feel that? (exposure #1)

News Announcer: I hate acting like a bully. I never want to do that! (shame associated with anger)

Therapist   : We are not ever talking about acting like a bully. We are just trying to explore that inner energy—and if you block it as you just did, you will not have the initiative to negotiate for yourself (disputing the logic of his shame reaction). So, could we try once more to look at those angry feelings that are part of your life force? (Therapist refocuses on the phobic affect for exposure #2.)

News Announcer: Well, in truth, I wanted to punch him in the face!

Therapist   : Can you let yourself feel that—just as if you were doing it? (Later) That is the energy you want to feel, but not act out. It is the energy that will help you drive a hard bargain in a negotiation (linking the inner feeling with appropriate expression).

Exposure should be done in a stepwise and supportive manner. In this case, the therapist helps the news anchor feel a little irritation before he could fully feel and appropriately control his anger.

In contrast, the anxious suitor's feelings of worthlessness and inadequacy imply much greater impairment to his sense of self that the other two characters. The major focus in his treatment would be to access the feelings of self-worth and acceptability that are blocked by shame. The physical experience of self-worth can often be accessed by an intervention called *changing perspectives*. If a person is not able to feel something one way, they can often access the feeling if it is once removed, as Father Gerald did earlier. The anxious suitor needs to imagine that other people in his life feel care or compassion for him before he can experience positive feeling for himself.

Therapist   : Who thought you were special when you were a child? Whose eyes lit up when they saw you?

The Anxious Suitor: No one.... (pausing)...Well, I suppose my Aunt Helen.

Therapist   :   How did you feel when you were in her presence?
                       (exposure to positive feeling for self)
The anxious suitor: I felt warm and happy. She just made me feel like she
                       loved having me around. (tears beginning to flow)
                       No one else in my family made me feel that way.
Therapist   :   I wonder if you could hold on to that feeling you had
                       with Aunt Helen and carry it with you?

Traditional forms of treatment tend not to focus directly on self-esteem, or on the desensitization of blocks to it. In contrast, positive self feelings is a major focus in STDP. Exposures, such as the one with the anxious suitor, must be repeated until shame is decreased and replaced instead with healthy pride, such as, "I am worthwhile and entitled to good things."

CLINICAL ISSUES AND SUMMARY

The treatment of performance anxiety is actually quite straightforward once the therapist understands how to use Malan's Two Triangles—and determine what core affect is blocked. Desensitization through exposure and response prevention helps a person to experience true feeling, and safely leave behind destructive inhibitions. The restructuring of the self enables the patient to gain strength and wholeness, leaving behind a host of negative self-statements and inadequate self-images. The sense of self often plays a pivotal role in anxieties and defenses associated with social phobia; concomitantly, positive feelings about the self often play a role in its resolution.

STDP incorporates many effective interventions from behavioral and cognitive therapies. However, STDP is primarily focused on the exploration and identification of conflicted, and thus avoided, feelings, which we consider the fundamental origin of maladaptive behavior. Nevertheless, the psychodynamic conflict is labeled in behavioral terms (*affect phobia*) and treated with desensitization techniques, because research-based behavioral interventions offer effective ways to resolve problems, including those arising from psychodynamic conflicts.

In summary, to understand the affect phobia imbedded in the Triangle of Conflict, the STDP therapist helps the patient develop a hypothesis concerning how the patient avoids feelings (defenses), why the patient is avoidant (anxieties), and what the patient is avoiding (the "true" or "phobic" affect). Thus the Two Triangles become operational by answering these questions that then guide the STDP interventions.

Common factors by Lambert and Bergin (1994) have been intentionally incorporated throughout the STDP process. Defense recognition was designed as a method for achieving awareness or insight. Defense relinquishing is the way we help build motivation. Affect experiencing is the process of exposure to and desensitization of conflicted feelings, and affect expression is the process of acquiring new learning about how to manage and convey those feelings appropriately. In addition, the STDP therapist constantly offers reassurance in an empathetic and caring manner, provides ongoing teaching so that patients can learn to articulate their experience, and gives encouragement for patients to face their fears and continue to practice repeated exposure to fearful and conflicted feelings.

This model of STDP has been developed and refined from research findings during the past 25 years. In addition to research supporting the efficacy of the common factors incorporated in STDP, there have been two randomized controlled clinical trials supporting the efficacy of this model. The first clinical trial (Winston, McCullough, Trujillo, et al, 1991) and two-year follow-up (Winston, Laikim, Pollack, Samstag, McCullough, & Muran, 1994) as well as a series of process studies (e.g., Foote, 1989; Makynen, 1992; McCullough et al., 1994; Salerno, Farber, McCullough, Winston & Trujillo, 1992) were conducted at Beth Israel Medical Center in New York City. The second clinical trial and two-year follow-up was conducted at the University of Trondheim in Norway, comparing STDP with cognitive therapy (Svartberg, Stiles & Seltzer, 2004). Currently, a large-scale process study is underway at the Norwegian University of Science and Technology in Trondheim, Norway, where the videotapes from these clinical trials are being extensively analyzed for change mechanisms that promote improvement (e.g., Johansen, Valen, Revheim, McCullough, Stiles, & Svartberg, 2004; McCullough, Kuhn, Andrews, Valen, Hatch, & Osino, 2004; Valen, McCullough, Stiles, & Svartberg, 2003), and are being compared with change mechanisms in videotapes from other theoretical orientations such as DBT (Linehan, 1993). This model is also being intensively examined in a single-case experimental design format conducted at Harvard Medical School with the goal of continually improving the treatment offered to our patients.

Of course, our movies might not be as entertaining without the hilarious failures of Father Gerald, the news anchor, and the anxious suitor. However, with their performance anxiety resolved, these characters just might have a chance of leading lives that are fuller, more peaceful, and ultimately more productive.

Emily Dickinson, a woman beset with severe social phobia (she rarely left her house) and performance anxiety (she never allowed her poems to be published while alive), nevertheless knew its cure in her heart and mind. She reminds us in her poem *1176*:

> *We never know how high we are*
> *Till we are asked to rise,*
> *And then if we are true to plan*
> *Our statuses touch the skies.*

The Heroism we recite
Would be a normal thing
Did not ourselves the Cubits warp
For fear to be a King-

REFERENCES

Barlow, D. H. (1988). *Anxiety and its disorders: The nature and treatment of anxiety and panic.* New York: Guilford.

Barlow, D. H. (Ed.). (1993). Clinical handbook of psychological disorders (2nd ed.). New York: Guilford.

Dickinson, Emily, Poem 1176, *The Complete Poems of Emily Dickinson,* Back Bay Books, 1976. (Paperback), edited by Thomas H. Johnson pg 522–523

Endicott, J., Spitzer, R. L., Fleiss, J. L., & Cohen, J. (1976) The Global Assessment Scale: A procedure for measuring overall severity of psychiatric disturbances. *Archives of General Psychiatry, 33,* 766–771.

Engstrom, Frederick W. (2004). *Movie clips for creative mental health education.* New York: Wellness Reproduction & Publishing.

Foote, J. (1989). Interpersonal context and patient change episodes. New York University, May 1989. *Dissertation Abstracts International, 51,* 12B.

Gabbard, G. (1994). *Psychodynamic psychiatry in clinical practice.* Washington, DC: American Psychiatric Press.

Johansen, P., Valen, J., Revheim, T., McCullough, L., Stiles, T., & Svartberg, M. (2004). *An analysis of defense mechanisms in short-term dynamic psychotherapy* and *cognitive behavioral therapy.* Presented at the Society for Psychotherapy Research, Rome, Italy, June 2004.

Lambert, M. J., & Bergin, A. E. (1994). The effectiveness of psychotherapy. In A. E. Bergin & S. L. Garfield (Eds.). *Handbook of psychotherapy and behavior change* (4th ed., pp. 143–189). New York: Wiley.

Linehan, M. M. (1993). *Cognitive–behavioral treatment of borderline personality disorder.* New York: Guilford.

Makynen A. (1992). The effects of continued confrontation on patient affective and defensive response. Columbia University Teachers' College, May 1992. *Dissertation Abstracts International, 54,* 01B.

Malan, D. H. (1979). *Individual psychotherapy and the science of psychodynamics.* London: Butterworth/Heinemann.

McCullough, L., Kuhn, N., Andrews, S., Kaplan, A., Wold, J., & Lanza, C. T. (2003). *Treating affect phobia: A manual for short term dynamic psychotherapy.* New York: Guilford.

McCullough, L., Kuhn, N., Andrews, S., Valen, J., Hatch, D., & Osimo, F. (2004). The reliability of the Achievement of Therapeutic Objectives Scale (ATOS): A research and teaching tool for brief psychotherapy. *Journal of Brief Therapy,* 2 (2), 72–90.

McCullough L., Winston A., Farber B., Porter F., Pollack J., Laikin M., Vingiano W., & Trujillo, M. (1991). The relationship of patient–therapist interaction to outcome in brief psychotherapy. *Psychotherapy, 28,* 525–533.

McCullough–Valliant, L. (1997). *Changing character: Short-term anxiety-regulating psychotherapy for restructuring defenses, affects, and attachment.* New York: Basic Books.

Salerno, M., Farber, B., McCullough, L., Winston, A., Trujillo, M. (1992). The effects of confrontation and clarification on patient affective and defensive responding. *Psychotherapy Research, 2,* 181–192.

Svartberg, M., Stiles, T.C., & Seltzer, M.H. (2004). Randomized, Controlled Trial of the Effectiveness of Short-Term Dynamic Psychotherapy and Cognitive Therapy for Cluster C Personality Disorders. *American Journal of Psychiatry.* 161: 810–817, May 2004.

Valen, J., McCullough, L., Stiles, T., & Svartberg, M. (September 2003). JakobsLadder: A web-based teaching tool for establishing reliability in raters. Presented at the Society for Psychotherapy Research, Weimer, Germany.

Wachtel, P. E. (1977). *Psychoanalysis and behavior therapy: Toward an integration.* New York: Basic Books.

Winston, A., Laikin, M., Pollack, J., Samstag, L., McCullough, L., Muran, C. (1994). Short-term psychotherapy of personality disorders: 2 year follow-up. *American Journal of Psychiatry, 151,* 190–194.

Winston, A., McCullough, L., Trujillo, M., Pollack, J., Laikin M., Flegenheimer W., Kestenbaum, R. (1991). Brief psychotherapy of personality disorders. *Journal of Nervous and Mental Disease, 179,* 188–193.

17

THE IMPORTANCE

OF NOVELTY IN

PSYCHOTHERAPY

BRETT N. STEENBARGER

SUNY Upstate Medical University
Syracuse, New York

What catalyzes change in psychotherapy? Consider several striking therapy cases:

☐ In a well-known example of brief therapy (Haley, 1984), Milton Erickson met with an insomniac client who tried every possible strategy for sleeping, only to face continued waking. Erickson asked him if he was willing to undertake a task; not surprisingly, the desperate man was prepared to try anything. His instruction was to not attempt sleep when he found himself awake at night. Instead, he was directed to use the opportunity of wakefulness to clean his floors meticulously with a small brush. No doubt more than a bit puzzled by the task, the man complied with Erickson's direction and shortly returned to therapy reporting that he had regained his ability to sleep. The labored floor cleaning was apparently so noxious that the man was willing to do almost anything to avoid the tedium—including sleep.

☐ A medical student client (Steenbarger, 2003) spent hours in front of her mirror, berating her weight and looks. She restricted her food intake, only to lapse into episodes of bingeing and purging. Proud of her ability to relate to her medical patients and assist them, she felt completely out of control when it came to her own eating. Interestingly, concerns over food intake were not troublesome during workday hours, but were all consuming at night and on weekends. Instructed to close her eyes and relax, she was taken through a guided imagery exercise and asked to imagine herself as her own patient. She was encouraged to visualize wearing her white doctor's coat at home and lovingly feeding her "patient" at dinnertime, utilizing all her sensitivity and talents. Almost immediately, she was able to apply her clinical skills to herself, ending the episodes of purging and moderating her food consumption.

❏ A boy was referred for truant behavior, but his mother refused participation in the therapy unless she was in the room at all times (Cummings & Sayama, 1995). The mother wrote a detailed, 40-page report of the son's history, but defensively insisted that the son was the patient—not her—and that she must be involved in all interventions with her son. The therapist not only agreed with the mother, but insisted that she serve as a cotherapist in the case. Stunned by the acquiescence, but concerned that her cotherapist role not be compromised, the mother initiated help for herself, gaining insight into her own patterns of guilt and overprotection. This allowed her to transfer her son's care to a needed male role model, sparking an elimination of the truancy.

Across these vignettes, a common element emerges: In each case, the therapist used an element of novelty to catalyze change. The client entered with one set of problem definitions and expectations, and was quickly helped to adopt very different perspectives and actions. In this chapter we shall explore how novelty is a core ingredient of successful therapy, opening the door to new patterns of thought and behavior.

DEFINING THE ISSUE

To be sure, there are a number of factors responsible for success in therapy. In the previous vignettes, success ingredients included client readiness for change (Prochaska, 2004), a positive working alliance (Bachelor & Horvath, 2004), and an emotionally charged helping setting that framed expectations for change (Frank & Frank, 1993). Note also that, in each case, the client entered therapy with one set of understandings regarding problems and solutions, and quickly adopted a radically different perspective. This novelty—defined in this article as fresh understandings, behaviors, and experiences introduced by a therapist to interrupt and alter established problem patterns—was central to breaking through resistances to change (Cummings & Sayama, 1995) and overcoming demoralization (Frank & Frank, 1993).

Budman, Friedman, and Hoyt (1992) observe that clients are typically stuck in cyclical patterns of repeating difficulties: "It is the therapist's job to disrupt these repeating cycles by introducing a novel perspective or by setting the stage for the client to be receptive to information in his or her natural environment that will open up options for change" (p. 348). Such novelty, they explain, "not only activates and arouses the client's interest, but disorients the client in a positive way and creates perturbations in the client's prior assumptions and established sets" (p. 348). Cummings and Sayama (1995) note that, "Doing something novel catapults the patient into treatment in spite of the resistance" (p. 44), challenging entrenched expectations. Tallman and Bohart (2004) describe the change process as a novelty-driven cycle of thinking, experiencing, and behaving. New thoughts promote new experiences, which facilitate new behaviors. These fresh behaviors, in turn, reinforce the new thoughts and encourage further experiences. Novelty, from this perspective, can take many forms: insights, experiences, and skills. Indeed, as we shall see, it is reasonable to surmise that a major function of the various schools of therapy is to systematize forms of novelty, entering the thinking–experiencing–behaving cycle at various points in the change process (Tallman & Bohart, 2004).

THEORY, CONCEPTUALIZATION, AND ASSESSMENT

Novelty is not intrinsic to therapist interventions, but instead is relative to clients' understandings. What is a novel skill or idea for one individual may be routine for another. Moreover, clients bring their distinctive, culturally derived worldviews to therapy (Pedersen, 2000), helping to shape what is novel. We cannot assess the role of novelty in therapy without entering the experience of both parties in the helping relationship. Fortunately, we have an extensive history of process and outcome literature to draw upon in understanding novelty's role as a facilitator of change.

Research emphasizes that outcomes in therapy are determined more by factors common to the various approaches than to their unique ingredients (Wampold, 2001). According to Lambert's (1992) well-known formulation, 40% of variance in clinical outcomes is attributable to client-related variables, 30% to the quality of the helping relationship, 15% to expectations regarding change, and only 15% to the techniques specific to therapeutic schools. Wampold (2001), reviewing meta-analytical studies of outcome, concludes that fully 70% of outcome variance is attributable to common therapeutic factors. This, he contends, supports a "contextual" model of change over a "medical" model. Individuals alter their thoughts, feelings, and actions not so much because of what is done to them as because the helping process affords them a different context for self-construal.

Frank and Frank (1993) refer to the rationales and procedures of therapy as "myths" and "rituals" (p. 44) that encourage a positive working relationship, increase expectations of change, provide new learning experiences, facilitate emotional arousal, and enhance a client's sense of self-efficacy. "All schools of psychotherapy," they contend, "bolster the patient's sense of mastery . . . by providing the patient with a conceptual scheme that explains symptoms and supplies the rationale and procedure for overcoming them, and by providing occasions for the patient to experience success" (p. 48). Novelty is thus central to change in two ways: creating fresh understandings of problem patterns and introducing new procedures for acquiring successful experience.

Reviewing process and outcome literature in brief counseling and therapy, Steenbarger (1992, 1994) finds support for a three-stage change process:

1. *Engagement*—An initial period of rapport building in which expectations and goals are established and a positive working alliance developed

2. *Discrepancy*—Initiation of interventions, typically under heightened conditions of client experiencing, that introduce experiences discrepant from the client's own

3. *Consolidation*—Opportunities to rehearse new, constructive action patterns that follow from the introduction of discrepancy so that these are internalized

Viewing novelty as discrepancy allows us to appreciate therapy as an evolutionary process, which introduces mutations into an existing "gene pool" of thoughts and behaviors. In this vein, Tallman and Bohart (2004) observe,

> The real therapy is living. What we call therapy is a special example of processes that occur outside of therapy. Therapy concentrates or distills the experiential and intellectual contexts of everyday life. Therapy can then be thought of as a prosthetic provision of contexts, experiences, and events which prompt, support, or facilitate client's self-healing. (p. 111)

Novelty is the essence of this "prosthetic provision." If clients, indeed, are the self-reflective, active agents in therapy portrayed in process research (Maione & Chenail, 2004), they will benefit from therapy to the extent that they can derive meaning from the explanations and procedures embodied by the various therapies. The presence of competing therapeutic schools may be less a function of scientific laxity than a reflection of the multiple, creative ways in which novel self-construals and actions can be introduced into an existing repertoire.

IMPACT ON CASE FORMULATION

An undeniable trend in the delivery of psychotherapy has been the development of manualized treatments for specific disorders (Barlow, 2001; Van Hasselt & Hersen, 1996). Although this movement has facilitated valuable research on therapeutic outcomes, it has also committed therapists to a stance in which the specific interventions distinguishing the various therapies are held to be the primary ingredients of change. Indeed, to the extent that adherence to manualized diagnoses and therapies defines good treatment, novelty in case formulation and intervention, such as that embodied in our introductory vignettes, must be tempered.

Wampold's (2001) review, however, finds that adherence to manuals accounts for very little variance in therapeutic outcomes. Instead of formulating cases as discrete diagnoses to be treated with standardized interventions, he recommends that treatments be tailored to clients' worldviews. Because clients enter therapy with "established patterns that yield unwanted consequences in terms of mood, behavior, and relationships" (p. 285) (Steenbarger & Budman, 1998), formulation must begin with a framing of client patterns and a reasoned consideration of therapeutic alternatives that could provide meaningful behavioral options. Budman et al. (1992), for example, describe how 13 therapists with differing therapeutic approaches use novelty to define and address client problems. Their methods included imagery exercises, rational disputation, reframing, experiences of therapist support, confrontation, and use of paradox. In each case, however, the case was formulated, not as a disorder to be treated or cured, but as a situation requiring fresh constructions and behavioral options.

Viewing case formulation as a form of social influence (Claiborn & Lichtenberg, 1989)—an attempt to alter rigidified client construals—rather than as a diagnostic exercise helps to explain several interesting findings from the psychotherapy outcome literature:

❑ The allegiance of therapists to particular therapeutic schools is more predictive of those schools' success than the procedures specific to those schools (Wampold, 2001). If case formulation is, in part, a persuasive process designed to help clients see themselves in a new light (Frank & Frank, 1993), we would expect therapists to be more persuasive if they, indeed, believe in the rationales and procedures they offer clients.

❑ Studies of change processes (Howard, Lueger, Marling, & Martinovitch, 1993) suggest that the first phase of change is an increase in client optimism and well-being. This typically occurs well before most of the interventions specific to the various approaches are initiated. If, however, novel case formulations help clients make sense of their problems and perceive new options for change (Frank & Frank, 1993), it would make sense that an increase in positive affect would precede actual symptom change and changes in functioning.

❑ One of the enduring findings in the outcome literature is that the quality of the therapeutic relationship is highly correlated with treatment success, regardless of the variety of therapy being conducted (Bachelor & Horvath, 2004; Lambert, 1992; Wampold, 2001). If case formulation is, at its root, an attempt to influence clients to adopt new understandings, one would expect the credibility and genuineness of the therapist to be crucial to change efforts.

These findings are consistent with the notion that therapist formulations function more as change catalysts (Cummings & Sayama, 1995) than as objective diagnoses that demand optimized treatments. Formulations, and the novelty embedded within them, are a central facet of change, not procedures that are undertaken prior to treatment proper.

CLINICAL STRATEGIES

How is novelty delivered across the array of therapeutic modalities? Table 17.1 summarizes several major therapeutic strategies and the ways in which they utilize novelty to catalyze change.

TABLE 17.1   Therapeutic Strategies and Novelty

Therapeutic Strategy	Specific Examples	Ways of Introducing Novelty
Psychoeducation	Introduce a depressed client to a cognitive conceptualization of problems	Help clients think about problem patterns in a new way
Interpretation	Link current emotional and behavioral patterns in a troubled relationship to past relationship conflicts	Help clients think about problem patterns in a new way
Miracle question	Focus clients stuck in unsatisfying careers on what they would be doing differently if the problem were miraculously eliminated	Help clients think about problem patterns in a new way
Exposure	Expose anxious clients to feared situations while they use coping skills	Help clients experience problem patterns in new ways
Corrective emotional experiences	Provide responses to low-self-esteem clients that are different from — and more constructive than — those experienced previously	Help clients experience problem patterns in new ways
Prescribed tasks	Place an arguing couple in a situation that interrupts their problem pattern by having them switch roles	Help clients experience problem patterns in new ways

Notice, in the table, that the first group of strategies has a "deductive" quality: They introduce novelty by first trying to alter client self-construals, with the understanding that such shifts will catalyze subsequent changes in experience. By challenging existing client schemas and introducing new ones, therapists hope to expand the client's behavioral repertoire. The second set of strategies might be described as "inductive"; they introduce new experiences directly, with the anticipation that these will coalesce into fresh client self-construals. By encouraging clients to do new things, therapists facilitate shifts in views of self and others.

The major approaches to therapy can be conceptualized as integrated collections of deductive and inductive change strategies. Each of the modalities introduces new views of client patterns and promotes novel experiences that support these views. Although the various schools of therapy may differ in the relative emphasis placed on deductive and inductive strategies, as well as strategies that are undertaken within and between sessions, they rely on a common evolutionary process: shaking up existing ways of thinking and behaving by introducing novel alternatives in the context of emotionally rich, caring, helping relationships.

The following is a summary of specific therapeutic modalities and some of the major inductive and deductive strategies they use to introduce novelty and facilitate change:

❑ *Behavior therapy* — Hembree, Roth, Bux, and Foa (2004) describe several strategies that typify behavior therapy, including psychoeducation (teaching clients about the sources of their distress), assignment of homework (for skill practice), presentation of a clear treatment rationale, skills training (stress inoculation, breathing training, structured problem solving, guided self-dialogue), and various forms of exposure to situations associated with distress (imaginal, in vivo, interoceptive). Craske and Barlow (2001) similarly describe the use of self-monitoring, cognitive restructuring, exposure, and relaxation training as central to behavior therapy. A typical sequence has therapists first describe and model skills, then encourage in-session skill enactment. Once it is clear that the client understands the rationale for the skill and can perform the skill adequately in session, homework exercises allow for further skill development and experiences of mastery. This is particularly the case with exposure-based therapies, which create vivid experiences of mastery by pairing exposure to problematic situations with rehearsal of coping skills. Clients with panic disorder, for example, may be asked to simulate sensations of anxiety by spinning in a chair and then practice self-control methods (breathing, rational self-talk). This permits them to experience threatening situations in an entirely new context, enhancing feelings of self-control. O'Donohue, Fisher, and Hayes (2003) describe nearly 70 empirically supported techniques utilized in cognitive behavior therapy, including assertiveness skills training, breathing retraining, contingency management, emotion regulation, mindfulness practice, motivational interviewing, stress inoculation training, and systematic desensitization. A careful reading of these methods suggests that they embody two components: (1) self-monitoring, assessment and psychoeducation to help clients view their patterns in fresh ways; and (2) in- and out-of-session skill practice to provide direct experiences of self-efficacy.

❑ *Cognitive therapy* — Beck and Bieling (2004) summarize the major strategies associated with cognitive restructuring methods, including problem solving, task assignments, activity monitoring and scheduling, psychoeducation, guided discovery of dysfunctional automatic thoughts, behavioral experiments designed to test the accuracy of those thoughts, imagery, and the use of coping cards and dysfunctional thought records to identify and challenge problematic automatic thought patterns. Psychoeducation typically educates clients about the cognitive model, helping them appreciate the connections between their ways of thinking and their feelings and behavior. Such education also helps clients understand the rationale behind the specific cognitive techniques. The aim of such techniques is to help clients understand, interrupt, and challenge their modes of processing self-relevant information. Although such methods as thought records and guided discovery assist awareness building, behavioral experiments and task assignments allow clients to experience their automatic thoughts directly in a new light. Young, Weinberger, and Beck (2001) describe the therapeutic relationship in cognitive therapy as an "investigative team" (p. 276) that tests client construals much as scientists test hypotheses. Such tests enable clients to appreciate, first-hand, limitations of their schemas, opening the door to new, adaptive constructions. O'Donohue et al. (2003), in their edited volume, describe a variety of empirically validated cognitive techniques, such as disputing irrational beliefs, conducting behavioral tests of negative cognitions, identifying and modifying maladaptive schemas, and defusing cognitions. Each of these methods begins with the presentation of a novel way of viewing thought patterns, followed by experiential exercises designed to test and revise existing assumptions.

❑ *Psychodynamic therapy* — Luborsky and Mark (1991) describe several strategies associated with STDP, including the formulation of a "core conflictual relationship theme"; the framing of symptoms as coping attempts; active clarification and interpretation of relationship themes as they appear in past and present relationships, as well as the therapeutic relationship; and the timing of responses based on shifts in the client's cognitive and emotional state. Levenson (2004) similarly describes the formulation of "cyclical maladaptive patterns" that occur across relationships, including the relationship with the therapist; strategies that provide new understandings, such as interpretation and clarification of cyclical patterns; and strategies that offer new experiences, such as therapist efforts to provide new relational experiences that subvert the maladaptive patterns. Psychodynamic schools associated with Peter Sifneos (Nielsen & Barth, 1991) and Habib Davanloo (Lakin, Winston, & McCulloch, 1991) stress the active role of the therapist in confronting maladaptive patterns and defenses, heightening client anxiety, and catalyzing fresh awareness. The formulations of psychoanalytical therapists provide clients with novel frameworks for self-perception, whereas the in-session behavior of the therapist—providing new responses and challenging old patterns—promotes experiential learning.

❑ *Solution-focused and strategic therapies*—Strategic therapies (Rosenbaum, 1990) utilize reframing, metaphor, symptom prescription, indirect suggestion, and directed tasks to alter client self-perceptions and undermine self-reinforcing cycles of problems and failed solutions. In solution-focused brief therapy (Steenbarger, 2004; Walter & Peller, 1992), problem talk is quickly shifted to goal-centered solution talk, emphasizing exceptions to the patterns and problems identified by clients. This focus on client strengths appears to be instrumental in providing clients with an experience of internal control (Beyebach, Morejohn, & Palenzuela, 1996), not unlike the experiences of mastery provided by cognitive behavioral therapies. Specific techniques in solution-focused brief therapy include the search for—and extension of—pretherapeutic change, active goal setting, the use of miracle and scaling questions to shift the therapeutic focus, and the emphasis on exceptions to existing patterns as potential solutions for subsequent rehearsal (Steenbarger, 2004). Central to the approach is the prescription of tasks that build upon client strengths/exceptions, undermining client problem definitions and fostering a sense of efficacy.

Although these modalities hardly exhaust the variety of therapeutic schools, they do cover a range of commonly encountered approaches to helping. At the level of technique, each operationalizes novelty similarly by facilitating new understandings and new experiences in the context of a supportive relationship. Note that many of the therapeutic techniques also place clients in unusual situations that arouse strong emotion, jarring their accustomed patterns. It may well be that the fostering of novel physical and emotional states is as important to therapeutic learning as the creation of new understandings and experiences (Budman et al., 1992).

KEY MISTAKES AND
MISCONCEPTIONS

Although it appears that novelty is necessary for change, it would be a mistake to assume that it is sufficient. The frequently encountered problem of relapse serves as a reminder that initiating change and sustaining it are different things. Steenbarger's (1992) review suggested that a period of consolidation—repetition of new patterns until they are overlearned—must follow the introduction of discrepant understandings and experiences for change to take root. After reading the case studies of such famous therapists as Milton Erickson, it is tempting to view change as a single moment when a lightbulb flashes in the client's mind. In reality, change occurs only once the novel becomes routine.

A second misconception is that novelty is valuable for novelty's sake—that any new framework is as good as any other. The reality is that fresh ideas and experiences that are insufficiently different from the client's own will not spark a cognitive and behavioral overhaul. Similarly, novelty that is jarring for clients, conflicting with their basic values, will be rejected out of hand (Budman et al., 1992). Some of the most powerful, novel frameworks are those drawn from client experience, but not yet salient for clients. As the following case study suggests, there is a sense in which novelty takes something familiar to the client and applies it to a new facet of life, opening the door to different ways of viewing and doing.

CASE STUDY

Dave is a professional trader at a large "daytrading" firm. This means that Dave makes frequent decisions about buying and selling, with few positions lasting more than a matter of minutes. Recent declines in market volatility have caused stocks to trade quite differently from when Dave first learned the business, making it more difficult to exit large positions at a chosen price level. As Dave's profit/loss balance has declined, he has become increasingly nervous about his income, especially given a large mortgage debt. Dave prides himself on the time and effort he has invested in his trading, and he is convinced that his house—located in an up-and-coming area of the city—is a fine investment as well. Desperate to avoid further losses, Dave has recently found it difficult to continue trading once he is profitable early in the day. Instead of taking full advantage of those days where he is experiencing success, he becomes unusually nervous and risk averse. He explains to his in-house counselor that he prefers to go home with a small gain rather than risk losing the money and going home yet again "in the red." Intellectually, Dave knows that cutting his winning days short in this manner is a recipe for long-term ruin, yet he is unable to continue trading once he is successful. "I don't want to risk my day," he explains to the counselor. "I can't do that to my wife; she worries so much about money."

When asked about his goals for counseling, Dave indicates that he wants to overcome his anxiety and trade confidently throughout the day. "I've invested too much to throw everything away now," he says, describing in detail the risks and hardships he undertook to begin a trading career. "It's like I'm sabotaging myself," he laments.

To Dave's surprise, the counselor does not attempt to talk him into strategies for fighting his anxiety and continuing his afternoon trading. Instead, the counselor praises Dave for his concern for his family and expresses relief that Dave vividly experiences his reluctance to lose money. "Could you imagine what would happen if you became overconfident when you were up money?" the counselor asks. "Your wife and kids would be nervous wrecks. At least you're sparing them that agony."

"But what should I do about my trading?" Dave implores. "I can't just go home at 10:00 AM just because I'm green for the day."

"Look, Dave," the counselor explains, "all we have to build on is your strengths, and goodness knows you have strengths as a trader. You yourself told me how much time and energy you invested to make this thing work. Who knows? Maybe you're a good investor, not just a good trader. Are you willing to make a different kind of investment in your trading career?"

Dave immediately nods. There is no doubt that he is motivated for change.

" Let's say you're up $5000 in the morning. How much of that money would you be willing to invest to have a good probability of making another five grand? Would you risk all 5000 to make another five?" the counselor asks.

"Of course not," Dave immediately responds. "Maybe 2000."

"OK," the counselor checks. "You're telling me that you could invest 2000 to make 5000 or more, and that you could be happy going home up 3000 on the day if your investment doesn't pay off that day?"

"Sure," Dave immediately replies. "I'd be fine if I could just know that I could go home up money."

"Then what do you say we give it a shot?" the counselor offers. "When you go up $5000 or more in a morning, I'm going to come into your office, and we'll figure out how much you're willing to invest in the afternoon. If the trade looks bad, maybe we'll invest nothing and go home early. If it looks good and the market's moving around, maybe we'll invest a couple grand and keep position sizes reasonable. But you'll always know that you'll go home with a profit, for your family's sake. You can be a good investor without taking major risks."

Dave loved the idea and immediately expressed optimism about the "investment" approach. By the end of the week, he had twice met with the counselor when he was profitable early in the day. On one occasion he lost the invested money and went home with slightly more than $3000 and no signs of anxiety. On the other occasion, he went on to have his first five-figure day in months. Over the next two weeks, he implemented the strategy several times with the counselor's assistance, reviewing his "investment" progress at the end of the day. His confidence-building breakthrough came in the fourth week, when he made a decision on his own and invested only a $1000 of morning profit in a nonvolatile market. This allowed him to end a very difficult trading day "in the green." Unable to risk his profits by trading, he found that he could put them to work as investments, overcoming a seemingly intractable pattern of risk aversion through a combination of discrepant viewing and doing.

SUMMARY

We have seen that the rapid and unexpected introduction of novelty is a central element in successful therapy, opening the door to new action patterns. In the case of Dave, novelty took the form of a "pivot chord" (Talmon, 1990) that shifted the focus from a problem—anxiety and nonperformance—to a solution: the capacity to make successful investments. As long as Dave thought of afternoon trading as a family-threatening risk, he experienced unbearable anxiety and found himself unable to trade. Once he could define afternoon trading as an investment that could actually benefit his family, he embraced it wholeheartedly. The novel construction of his situation, drawing upon an existing strength, convinced him to try his hand at controlled trading after he was profitable early in the day. To his delight, he found that he could lose money and still feel good about his role as family provider. Such new experiences cemented the investment theme in his mind, reinforcing the new behavioral pattern. Dave's case neatly illustrates the interplay between deductive strategies (novel ways of viewing) and inductive ones (novel ways of doing) in catalyzing and consolidating change.

REFERENCES

Bachelor, A., & Horvath, A. (2004). The therapeutic relationship. In M. A. Hubble, B. Duncan, & S. D. Miller (Eds.). *The heart and soul of change: What works in therapy* (pp. 133–178). Washington, DC: American Psychological Association.

Barlow, D. H. (Ed.). (2001). *Clinical handbook of psychological disorders: A step-by-step treatment manual* (3rd ed). New York: Guilford.

Beck, J. S., & Bieling, P. J. (2004). Cognitive therapy: Introduction to theory and practice. In M. J. Dewan, B. N. Steenbarger, & R. P. Greenberg (Eds.). *The art and science of brief psychotherapies: A practitioner's guide* (pp. 15–50). Washington, DC: American Psychiatric Press.

Beyebach, M., Morejon, A. R., Palenzuela, D. L., et al. (1996). Research on the process of solution-focused therapy. In S. D. Miller, M. A. Hubble, & B. L. Duncan (Eds.). *Handbook of solution-focused brief therapy* (pp. 299–334). San Francisco, CA: Jossey-Bass.

Budman, S. H., Friedman, S., & Hoyt, S. F. (1992). Last words on first sessions. In S. H. Budman, M. F. Hoyt, & S. Friedman (Eds.). *The first session in brief therapy* (pp. 345–358). New York: Guilford.

Claiborn, C. D., & Lichtenberg, J. W. (1989). Interactional counseling. *Counseling Psychologist, 17*, 355–453.

Craske, M. G., & Barlow, D. H. (2001). Panic disorder and agoraphobia. In D. H. Barlow (Ed.). *Clinical handbook of psychological disorders: A step-by-step treatment manual* (3rd ed., pp. 1–59). New York: Guilford.

Cummings, N., & Sayama, M. (1995). *Focused psychotherapy: A casebook of brief, intermittent psychotherapy throughout the life cycle.* New York: Brunner/Mazel.

Frank, J. D., & Frank, J. B. (1993). *Persuasion and healing: A comparative study of psychotherapy* (3rd ed.). Baltimore: Johns Hopkins University Press.

Haley, J. (1984). *Ordeal therapy.* San Francisco: Jossey-Bass.

Hembree, E. A., Roth, D., Bux, D. A., & Foa, E. B. (2004). Brief behavioral therapy. In M. J. Dewan, B. N. Steenbarger, & R. P. Greenberg (Eds.). *The art and science of brief psychotherapies: A practitioner's guide* (pp. 51–84). Washington, DC: American Psychiatric Press.

Howard, K. I., Lueger, R. J., Marling, M. S., & Martinovitch, Z. (1993). A phase model of psychotherapy outcome: Causal mediation of change. *Journal of Consulting and Clinical Psychology, 61*, 678–685.

Lakin, M., Winston, A., & McCulloch, L. (1991). Intensive short-term dynamic psychotherapy. In P. Crits–Christoph & J. P. Barber (Eds.). *Handbook of short-term dynamic psychotherapy* (pp. 80–109). New York: Basic Books.

Lambert, M. J. (1992). Psychotherapy outcome research: Implications for integrative and eclectic therapists. In J. C. Norcross & M. R. Goldfried (Eds.). *Handbook of psychotherapy integration* (pp. 94–129). New York: Basic Books.

Levenson, H. (2004). Time-limited dynamic psychotherapy: Formulation and intervention. In M. J. Dewan, B. N. Steenbarger, & R. P. Greenberg (Eds.). *The art and science of brief psychotherapies: A practitioner's guide* (pp. 157–188). Washington, DC: American Psychiatric Press.

Luborsky, L., & Mark, D. (1991). Short-term supportive-expressive psychoanalytic psychotherapy. In P. Crits–Christoph & J. P. Barber (Eds.). *Handbook of short-term dynamic psychotherapy* (pp. 110–136). New York: Basic Books.

Maione, P. V., & Chenail, R. J. (2004). Qualitative inquiry in psychotherapy: Research on the common factors. In M. A. Hubble, B. L. Duncan, & S. D. Miller (Eds.). *The heart and soul of change: What works in therapy* (pp. 57–90). Washington, DC: American Psychological Association.

Nielsen, G., & Barth, K. (1991). Short-term anxiety-provoking psychotherapy. In P. Crits–Christoph & J. P. Barber (Eds.). *Handbook of short-term dynamic psychotherapy* (pp. 45–79). New York: Basic Books.

O'Donohue, W., Fisher, J. E., & Hayes, S. C. (Eds.). (2003). *Cognitive behavior therapy: Applying empirically supported techniques in your practice.* Hoboken, NJ: Wiley.

Pedersen, P. (2000). *A handbook for developing multicultural awareness* (3rd ed.). Washington, DC: American Counseling Association.

Prochaska, P. O. (2004). How do people change, and how can we change to help more people? In M. A. Hubble, B. Duncan, & S. D. Miller (Eds.). *The heart and soul of change: What works in therapy* (pp. 227–258). Washington, DC: American Psychological Association.

Rosenbaum, R. (1990). Strategic psychotherapy. In R. A. Wells & V. J. Giannetti (Eds.). *Handbook of the brief psychotherapies* (pp. 351–404). New York: Plenum.

Steenbarger, B. N. (1992). Toward science–practice integration in brief counseling and therapy. *Counseling Psychologist, 20,* 403–450.

Steenbarger, B. N. (1994). Duration and outcome in psychotherapy: An integrative review. *Professional Psychology: Research and Practice, 25,* 111–119.

Steenbarger, B. N. (2003). *The psychology of trading.* New York: Wiley.

Steenbarger, B. N. (2004). Solution-focused brief therapy: Doing what works. In M. J. Dewan, B. N. Steenbarger, & R. P. Greenberg (Eds.). *The art and science of brief psychotherapies: A practitioner's guide* (pp. 85–118). Washington, DC: American Psychiatric Press.

Steenbarger, B. N., & Budman, S. H. (1998). Principles of brief and time-effective therapies. In G. P. Koocher, J. C. Norcross, & S. S. Hill (Eds.). *Psychologists' desk reference* (pp. 283–286). New York: Oxford University Press.

Tallman, K., & Bohart, A. C. (2004). The client as a common factor: Clients as self-healers. In M. A. Hubble, B. L. Duncan, & S. D. Miller (Eds.). *The heart and soul of change: What works in therapy* (pp. 91–132). Washington, DC: American Psychological Association.

Talmon, M. (1990). *Single session therapy.* San Francisco: Jossey-Bass.

Van Hasselt, V. B., & Hersen, M. (Eds.). (1996). *Sourcebook of psychological treatment manuals for adult disorders.* New York: Plenum.

Walter, J. L., & Peller, J. E. (1992). *Becoming solution-focused in brief therapy.* New York: Brunner/Mazel.

Wampold, B. E. (2001). *The great psychotherapy debate: Models, methods, and findings.* Mahwah, NJ: Lawrence Erlbaum Associates.

Young, J. E., Weinberger, A. D., & Beck, A. T. (2001). Cognitive therapy for depression. In D. H. Barlow (Ed.). *Clinical handbook of psychological disorders: A step-by-step treatment manual* (3rd ed., pp. 264–308). New York: Guilford.

18

INTERRUPTION REPLACES TERMINATION IN FOCUSED, INTERMITTENT PSYCHOTHERAPY THROUGHOUT THE LIFE CYCLE

NICHOLAS A. CUMMINGS

University of Nevada, Reno
and Cummings Foundation for Behavioral Health

Much has been written regarding the difficulties surrounding termination, not the least of which is the frequent return of the presenting symptoms that initially brought the patient to psychotherapy. Faced with termination and fearing the consequences of severing a dependency on the psychotherapist, the patient unconsciously responds with a resurgence of symptoms that had disappeared during the course of treatment. Another consequence not often discussed is the implication that the patient has overcome all difficulties and it would be a betrayal of the therapeutic process to seek treatment again at some future time. Thus, there is a reluctance to resume treatment, and if necessity drives the patient, often a new therapist is sought to avoid the embarrassment. Treatment may be unnecessarily prolonged in one instance, and needed treatment may be avoided in the second. In the model discussed in this chapter, the patient is appraised that treatment is being interrupted, not terminated, and the patient is encouraged to contact the psychotherapist if the vicissitudes of one or more of the future stages of life require assistance (Cummings, 2001).

A model in which psychotherapy is seen as a continuous process, even between intermittent episodes of treatment, renders termination with all its attendant problems unnecessary. Pioneered by me and my colleagues a half century ago, hundreds of psychotherapists have received hands-on training in focused, intermittent psychotherapy throughout the life cycle, and much has been written on the subject (see, for example, Bloom, 1991; Cummings, 1990, 1991; Cummings and Cummings, 2000; Cummings and Sayama, 1995; Cummings and VandenBos, 1979). It is not within the scope of this chapter to describe the entire model; only those aspects that pertain to the substitution of interruption for termination are addressed. This substitution would seem to be a simple procedure until one confronts all the complexities involved. Performed correctly, psychotherapy becomes a continuous process throughout one's life. It is resumed whenever problems in life's cycle make it necessary, while progress continues within the patient between episodes of treatment. For some patients the initial episode of treatment is sufficient; others return once, twice, or more; while still others may be seen for a session or two once every two or three years for the rest of their lives. In any case, the problems of termination are eliminated, because the patient sees therapy to be open and available even if she or he never returns.

The problems of termination are only slightly ameliorated by the therapist's exhortation that the patient is free to resume treatment any time in the future. Termination by definition refers to a discrete episode of treatment that has a beginning and end; thus, resuming treatment means to the patient she is beginning a second episode and that something was missed the first time around. Furthermore, she has not been given silent ways of continuing the therapy without the psychotherapist, a procedure that clearly defines psychotherapy as a continuous process that may reinvolve the psychotherapist at any time the self-process bogs down. Thus, the strength of the treatment experience carries over and continues during periods of interruption, whether they are six months or 20 years. The patient continues the therapy, talking to the therapist and finding the answers "in his or her head" whenever difficulties arise. When the answers are not forthcoming, the patient knows it is time to make a return appointment. Psychotherapists are mobile and over a life span one's therapist may have moved or retired. Experience demonstrates that a patient easily relates to a new psychotherapist as long as the successor psychotherapist is skilled in this model.

It is usual, but nonetheless startling, to see a patient after several years who begins talking as if the last session was two weeks ago. This attests to the continuous nature of the treatment, and reflects a different type of transference than that fostered in traditional psychotherapy. The patient has learned to be her own therapist, and one who knows when she needs the psychotherapist. Return appointments, no matter how many months or years may intervene, are usually comprised of one to three sessions, demonstrating a learned self-reliance that only occasionally needs tweaking.

To substitute interruption for termination successfully, the strength of the transference must be diminished while the intensity of the therapy is increased. This seems contradictory inasmuch as the intensity of the psychotherapy often parallels the depth of the transference. However, the patient's attachment and dependency are variables that can complicate and delay termination. It was Freud (1933) who first postulated that a neurosis is treated by substituting a "transference neurosis" (i.e., attachment and dependency in the treatment situation). The problem, then, was to work through and resolve the transference neurosis — a process that was seen as protracted, making psychotherapy a long-term undertaking not because of the nature of the presenting symptoms, but because of the necessary way of addressing them. Stated in another way, the cure was worse than the disease.

Depending upon the type of psychotherapy, the approach of the psychotherapist, and the personality of the patient, all psychotherapy more or less fosters dependency. In our model, the fear of losing the therapist is eliminated by a prescription to return to psychotherapy as needed. In addition, the patient has learned techniques that continue the therapeutic process. As in the intervening week between sessions when the patient is assigned homework and has been taught to talk to the therapist in her head, after interruption the patient continues this procedure, assigning her own homework and carrying on an imaginary conversation with the therapist. Surprisingly, most of the time answers or solutions to her problems will be forthcoming. When an answer is not forthcoming, she is encouraged to resume sessions with the psychotherapist.

The concept of medical necessity is irrelevant in this model, because years of experience and research have shown that focused, intermittent psychotherapy administered before there is absolute necessity prevents later serious episodes that would require much more intensive treatment (Cummings & Cummings, 2000). Thus, early intervention is not only therapeutically desirable, sparing the patient prolonged and even increased distress, but it is also cost-effective in that it prevents the need for more costly interventions at a future time. In summary, the model eliminates unnecessary sessions prompted by the threat of termination by creating a therapeutic process that continues in the absence of the psychotherapist. Returning to see the psychotherapist is only an aspect of this continuous process. Furthermore, returns to treatment are brief and are usually one to three sessions, resulting in a life span of therapy that is most often less in session totals than the usual traditional therapy followed by termination.

There are clinical strategies for implanting continuous psychotherapy throughout the life cycle, each of which is part of a well-defined series of three steps.

STEP 1: DIMINISHING THE TRANSFERENCE THROUGH A THERAPEUTIC PARTNERSHIP

The key to diminishing the transference is the establishing of a true partnership between the therapist and the patient, and then unrelentingly implementing it despite any dependency on the part of the patient. That this is accomplished for the benefit of the patient is reflected in the psychotherapist's empathy, understanding, and patience in the process, all of which do not detract from its determination. The cornerstones of this partnership are the therapeutic contract, homework, and fostering resiliency.

THE THERAPEUTIC CONTRACT

At the appropriate time in the first session the psychotherapist presents the therapeutic contract, which makes clear the therapy is primarily the responsibility of the patient, whereas the therapist acts as a catalyst. The language is varied in accordance with the patient's socioeconomic status and level of education, but the message is always the same. The appropriate time is after the psychotherapist has skillfully and rapidly fostered bonding and other aspects of the therapeutic alliance. In its succinct form, the therapeutic contract states the following:

> I shall never abandon you as long as you need me, and I shall never ask you to do something until you are ready. In return for this, I ask you to join me in a partnership to make me obsolete as soon as possible.

This contract is not presented in a perfunctory manner; rather, it is discussed until the patient fully understands and accepts its impact. It is made clear that although the patient will not be asked to do something for which he is not ready, it is made clear that once patient and therapist determine readiness, the patient is required to move forward. This is the essence of the partnership, and differs markedly from the model in which the therapist more or less passively awaits for the patient to initiate the next step comfortably.

HOMEWORK

It is the homework, more than anything else, that results in the patient's realization this is, indeed, a partnership. Homework is assigned after the first session and every session thereafter, and is enforced in a variety of ways. When the patient has agreed to the therapeutic contract and the homework is in keeping with the three characteristics described in the next paragraph, enforcing the homework is not an issue. In the rare instances when the homework is not completed, the session first addresses the reasons and their implications, with a revisit to the therapeutic contract.

There is no cookbook from which homework is arbitrarily assigned. Rather, the homework is tailored to be meaningful to each patient's goals and therapeutic contract, and three requisites must be fulfilled in each and every homework assignment: (1) the patient must be capable of doing it, but (2) it must be difficult enough so that the patient achieves a sense of accomplishment, and (3) it represents the next step in this patient's goal in therapy. (For a more comprehensive discussion of homework, see Chapter 12.)

LEARNING RESILIENCY

Promoting resiliency in the patient is a certain way to diminish the transference, while at the same time increasing appreciation of the therapist as catalyst rather than a person upon whom to rely unduly. It must be emphasized that, in this role, all the characteristics of compassion and understanding that are the hallmarks of a good psychotherapist are present, but this is coupled with decisiveness in insisting the patient proceed to the next step in spite of fears and objections. The focused psychotherapist must possess a set of qualities that encompasses an understanding of when the patient is ready as well as the reasons for the patient's reluctance, and then have the ability to inspire the patient to move forward. Misjudging a patient's readiness is a sign the therapist lacks empathy and understanding, and excusing a patient when the optimum time to move forward has come is a sign that the therapist lacks skill as well.

Self-esteem must be achieved; it cannot be handed to the patient by well-intentioned but overblown praise. This may make the patient feel good, but only temporarily. As patients overcome their learned helplessness (Seligman, 1975) and achieve self-efficacy (Bandura, 1977), a therapeutic excitement develops that facilitates success in the next discrete therapeutic task. Patients discover their resiliency and enjoy exercising and enhancing it. Much of the excitement has to do with the mutual appreciation this was accomplished by the patient, while the therapist acted as catalyst. The confidence that ensues not only adds to the vitality of the therapeutic experience, it also creates the platform upon which the patient will continue the therapy alone after interruption of the formal sessions. In this way therapy is continuous, even though the presence of the therapist is intermittent throughout the life span.

STEP 2: RAISING THE INTENSITY OF THE TREATMENT EXPERIENCE

A strong transference can enhance therapy, but it also can prolong it, because the attachment to the therapist must be resolved before the patient has the courage to terminate. On the other hand, diminishing the transference to avoid protracted treatment without increasing the intensity of the therapeutic experience can result in a lowering of expectation and lack of progress. Enforcing the therapeutic contract and the homework raises the intensity of the therapy, as will promoting the excitement that comes with new-found resiliency. Increasing the intensity of therapy must compensate for the diminished transference to the degree that it not only accelerates treatment, but it also is sufficient to carry the individual through a number of hiatuses in therapy throughout the life span. The following additional techniques can be only briefly described, and the reader is referred to textbooks for a fuller exposition of the methodology (Cummings & Cummings, 2000; Cummings & Sayama, 1995).

THE FIRST SESSION MUST BE THERAPEUTIC

By making the first session therapeutic, the therapist is hitting the ground running. It enables the patient to see that help is not only possible, but probable. The concept that the first session must be devoted solely to taking a history or getting acquainted is outmoded, and often results in the patient feeling so overwhelmed he does not return for the second session. History taking is important, but the therapist can always glean and then respond to something useful during the first session so that the patient experiences a therapeutic benefit. For example, after the patient concludes a litany of what, to her, is a monumental problem, the therapist can recall that he saw a woman with a similar problem several years ago and the outcome was very positive. By making certain the demographics of the previous patient fit the current one, the troubled patient not only identifies with her, but immediately experiences hope, the therapeutic alliance is strengthened, and the intensity of the therapy is increased. Such a patient will eagerly return for the second session.

PERFORM AN OPERATIONAL DIAGNOSIS

The reason most often proffered by the patient regarding why he is here is seldom, if ever, the actual one. The operational diagnosis asks one thing: Why is the patient here today instead of last month, last year, or next year? If the patient responds that he is an alcoholic, this is not the real reason, because he has been an alcoholic for more than ten years. What is it about his alcoholism that brings him in today instead of ten years ago? The real reason might be that he has just received his third DUI (driving under intoxication) arrest and he is facing six months in jail. Skillfully discerning the operational diagnosis, along with the implicit contract that accompanies it, remarkably intensifies psychotherapy.

ELICIT THE IMPLICIT CONTRACT

Although the operational diagnosis tells the therapist why the patient is here now, the implicit contract reveals what the patient actually wants out of psychotherapy. In the example of the alcoholic with his third DUI arrest, this might be to enlist the therapist as an ally toward getting probation instead of jail time. All the while, however, the patient is offering an explicit (rather than implicit) contract—ostensibly that he wants help in quitting drinking. Skillfully bringing out into the open the implicit contract will cut through the resistance and manipulation; clarify the therapist's role as a healer, not an advocate; and solidify the therapeutic goal as abstinence.

Performing the operational diagnosis and eliciting the implicit contract will markedly intensify the therapeutic process. Misjudging either or both will equally diminish the intensity. Patients want to impress the therapist and will say the right things, or whatever they believe the therapist wants or needs to hear. Missing the real reason why the patient is here now, or inadvertently accepting the explicit, rather than the implicit, contract results in the therapist having feet of clay. The intensity of the therapy is lowered accordingly. Experience has shown that therapists are prone to accept the explicit contract and miss the implicit contract along with the operational diagnosis. A certainty that the implicit contract has been elicited often results in the later discovery this was, in actuality, the explicit contract. (For further discussion and more examples see Chapter 9.)

DO SOMETHING NOVEL IN THE FIRST SESSION

In this "era of psychology," patients are seldom completely naive about psychotherapy. They come to the first session with certain expectations derived from watching movies or television, their reading, friends who have been in treatment, or from their own previous psychotherapy. Patients who have seen a number of psychotherapists with only a modicum of success are no longer a rare phenomenon, especially among those with personality disorders. Thus, the first session has been preceded by a number of re-hearsals within the patient's mind, all of which are easily discernible to the skilled and experienced therapist from how the patient presents himself. Doing something therapeutic that is both unexpected and novel often cata-pults a wishy-washy patient into intensity. A well-timed and nicely crafted paradox may quickly change the attitude of a patient who was expecting the therapist to "do it all for me." A well-delivered opinion that the unmotivated or manipulative patient need not continue in therapy will not only turn a patient around, but will result in an impressive surge of motivation. (There is more discussion of this in Chapter 9, but for a wide range of novel and innovative interventions for the first session, see Cummings and Cummings (2000) and Cummings and Sayama (1995).

ENFORCE THE HOMEWORK

More than anything else, enforcing the homework amplifies the intensity and drives home the realization that the therapeutic process is, indeed, a partnership. As part of the therapeutic contract that makes therapy a partnership, the patient upholds her side of the agreement by doing her homework, and forfeits the session if she comes in without having completed it satisfactorily. Timid therapists have difficulty sending a patient home, especially if she is cleverly screaming for help, saying, "Today I need you more than ever and you are not letting me have my appointment." The appropriate response from the therapist is, "If you need these sessions so much, do your homework so you can derive benefit from them. Remember, this is a partnership. You do your work and I'll do mine."

Experience has demonstrated that about 40% of patients will test the rule and be sent home once for not completing the homework. Once the patient is sent home, there is rarely the forfeiture of a second session; rather, it is the patient who was excused the first time who is likely to repeat the behavior. If care has been taken to assign the homework properly in accordance with the aforementioned three requirements, there is no reason to excuse the patient. The same timid therapist will fear the patient will quit treatment if the rule is enforced. To the contrary, it is the patient who is excused who is likely to drop out of treatment. Enforcing well-designed and appropriate homework increases the intensity of the treatment and motivates the patient to continue.

STEP 3: CLINICAL STRATEGIES FOR IMPLEMENTING THE INTERRUPTION

In traditional therapy the subject of termination is usually first brought up by the patient, who then quickly backs away when the therapist seems to concur. The therapist's response has been premature, awakening fears of separation and prompting barriers to ending treatment. As previously mentioned, the most frequent is the resurgence of initial symptoms that had long disappeared. The message is clear: The patient is frightened. The dependency is threatened. A similar, although somewhat less intense fear may arise in approaching interruption, even though all along the attachment to the therapist has been deemphasized and self-reliance has been cultivated. Nonetheless, interruption requires that it be approached skillfully so the patient is prepared for the continuation of treatment in the absence of the psychotherapist.

Paramount is the requirement that interruption is understood so that its impetus always comes from the patient. This does not mean the therapist is not active in the process, but that she is obliquely so. There is therapeutic guidance analogous to that of the homework, completed by the patient, but assigned by the therapist, who anticipates the next level of therapeutic progress. Just as, ultimately, it is the patient who decides the future by determining the outcome and direction of the completed homework, similarly the therapist is guiding the interruption, but the patient sees it as his decision to interrupt. The patient who is comfortable with the ongoing nature of therapy without the psychotherapist manifests no resurgence of symptoms or other difficulties.

AUGMENTING THE READINESS

Generally it can be expected that psychotherapy will progress rapidly, because self-reliance has been a major consideration from the onset of treatment. The patient will signal a readiness, actually not yet embraced by the patient, by musing how long she might need to continue coming. The therapist is careful not to jump on this; rather, with jocularity says, "I think you may be getting ready to fire me." The patient may seem surprised, but usually laughs along with the therapist, who then ignores the aside and recapitulates the therapeutic contract, "I shall never abandon you as long as you need me." This is the apparent emphasis, while the therapist then muses seemingly with another aside about the characteristics of continuous psychotherapy, reflecting on how the patient continues to grow after interruption, and that the patient is encouraged to resume the sessions with the therapist at any time. It is pointed out to the patient there are future times, following unforeseen events and unexpected complexities of life, that the patient may need the therapist again, and the promise in the therapeutic contract includes such future eventualities, whether this be two months or 20 years. Then the therapist abruptly drops this seeming tangent and attends with the patient to other matters.

AUGMENTING THE DECISION

If the timing and sequence are as described, invariably in the following session the patient suggests there seems to be no need to keep coming in and she will ask if the therapist agrees. The therapist must, at this point, throw it back to the patient. However, the therapist must take time to point out it has been the patient who has made all the progress and the patient can continue the problem solving in the absence of the therapist. "Many patients find it helpful when there is a problem to talk to me in their heads. You know by now what I am likely to say, and you will be pleased how you come to your own conclusions just as you have here. My patients tell me they always get an answer, and when they do not, they know it is time to call and make an appointment to come in." If the therapist has read the patient correctly, and has appropriately augmented both the readiness and the decision to interrupt, the typical patient will nod assent. Interruption usually results after such a session. The patient is satisfied that the goal has been reached, has the security of knowing returning to psychotherapy is an encouraged option, and has a modus operandi for continuing the problem solving on her own. The word *termination* has never been uttered.

OVERCOMING THE OCCASIONAL GLITCH

Occasionally there will be a patient who, after showing readiness, does not take the second step in the following session, but in the one after that. In such instances the therapist must exercise restraint and not try to augment the decision prematurely. There are some patients who are uncertain and do not want to interrupt yet, even though they had expressed what is defined here as readiness. Again, if the therapist has read the patient correctly, this occasional balking can be addressed by assigning a specific homework. The patient is asked to write down five reasons therapy should be interrupted, and five reasons why it should not. Almost invariably the patient will relate in the next session that the five reasons to interrupt came easily, but he could come up with only two or three reasons why the sessions should continue, and then only after much thought over several days.

THE HIATUS

During periods of interruption it is common for most patients to write to the psychotherapist. Most often it is a holiday card with a greeting and a brief message that things are going well. At other times it may be a letter, sometimes a very long letter, describing a difficulty and how it was overcome. Still other patients will ask for advice or reassurance that they did the right thing. The psychotherapist responds warmly to all communications, indicating how pleasant it is to hear from the patient, but carefully avoids any advice, admonition, or therapeutic insight. The patient is complimented for continuing to solve life's problems, but if help is asked for in the letter, the response should merely ask the patient if she thinks it is time to come in. More often than not, the next written communication will report that the problem has been solved.

HALF A CENTURY
OF EXPERIENCE

I began using this model in 1950 and began actively teaching it a few years thereafter in clinical case conferences to the psychiatry department at Kaiser Permanente in San Francisco, where I was chief psychologist. It became the model used in the government's Hawaii Project and with the thousands of psychotherapists working with American Biodyne nationally, as well as with hundreds of psychotherapists in independent practice who attended training sessions. Unfortunately most data are scattered, essentially incomplete, and usually impossible to access. As a follow-up, I surveyed 243 patients I had personally treated using this model, and who had their initial sessions between 1961 and 1965. These are all the patients I had seen in my own independent practice during this time period, and whose records were readily available. Their records were surveyed for up to the four decades following the initial session (Cummings, 2001).

You will note from Table 18.1 that 56 patients (23%) were never seen again beyond the initial episode that averaged 8.1 sessions. Another 39 patients (16%) had one return episode, with the initial episode averaging 6.2 sessions and the second episode averaging 3.4 sessions. The smallest group of 17 patients (7%) had three to five return episodes, with the first episode averaging 6.4 sessions and the return episodes averaging 3.5 sessions. The largest group of 131 (54%) availed themselves of 6 to 12 return episodes, with the sixth episode averaging 6.1 sessions and subsequent episodes averaging 2.9 sessions.

It is clear from these results that more than half the patients seen availed themselves of the model of focused, intermittent psychotherapy throughout the life cycle throughout a 35 to 40-year period. It is clear also that in this model there is considerable generalization of therapeutic effect, for subsequent episodes average only about three sessions for all patients returning for more than three episodes. In succeeding episodes often only one session is needed. By adding the average number of sessions per episode for those in the 12-return episode group, the total number of sessions is only 40.9 over a 35 to 40-year span. This model is not only responsive to the needs of these patients, but also meets the most stringent standards of cost-effectiveness imposed by third-party payors today.

TABLE 18.1   Tabulation of 243 Patients Initially Seen By Me in Focused Psychotherapy from 1961 to 1965 by Episodes and Number of Sessions per Episode, with Follow-up Tabulation for 40 Years

No. of Episodes	Average No. of Sessions per Initial Episode	Average No. of Sessions per Subsequent Episodes	n	% of Total
1	8.1	0.0	56	23
2	6.2	3.4	39	16
3–5	6.4	3.5	17	7
6–12	6.1	2.9	131	54
Total			243	100

CASE ILLUSTRATIONS

Two cases are described here because they illustrate the two extremes of the model. The first is the case of Gregory (Cummings, 2001) who was seen twice, had a 22-year hiatus, after which there was just one more session. It startled even the therapist with its degree of success. The second is Steve, a physician who was first seen as an undergraduate, and continued intermittent sessions throughout medical school, his marriage, divorce, remarriage, the birth of his children, and his career over a 39-year period, with a total of 43 sessions to date.

GREGORY: SORRY I AM BACK SO SOON

A man of 26 was openly distraught during the first session because his wife was leaving him. He said he would do anything to hold the marriage together, but he was vague and evasive when asked, "If your wife were here, what would she say was her reason for leaving you?" His explicit contract, which stated he was here to save the marriage, did not seem to reflect the whole story, and repeated probing eventually revealed that his wife had been complaining for some time that he was gambling too much. He attempted to dismiss this by jocularity, asking, "What is wrong with placing a little wager once in a while?" It soon became apparent, however, that Greg was a compulsive gambler whose addiction had not only deprived the family of necessities, but had plunged them into debt. Nonetheless, the patient persisted in his denial, and repeatedly asked the psychotherapist to intercede with his wife and ask her to postpone the divorce while they both sought marital counseling. The implicit contract was "save my marriage without interfering with my gambling." Greg was given the homework assignment to give the therapist no less than five valid reasons why his wife should not leave him now, and to list five additional reasons why he should be allowed to continue gambling for an indefinite period while the couple is in marital counseling.

Greg returned for his second session stating he was unable to do his homework as assigned. He came up with more than 30 reasons why he should quit gambling now, accept the fact that he is a compulsive gambler, and do whatever necessary never to gamble again. The therapist intimated that although Greg's new-found resolve was commendable, he needed help and discussed with him Gamblers Anonymous and a group program available in the current treatment setting. Greg said he would think about it, left, and never called for a third appointment. In my mind, the therapy was a failure, and I made a note in the chart to that effect.

Twenty-two years later, Greg called for his third appointment. His 19-year-old son was involved in a fatal auto accident, and the patient feared that in his severe emotional upset he might weaken and gamble. He felt and recognized the craving, which was disguised as, "What the hell? What did being clean get you?" He described in the session how ashamed he had been with his own behavior two decades ago, but even more ashamed with his rationalizations that attempted to justify his continued gambling in the face of his inability to provide basic necessities for his spouse and children. "You said just the right thing to me, and I'm back for a refresher that will get me through the next 22 years." Greg had not even made as much as a so-called "innocent wager" in the 22 years following his first appointment. During those years when he was tempted, he would talk in his head to the therapist and "I always got the right answer." One such time he asked what would be the harm if he bought a lottery ticket? He heard the therapist reply, "You want me to say it's okay, but you know the real answer to your question." He did not buy the ticket. Another time he was tempted to enter the Publishers' Clearinghouse Sweepstakes, and laughed when he heard me say, "Now your denial is approaching the absurd." After we discussed his bereavement and he received encouragement to grieve, Greg left satisfied he was good for another 22 years, and subsequent holiday cards confirm he has remained abstinent and has worked through his mourning.

STEVE, THE RELUCTANT PHYSICIAN

A midday panic phone call from Steve resulted in my giving him an appointment during what would have been my dinner hour, because I was booked that day until midnight. He had first spoken with my secretary, learned my schedule was full, and surmised how I had accommodated the urgency of his request. He began the session expressing gratitude. Steve was a tall, handsome, but somewhat obsequious 20-year-old man who was a junior in college and had aspirations to go to medical school. He was taking the appropriate premedical courses and had an almost straight A grade point average until this last academic quarter, in which his performance in two of his physical science courses had fallen precipitously. His presenting complaint was that he suddenly was unable to concentrate on his studies, especially his science courses, and suggested that he probably did not really want to go to medical school after all. His father was a construction worker and Steve was the first in his family to go to college. "My family is all blue collar; what makes me think I can be a doctor? I'm not smart enough." His almost three-year history of excellent grades, plus the sudden onset of his inability to concentrate, made me doubt the etiology he so readily proffered. Probing got us no where until I asked about the man who referred him to me, a university professor and my casual acquaintance of several years. Steve broke out into a sweat. With difficulty he spoke of this man's sexual interest in him, his own capitulation to sexual encounters in which he passively submitted, but did not reciprocate. Shaking and sweating, he confessed, "I'm afraid I might be queer," and went on to say if his burley father knew what he was doing he "would beat me to death with a cement shovel." Steve was also afraid of the professor, in whose class he was doing poorly, and opined that if he broke off the sexual relationship the professor might well give him the failing grade he deserved. A number of issues were discussed: It is not the end of the world to be gay, but a lifestyle choice for many men and women. The professor would not be forcing himself on the patient, and would have no right to do so, were Steve to say no. If the professor used the threat of poor grades he would be guilty of sexual harassment and would thus be more vulnerable than Steve. The therapist discerned that Steve was ready to confront the issue and was given a choice for homework: either stop submitting to the sexual encounters or continue them as an active, willing participant. Expressing considerable fear, the patient accepted the assignment. Recognizing the danger, this intervention was undertaken with a great deal of forethought. It catapulted the therapy into a remarkable intensity, and it was successful.

During the second session Steve described without embarrassment how he participated in the next sexual encounter with the professor, and found out to his amazement that he did not enjoy it, it was somewhat repugnant, but he did not fear it. He realized that all his attraction since his earliest memory was for girls and women. The professor accepted without animosity the decision that Steve would no longer have sex with him. The therapist asked about masturbatory fantasies, because these are psychologically more definitive than verbalizations. He reported these were entirely heterosexual, as were his earlier nocturnal emissions, and it had never even occurred to him that he might have a homosexual fantasy. Yet like a lot of shy men who are awkward with women, he thought this meant he might be gay. His poor concentration had abated, and Steve's homework was to catch up on the lab assignments in which his falling behind was contributing to his poor grades. This might mean burning the midnight oil for a time. As for Steve's professor who referred him, he never asked about Steve and, because of the complicated relationship, the therapist did not contact him to acknowledge the referral.

The next six sessions involved rather emotional discussions of Steve's strong ambivalence to his sometimes bullying father whom he both feared and admired, and of a rather cold mother whom he could never really please. He feared that with his humble background if he should graduate with his medical degree he would look like "a blue collar worker in a white coat," be scorned by his colleagues, and avoided by patients. Steve was doing well, and on the ninth session the treatment was interrupted.

Steve was not seen again until he had graduated, had applied to medical schools, and was experiencing an excruciating wait to hear whether he was admitted. His father had finally not only accepted Steve's decision to go to medical school, but had been crowing to everyone that there would soon be a doctor in the family. During the wait, many of Steve's insecurities had returned, and were now coupled with the fear of possibly having to disappoint his father. He was in near panic. His inability to concentrate had returned, and he doubted he could succeed in medical school even if he were accepted. During the third session of this second episode Steve learned he had been accepted by the University of California at San Francisco medical school, just down the street from the therapist's office. He was ecstatic, because he could continue to have access to the therapist. Steve was given homework designed to help him understand his panic state, and how to handle it in his future life because he again might be overwhelmed with self-doubt. Treatment was interrupted after the fourth session.

Steve was seen again in the middle of his second year in medical school. He was doing very well in his studies, but his life was now complicated by his swift marriage to a nurse. Lenora was an aggressive borderline personality disorder who decided she wanted to marry a doctor, and shy Steve did not have a modicum of a chance to object. His wife was a difficult, unpredictable, and volatile woman, but Steve was enjoying the torrid sex and he decided not to disrupt his studies with what would be a nasty separation. During the next two years he was seen occasionally for a total of nine sessions as might be required to help him make the best of a bad marriage. Eventually Lenora did herself in by a series of turbulent extramarital affairs and Steve divorced her shortly before embarking on his residency. Having found an established and far more exciting surgeon, Lenora did not contest the divorce.

Steve accepted a residency in internal medicine in a prestigious northeastern hospital, but he kept in touch with an occasional letter that indicated he was doing well and was also dating. Four years elapsed, Steve had completed his residency, and he returned to the San Francisco Bay area to join a large group practice in an upscale suburb. He came in for one appointment, mainly to update the psychotherapist and reestablish a connection. Although this episode was limited to one session, episode 5 two years later consisted of six sessions, two of them conjointly with his fiancée, whom he married shortly thereafter. In accordance with their intention, Steve's spouse bore three children in rapid succession, two girls and one boy. She had interrupted her career as a business executive to become a stay-at-home mom.

Seven years after Steve had joined his group practice, troubles emerged among the physician partners. Managed care was beginning to take its toll, the cost of malpractice insurance was skyrocketing, and competition was keen. The Bay Area had become a very desirable place to practice, resulting in an influx of too many physicians with not enough patients. The group practice members annually rated each other's performance, and the emerging score determined how much of the divisible profit each physician member would receive at the end of the year. Steve was always rated at the bottom, which he accepted, but now that the practice's revenue had dropped, there was talk of drastically restructuring the group, with the senior physician arguing that they should let Steve go because of his poor performance. Steve, now a husband and father of three children, was shaken and reinstated his psychotherapy sessions. He manifested the same kind of lack of concentration that he had shown on his very first visit. The senior physician was somewhat of a bully, and reminded Steve of his father. It readily became apparent that Steve's performance in practice did not match his scholastic achievements. He was unsure of himself, was wishy-washy with patients, and would say to them upon prescribing a medication or a regimen, "We'll try this, and if it doesn't work we'll try something else." Patients shunned Steve, seeing him to be poorly trained where in actuality he was more highly trained than most of his colleagues. It became clear that Steve felt inferior to his partners, all of whom came from upper middle class educated families. He had become the blue collar worker in a white coat. We spoke of many things, not the least of which was that the placebo effect accounts for 30% of successful medical treatment, augmenting the pharmacological benefit. A skilled physician strives to strengthen the placebo effect by presenting a positive demeanor. During the course of 11 sessions Steve not only became a confident physician, but a favorite with the patients. He worked through his fear of the managing physician, and within a few months became his right hand in the partnership, and as serendipity he found himself reconciled with his father. He remembered how hard his father worked in heavy construction, always putting food on the table, even in lean times. He had feared he would never be a breadwinner like his father. The last few years of his father's life were a joy to Steve, and he only regretted that no matter what he did he could not break through his mother's coldness and aloofness. She took these to the grave, but long before she died, Steve discovered that much of his shyness with women had been the belief he could no more please them than he could his mother. He realized also that a great deal of his father's anger was displaced from his cold wife; yet he never raised his voice to her and was loyal to the end.

A little more than a decade passed before Steve was seen again. His children were doing well in school and he had been named the managing partner of the group that had expanded considerably in size. His wife and children were complaining that he spent all his time at work, almost totally neglecting the family. At Steve's request he was seen along with his wife and three children. The latter were not shy about voicing their disappointment with their father, who acknowledged they had a right to complain. Steve was seen alone for two more sessions, during which he was able to liken his behavior to that of his mother, who was always too busy with her own activities to spend time with the family. He changed his behavior rapidly and markedly.

Steve was seen once two years ago. He had no complaints, and just came in to bring the therapist up to date and to express his gratitude for the very happy life he had with his family and his work. In almost four decades Steve was seen 43 times, including the sessions with his wife and with the children. This is an average of a little more than once a year, a parsimonious number in the light of the excellent outcome. It is doubtful that the same outcome would have been possible without the model of focused, intermittent psychotherapy throughout the 40 years of Steve's life, addressing a number of vexing problems as they unfolded over time.

SUMMARY

By replacing termination with interruption, psychotherapy is spared the difficulties that result in needless sessions on the one hand, and a reluctance to seek future treatment when new problems arise. It is facilitated by a model of focused, intermittent episodes of psychotherapy as needed throughout the patient's life span, which is the way all health care is dispensed (Cummings & VandenBos, 1979). The physician does not continue to see the patient after the pneumonia is cured, but it is understood that the patient returns to treatment in the future should she break a leg or become ill with influenza. Half a century of experience has demonstrated that patients like this model and utilize it accordingly. In addition, tracking these patients reveals that the approach is cost-effective and meets the requirements of even the most stringent rules of third-party payors. The model may seem deceptively simple, and some training and experience are required before the psychotherapist who is used to the termination model is able to implement correctly the interruption sequence (Pallak, Cummings, Dorken, & Henke, 1994).

REFERENCES

Bloom, B. (1991). *Planned short-term psychotherapy*. Boston, MA: Allyn and Bacon.

Bandura, A. (1977). Self-efficacy: Toward a unifying theory of behavioral change. *Psychological Review, 84*, 191–215.

Cummings, N. A. (1990). Brief, intermittent psychotherapy throughout the life cycle. In J. Zeig & S. Gilligan (Eds.). *Brief therapy: Myths, methods, and metaphors* (pp. 169–184). New York: Brunner/Mazel.

Cummings, N. (1991). Brief, intermittent psychotherapy throughout the life cycle. In C. Austad & W. Berman (Eds.). *Psychotherapy in managed healthcare* (pp. 35–45). Washington, DC: American Psychological Association.

Cummings, N. A. (2001). Interruption, not termination: The model from focused, intermittent psychotherapy throughout the life cycle. *Journal of Psychotherapy in Independent Practice, 2*, 3–16.

Cummings, N., & Cummings, J. (2000). *The essence of psychotherapy: Reinventing the art in the era of data*. San Diego, CA: Academic Press.

Cummings, N., & Sayama, M. (1995). *Focused psychotherapy: A casebook of brief, intermittent psychotherapy throughout the life cycle*. New York: Brunner/Mazel.

Cummings, N., & VandenBos, G. (1979). The general practice of psychology. *Professional Psychology, 10,* 430–440.

Freud, S. (1933). *Collected papers.* London, UK: Hogarth.

Pallak, M., Cummings, N., Dorken, H., & Henke, C. (1994). Medical costs, Medicaid, and managed mental health treatment: The Hawaii Study. In N. Cummings & M. Pallak (Eds.). *Managed care quarterly* (vol. 2). Frederick, MD: Aspen Publishers.

Seligman, M. (1975). *Helplessness: On depression, development, and death.* New York: Alfred A. Knopf.

19

SUICIDAL PATIENTS: THE ULTIMATE CHALLENGE FOR MASTER PSYCHOTHERAPISTS

JANET L. CUMMINGS

University of Nevada, Reno
and Cummings Foundation for Behavioral Health

For the master psychotherapist, the diagnosis, goals, and treatment plan serve as guidelines but are not utilized in a rigid cookbook fashion. Instead, the master psychotherapist sees psychotherapy as a journey that sometimes takes some unexpected turns. Although such elements as the operational diagnosis and implicit contract provide a road map to the treatment plan (Cummings & Sayama, 1995), the psychotherapist often finds obstacles along the journey that necessitate taking an alternate route. In other words, the master psychotherapist is not someone who can develop a flawlessly detailed treatment plan and follow it without deviation; rather, he is someone who can develop a plan that serves as a general guideline while maintaining the flexibility and adaptability necessary to implement a treatment plan in the real world. The master psychotherapist is not someone who develops and executes only the most successful of interventions. Rather, he has the skill and creativity to make a U-turn and create a new intervention when one attempt at intervention falls flat. The master psychotherapist can vary the pace of the treatment in response to cues from the patient. He can wait until the most opportune moment for an intervention, realizing that timing can be everything. When the master psychotherapist encounters resistance from the patient, he is able to decide the most effective way to counter or bypass the resistance to remain on track, moving toward the goal.

However, the psychotherapist managing a suicidal patient may not have the luxury of developing another intervention after one intervention fails. He may not be able to reevaluate the diagnosis and treatment plan, because there is no second chance following a patient's suicide. An error in the treatment of a suicidal patient can be lethal to the patient, as well as devastating to the patient's loved ones and to the therapist. These facts create a certain level of fear and anxiety in most psychotherapists, who in turn often end up mismanaging their suicidal patients as a result of their own anxiety.

On the other hand, master psychotherapists have learned to trust their own clinical judgments and act out of confidence in their knowledge of the suicidal process and their ability to determine the patient's true potential for lethality. Master psychotherapists have abandoned the misbeliefs that prevent most of their colleagues from managing their suicidal patients effectively. These misbeliefs were first summarized as four outmoded attitudes by Cummings (1996).

OUTMODED ATTITUDES (OR MISBELIEFS)

MISBELIEF #1: EVERYONE WHO THREATENS SUICIDE NEEDS A PSYCHIATRIC HOSPITALIZATION

In trying to avoid the loss of human life and the devastation that follows, many therapists err by relying too heavily upon psychiatric hospitalization for suicidal patients. For some therapists, the psychiatric hospital is the only intervention used to prevent suicide, and some therapists routinely hospitalize any patient who expresses suicidal ideation with even the vaguest plan. Even though only 1 of 23 patients who threaten suicide is truly lethal (Cummings, 1996; Cummings & Sayama, 1995), many clinicians hospitalize all patients who threaten suicide because of their own inability to differentiate the lethal patient from the nonlethal patient or because they have no other interventions at their disposal.

Many therapists have hospitalized patients unnecessarily to hide their own incompetence and insecurity about managing suicidal patients. Rather, it should be the therapist's obligation to hone her skills to be able to differentiate the lethal from the nonlethal patient and to treat each appropriately. This will take practice and, most likely, further education. However, even a therapist who can accurately assess 12 of the 23 patients threatening suicide as nonlethal will reduce his unnecessary psychiatric hospital admissions for suicidality by more than 50%. As the therapist becomes increasingly adept at differentiating the lethal patient from the nonlethal patient, he may eventually be able to pinpoint that 1 out of 23 who is lethal, and to have confidence in her judgment that the other 22 of 23 patients are not lethal. It is this ability, more than any other in a psychotherapist's repertoire, that qualifies her as a "master psychotherapist."

MISBELIEF #2: UNNECESSARY HOSPITALIZATION CAN'T HURT, SO IT'S BETTER TO BE ON THE SAFE SIDE

The routine hospitalization of patients threatening suicide is extremely inefficient from a cost containment standpoint, because patients, families, employers, and insurance companies are paying for 22 unnecessary hospitalizations for each necessary one. More important, however, unnecessary hospitalizations do a tremendous disservice to many patients, not just economically, but psychologically as well. For example, unnecessary hospitalization of histrionic patients causes them to think of themselves as much crazier than they really are, which in turn can actually increase their future risk of suicide rather than diminish it. Unnecessary hospitalization of borderline patients teaches them to continue using suicidal threats and gestures to manipulate their therapists. In other words, therapists give these patients a trump card that they can pull out and use to manipulate their therapists at any time. Many borderline patients look for a ticket into the hospital whenever life becomes stressful and, with repeated hospitalizations, can lose all motivation to learn to handle problems outside the hospital. For these reasons, unnecessary hospitalization can be deleterious to further treatment or can actually increase lethality in previously nonlethal patients.

MISBELIEF #3: THE BEST INTERVENTION IS TO TAKE RESPONSIBILITY FOR THE SUICIDAL PATIENT'S LIFE

Most people who suicide do so *at* someone else. By taking responsibility for a suicidal patient's life, the therapist volunteers to substitute for the person at whom they wish to suicide. Then, the patient can suicide *at* the therapist. Master psychotherapists, on the other hand, use their skills to help the patient find his own will to live based on his individual reasons for deciding to resist the temptation to suicide. In so doing, the patient takes ownership of his decision not to suicide and will likely continue to resolve life's difficulties in healthier ways.

MISBELIEF #4: NONMEDICAL PRACTITIONERS CANNOT MANAGE SUICIDAL PATIENTS AND MUST ENLIST A PSYCHIATRIST

Although it is appropriate to contact a physician when a patient is in need of medication, it is not necessary to involve physicians in every case when a patient threatens suicide. Nonmedical practitioners, with the proper training and experience, *can* learn to manage suicidal patients effectively.

Most psychiatrists and many psychotherapists believe that all depressed persons should be placed on antidepressant medication. This is an erroneous assumption, because antidepressant medication can actually increase the risk of suicide in some cases (Cummings, 2004). For example, schizophrenics who are placed on antidepressant medication (particularly selective serotonin reuptake inhibitors) without antipsychotic medication may become increasingly violent and more at risk for both homicide and suicide. In depressed "bipolars," antidepressant medication (particularly in the absence of mood-stabilizing medication) can bring about undesirable results, including a "switchover" to mania and the increase in energy level necessary to act upon suicidal thoughts.

Many depressed patients become more lethal during early treatment with antidepressant medication (Cummings, 2004). In many cases, vegetative signs of depression (including psychomotor retardation) improve before the cognitive symptoms of depression (e.g., hopelessness). The result is an individual who subjectively feels every bit as depressed and hopeless, but who suddenly has the energy and wherewithal necessary to plan and execute her suicide. To compound the problem further, many psychiatrists and psychotherapists breathe a sigh of relief when a patient is placed on anti-depressant medication and begins to show improvement in the vegetative signs of depression. Instead of becoming more vigilant because of the increased risk for suicide, they become less vigilant as a result of their erroneous belief that the medication will keep the patient safe.

Most therapists who wish to manage suicidal patients effectively will need additional training, because trying to learn by trial and error can be dele-terious, or even lethal, to patients. The remainder of this chapter serves as an illustration of what can be done by master psychotherapists in the manage-ment of suicidal patients. However, it is not meant to provide exhaustive training on the subject, and most therapists will need additional training and consultation beyond what this illustrative chapter provides.

Master psychotherapists, those who can differentiate lethal patients from nonlethal ones and who can treat each appropriately, have the following knowledge and skills:

1. They understand the three-stage suicidal process and can recognize the warning signs associated with each of the three stages.
2. They know how to intervene and prevent what would otherwise be the imminent death of their lethal patients.
3. They are adept at developing individually tailored treatment interven-tions for their nonlethal patients.

It is my intention in the remainder of this chapter to outline the three-stage suicidal process and the warning signs associated with each stage, to discuss a limited repertoire of effective treatment strategies for lethal patients, and to offer some strategies for effectively treating nonlethal patients.

THE SUICIDAL PROCESS

Most suicidal persons follow a distinct three-stage process (Cummings, 1996; Cummings & Cummings, 2000; Sattem, 1989). The notable exception to this rule is the paranoid patient, and this exception is discussed separately later in this chapter. During this process, suicidal persons decide whether to end their lives. If they decide to end their lives, they choose the time, location, and method of their own deaths. The suicidal process can be interrupted at any point with intervention, or may simply be abandoned if the patient decides not to suicide. However, if the process runs its full course, the end result is a suicide attempt or completion.

As individuals move through the suicidal process, they often exhibit the following verbal, nonverbal, and tactile indicators of lethality (Sattem, 1989).

VERBAL INDICATORS

Most suicidal people tend to be more open to discussing their lethality earlier in the process, and may complain about the problems in their lives and express the desire to die with anyone and everyone who will listen. They tend to talk about their lethality less later in the process, because others may have indicated they are tired of listening or because the suicidal individuals feel that others don't understand or care. Suicidal people commonly talk about death and suicide in general, but don't always readily tell others of their own suicidal ideation. For example, upon learning that a commercial airplane crashed, they may express the view that the deaths of the passengers and crew were a blessing to relieve them of the difficulties of life rather than a tragedy. It is important to note that not all suicidal persons openly discuss their suicidal ideation. In fact, some people suicide without ever having discussed their suicidal ideation or intent with anyone.

As people move through the suicidal process, their verbal expression becomes increasingly right-brain dominated. Tasks generally attributed to the left brain become increasingly difficult for them. They often talk of being overwhelmed with feelings and unable to concentrate. They may seem increasingly less logical and more emotional and creative in their speech or writing. It is not uncommon for people to become increasingly artistic, or to exhibit artistic abilities for the first time in their lives, as they move through the suicidal process. These people may compose music or write stories and poetry for the first time, and their artistic expressions may contain themes of hopelessness or death.

NONVERBAL INDICATORS

Suicidal persons continue listening to or performing their usual styles of music, because their tastes in music seldom change dramatically as they move through the suicidal process. However, they often narrow their focus more and more, until they are listening to or performing only very few songs, or perhaps only one song. Their choice of focus has meaning to them and will generally tell something about their pain source or their changing view of death as relief rather than as tragic.

Suicidal persons' artistic expression tends to focus on themes of death, suicide, pain, and hopelessness. In drawings, the body size of figures may be quite reduced, reflecting low self-worth, and the necks or wrists may be omitted or slashed. Dark colors or heavy lines are often used.

TACTILE INDICATORS

Although not all suicidal persons exhibit tactile indicators, these signs are quite powerful in those who do show them. Suicidal persons can selectively hide their verbal and nonverbal indicators from others, yet have much less ability to prevent tactile indicators from becoming apparent to those around them.

Suicidal persons often withdraw from other people. They stop touching other people and stop allowing others to touch them. They often avoid touching themselves, which is often evident from their neglect of grooming and personal hygiene. Some suicidal persons will remove or cover the mirrors in their homes, because they no longer wish to look at themselves. They may also remove photographs of themselves and family members from display in their homes and work places, because they no longer wish to view themselves or their loved ones. In so doing, the suicidal person may be disengaging from others (and even from himself) to make it easier to end his life.

Some suicidal people rest or sleep in the fetal position. Others experience a number of injuries, as they become less careful and more accident prone. In some cases, suicidal persons exhibit nervous touching of their wrist and neck areas, because these areas become irritation points for them, even if they are not considering a suicide method involving these areas.

These verbal, nonverbal, and tactile indicators of suicide differ greatly from individual to individual. Some suicidal persons exhibit a number of these indicators, whereas other persons may exhibit relatively few. Some patients will show more of one type of indicator than the others. However, the following three-stage process applies to all suicidal persons except paranoids.

STAGE 1: IDEATION

People in this first stage of the suicidal process are considering suicide as a possible solution to their problems and relief from their pain. They may spend a lot of time thinking about death and suicide, but are generally very afraid of suicide and of their own suicidal thoughts. Because of this fear, they have a difficult time planning their suicides and are likely to think about a number of possible methods. They often fantasize about dying from natural causes or wish they would be killed in an accident, but do not have a specific plan for their suicide.

In stage 1, people commonly verbalize their feelings of ambivalence, talking about both their desire to die and their fear of death. In speaking with those patients who talk openly of their suicidality, the therapist will generally note that the patient's fear of death greatly outweighs its appeal at this point. In stage 1, the tactile indicators are still absent or minimal whereas the non-verbal indicators may just begin to be evident.

Stage 1 generally lasts at least several months and can go on for years (Sattem, 1989). Some people spend most of their adult lives toying with the idea of suicide and are chronically in this stage. People in stage 1 may or may not move on to subsequent stages, so stage 1 is not time limited.

STAGE 2: PLANNING

In stage 2, the attraction to suicide becomes more salient than the fear of suicide, although these people still maintain some fear of suicide and have not decided to die. Although some ambivalence remains, an individual in this stage is able to formulate a very specific plan for her suicide, choosing the exact time, location, and method of her own death.

Master psychotherapists realize that a patient's choice of method gives insight into his potential for lethality. A person who is very seriously contemplating suicide will generally select a very lethal method and will choose a time and place for his death that affords minimal chance that someone will find him, intervene, and thwart the plan. On the other hand, the person whose plan includes less lethal means and a greater likelihood of rescue may make suicidal gestures but is unlikely to be lethal. The noteworthy exception to this rule is the histrionic personality, who sometimes miscalculates the rescue and inadvertently dies from what was intended only as a gesture (Cummings, 1996; Cummings & Sayama, 1995).

As a person moves through stage 2, she likely will show a decrease in verbal indicators with an increase in nonverbal and tactile indicators. By late in stage 2, verbal indicators may be minimal or completely absent. Stage 2 generally lasts at least a few weeks and sometimes months, but rarely does it last for more than a year (Cummings, 1996; Sattem, 1989). Once the individual has made specific plans, she feels tremendous pressure to decide either to die or not to die. Simply put, the ambivalence characteristic of stage 2 is so painful that the individual feels that he must make a decision one way or the other.

STAGE 3: AUTOPILOT

A suicidal person moves from stage 2 to stage 3 at the precise moment she decides to commit suicide. Instantly upon making the decision to die, that decision becomes repressed, or unconscious, and the person goes on "autopilot" (Cummings & Sayama, 1995). Although people at stage 1 and stage 2 in the process are not lethal, those who reach stage 3 are lethal, even though they are no longer aware that they have decided to die.

In stage 3, there is generally a complete absence of, or at least a marked decrease in, the verbal, nonverbal, and tactile indicators previously discussed. The person on autopilot will inevitably show a dramatic elevation in mood, with remission of depressive symptoms, as he enters stage 3. He has not resolved the problems that led him to feel suicidal to begin with. Rather, he feels a tremendous sense of relief for having made the decision to suicide. The painful ambivalence characteristic of stage 2 has been resolved.

Even though the patient has made the decision to suicide, she will give someone a clue that she has decided to die. A patient in psychotherapy will give that clue to her psychotherapist. Unfortunately, these clues are seldom recognized by loved ones or by therapists. Rather, friends, family, and mental health professionals are all too busy breathing a sigh of relief when they see the remission of depressive symptoms that stage 3 brings.

Stage 3 seldom lasts more than 48 hours (Sattem, 1989). Even though an individual may wrestle for some time with the decision to suicide while in stages 1 and 2, once the decision is made, he tends to carry out that decision quickly and decisively.

INTERVENTIONS FOR LETHAL
STAGE 3 PATIENTS

As mentioned previously, persons in stage 3 usually give someone a clue that they have decided to suicide. In cases when the suicidal individual has been discussing her ideation and planning with a family member, close friend, or therapist, she will inevitably give that person a clue that she has decided to die. The human will to live is so powerful that, even though the decision to die has been made, the individual gives one final opportunity for intervention.

Unfortunately, however, these clues are more often than not overlooked until after the suicide. Because stage 3 brings an elevation in mood and remission of depressive symptoms, family, friends, and even therapists tend to feel relieved and become less vigilant rather than more vigilant. They fail to look for clues to lethality or consider the possibility that the suicidal person is on autopilot. Once the patient has completed suicide, however, these clues often become blatantly obvious and serve to accentuate the guilty feelings in the survivors.

The type of clue given is highly individual, making an exhaustive list impossible. However, some general types of clues are common:

1. The patient may make a reference to getting his affairs in order. He may mention, as a casual aside that may easily be missed, his plan to revise a will or otherwise get his personal papers in order.

2. The patient may make a reference, again as a casual aside, to disposing of some personal or real property (via sale or gift), often without mentioning that she will no longer be needing the property.

3. The patient may make a casual reference to canceling some plans, without saying that he does not plan to be alive at the time. The clue may be a simple statement that the patient feels better and does not need to schedule a follow-up psychotherapy appointment, or it may be the cancelation of an appointment with no mention of rescheduling.

4. The patient may state, again as a casual aside, that she has no resources or hope left.

It is imperative to note that stage 3 patients will not disclose their intention to commit suicide if asked with the usual psychotherapeutic probes. It is possible that these patients lie in the face of such probes to avoid hospitalization or other intervention to thwart their plans. However, it is more likely that they deny their intent to commit suicide because their decision has gone unconscious and is out of their awareness.

Despite the clues that patients give to indicate their decision to suicide, the lethal stage 3 patient often goes undetected. Knowing this, it is imperative that the therapist working with patients who are considering suicide take the following steps (Cummings, 1996; Cummings & Sayama, 1995):

1. Be alert when a depressed patient who doesn't seem to improve suddenly gets markedly better, especially if there is an absence of any psychological reason for the sudden improvement. Recognize that the patient may have decided to suicide and may be on autopilot.

2. Instead of relaxing when a depressed patient finally seems to get better, the therapist should become more vigilant than ever and look for any words or action that might be a clue of a decision to suicide. The clue may be very subtle, such as a casual aside, and could easily be missed if it is inserted in more interesting verbage. It is my experience that the clue is generally presented much like an implicit contact (discussed in Chapter 10; (see also Cummings and Cummings, 2000; Cummings and Sayama, 1995). Therefore, the psychotherapist who has become adept at recognizing implicit contracts will likely have a distinct advantage when it comes to recognizing these stage 3 clues.

3. If there is any suspicion that a patient may be on autopilot, the therapist should forcefully confront him by saying, "When and how did you decide to kill yourself?" The question should be repeated as many times as necessary until the patient convinces the therapist that he has not decided to die (which will be the case two out of three times) or until the patient can no longer remain on autopilot and confesses his plan and intent to suicide. Remember, it is better to apologize to those two out of three patients for falsely accusing them than to risk a suicide by failing to take this step. It should be noted that this is an in-your-face confrontation, not a gentle probe. The master psychotherapist knows when to be gentle and when to be forceful, and this is one time when the force behind the words is as powerful as the words themselves. Without appropriate forcefulness, the intervention will not succeed in jolting the patient off autopilot.

4. If a patient on autopilot, when confronted, remembers and confesses her decision to suicide, the therapist should discuss the plan with her. This discussion should be meticulous and cover every detail of the plan. It is best to repeat this discussion as many times as necessary for the therapist to be certain the plan can no longer become unconscious. It may be helpful in some cases to "dismantle" the plan. This can be accomplished in a number of ways, depending upon the details of the plan, but may include such things as having the patient dispose of the lethal means or having the patient alert others to the plan so that they do no leave her alone, thus minimizing opportunity for the plan. Because master psychotherapists know that they cannot take responsibility for a patient's life, they realize the importance of encouraging the patient to dismantle the plan rather than doing it themselves.

Because master psychotherapists are familiar with the suicidal process, they are able to recognize suicidal patients who are reluctant to disclose their suicidality. As important, they are able to recognize patients who are not in the suicidal process, but who are threatening suicide manipulatively. In cases of the latter, master psychotherapists are able to deal with the manipulation in other therapeutic ways, because they are not fearful that these patients will suicide. Borderline patients often threaten suicide in ways that frighten their psychotherapists into acquiescing to their demands. Master psychotherapists, however, realize that borderline patients only suicide after they have gone through the same suicidal process that other suicidal patients do.

MANAGING LETHAL PARANOID PATIENTS

Paranoid patients warrant a separate discussion because they do not follow the same three-stage suicidal process that other suicidal patients follow and because they require much different intervention. Paranoids use projection as their main defense mechanism and, in so doing, are unaware of their own suicidal feelings. These patients do not need to go on autopilot to carry out a decision to suicide, because they are unaware of their suicidal ideation long before they are ready to carry out their plan. Furthermore, they may not view suicide as death, but rather as achieving freedom from and invulnerability to life's problems by going on to a higher plane of existence.

Because lethal paranoids express their suicidal ideation via projection rather than directly, many therapists fail to recognize their lethality. When a paranoid says that someone (the CIA, space aliens, or the ever-present "they") are planning to kill him, he really is planning to kill himself but is projecting those suicidal feelings onto the CIA, space aliens, or whomever else. Likewise, if a paranoid says that she is aware of a plot to kill someone else, it means that she herself is experiencing homicidal ideation toward that person.

Many suicide notes from successful suicides have a paranoid quality to them (Cummings & Sayama, 1995). Furthermore, many dual deaths (i.e., one or more homicides followed by a suicide) are perpetrated by paranoids who believe they are helping themselves and their loved ones go on to some higher existence, where they can be together without interference from those conspiring against them and the problems they are experiencing in this world (Cummings, 1996; Sattem, 1989).

Although the intervention of contracting with patients to abstain from suicide for specified periods of time is discussed later in this chapter, it is important to note here that such contracting is ineffective with paranoids. These patients do not recognize themselves as being suicidal in the first place. Furthermore, they generally do not believe in death but, rather, in some higher level of existence. Paranoids simply do not keep contracts.

Anyone who has ever tried to reason with a paranoid realizes that this is an exercise in futility. Trying to talk him out of his delusion will only convince the paranoid that the therapist is in collusion with whomever he believes wishes to harm him or is otherwise conspiring against him. Although the therapist must ask very specific questions to get information from a paranoid, the information can be elicited without causing him to distrust the therapist. Master psychotherapists are adept at joining the patient's delusion and can ask questions about the delusions in ways that someone who truly believed the delusions might. The master psychotherapist can use the patient's response to assess his risk for lethality without challenging the patient's delusion. He can adeptly inquire about how "they" plan to harm the patient or someone else, as well as the patient's perception of when the harm is likely to occur. (For a more complete discussion of "joining the delusion," see Cummings and Sayama, 1995, and Fromm–Reichman, 1950.)

Paranoid patients in imminent danger of suicide or homicide need two interventions: (1) containment (psychiatric hospitalization on a locked unit with constant supervision) and (2) antipsychotic medication. The patient should not be released from the hospital until she is stable on antipsychotic medication and is no longer a danger to herself or others. She must continue in outpatient treatment (including both antipsychotic medication and supportive psychotherapy); otherwise, she may become suicidal and/or homicidal again quite quickly. It cannot be overstated that other interventions, no matter how effective with nonparanoid patients, will fail when used with a lethal paranoid.

INTERVENTIONS FOR NONLETHAL PATIENTS

Although this chapter has outlined very specific interventions for lethal stage 3 and lethal paranoid patients, the number and diversity of interventions that can be effective with nonlethal patients are virtually unlimited. For this reason, master psychotherapists find working with nonlethal suicidal patients to be challenging and enjoyable, because the psychotherapist has the flexibility to tailor interventions to each specific patient. In developing an intervention, the therapist can consider whether the patient is in the suicidal process or merely making manipulative threats, as well as the patient's personality style, diagnosis, and worldview. Although an exhaustive list of interventions would be impossible, several basic types of interventions are commonly used by master psychotherapists.

THE CONTRACT

Along with psychiatric hospitalization, the contract is a commonly used (and misused) intervention. Usually, the therapist asks the patient to promise not to commit suicide while in treatment with the therapist. The patient is often asked to sign a paper (usually a one-size-fits-all form) as part of the agreement.

There are some inherent problems with this intervention:

1. Some individuals are incapable of keeping contracts. These include paranoids (as previously discussed) and those with dementia or other organic memory problems who simply may not remember that they have a contract in place. Other patients may forget the contract or simply choose to violate it when they are intoxicated from drugs or alcohol.

2. Individuals in stage 3 of the suicidal process are on autopilot, with no conscious awareness of their imminent suicide. It is highly unlikely that contracts would have any impact on these patients.

3. Simply put, a contract in effect for a long period of time may be too difficult for many depressed and suicidal patients to keep.

4. Such contracts may lull the therapist into a false sense of security, thus preventing him from creatively using other interventions.

Master psychotherapists do use contracts with their suicidal patients, but not in the way that most therapists use them. The master psychotherapist may creatively utilize a series of short contracts, renewable with each contact with the patient. The psychotherapist can ask the patient at each contact (face-to-face or telephone) how long a time period would be appropriate for the next contract. The psychotherapist then schedules the next contact with the patient accordingly. Some suicidal people may only be able to contract for short periods of time (hours) at the beginning, and the psychotherapist extends the length of the contract only as the patient is able keep the contract for longer periods of time. To utilize this type of intervention effectively, the psychotherapist must realize that there is nothing magical about weekly 50-minute sessions. With suicidal patients, it is often advantageous to schedule shorter but more frequent contacts. Although some face-to-face contacts are necessary to look for nonverbal and tactile indicators of suicide, telephone contacts may be used in between the face-to-face contacts when very frequent contacts are needed.

BURSTING THE PATIENT'S BALLOON

In cases when the patient wishes to punish some other person or persons with her suicide, the psychotherapist can allow the patient to express her fantasies about her suicide. She is encouraged to talk at length about who will find her, how others will find out about the suicide, and what everyone's reactions will be. The psychotherapist listens intently to discover who the patient intends to punish with the suicide. Once the intended victim has been discovered and the patient has shared all her fantasies about the suicide, the master psychotherapist explains that the patient will not get the desired outcome and the intended victim will not actually suffer as much as the patient would hope. For example, a patient angry at his estranged spouse may be told that the spouse will likely go through a period of grieving, but then will go on with her life and will probably find a new love interest once the patient is gone.

A variation of this type of intervention can be very effective with histrionic patients. These patients fear disfigurement much more than they fear death (Cummings & Sayama, 1995). After listening to the patient's fantasy, the master psychotherapist explains how she will likely be disfigured as a result of the chosen method, regardless of whether the method succeeds. Because histrionics generally choose neat suicide methods (such as pills) rather than messy methods (such as gunshot), this can be a challenge.

I have had success in describing to histrionic patients the disfigurement that can result if the patient does not die but is left brain damaged, such as incontinence and fine motor problems that interfere with the ability to groom oneself. I have also had success in explaining to these patients that a lengthy coma prior to death could leave facial disfigurement for all to behold at the funeral. Rather than risk disfigurement, many histrionic patients prefer to work in therapy to learn to live successfully.

FINDING ANOTHER WAY TO THE DESIRED OUTCOME

This technique is similar to the previous type of intervention in that the master psychotherapist listens intently to the patient's fantasies of what he hopes to accomplish by suiciding. Then, the psychotherapist helps the patient see that he may be able to get the same outcome without committing suicide and further helps the patient realize that he can be alive to enjoy the outcome. For example, a patient who is angry at an estranged spouse may decide to seek a fair settlement in divorce court rather than die and leave all the joint assets to the spouse. Amazingly, I have had a number of successes in helping patients realize that having a happy and fulfilling life may provide better vengeance than their suicide ever would.

TEACHING SELF-MONITORING

Some suicidal patients enter a panic state with each suicidal thought and frantically call their therapists several times per day as a result. These same patients may not see improvement in themselves when they do begin to recover from their depression. It can be helpful in these cases to teach the patient to rate her suicidality on a scale, such as a zero to ten-point scale. The patient can be instructed to call the therapist only if her suicidality gets above a certain level, say eight points on the zero to ten-point scale. The patient can also be instructed to chart her suicidality so that she can later see improvement. Using this technique, I have reduced crisis calls from suicidal patients by as much as 90% within a few weeks.

UTILIZING SUPPORT

Many therapists view psychotherapy as only what happens inside the psychotherapy office. This narrow view leads many therapists to fail to recognize outside support that may be available to patients. On the other hand, master psychotherapists are willing to look for and utilize outside social support for their nonlethal suicidal patients. Many patients have families, circles of friends, and religious institutions that can offer tremendous support. However, many depressed and suicidal patients are unable to recognize and utilize the support that is at their disposal. The psychotherapist can help the patient recognize available social support and can assist in mobilizing that support for the patient. I have (with consent from the patient) mobilized support for suicidal patients from family and other social networks on a number of occasions. Although this may seem like extra effort, or at least effort that may not be reimbursable, it has proved to be time well spent both in terms of effective treatment and in terms of preserving the psychotherapist's limited time and resources by creating a situation in which the psychotherapist is not being called upon to be the patient's only source of support. Furthermore, the patient learns to continue to recognize and utilize his available support systems long after psychotherapy has been interrupted.

PSYCHOJUDO

In psychojudo, some of the principles found in the Japanese martial art of judo are applied to the psychotherapy process. The martial art suggests that using the opponent's resistance and converting it into momentum can be more effective than fighting the opponent head on. When faced with an opponent's onslaught, the judo student is taught to keep the opponent moving, but to redirect that movement slightly, rather then trying to stop the onslaught. Thus, an individual trained in judo can overcome a much larger, stronger opponent by using the opponent's momentum to throw her off balance.

When applied to psychotherapy, the principles of judo suggest that a patient is entitled to his resistance, and that attempts to strong-arm the resistance will inevitably cause the therapist to be overpowered and the progress toward the goal to be thwarted. Instead, the psychotherapist goes with the patient's resistance and turns it into momentum for change and progress toward the goal. (The principle of using the patient's resistance and other principles of psychojudo are outlined in detail in Cummings and Sayama, 1995, and Cummings and Cummings, 2000.)

When applied to suicidal patients, the principles of psychojudo suggest that it may be deleterious to some patients for the therapist to challenge or try to counter directly their suicidal threats. This is especially true in cases when patients are threatening suicide to manipulate the therapist. The principles of psychojudo that apply to the management of suicidal patients are as follows:

Prescribing the Resistance

In cases when a patient is not suicidal but is threatening suicide manipulatively, a paradoxical intervention can be used to disarm the patient and use her obstinance to defuse the attempts at manipulation. I use the paradoxical technique called *prescribing the symptom* (Watzlawick, Weakland, & Fisch, 1974) with such patients. When the patient makes a manipulative suicide threat, the master therapist responds by instructing the patient to decide upon a dramatic (or outrageous) method. The patient may be told that the method must be worthy of being the psychotherapist's first suicide or that the method must be worthy of inclusion in a book or chapter on suicide that the psychotherapist intends to publish. In fact, the selection of the method is said to be so important that the patient must give it great consideration, and is told to do so for his homework. When the patient returns for the next session, he is asked what method has been selected. No matter what the patient says, the psychotherapist dismisses it as not worthy of being her first suicide or of inclusion in a book or chapter on suicide. The patient is told to come up with a better plan for his homework assignment. Again, the psychotherapist deems the patient's plan as unworthy, and again instructs the patient to think of a more dramatic plan. This continues until the patient tires of the game and decides to stop threatening suicide in order to end it.

Humoring the Resistance

The use of humor is particularly effective with borderline patients, who enjoy playing psychological games. The more outrageously the patient behaves, the more outrageous the psychotherapist can (and must) be in his use of humor (Cummings & Sayama, 1995). For example, I have disarmed many borderline patients threatening suicide in the midst of their tale of woes by saying, "It would be a shame if you killed yourself before you had a chance to tell your story on *Geraldo Rivera* or *Rikki Lake*." When said in a tongue-in-cheek way, such statements get both the therapist and the patient laughing. The laughter disarms the patient and causes him to stop threatening suicide (at least for the time being).

Mobilizing Rage in the Service of Health

When a patient is experiencing a reactive depression, he may have internalized his rage at another individual. He then unconsciously punishes that individual (the introject) by punishing himself with depression. In some cases, the depression (internalized rage) progresses until the patient "murders" the introject by killing himself. In such cases, supportive psychotherapy will generally backfire, because the therapist's attempts to encourage and reassure the patient are taken as attempts to exonerate the object of the internalized rage. Thus, the internalized rage intensifies and the patient becomes more at risk for suicide.

The principles of psychojudo suggest that the appropriate treatment for reactive depression (internalized rage) is to externalize the patient's rage. The therapist can behave in ways that mimic the person who is the object of the patient's internalized anger, thus provoking the patient to anger. As an alternative, the therapist can provoke the patient to anger by constantly singing the virtues of the object of the patient's anger and by continually assigning the patient to be unrealistically nice to that person. The result of this technique is that the patient becomes enraged at the therapist, who substitutes for the real object of the rage. The rage is externalized and the depression remits. (This technique is described in detail in Cummings and Sayama, 1995, and Fromm–Reichman, 1950.)

In some cases, the technique of mobilizing the patient's rage may be used to overcome momentary obstacles. For example, if the psychotherapist feels uncertain that the patient will follow through on important homework, he may express doubt about the patient's willingness or ability to follow through to create a sense of righteous indignation in the patient, who will then follow through on the homework to prove the psychotherapist wrong.

CASE ILLUSTRATION: DESTINY

Destiny was a 28-year-old female borderline who had utterly defeated a number of psychiatrists and psychotherapists since she had first entered the mental health system at the age of nine. At various times in her life she had been assigned a number of psychiatric diagnoses, including attention deficit disorder, anorexia/bulimia, substance abuse, PTSD, multiple personality disorder, bipolar disorder, gender identity disorder, and schizophreniform disorder. She had a history of countless psychiatric hospital admissions and had been on just about every possible psychotropic medication at one time or another.

Destiny had wrecked havoc in a large health care system in which she had been a subscriber for the past several years. She used all the usual borderline tactics. She frequently "no-showed" for appointments, only to abuse after-hours crisis services later the same day. When providers in the system tried to contain her, she would complain to the insurance company and the licensing boards over her various treatment providers. When all else failed, Destiny would play the suicide card. She would threaten suicide to her psychiatrist or psychotherapist, or simply show up at the psychiatric hospital and use her threats of suicide as a ticket for admission. Destiny's providers, as well as the entire health care system, were so afraid of her that they seldom said no to any of her demands. Instead of containing her, they allowed her to get increasingly out of control. One can only imagine that the health care system threw a big party and celebrated with champagne when Destiny's employer decided to purchase a different benefit package with a different mental health provider company. This new benefit package happened to include Biodyne benefits, and I was the unfortunate Biodyne psychotherapist to whom Destiny was assigned.

Destiny was a very large woman who had a "hardened" look to her, which caused her to look much older than her chronological age. When I first greeted her in the waiting room, the look of contempt on her face indicated that she planned to "eat me for lunch."

At the beginning of the first session, Destiny launched into a well-rehearsed litany of complaints about her abusive childhood and how everybody has victimized her throughout her entire life. I deliberately appeared disinterested and waited for Destiny's response. She became visibly angry and said, "What's the matter with you? You're a shrink and you're supposed to listen to me." I replied, "I haven't heard anything real interesting so far. I've been doing this for awhile, and I haven't heard anything new or exciting lately. Can you do any better?" The session continued with a number of rounds in which Destiny tried to come up with a story dramatic enough to spark my interest, followed by the admonition that she would have to do better. When Destiny began to talk of her many previous suicide "attempts" (which were actually gestures), I said, "Well, I guess that's pretty good. It's *Oprah* material, maybe *Rikki Lake* material, but it won't get you on *Jerry Springer*." At this point, Destiny and I both chuckled. The patient was very manageable for the remainder of the session, apparently conceding that I had won that particular battle. I knew, however, that she would strategize and have a new battle plan before the next session.

The next several sessions were a psychojudo match in which Destiny came at me with one onslaught after another and I redirected her momentum rather than strong-arming it. For example, Destiny seemed unexpectedly sedate at the beginning of the second session. After being remarkably quiet for ten minutes or so, she announced that she had taken a lethal dose of pills before coming to the appointment and that the pills were starting to take effect. She said that she expected to pass out at any minute. I casually reached into the desk, pulled out a telephone book, and started thumbing through the government pages. After a few minutes, Destiny asked what was going on. I replied, "I'm trying to find the number for the coroner. But there's no listing. Oh, I know what's wrong. I'm looking at state agencies instead of county agencies." There was silence as I continued looking at the phone book. I broke the silence by saying, "There's no listing for 'coroner.' I think I need to try 'medical examiner.' " Destiny became incensed, and demanded to know what was going on and why the coroner was going to be called. The response completely disarmed her: "I don't want you dying in my office. I wouldn't know what to do with a dead person. I figured you should die at the morgue since they know what to do with dead people there. And if you die before they get here, at least they can take you away and I can get my office cleaned up before my next patient." Destiny sat with a smirk on her face, trying to contain her amusement, but burst into uproarious laugher. She then confessed that she had not actually taken the pills.

A few days after the second session, Destiny telephoned after hours, demanding admission to the hospital because of her suicidality. I had anticipated an after-hours call from this patient and had requested that the answering service notify me (rather than the on-call therapist) should she call. When I refused to authorize (precertify) the hospital admission, Destiny became irate and threatened to kill herself right after making a complaint about me to the State Board of Psychologist Examiners. I responded by saying, "Will you be killing yourself before or after your appointment with me this Thursday? If you're going to kill yourself before the appointment, I need to know so I can give that time slot to someone on the waiting list." Destiny told me (quite loudly) that she wanted her appointment and did not want me to give it to anybody else. Thus, I was certain that she would be alive (and as cantankerous as usual) at her next scheduled appointment.

Destiny arrived for the third session with blood dripping from both wrists, having cut her wrists on the way into the session. The cuts were obviously not lethal, and I handed her a box of tissue to blot the blood and asked that she try not to drip blood on my carpet. I then asked her if she would like a couple Band-Aids. Destiny yelled, "You suck!" which I took as an admission of defeat in that particular round of psychojudo.

Ultimately, Destiny became part of a 20-week group treatment program at Biodyne designed specifically to manage borderline patients. (For a description of this program, see Cummings and Sayama, 1995.) She learned to identify with healthier coping styles, stopped threatening suicide, and became a very manageable (and sometimes even likable) patient. She continues to see me occasionally. Every once in awhile, Destiny tries to pull one of her manipulation tactics on me, just to reassure herself that I am still strong enough to help her avoid self-destruction.

SUMMARY

The finality of suicide constitutes a formidable challenge to psychotherapists, most often prompting them to overly hospitalize these patients so as to be on the safe side. However, unnecessary hospitalization, the belief that only a psychiatrist can manage suicidal patients, or the converse, attempting to take responsibility for a patient's life can all be counter-productive and even harmful to the patient, increasing the risk of suicide. The master therapist can differentiate the lethal patient from the non-lethal patient and proceed appropriately to prevent both death in the first, and eliminate repetitive threats and attempts at suicide in the latter.

Master therapists (1) understand the three-stage suicidal process and can recognize the warning signs with each, (2) know how to intervene and prevent what would otherwise be the imminent death of their lethal patients, and (3) are adept at developing tailored treatment interventions for their non-lethal patients. There are verbal, nonverbal and tactile indicators of lethal suicide, and there ate three stages in the lethal process: ideation, planning, and autopilot. Having missed indicators and the first two stages, autopilot is the last opportunity to intervene and prevent the suicide, but this autopilot is usually manifested and disguised in outward improvement and the imminent lethality is missed by the therapist. Recognizing the autopilot, along with steps to confront and prevent death is an imperative by a skillful therapist.

Paranoid suicidal patients can be quite lethal and they require a much different approach than recognizing the three stages of lethality as they manifest a different set of warning signs. Furthermore, the lethality of non-lethal patients can be increased by a well-intentioned therapist who either takes their threats too seriously or too lightly. A number of tailored approaches for these patients are described.

REFERENCES

Cummings, J. (1996). Managing suicidal patients: The ultimate test in overcoming outmoded attitudes. In N. Cummings, M. Pallak, & J. Cummings (Eds.). *Surviving the demise of solo practice: Mental health practitioners prospering in the era of managed care* (pp. 279–298). Madison, CT: Psychosocial Press.

Cummings, J. (2004). *Psychopharmacology overview*. Scottsdale, AZ: The Nicholas & Dorothy Cummings Foundation.

Cummings, N., & Cummings, J. (2000). *The essence of psychotherapy: Reinventing the art in the new era of data*. San Diego, CA: Academic Press.

Cummings, N., & Sayama, M. (1995). *Focused psychotherapy: A casebook of brief intermittent psychotherapy throughout the life cycle*. New York: Brunner/Mazel.

Fromm–Reichman, F. (1950). *Principles of intensive psychotherapy*. Chicago: University of Chicago Press.

Sattem, L. (1989). Suicide prevention. In J. Cummings (Producer) & K. Knight (Director). *A psychological autopsy* [film]. Dayton, OH: Wright State University TV Center.

Watzlawick, P., Weakland, J., & Fisch, R. (1974). *Change: Principles of problem formation and problem resolution*. New York: WW Norton.

AUTHOR INDEX

NOTE: Italicized page numbers
refer to names appearing
within the references.

INDEX

restructuring defensive and affective patterns, 270–273

Two Triangles, 269

of self-assigned Ericksonian tasks, 235–236

transference, 108–111

Case formulation, 8; *see also* temporal structure of therapy

in experiential sessions, 171–172

in integrative behavioral couple therapy, 242–243

therapeutic alliances, 42–43

transference, 101–102

using novelty, 280–282

Catatonics, garlic, 163

Causal relations, 3

Census Bureau, United States, 73, 85

Change; *see also* experiential sessions; therapeutic alliances

fear of as resistance, 129–130

in integrative behavioral couple therapy, 244–247, 255

and novelty, 278–280

readiness to, 18, 26, 174, 194–195

transtheoretical model of, 12–13, 120–121, 194–195

Change talk, 20

Changing perspectives, 272–273

Characters, indiscriminate, in story-making, 66

Childhood conditioning for panic attacks, 150

Children and motivational interviewing, 30

Chronic illness and chronic depression, 153–154

Chronicles, 119

Classical transference, 99–100

Clients; *see also* manipulation; resistance; suicidal patients; therapeutic alliances; transference

commitment to change, 25–28

cultural influences in, 74–76

and interruption of therapy, 298–299

in narrative psychotherapy histories, 64–65

as narrators, 58, 59–60

versus patients, 119–120

power and motivation of, 119

self-assigned Ericksonian tasks, 235

strengths of, 16, 122, 224

unique personalities of, 2–3, 130–131

Clinical Decision Making in Behavior Therapy: A Problem Solving Perspective, 220

Clinical judgment, 125

Clinical observations, 61–62

Clinical strategies; *see also* experiential sessions; homework; integrative behavioral couple therapy (IBCT); motivational interviewing (MI); resistance; transference

for implementing interruption of therapy, 298–300

narrative psychotherapy, 62–68

client histories, 64–65

current issues, 63–64

selected elements of story-making, 65–68

novelty, 282–285

for performance anxiety in STDP, 273–275

skills training, 218–219

therapeutic alliances, 43–48

metacommunication, 44–46

rupture resolution, 46–48

Clues to lethality of suicidal patients, 316–317

Cognitive therapy, 284

Collaborative homework assignments, 193–196

Commitment, 123

Commitment to change, 25–28

Communication training, 244

Competencies, *see* skills training

Complainants, clients as, 120

Complete Tales of Winnie-the-Pooh, The, 113

Compliance problems with bipolar patients, 154–155

Compliant persons, 230

Component skills, 217

Compulsions, 156–157

Skills training (*continued*)
useful resources, 219–220
varied approaches to, 212
Skillstreaming the Adolescent, 210
Social influence, case formulation as, 281–282
Social phobia, *see* performance anxiety
Social skills training, 212
Social support for suicidal patients, 322–323
Socioeconomic status and skills training, 216
Sociopaths, schizophrenic, 163
SOCRATES (Stages of Change Readiness and Treatment Eagerness Scale), 18
Solution-focused therapy, 120–121, 227–228, 285
Somatization, 74
Some Stories Are Better Than Others, 113, 124–125
Special populations and motivational interviewing, 30
Specific goals, 193
Splitting identification, 160–161
Stages of change model, *see* transtheoretical change model
Stages of Change Readiness and Treatment Eagerness Scale (SOCRATES), 18
Stages of treatment, 115–116
Status quo, maintenance of through acceptance, 255
STDP, *see* short-term dynamic psychotherapy
Stereotypes, 78–81
Stigma reduction in skills training, 214
Stories
in client history, 65
making, 56–57
psychotherapeutic, 58–59
remaking, 62–63, 69
unfinished, 68
and ways of seeing, 124–125
Strategic therapy, 285
Strengths of client, 16, 122, 224

Stress, 150, 212, 215–216
Strong-arming resistance, 131–132
Subjectivity in therapeutic alliance, 41
Success of treatments, 281–282
Suicidal patients, 309–327
borderline, 160–161
case example, 325–327
interventions for lethal, 316–318
interventions for nonlethal, 320–325
contracts, 320–321
psychojudo, 323–325
self-monitoring by patient, 322
transforming suicidal fantasies, 321–322
utilizing outside social support, 322–323
management of paranoid, 318–320
and manipulation, 90–91
misbeliefs regarding, 310–313
overview, 309–310
suicidal process, 313–316
Summarizing in motivational interviewing, 23
Support for suicidal patients, 322–323
Sycophants, 88
Symbolic tasks, 231–233, 235
Symptom prescription, 229–230, 234–235
Systemic techniques, 224

T
Tactile indicators of lethality, 314
Taking sides trap, 28–29
Tasks
agreed-upon homework, 193–196
in Ericksonian therapy, 223–237
case example of self-assigned, 235
congruent homework tasks, 226–228
gift wrapping, 225–226
incongruent tasks, 228–234
in-session, 234–235
overview, 223
setting goals, 223–225
prescribed, 282
in skills training, 219
and therapeutic alliance, 38, 43